D1064127

beyond **BLACKFACE**

beyond

BLACKFACE

African Americans

AND THE CREATION OF

American Popular Culture,

1890–1930

EDITED BY W. Fitzhugh Brundage

The University of North Carolina Press

CHAPEL HILL

THIS BOOK WAS PUBLISHED WITH THE ASSISTANCE OF THE
H. Eugene and Lillian Youngs Lehman Fund of the University of North Carolina Press.
A complete list of books published in the Lehman Series appears at the end of the book.

The paper in this book meets the guidelines for permanence and durability of the
Committee on Production Guidelines for Book Longevity of the Council on Library Resources.
The University of North Carolina Press has been a member of the
Green Press Initiative since 2003.

Library of Congress Cataloging-in-Publication Data
Beyond blackface : African Americans and the creation of American popular culture,
1890–1930 / edited by W. Fitzhugh Brundage.
p. cm.
Includes bibliographical references and index.
ISBN 978-0-8078-3462-6 (cloth : alk. paper) — ISBN 978-0-8078-7184-3 (pbk. : alk. paper)
1. African Americans in mass media. 2. African Americans in popular culture. 3. Mass
media—United States—History. 4. African Americans—Race identity—History. I. Brundage,
W. Fitzhugh (William Fitzhugh), 1959–
P94.5.A372U536 2011
305.896′073009041—dc22   2010053996

cloth   15 14 13 12 11 5 4 3 2 1   paper   15 14 13 12 11 5 4 3 2 1

Portions of Clare Corbould, "At the Feet of Dessalines: Performing Haiti's Revolution
during the New Negro Renaissance," have been reprinted by permission of the publisher
from "Haiti, a Stepping-Stone to Africa," in *Becoming African Americans: Black Public Life in
Harlem, 1919–1939*, by Clare Corbould (Cambridge, Mass.: Harvard University Press,
© 2009 by the President and Fellows of Harvard College), 168–90.

Contents

Acknowledgments

During the gestation of this volume I have acquired an uncommonly long list of debts. To the contributors, I am grateful for their creativity, generosity, and patience. It has been a pleasure to work with scholars whose work I admire greatly. This volume was also made possible through the generosity of the community at the University of North Carolina. The conference that anchored and enriched this volume was made possible through the generous support of the Center for the Study of the American South, the Office of the Associate Dean of Social Sciences, the Diversity Initiative Fund, the University Program in Cultural Studies, the Associate Provost for International Affairs, the Department of History, the Department of English, the Curriculum in American Studies, the Institute for the Arts and Humanities, the Sonja Haynes Stone Center for Black Culture and History, the Department of Dramatic Arts, and the University of North Carolina Press. More specifically, special thanks are due for Violet Anderson, Barbara Call, McKay Coble, Peter Coclanis, Lisa Eveleigh, Herb Garman, Karen Gil, Hilary Green, Larry Grossberg, Joseph Jordan, Joy Kasson, Lloyd Kramer, Joyce Loftin, John McGowan, Cookie Newsom, Nancy Schoonmaker, David Silkenat, Olympia Snowe, and Harry Watson.

I also am indebted to the members of the Chapel Hill academic community who contributed to the conference: Matt Harper, Trudier Harris, Kenneth Janken, Greg Kaliss, John Kasson, Mark Katz, Laurie Maffly-Kipp, Charlene Regester, and Lyneise Williams.

At the University of North Carolina Press, Chuck Grench has been tolerant and patient beyond all explanation. One of the pleasures of being a member of this community has been working closely with Chuck and the rest of the UNC Press staff.

Finally, I eagerly await Armistead's book(s). And no words are adequate to express my gratitude to and love for Susan.

Working in the "Kingdom of Culture"

African Americans and American Popular Culture, 1890–1930

W. FITZHUGH BRUNDAGE

Ethel Williams's and Johnny Peters's exuberant vaudeville interpretation of the Texas Tommy dance, Louis Chauvin's virtuoso performances of piano rags, Bert Williams's winsome pantomime in the Ziegfeld Follies, Oscar Micheaux's brash experiments in cinema, and Hubert Julian's daredevil stunts in and over Jazz Age Harlem. These are a few milestones of African American artistry and cultural innovation at the dawn of the twentieth century. Virtually every facet of popular culture in the United States displayed black influences. Black faces—Aunt Jemima, Uncle Ben, and other icons—graced the most popular mass-produced products that filled American pantries. African Americans had always been present—even when unacknowledged—in American culture and life, but now their conspicuous presence as both subjects and innovators of popular culture was unmistakable and unprecedented.

The rise of blacks in American mass culture between 1890 and 1930 coincided with the heyday of what historian David Nasaw has described as the era of "public amusements." A proliferation of commercialized mass entertainment, ranging from phonograph parlors and silent-film palaces to professional sports events and dancehalls, transformed American leisure. In huge numbers, Americans of all classes and backgrounds sought out these and other forms of commercial leisure. By exploiting the era's dizzying technological innovations, mass-culture entrepreneurs produced accessible and alluring forms of entertainment that accelerated the nation's emerging consumer economy.[1]

This new prominence of mass entertainment, and of blacks in it, accentuated contradictions in American attitudes about both race and culture. At century's end, white Americans engaged in strenuous debate over their "Negro problem." The Civil War had left unresolved the status of African Americans as citizens. White Americans recognized that blacks would no longer be slaves, but few imagined a future in which blacks would attain equality with whites. Some self-proclaimed experts predicted that the laws of evolution doomed blacks to eventual extinction. Others awaited an inevitable race war during which whites would annihilate blacks. Perhaps most whites assumed that blacks were consigned by nature and tradition to inferiority for generations to come. Most speculations about the future of black Americans revealed the mixture of loathing, fear, envy, and curiosity that whites harbored toward African Americans.[2]

Evidence of whites' fear and loathing of blacks was plentiful. At century's end, legalized segregation swiftly expanded and racial discrimination intensified, circumscribing virtually every life choice of blacks, especially in the South, where the era of Jim Crow had dawned. An epidemic of lynchings, racial affrays, and riots against blacks underscored the proclivity of whites to employ violence to impose their will. And the figure of the depraved black criminal assumed a prominence in newspapers, fiction, plays, songs, and early films far out of proportion to his actual numbers. With good cause, historians have referred to the era as "the highest stage of white supremacy" and "the nadir" of American race relations.[3] Yet efforts to quarantine and demonize blacks failed to overcome either black resistance to their oppression or the fascination that black culture possessed for whites. Even while some whites professed revulsion and contempt for African Americans, others enthusiastically appropriated and consumed black culture.

Because African American artistry and representations of African Americans were so conspicuous in the emerging mass culture of the era, blacks were acutely sensitive to the power of popular culture to shape their public identity and, indeed, their status as citizens. As W. E. B. Du Bois explained, the dilemma African Americans faced was that their identity as Americans was, in the eyes of the white majority, contingent. Blacks constantly had to prove themselves worthy of tolerance from, let alone inclusion in, American society. By necessity, blacks acquired a "double consciousness," a keen sense "of always looking at one's self through the eyes of others."[4] In this milieu, representations of African Americans in mass culture exerted inordinate influence over both whites and blacks. Earlier forms of popular culture, especially minstrelsy, had also shaped perceptions of African Americans and circumscribed the careers of black artists who aspired to other modes of artistry. But now in an age of commercialized leisure and proliferating technologies of mass culture, African Americans faced the prospect that new forms of mass culture would perpetuate and even intensify inherited stereotypes of blacks. African Americans, ranging from Scott Joplin and Oscar Micheaux to W. E. B. Du Bois and the founders of Black Swan Records, understood the importance of securing a toehold in the cultural marketplace of the twentieth century. Only by doing so could they give voice to their loftiest ambitions and their claims to equality in an age of strident white supremacy.

The politics of black expressive culture at the dawn of the twentieth century defied simple description or categories. "Precisely because African Americans have had more control over their own culture than many other aspects of their world," historian Waldo Martin writes, "culture has always been a critical battleground in their freedom struggle." As Martin has explained, black culture was inevitably politicized while black culture informed black political aspirations and programs. The exigencies that African Americans faced dictated that culture and politics should overlap and merge. Thus, black cultural and political expression gave voice simultaneously to black ambivalence toward, alienation from, affirmation of, and optimism in the nation and their place in it. But although politics suffused the emerging mass culture created by African Americans during the early twentieth century, we should avoid reducing their creativity to sublimated politics. Instead, their quest was to create an expressive culture that acknowledged, in ways that were previously inconceivable, their full and complex humanity.[5]

When African American artists and entrepreneurs entered the cultural marketplace of the early twentieth century they could not escape ongoing debates over the relative worth and respectability of popular culture. These debates reflected deep anxieties that the nation's accelerating cultural heterogeneity would erode the prestige and influence of "high" culture. The nation's cultural arbiters—editors, critics, orchestra leaders, educators, ministers—had only recently succeeded in distinguishing "high" from "low" culture, and they were loath to see their work undone. This hierarchy of high and low culture, as well as the campaign by many African Americans to demonstrate their "respectability," severely circumscribed black creative opportunities. Consequently, black artists and entrepreneurs continually tested the cultural and social conventions that circumscribed them. Both because and in spite of the myriad boundaries that constrained their creativity, blacks fashioned music, dance, and visual arts that straddled, ignored, or subverted the dictates of high and low art. Because of who they were—members of a purportedly debased race—black entertainers transgressed prevailing ideas of culture, art, and leisure whenever they experimented with any cultural expression that diverged from those already associated with African Americans.[6]

The bifurcation of American culture into high and low was a corollary of the ascendant ideal of culture championed by cultural elites. For them, culture and civilization were indistinguishable. The purpose of culture was to refine, inspire, and morally elevate an individual. Culture was inseparable from traditional moral discipline; it was gained through a proper upbringing, and it enabled men and women to keep their baser instincts in check. Culture was polite manners, a code of personal conduct, and an appreciation of the arts. Those who possessed culture were thought to be civilized; those who lacked it were philistines, or worse, savages. The latter category, predictably, included an assortment of people that cultured whites feared or disliked—the lower classes, non-Europeans, and people whose skin color was not white. Such people were to be scorned because their behavior could only degrade, not elevate.

These cultural arbiters envisioned a world that revered moral purity. To bring this world into being, they strove hard to encourage purity and to impose order—moral order, social order, and public order—on an American society beset by headlong change. In an industrializing, urbanizing nation absorbing millions of immigrants from alien cultures and assimilating millions of former slaves into the polity, the guardians of culture predictably harbored fears of cultural fragmentation and moral anarchy. In response, they advocated cultural standards and nurtured institutions intended to protect high culture from the disorderly and debasing influence of the uncouth lower orders.[7]

Their ambitious campaign took many forms, including the retreat of elites into private spaces (better to cede public space to the masses than to have to share it with them), the transformation of public spaces by strict rules of behavior, and the inculcation of cultural preferences on the broader American public. The behaviors that were targets of this campaign were diverse but unmistakable. Besieged by ill-bred and ignorant people who impeded the contemplation of the perfect and the sublime—the main purpose of the arts—orchestra conductors inveighed against audience unruliness and playbills coached audiences in proper listening posture and polite exiting, while cultural critics tutored readers in the subtleties of high culture. Whatever particular form the promotion of high culture took, it aimed to tame the American masses and instill in them proper deference to it.

High culture necessarily was set against its antithesis—low culture. The purported attributes of low culture need not delay us long. Low culture was uninhibited, crude, and simple; it aroused animalistic responses from audiences and encouraged debased behavior. At its worst, it flirted with barbarism by corrupting the senses and corroding the soul. While high culture was unmistakably European in origin, low culture was the unfortunate creation of inferior and darker "races." Inevitably the least civilized races performed and consumed low culture.

This hierarchy of culture dictated the creative opportunities available to all popular performers and artists in the United States. Artists, entrepreneurs, and consumers alike had to elect whether to align themselves with high or low culture. Although the boundaries between high and low culture were never as stark or impenetrable as the defenders of high culture would have liked, generations of performers nevertheless faced the choice of following the dictates of arbiters of culture to cultural legitimacy or embracing low culture and the risk of acquiring the identity of cultural philistines.[8]

For African Americans, careers in and access to high culture verged on inconceivable. Professional African American actors during the nineteenth century, for instance, had almost no prospects of performing Shakespeare or other venerable works of the stage. Instead, they were consigned to minor roles or characters that were consonant with prevailing stereotypes of primitive, buffoonish blacks. A few ambitious black actors exiled themselves to Europe in search of greater opportunities. Ira Aldridge decamped to England in 1824, where he sustained a four-decade-long career performing as Othello, Hamlet, King Lear, and nearly four dozen other roles. Even more remarkable, Aldridge, adorned with a wig and greasepaint, periodically appeared as white European characters. Not until three-quarters of a century after his death in 1867 would black actors in the United States enjoy comparable opportunities.[9]

Even blacks who were steeped in high culture and were proficient in its forms could not anticipate any recognition of their mastery. Sculptor Meta Warrick Fuller endured repeated frustrations common to black artists who aspired to create high art. Born into the ranks of the "Negro aristocracy" of Philadelphia in 1877, Fuller grew up with the trappings of Victorian respectability and exceptional educational opportunities. During high school she earned a scholarship to the Pennsylvania Museum School of the Industrial Arts, where her teachers urged her to continue her training in France. Arriving in Paris in 1899, she came under the tutelage of painter Henry O. Tanner and renowned sculptors Augustus Saint-Gaudens and Auguste Rodin. While honing her sculpting technique and mastering the aesthetic language of the Romantic Symbolist school of art, she deliberately avoided African or African American themes.[10]

When W. E. B. Du Bois met Fuller while in Paris in 1900 he encouraged her to "make a speciality of Negro types." She demurred. Her reluctance almost certainly reflected the dilemma African American artists confronted when selecting their subject matter. Prevailing aesthetic conventions of sculpture, rooted in the classical tradition and distorted by racism, inhibited efforts to fashion representations, particularly heroic images, of African Americans. The artistic challenge of depicting African Americans in sculpture was especially daunting because there was virtually no precedent for sculptural depictions of African Americans. Moreover, Fuller already had acquired a reputation for her perceived "grotesque" renderings of mythical and biblical themes. To apply this technique to African American topics ran the risk of having both her creations and her subjects dismissed by white patrons and critics as primitive and bizarre, thereby worsening the artistic marginalization of African Americans.[11]

Circumstances eventually led Fuller to reconsider. She had pursued an education and a career as an artist with the assumption that her identity as a black woman was irrelevant. But the conditions she encountered when she returned to Philadelphia in 1903 compelled her to revise her expectations. Despite the accolades she had earned in Paris, few white connoisseurs regarded her as a legitimate artist or were interested in her sculpture. Her art and her racial identity, she came to recognize, could not be separated. When she was offered a commission to create a diorama tracing the history of blacks in America for an international exposition in Jamestown, Virginia, in 1907 she eagerly accepted. With no likelihood of displaying her sculpture in museums and galleries, Fuller grasped the opportunity to reach the potentially huge audience of exposition visitors. Casting aside her previous refusal to take up African American themes, Fuller refashioned both her art and her identity as an artist when she made her elaborate diorama of black history.[12]

For Ira Aldredge, Meta Warrick Fuller, and other African Americans, the bifurcation of high and low culture dictated how and where they pursued their craft as well as who their audience would be. If they strove to advance the goals of high culture they stood little likelihood of garnering respectability, at least in the eyes of the nation's white arbiters of culture. But if they accepted the roles that were consigned to them by prevailing racial stereotypes and notions of low culture, they might never be able to give expression to the full range of either their talents or their race's aspirations. They would, in effect, contribute to their own dehumanization.

Some African Americans resisted these Procrustean choices by striving to elevate the prestige of their artistry. They did so by insisting that some African American cultural forms dismissed as low and "vulgar" properly belonged within high culture. As a composer of songs irrevocably associated with disreputable nightlife, Scott Joplin was an unlikely proponent of revisions to the canon of high culture. Emerging from obscurity in the Reconstruction-era southern hinterlands, he built his reputation as one of the most brilliant American composers of the 1890s. He came to resent that his ragtime compositions retained the stigma of low culture, so he set out to revise the reputation and performance of ragtime. For Joplin, ragtime was America's most important contribution to the world's musical heritage, and he demanded that the music be accorded appropriate respect. He published texts explaining the proper performance of ragtime and committed himself to demonstrating its aesthetic sophistication. Too many interpreters of ragtime, he complained, played the music without appropriate solemnity. Appalled by the grotesque and stereotypical depictions of blacks that littered contemporary sheet music, he insisted that the illustrations that graced his music depict African Americans as dignified, elegant, and modern. Intent on cementing his reputation as a composer of enduring greatness while also burnishing the reputation of American music, he threw himself into composing an opera in the final years of his life.[13]

On almost every count, his opera, *Treemonisha*, was ill suited for its age. It told the story of a young black woman coming of age in Arkansas during the years following the Civil War. Treemonisha, the title character, struggles to lead her community out of ignorance and superstition by instilling in them a love of education. Although Joplin insisted that his opera was not a ragtime composition, most contemporary Americans thought of Joplin strictly as a ragtime composer. Joplin's depiction of superstition and ignorance among rural southern blacks, alas, was unlikely to hold much allure for elite or urban black audiences. And the idea that recently freed blacks were an apt subject for an opera was inconceivable to most whites. That Joplin died virtually ignored and broke, having never heard his opera performed, revealed how hard it was to lift the reputation of a low-culture genre such as ragtime.[14]

Aida Overton Walker, one of the leading black choreographers and dancers of the early twentieth century, was more successful than Joplin at dissolving the boundaries between high and low culture. Since the early nineteenth century black dance, at least as interpreted by whites, had earned a conspicuous place in American theater. One black dancer, William Henry Lane, the "Master Juba," broke the color barrier during the 1840s and garnered an international reputation as a minstrel performer.[15] But not until late in the century did black dancers gain a spot on the stage beyond the forms associated with minstrelsy, and even then they did so principally as performers of the wildly popular, plantation-derived "cakewalk" dance.[16] Assumptions about black primitivism and white cravings for "authentic" performers now elevated black dancers as the ideal interpreters of cakewalks, which were at once raucous and athletic. Overton Walker was a beneficiary of these new opportunities for black dancers. Born in 1880 in Richmond, Virginia, she grew up in New York City. While still a teenager she joined a series of black touring companies, including the Black Patti Troubadours, one of the most successful black shows of the era. In 1898, she secured a place in the company of the internationally renowned comedy duo Bert Williams and George Walker, for whom she soon became the principal choreographer. Although she won her initial fame as a cakewalk dancer, she used her position with Williams and Walker to expand the repertoire available to her and other black dancers.[17]

One of her most audacious innovations was her 1908 adaptation of *Salome*, first for a Williams and Walker production and then as part of her own show. Salome's unfettered and seductive dance before Herod in the New Testament had already provided inspiration for several noted white women choreographers interested in depicting female physical expression and sensuality. Beyond the contemporary craze for exotic "Oriental" dances, the notoriety of both Oscar Wilde's play *Salome* and composer Richard Strauss's opera of the same name encouraged Overton Walker to tackle the role of Salome. It, however, was fraught with risks. Variety audiences were unprepared for Overton Walker's graceful choreography that avoided the vulgar excesses of popular black comedy. Members of the black middle class, who condemned any endeavor that undercut images of black respectability, could be expected to criticize anything as risqué as Salome's dance. Nevertheless, Overton Walker's performances as Salome won her grudging respect from both black and white critics by skillfully playing to their expectations. For whites, Overton Walker's race made her ideally suited to assume the role of Salome. A reviewer in *Vanity Fair* concluded, "Her Pantherine movements have all the languorous grace which is traditionally bound up with Oriental dancing."[18] Skeptical blacks, meanwhile, could be reassured that Overton Walker's performance of Salome's dance drew upon high culture for its inspiration and was a chaste display of feminine grace and artistry.[19]

To a greater degree than even Overton Walker, William Grant Still found ways to confound the high and low categories. Born in Mississippi in 1895 and educated at Wilberforce University, Still needed only to recall the frustrations of Will Marion Cook, a brilliant black violinist at the turn of the century, to be reminded of the obstacles to black musicians succeeding in the realm of high culture. Unable to secure a career as a soloist, Cook had settled on a career as a composer for black theater. Still, like Cook, was a conservatory-trained musician who aspired to compose symphonic music. But whereas Cook, his senior by thirty years, had had no viable alternative to the low culture world of black theater, Still successfully straddled the divide between high and low culture. While composing symphonic music during the 1920s he worked as an arranger for bluesman W. C. Handy's band, played in the pit orchestra for Noble Sissle and Eubie Blake's Broadway musical *Shuffle Along*, and was the recording manager of the Black Swan Phonograph Company, the first African American–owned and -operated record company. Subsequently, he kept his hand in popular music during the 1930s by arranging music for popular radio broadcasts as well as for Hollywood films.[20]

Still and his predecessors contended not just with white defenders of high culture but also with African American cultural elites who espoused racial uplift through the politics of respectability. As W. E. B. Du Bois pointed out, African Americans maintained an exaggerated self-consciousness and cultural defensiveness in the face of white claims of superiority. To rebut such claims, many prominent blacks dwelt on the importance of blacks attaining collective and individual respectability. Respectability was never just an unthinking mimicry of whites and white norms. The focus on individual behavior and attitudes, which was a concern shared by black women's and men's voluntary groups as well ministers and secular leaders, represented an assertion by blacks of their will and agency to define themselves. By adhering to a code of temperance, thrift, polite manners, sexual purity, cleanliness, and rectitude, blacks could contradict racist stereotypes about their inherent inferiority. They also could reject claims that wealth or status defined their self-worth, thereby extending the claim of respectability to the most menial members of their community. This inclusiveness across class lines helps to explain why the language of respectability had such resonance among blacks.[21]

Yet the dictates of black respectability often pitted black artists and entrepreneurs against black cultural arbiters. For middle-class blacks anxious to defend their respectability, popular genres of music, especially ragtime and the blues, were offensive both on aesthetic grounds and because they elicited mockery from whites. During the 1890s and first decade of the twentieth century many blacks denounced the lyrics and imagery of such "coon songs" as Ernest Hogan's enormously popular "All Coons Look Alike To Me" (1896). That the song was written by a black man did nothing to lessen the damage of its mean-spirited lyrics. (Crowder failed to appease his black critics when he pointed out that he had replaced the word "pimps" with "coons" when he published the song.) The *Negro Music Journal*, for instance, claimed to speak on behalf of the upstanding black community: "White men also perpetuate so-called music under the name 'ragtime,' representing it to be characteristic of Negro music. This also is a libelous insult. The typical Negro would blush to own acquaintance with the vicious trash put forth under Ethiopian titles. If the *Negro Music Journal* can . . . help to banish this epidemic it will go down in history as one of the greatest musical benefactors of the age."[22] In later years successive generations of frustrated black cultural arbiters would add moving pictures, vaudeville, jazz, and other expressions of mass culture to the distractions that lured black audiences away from "the classics."[23]

Although the ideology of black respectability, along with the hierarchy of high and low culture, defined and restricted black creative opportunities, black artists and entrepreneurs continually tested the boundaries that circumscribed their work. While white artists and cultural entrepreneurs had the option of pursuing "middlebrow" culture that was both accessible and, increasingly, respectable, ambitious blacks pioneered cultural expressions that defied conventional genres. When the Black Patti Troubadours performed on stage from Argentina to Australia during the 1890s, they mixed the sacred and profane; their repertoire included sublime opera, solemn spirituals, and raucous cakewalks. After the turn of the century, the Whitman Sisters of Lawrence, Kansas, parlayed their dancing and musical talents, extremely light skin color, and respectable upbringing as the daughters of a prominent minister into a popular vaudeville act that elevated black theater to new respectability and eroded the boundaries that separated secular, commercial entertainment from religious performances. Beginning in the late 1920s Duke Ellington's band defied easy categorization by fusing lush and complex orchestral arrangements with swinging jazz polyrhythms and unpredictable and edgy improvisation, thereby creating simultaneously sophisticated concert and toe-tapping dance music. Who could say whether Ellington and his orchestra were practitioners of high or low culture?[24]

By the time that Ellington's orchestra was refining swing jazz, the grip of the cult of high culture and respectability had loosened considerably. World War I had called into question the presumptive supremacy of Anglo-European civilization. After witnessing Western Europe destroying its youth on blood soaked fields, black Americans could not easily subscribe to the belief that they should measure their progress against the standard of Western civilization. The revival of Pan-Africanism, dramatized by the 1919 Pan-African Congress that coincided with the Paris Peace Conference, stirred hopes among blacks that the future of blacks, and even the world, would be settled in Africa. At the same time, Marcus Garvey's Universal Negro Improvement Association attracted hundreds of thousands of black men and women, including some in the rural South, to the causes of African redemption and civilization. By the 1920s interest in Africa and the African diaspora, including especially Haiti, dominated African American intellectual life, extending from the "New Negro" movement to popular drama and even the new mass art form of cinema. This diverse cultural movement prompted blacks to reconsider Africa's legacy in the Americas and their own relationship to their ancestral continent. Together, the waning of the ideology of civilization and the Pan-Africanist revival worked to glorify the primitive and to undermine the idea that African Americans should slavishly defer to the conventions of contemporary white civilization. The presumption that the black masses were a crude and immature race striving to overcome the legacy of their barbarous ancestors and slavery while inching up the ladder of civilization seemed glaringly obsolete. By the 1920s, black intellectuals and leaders evinced less and less embarrassment about the black masses. Historian Wilson Jeremiah Moses explains, they "became acceptable to the black world—more than incidentally—at the same time that they were becoming more acceptable to the white."[25]

As the sanctity of high culture eroded during the 1920s, black cultural arbiters called for a new black aesthetics to take its place. But serious disagreements arose over the manner and degree to which black artists were obligated to engage with and represent the experiences of African Americans. This debate about the politics of art framed the significance that black intellectuals assigned to the popular culture of their age. The older aesthetics of high culture had held popular art at arm's length. But now it was open to reconsideration. Yet when black intellectuals hashed out a new aesthetics during the 1920s, they returned invariably to formal aesthetics and slighted the unpretentious, intuitive, spontaneous, and democratic aesthetics of popular culture.

The evolution of Du Bois's ideas about black aesthetics are suggestive. Enthralled by the high culture of Europe while traveling on the continent during the early 1890s, Du Bois expressed conventional attitudes toward the "education" and "soul training" engendered by contemplation of the sublime. Like many aesthetes of his age, Du Bois lamented that the United States fostered "vigor" and "ingenuity" rather than beauty. To compensate for these failings and to nurture an appreciation of beauty among African Americans, Du Bois toured the South lecturing on "The Art and Art Galleries of Europe" and circulating cheap reproductions of great European works. By 1903, when Du Bois's *Souls of Black Folk* was published, he was urging blacks to enrich themselves and the nation by becoming workers in the "kingdom of culture." Betraying his romantic interpretation of racial identity, Du Bois saluted African Americans for using art to express their unique racial essence. He believed these gifts were manifest especially in black music, proclaiming, "There is no true American music but the wild sweet melodies of the Negro slave." His admiration of slave spirituals, however, did not translate into an embrace of contemporary black popular culture, which, to Du Bois's dismay and disgust, he found vulgar and, worst of all, commercial.[26]

By the 1920s, Du Bois had revised his vision of the "kingdom of culture." No longer did he insist that aesthetic experience needed to be quarantined from everyday life. And now Du Bois looked to art not to express but rather to render irrelevant racial identity. In "Criteria of Negro Art," published in 1926, Du Bois answered the question of what have "we who are slaves and black to do with Art." Because blacks had been thrust to the margins of American society, they developed "a certain distaste for the tawdry and flamboyant" that regrettably characterized American culture. It consequently fell to black Americans to undertake "the creation of Beauty." The beauty that Du Bois had in mind was "not a servile imitation of Anglo-Saxon civilization," but instead a beauty that would revitalize America's impoverished democracy and counter the nation's capitalist excess. This beauty, however, was not some "eternal and perfect Beauty" that exists apart from "Truth" and "Freedom." To the contrary, "they are for me unseparated and inseparable." Empowered by this belief, Du Bois concluded that art and propaganda are also inseparable. "I do not care a damn," he announced, "for any art that is not used for propaganda."[27]

Du Bois's position on art as "propaganda" was more subtle than his rhetoric would suggest. His intent in the essay was to challenge the aesthetics of both white cultural voyeurs such as Carl Van Vechten, who romanticized black decadence, and black artists such as Alain Locke, who postured as "wailing purists." Du Bois had been troubled by Locke's introduction to *The New Negro* collection, published the year before Du Bois's essay. As the self-appointed spokesman for a new generation, Locke dismissed the "guarded idealization" of Du Bois and his ilk along with their presumption that "art must fight social battles and compensate social wrongs." Locke admonished young artists to unshackle themselves from this tired moralism and to embrace their racial identity in the service of art, rather than to enlist art in the service of their race. At the heart of the debate between Du Bois and Locke was whether politics and aesthetics were complementary or antagonistic; Du Bois held the former belief, and Locke the latter.[28]

These lofty debates about aesthetics, politics, and race were far removed from the speakeasies where jazz and blues musicians were refining their own vernacular aesthetic, the dancehalls where black dancers experimented with flamboyant movement, and the diverse venues where most blacks sought entertainment and perhaps found beauty. Neither Du Bois's nor Locke's aesthetics encouraged black intellectuals or cultural arbiters to take seriously the cultural innovation fomented and consumed by the black masses. Wed to ideals of pure culture and hostile toward the mass-consumer marketplace and popular culture, Du Bois, Locke, and other black intellectuals of the early twentieth century had, at best, modest success molding the habits and preferences of most black consumers. As long as leading black intellectuals and critics were committed to genteel Victorian moralism or effete modernist aesthetics they misunderstood or overlooked the popular culture of their day.

Without an ongoing and far-reaching shift in American attitudes toward leisure it is unlikely that the plethora of popular amusements and technological innovations of the era would have been embraced by American consumers. Commercialized leisure was a corollary of the routinized work rhythms that accompanied industrialization. As work became more regular and structured, so too did leisure. The accelerated pace and intensity of industrial work, as compared to the ebb and flow of earlier work rhythms, transformed "free time" into a respite from the hurly-burly and tedium of work. For workers leisure time increasingly offered an opportunity to express elements of their personality and sense of self that were unwelcome in the modern workplace. So black domestics in Atlanta sought release in the city's nightspots, shop girls in New York City toyed with the boundaries of propriety by flirting with men in dancehalls, and thrill seekers in Lexington, Kentucky, marveled at the sounds and images that their coins bought at nickelodeons. When leisure time became more regimented, it became more valuable both to workers off the clock and to entertainers and entrepreneurs eager to fill it.[29]

Before Americans could embrace commercialized leisure they had to surrender, or, at the very least revise, inherited notions about the virtues of self-sufficiency. In the agrarian society of the nineteenth-century United States, ownership of land or possession of an artisanal skill were the aspirations of most American men. Nineteenth-century Americans purchased consumer goods, of course, but the value they assigned to independence placed restraints on consumerism. By the early twentieth century economic self-sufficiency was no longer a realistic aspiration for the majority of Americans who were now urbanites and wage earners.[30]

No longer autonomous economic actors, the vast majority of Americans looked for new ways to redefine their self-worth so that work was more than meaningless drudgery. Men were still providers, but what did it mean to be providers if a male wage earner could no longer control his work? Women, likewise, were still expected to be nurturers of families and children, but this role increasingly entailed participating in the marketplace as consumers of mass-produced goods. American men and women, then, had to reconcile their roles as husbands and wives, workers and homemakers, with the economic and social realities of the nation's industrial and consumer economy.

More and more Americans elected to define themselves by what they purchased. In the process they forged "communities of consumption" peopled by like-minded consumers who experimented with new and similar expressions of self. These communities were about more than escapism or mindless consumption. Immigrants, for example, could camouflage their origins and escape suspicion by adopting the latest fashions. The young took advantage of commercialized leisure to experiment with new modes of courtship while the newly urbanized, whether from the prairies of Minnesota or the piney woods of Texas, could dust themselves off by sporting urbane styles. And African Americans could escape the exclusion and humiliation of segregation by establishing and patronizing black dancehalls, theaters, sporting events, and recreational facilities.

Madam C. J. Walker's thriving hair-culture business during the first third of the twentieth century illuminates many of the essential traits of the communities of consumers that emerged among African Americans. Born of former slaves in Louisiana shortly after the Civil War, Walker (née Sarah Breedlove) was orphaned before marrying and becoming a mother at a very young age. She toiled for years as a servant and laundress before her thinning hair prompted her experiments with home remedies to restore hair loss. Convinced of the efficacy of her remedies, she launched a line of hair-care products. Within a decade she had married a prominent newspaperman in Indianapolis, taken the name of Madam Walker, incorporated her business, and begun marketing her goods nationally through door-to-door sales and a mail-order business. By then, she was well on her way to becoming the wealthiest African American female entrepreneur of the age and a noted patron of black causes and black artists.

Walker's success was inconceivable without women's new enthusiasm for transforming their self-images and new sense of identity as consumers. Like other cosmetic and hair-product entrepreneurs, Walker had to overcome older aesthetics of female beauty that looked askance at cosmetics. Walker's task was eased by the era's cult of celebrity that introduced American women to images of actresses, singers, dancers, professional beauties, and others who made ample use of beauty products. Magazines, newspapers, druggists, and department stores were slow to market cosmetics, but by the 1910s even they had abandoned their skepticism about the propriety of the trade. Walker's greatest commercial advantage was her skill at adapting her merchandising strategy to preexisting networks among black women. Black women had long engaged in collective hair grooming; now Walker offered some of them an opportunity to escape the drudgery of housekeeping and laundering and instead earn a living as sales agents and beauty-shop proprietors who catered to other black women. At the same time Walker and her agents could strike a blow against prejudices about African American appearance. Refusing to promote the emulation of white beauty—light skin and straight hair—Walker endorsed an aesthetic of black beauty that drew attention to "the inner worth" and personal dignity of black women. Walker's revaluation of black female beauty overcame early opposition from ministers and black elites, and by the end of the 1910s her agents and those of her competitors were ubiquitous wherever African Americans lived. By then, as historian Kathy Peiss notes, "commercial beauty culture was something much more than an isolated act of consumption or vanity."[31]

Madam Walker's rise from an impoverished childhood to life as a millionaire cosmetics entrepreneur was an exceptional rags-to-riches saga. Few if any of the consumers of her products enjoyed comparable fortune, but they did experience expanding economic opportunities that provided the discretionary funds that grew Walker's bottom line and fueled the explosion of black popular culture. The majority of blacks, of course, barely advanced beyond poverty. But a significant minority acquired property and clawed their way into the middle class. During the late nineteenth century black farmers steadily accumulated land, eventually holding title to 15 million acres by 1910. Virtually every southern town of note boasted a black business district that served as a center of business and leisure. Even in the rural hinterland, black incomes in the three decades after Appomattox more than doubled, and may have even grown more rapidly than did white incomes. By 1900, black families had sufficient means to afford life's necessities *and* to splurge occasionally on leisure, travel, and culture. As the economic resources in black hands grew, so too did the opportunities for black creativity and consumption of everything from cosmetics to commercialized leisure.[32]

Madam Walker's extraordinary life was emblematic of the black experience in one other important regard; like her, more and more blacks joined the quickening diaspora of African Americans across the nation. With each decade the ranks of blacks who moved from the southern countryside to the city, and from the South to the North and West, swelled. Walker's trek took her from rural Louisiana north to St. Louis, then west to Denver and back east to Indianapolis before concluding outside New York City. Vaudevillian Bert Williams would also settle in New York City after moving as a child from Florida to southern California. Once he began his performing career, he headed north to San Francisco and eventually east to Cleveland. Filmmaker Oscar Micheaux made his way to New York City after a youth spent on the plains of Illinois, Kansas, and South Dakota, followed by early career stops in Chicago and Roanoke, Virginia. For Walker, Williams, Micheaux, and their contemporaries, geographic mobility was perhaps the most tangible expression of freedom after slavery. Moreover, the opportunity to move as their careers required was essential to their artistic and commercial success. Black mobility, of course, took more quotidian forms as well, as when African American revelers bought reduced fare railroad tickets to attend festivities in the cities of the New South and when black booksellers crisscrossed the nation selling Booker T. Washington's writings and other popular works by black authors.[33]

The trend was unmistakable; blacks were becoming increasingly mobile, urban, and urbane. Without the ongoing redistribution of African Americans across the nation the diffusion of black culture and its broader impact on mass culture almost certainly would have been greatly diminished. This movement of blacks from the countryside to the nation's cities led to the emergence of islands of black commerce and culture from Pittsburgh to Milwaukee and San Francisco. Bonds of family and place continued to link residents of burgeoning black communities to their former homes, and consequently all manner of black culture circulated from countryside to city and back again. Thus the railroads that made possible the careers of itinerant performers such as Scott Joplin and the Whitman Sisters also carried migrants to Chicago and Philadelphia, and in turn distributed the *Chicago Defender*, the recordings of Bessie Smith, and the beauty products of Madam Walker across the nation's hinterland.[34]

We may be excused for assuming that rural blacks in the Deep South, who made up a large portion of the nation's African American population and endured the most intense combination of poverty and oppression, were cut off from these cultural exchanges. In fact, even in the depths of the Mississippi Delta blacks were eager consumers of and contributors to the latest popular culture. At the beginning of the century, when W. C. Handy and other black orchestra leaders started touring the Delta, they began to fashion a musical genre that drew on white brass band and rural black music. The resulting hybrid was warmly embraced by black audiences and emulated by local musicians. Even while local artists continued to hone their distinctive version of the blues, they adapted and mastered each new genre of popular music. The repertoire of Delta musicians was much more eclectic that extant recordings would suggest—likewise the listening preferences of Delta blacks. By the 1930s, recordings by swing bands and crooners filled the jukeboxes in the region. A 1942 survey of favorite radio performers in the Delta offers a telling measure of the region's participation in contemporary national popular culture; topping the list were big bands, gospel acts, country music stars, and a Broadway show-tune singer, but only one blues artist.[35]

Rising rates of black literacy and education facilitated this widening and accelerating diffusion of black culture. Despite white opposition and paltry educational resources, the percentage of blacks who were literate rose from less than one-third in 1870 to more than three-quarters by the turn of the century. Although the educational opportunities available to southern blacks lagged far behind those available to whites, by the turn of the century one-third of eligible black children attended school. Conditions continued to improve, although only gradually and unevenly, so that by World War II, two-thirds of black children of age attended school and more than one-fifth of eligible black children were enrolled in high school.[36]

From the ranks of these literate African Americans came not only black writers, journalists, and lyricists, but also the black consumers who bought black newspapers, sheet music, poetry, and other black creative endeavors. John Edward Bruce's and James Weldon Johnson's careers, for example, would have been inconceivable in the absence of advancing black literacy and education. Bruce himself was born a slave in Maryland in 1856. Although largely self-educated, he had done a brief stint at Howard University before beginning his career as a journalist for a black newspaper in 1874. At the age of twenty-three, he launched his own newspaper, and by the 1880s he was a widely published correspondent under the pen name Bruce Grit. Like most black newspapermen, Bruce had to hustle to make a living. The prospects of transforming the swelling ranks of literate blacks into a community of subscribers enticed him and others to launch one black newspaper after another. A similar ambition to reach black magazine readers inspired Bruce to exploit the popularity of the detective genre to promote Pan-Africanism by writing a serialized story about "The Black Sleuth," an African prince who astounds white Americans with his feats of detection.[37]

Johnson, who was a generation younger than Bruce, was the beneficiary of educational opportunities in the New South that Bruce had never enjoyed. Born in 1871 to transplanted Bahamian parents in Jacksonville, Florida, Johnson attended public schools, earning his diploma at the age of sixteen. He subsequently graduated from Atlanta University and then, at the age of twenty-three, returned to his hometown to become principal of his former school. He trained for and passed the bar but the allure of a life in theater drew him to New York, where, along with his brother, he prospered as a composer, lyricist, novelist, poet, and man of letters.[38]

Black culture, of course, did not require literacy. Blacks had sustained a rich culture even during slavery when law and tradition suppressed literacy among African Americans. Yet literacy was important if blacks were to participate in mass-produced culture and, equally important, were to have a measure of influence over their representation in mass culture. Otherwise, literate blacks or whites, in the role of lawyers, producers, entrepreneurs, and managers, were certain to have decisive influence over the commercialization of African Americans' creations. Countless black artists who lacked literacy were prevented from translating their artistry into a form that could be mass marketed. For example, the music publishing industry of the late nineteenth century ignored many popular forms of black music, in part because many of their creators and practitioners could not read or write musical notation. Of course, some of these forms of black music could not easily be transcribed into conventional musical notation. Established musical notation could not capture the subtle alterations in tone, tempo, or the quarter-notes (the notes between the notes, so to speak) that were so essential to black music. Consequently these genres fell outside the canon of published music and of the processes of the popular music industry, and would remain so until the recording revolution of the twentieth century and subsequent transcription by musically trained black and white musicians. To the extent that the popular-music industry captured the remarkable burst of black musical innovation at the end of the nineteenth century it was dependent on Scott Joplin, James Weldon Johnson, Will Marion Cook, W. C. Handy, and other trained musicians who were fully conversant in musical composition and notation.[39]

The differing degrees of commercialization of various forms of black music are a reminder that the prominence of blacks and black artistry in commercialized mass culture was hardly inevitable. After all, at the end of the Civil War, the overwhelming majority of African Americans were indigent and illiterate freedpeople in the rural South. There, they had participated in the region's and the nation's cultural life, but so long as they remained isolated by geography, illiteracy, and poverty, they were severely limited in their capacity to participate in the nation's emerging mass culture. Greater mobility, improving education, and advancing wealth were prerequisites for the explosion of black culture in turn-of-the-century United States.

The "kingdom of culture" that most black performers labored in was a world of commercialized leisure, mass produced for mass consumption. The era's ascendant forms of popular art exploited electricity and the age's other technological innovations, making possible mechanical reproductions of art and entertainment on a previously unimaginable scale. Yet while these innovations made popular culture cheap and accessible to a huge swath of the nation's public, they also represented a challenge to black entrepreneurs who participated in the marketplace of popular culture. In addition to the expense of the latest technology, successful entrepreneurs needed the means to reach potential audiences. Although blacks had sufficient disposable income to enjoy commercialized leisure by the beginning of the twentieth century, they lacked access to the capital that some of their white competitors possessed. And while white artists, businessmen, and consumers traversed the boundaries of Jim Crow when whim or profit dictated, black entrepreneurs, no less than black performers, had to adjust virtually every aspect of their business to take account of racial segregation.

African Americans predictably first gained a foothold in the cultural market as performers. As the de facto laborers of the entertainment industry, performers had few fixed costs, needed little if any access to credit, and had only to secure the necessities of their craft—instruments, costumes, equipment, and, perhaps, talent—to enter the marketplace of popular culture. The itinerant black bluesmen who performed on the streets of Durham, North Carolina, or in the blind tigers of Mississippi were exemplars of the new, if seldom lucrative, opportunities available to black performers in the early twentieth century. At the very least, black musicians, comedians, and actors now could scratch out a better livelihood as entertainers than in many other occupations open to blacks. W. C. Handy, before achieving fame as a band leader and popular composer, experimented with several careers, including teaching, carpentry, shoemaking, and plastering. He eventually settled on a career in music because it was at least as lucrative as the alternatives and provided an outlet for his creativity.[40]

A few black performers even achieved extraordinary fame and wealth. Bert Williams, at the peak of his fame as a singer and comedian during the 1910s, was one of the highest-paid stage performers, regardless of race, in the United States. Jack Johnson, the controversial black heavyweight boxer, earned hundreds of thousands of dollars for some of his title bouts, and perhaps equal sums for endorsing patent medicines and other products. At a time when blacks faced concerted campaigns to drive them from almost all skilled or well-paid trades, the possibility of replicating Williams's or Johnson's success must have whetted the ambitions of countless would-be black performers.[41]

Other blacks whose talents lay in business rather than performance carved out niches for themselves as impresarios, managers, and intermediaries between the white cultural marketplace and black performers.[42] In such instances, blacks marketed their knowledge of and networks with black artists. Clarence Williams, a jack of all trades, demonstrated the possibilities open to black impresarios who possessed both an eye for talent and business acumen. Born in Plaquemine, Louisiana, in 1898, Williams joined a traveling minstrel show at the age of twelve. After moving to New Orleans he supported himself by shining shoes, doing odd jobs, and singing. From the beginning of his career, he honed his skills not just as a performer but also as a composer, music publisher, and manager. While still a teenager Williams began managing New Orleans saloons and dancehalls, including his own cabaret. After concluding that Chicago was replacing New Orleans as the center of black popular music, Williams moved there in 1920 and opened a string of record and music stores. When, in that same year, Mamie Smith achieved extraordinary success with her recording of "Crazy Blues," Williams shifted to managing black women blues singers. He began by promoting the career of his wife, Eva Taylor, and settled in New York City, which had emerged as the center of the music publishing and recording business. Within months of his arrival, he helped Bessie Smith launch her renowned career as a blues singer with Columbia Records. In addition to accompanying her on piano, he wrote or cowrote many of her most popular songs and released them under his own publishing company. Based on his reputation as a talent scout, Williams signed on as the artist and repertoire director for Okeh Records, a white-owned record label that targeted African American consumers. Tapping his varied talents, he arranged recording sessions for Okeh artists, supplied them with songs, published their compositions, and managed their business affairs. Simultaneously he continued to record under his own name and in 1927 even composed and produced a musical, *Bottomland*. After decades in the music business, Williams sold his extensive back catalog of tunes to Decca Records for $50,000 and retired in 1943. (Apparently, idleness did not suit him. He then bought and ran a used-goods store to keep himself busy.)[43]

The exceptional career such as Williams', however, did not substantially improve the precarious position of black entrepreneurs in the entertainment industry. Williams gained a toehold in several sectors of the industry that were otherwise beyond the reach of most blacks of his generation. By publishing his own songs as well as those of performers whom he managed, Williams established a black presence in music publishing. But the bulk of music publishing remained securely in the hands of the huge publishing houses that had secured control over the market in the late nineteenth century. As late as the 1910s, New York City, the center of music publishing, had only one major publishing firm run by African Americans. This notable exception was the Gotham-Attucks Publishing Company, founded in 1905. The company was preceded by two smaller short-lived enterprises, the Attucks Music Publishing Company, founded by Bert Williams and several other noted songwriters, and the Gotham Music Company, which included among its founders bandleader James Reese Europe and composer

Will Marion Cook. When the two companies merged they brought together most of the luminaries in black musical theater and songwriting. The firm's catalog consisted largely of songs from popular Broadway shows associated with Williams and his partner George Walker. As long as ragtime and "coon songs" remained popular, the company provided an important outlet for black artists who rejected the trite, degrading lyrics and illustrations that marred popular music associated with African American life and themes. Gotham-Attucks, however, could not compete with major white publishers such as Joseph Stern, Jerome H. Remick, or E. T. Paul, which could afford to advertise widely and publish songs in diverse arrangements (voice, solo piano, guitar, orchestra, etc.) appropriate for any potential performer. By 1911, most of the company's composers and lyricists had migrated to other well-established publishing houses, and Gotham-Attucks rapidly declined.[44]

As in music publishing, neither talent nor business savvy enabled blacks to stake a claim in the early recording industry. Despite the popularity of black singers and performers beginning in the 1890s, the recording industry remained controlled by white businessmen and inventors who ignored both black artists and consumers. Because these industry executives retained proprietary rights to most recording technology until World War I they could dictate who and what was recorded. Intent on establishing the cultural respectability of the new technology, Thomas Edison and his competitors sought to limit its use to disseminating edifying art, such as classical leider, opera, and chaste popular songs appropriate for the parlor. Such attitudes ensured that the rare black voices heard on the earliest recordings were musical curiosities that, often as not, exploited the stereotype of the happy, carefree "coon."

Although George W. Johnson's immensely popular "Laughing Song" was one of the best-selling recordings of the 1890s, Johnson's career revealed the limited possibilities that the new technology then held for black performers. Born a slave in Virginia before the Civil War, Johnson eventually made his way to New York City. There in 1889 he was overheard whistling a song and was invited to record a cylinder for the infant recording industry. Noted for his whistling and raucous laugh, which he delivered on pitch, Johnson developed two performances that made him famous, "The Whistling Coon" and "The Laughing Coon." Issued in 1890, these two songs sustained Johnson's career for nearly two decades. Because no method of mechanical duplication of recordings had yet been perfected, Johnson could make only a few records at once by singing into several synchronized recording machines. In this fashion, by 1894 he reportedly had recorded more than 25,000 cylinders, for which he was paid twenty cents apiece.[45]

Before World War I, only a tiny number of black performers cut records, and most of them only after gaining appreciative white audiences. Thus, once Bert Williams was established as one of the most popular stage performers of the era he was recorded and subsequently became one of the industry's major stars. And after James Reese Europe acquired national fame as the preferred accompanist of celebrity dancers Irene and Vernon Castle he and his orchestra were invited to record. Otherwise white record executives were little inclined to use expensive technology to produce records of black performers that they assumed whites would not buy and blacks could not afford to buy.[46]

After 1916 the cost of entry into the industry eased when many patents on recording technology expired. By then the price of phonographs had fallen to a point that virtually any music enthusiast could afford one. Simultaneously a new generation of entrepreneurs pioneered a new approach to marketing recorded music. In the early stages of the industry record companies had concentrated on the manufacture of recording technology and record players (which were by then the size of furniture). The records themselves were almost an afterthought. From the record companies' perspective, records were a sideline used to promote the sale of record players. From the consumers' perspective, however, the primary commodity was the records, not the phonograph that was bought only once. Early record companies also had little connection with the impresarios involved in music publishing or artistic management. Recognizing the underserved market of potential record consumers, including hitherto ignored African Americans, executives at the new record companies of the late 1910s and early 1920s focused almost exclusively on producing records. Beyond building relationships with music impresarios and experimenting with new marketing strategies, the new companies catered to all manner of markets—ethnic, religious, regional—that had been ignored by the older record companies. Soon, previously unrecorded genres, ranging from jazz and "hillbilly" music to religious sermons, were widely available to consumers, and black performers, such as Mamie Smith, became popular stars.[47]

The cumulative effect of these changes in the recording industry exacerbated the resentment and impatience of black performers and managers, who watched as white recording companies bought songs from them and then used white artists to record them. Black performers also chafed when white record executives dictated the style and manner in which they performed when recording. These frustrations led Harry Herbert Pace to launch the first successful black-owned record company in 1920. Born in 1884 in Georgia, Pace was a precocious student who graduated valedictorian of his class in Atlanta University at age nineteen. There he had become a disciple of W. E. B. Du Bois, with whom he subsequently worked as business manager of Du Bois's short-lived journal, *Moon Illustrated Weekly*. When the journal failed, Pace worked in printing, banking, and insurance, first in Atlanta and later in Memphis. While in Memphis he befriended W. C. Handy, with whom he began writing songs and cofounded a music publishing company in 1912. Eight years later, Pace moved to New York to launch his Black Swan Record Company. With borrowed capital (probably from Du Bois, Bert Williams, and other members of the company's board of directors) Pace incorporated the company, lined up a recording studio and pressing plant, and, in April 1921, began releasing records.

For Pace and his investors, Black Swan Records was a milestone in both black culture and business. The company pledged to record what Du Bois called "our best voices" and "best music," as opposed to the "comic darky songs" proffered by white companies. With offices in a Harlem brownstone, a fifteen-person office staff, seven district managers, and an eight-man orchestra directed by William Grant Still, Black Swan brought together black talent in performance and composition *with* black business acumen and capital. With tacit nods to the New Negro ethos, Pace sought to harness the new consumer habits of blacks to the cultural marketplace. Company advertisements boasted that Black Swan records were "the only genuine colored records; others are only passing for colored."[48]

Just as Pace sought to loosen the grip of whites on record production, so too he sought to create new, black-controlled avenues to disseminate and promote his records. The company advertised widely in black newspapers and built up a national distribution network. Pace adopted an innovative marketing strategy of staging a musical revue to promote the label's artists and their recordings. From fall of 1921 until the summer of 1922, the Black Swan Troubadours, headlined by rising blues star Ethel Waters and accompanied by bandleader Fletcher Henderson, toured the East, Midwest, and South. While in Louisiana the troupe even performed on radio, then still a curiosity. Taking advantage of the press attention and large audiences that the tour garnered, Pace strove to make Black Swan records easily available to black consumers. Virtually any business that catered to a black clientele, from barber and beauty shops to pool halls, drug stores, furniture dealers, and newsstands, was a prospective record distributor. His aggressive marketing strategy was popular with black merchandisers, who were keen to sell records, and black newspapermen, who were eager for more advertising money from record companies. Retailers and newspapers in turn promoted record-buying campaigns of black artists on the Black Swan label as an expression of race pride. Together, the popularity of recordings by Ethel Waters and other Black Swan artists along with adept marketing generated sales of 400,000 records during the company's first year.[49]

Black Swan's early success, however, proved impossible to sustain. The popularity of black women singers such as Waters and Mamie Smith led other record companies to sign blues singers. By 1924, Black Swan was competing in a marketplace crowded with competitors such as Okeh, Columbia, Aeolian, Brunswick, and Victor, all of which had deeper pockets than Pace's company. Moreover, the white-owned labels signed many of the most popular new performers of the era, including Bessie Smith and Louis Armstrong, while also luring away with generous contracts some of Black Swan's artists. By 1923 the conundrum the company faced was clear; it no longer had a unique product, black popular music, and it could not compete with better-financed white labels. After producing more than 180 recordings and selling hundreds of thousands of copies of them, Black Swan closed in the summer of 1923.[50]

The challenge to which Pace and his short-lived company succumbed was inherent to the American marketplace of popular culture.[51] Black entrepreneurs faced almost insurmountable barriers when competing head to head with white-owned businesses. Black businessmen such as Pace could urge black consumers to buy products produced by black-owned companies in the name of "race pride," "self-help," and "mutual benefit," but black consumers seldom made their consumption choices solely on the basis of racial considerations. Whereas thriving black service businesses, ranging from Madam Walker's beauty parlors to undertakers and barbers, faced few white competitors, black entertainment businesses competed in a marketplace where black consumers had ample reason and opportunity to purchase goods and services from white-owned companies. Indeed, as black music forms came to dominate popular music during the late 1910s and 1920s, the challenges to black cultural entrepreneurs grew. Black entrepreneurs could not conceivably achieve, let alone sustain, a monopoly of black performers and popular culture.

Recorded music, then, was peculiarly adaptable to a mass-consumer market that bridged previously stark divisions in American audiences. Because recorded musical performances were, in a literal sense, disembodied from the black performers who made them, they were not subject to the conventions of racial etiquette that dictated black and white interactions in public spaces. White patrons who might never have entered a speakeasy on Chicago's South Side to hear Louis Armstrong or a Philadelphia nightclub to hear Bessie Smith could listen to their records without crossing uncomfortable racial boundaries. In the absence of recordings, black audiences and musicians such as Louisiana bluesman Lead Belly might never have heard popular Tin Pan Alley songs performed by leading white singers. Because of recordings, the boundaries of race, region, and class that had dictated access to popular music now became permeable. Previously, the music of any specific social group was essentially its own. The advent of mass-produced and cheap recordings made such music instantly available anywhere at the turn of a crank. Even while the white-owned record companies developed special "race records" to cater to blacks, neither record executives nor record retailers had an interest in impeding record sales to any potential audience. In such a fluid and open commercial marketplace for recorded music, black entrepreneurs stood at a distinct disadvantage.

In other sectors of the entertainment industry, the geography of race did circumscribe, to a degree, many competitive advantages of white-owned businesses. Producers and aficionados of live entertainment, unlike record buyers, could not ignore the racial segregation etched into the landscape of virtually every American town or city. Both laws and customs restricted interracial mingling, so that even while black and white popular culture deeply influenced each other, they retained separate performance spaces and distinct performance traditions.[52] This separateness was at the very center of much of the cultural innovation of the era. White curiosity about African Americans could no longer be satisfied, as it had been during much of the nineteenth century, by white performers in blackface and white parodies of black culture. For whites to gain access to the world of black culture they had either to accede to a more porous segregation or to enter African American spaces. In fact, both occurred during the early twentieth century. But when whites or blacks ventured out in search of entertainment performed by the other race or in spaces frequented by them, they had to comply with, skirt, or ignore established racial boundaries. That blacks and whites would test these boundaries was inevitable once black culture captured the American imagination and, no less important, white authorities used zoning ordinances to isolate commercialized vice in black neighborhoods. Whether on Beale Street in Memphis, 18th and Vine Streets in Kansas City, 35th and State Streets in Chicago, or 125th Street in Harlem,

by the 1920s black neighborhoods often were famed for nightlife that attracted both white and black revelers.[53]

Black businessmen found their most secure and lucrative opportunities serving black audiences with neighborhood theaters, clubs, and movie
houses. Small in size and usually only modestly capitalized, these enterprises
promised black consumers the latest entertainment in an environment free
of white prejudice or insults. There, black patrons were not segregated in
the worst seats in the house or subject to harassment from either the management or white customers. These venues also catered to the diverse tastes
and constituencies of their neighborhoods by offering preferred accommo-
dations and "high-tone" entertainment for the black bourgeoisie and inexpensive and rustic performances targeted to recent arrivals from the rural
hinterlands. Often accorded a special place of pride in their communities,
black-owned theaters and nightspots such as the Pekin Café in Chicago, the
New Standard in Philadelphia, and the Gem in Lexington, Kentucky, were
vital spaces where generations of blacks participated in mass culture.[54]

Black entrepreneurs such as Sherman H. Dudley, a black vaudevillian
and theater owner, had a decided advantage over their white competitors
when it came to anticipating black consumer habits and desires. Born in
Dallas around 1870, Dudley developed his stage skills in various minstrel
troupes, including his own Dudley Georgia Minstrels. By the late 1890s he
expanded his repertoire by writing, producing, and performing in musicals. His years of experience touring and managing gave Dudley a keen
understanding of both the entertainment business and the hardships that
black performers experienced at the hands of white businessmen. Moreover, he understood that the consolidation of the black entertainment industry offered the best means to bring order and a measure of fairness to
what had been a haphazard and regional business. In 1911 he began buying
vaudeville and movie theaters in the South and in Philadelphia, Indianapolis, Cleveland, St. Louis, and Kansas City. Within a few years his holdings
expanded to include theaters in Washington, D.C., Philadelphia, Virginia,
and Georgia. At the same time he began to book shows for black communities across the East, South, and Midwest. Dudley's next move was to organize the Southern Consolidated Circuit, which booked touring companies
into black theaters in northern cities and across the South. His influence
over black theaters continued to grow even after movies began to threaten
the popularity of vaudeville. In 1920 he assumed a major role in the Quality
Amusement Corporation, a booking agency that managed films as well as
operas, musicals, plays, and other acts. Yet none of these enterprises was

sufficient to dominate the increasingly complex and national market for popular entertainment. Eventually, during the 1920s, the Theater Owners Booking Association (TOBA), made up of black and white theater owners, including Dudley, emerged as the dominant booking agency for black entertainment. Dudley retained his controlling interest in the Southern Consolidated Circuit, his chain of theaters, and produced several successful touring shows, even as he devoted much of his time to his thoroughbred horses and Maryland estate. Beyond his significance as a popular performer and playwright, Dudley is notable for speeding the economic integration of what had been an unsystematic and decentralized industry. His far-flung theater empire demonstrated that black entrepreneurs could retain a stake in the industry even as it consolidated.[55]

As long as black cultural entrepreneurs served black audiences, and the occasional white cultural voyeur, in black neighborhoods they were unlikely to face stiff competition from white rivals. But in the largest cities, especially after Prohibition drove much of the vice trade into black and working-class neighborhoods, white businessmen sought to capture the most lucrative portions of commercial nightlife. Many of the tony "black and tan clubs" that drew black, white, and, on the West Coast, Asian patrons, were owned by whites, as were the ritziest movie theaters that catered to blacks in major cities. Such businesses might employ black ushers and managers, but white executives oversaw the staffs and pocketed the profits. The most prestigious and lucrative clubs of the era were virtually always in the hands of whites. For instance, Harlem's famed Cotton Club, frequented by George Gershwin, Al Jolson, Mae West, and other white celebrities of the era, had its origins in a club owned by the boxer Jack Johnson, but enjoyed its greatest notoriety, and profits, while run by Owney Madden, a white gangster. Throughout the 1920s and early 1930s, the club refused admittance to blacks even while risqué black dancers, accompanied by superb black orchestras led by Fletcher Henderson and Duke Ellington, performed the club's signature stage shows.[56]

White Americans' growing familiarity with, easier access to, and potential economic control of black culture posed a dilemma for all black cultural entrepreneurs. Which market—white, black, or both—should they serve? One possible answer was to foster and market autonomous black culture to black audiences and consumers. Especially during the late 1910s and 1920s, prominent voices within the black community, including leading newspapers, ministers, and business leaders, appealed to blacks to harness their consumption to the collective advancement of the race. Thus, the

Chicago Defender urged blacks to purchase Mamie Smith's early recordings in order to promote blacks as recording artists, and the *Philadelphia Tribune* exhorted its readers to patronize impresario John T. Gibson's various venues.[57] In Chicago, Harlem, and other large centers of black population, blacks envisioned creating separate economies where a symbiosis between black production and consumption would free them from dependence on white capital.

But such appeals from advocates of black cultural separatism had to offset powerful countervailing commercial and cultural forces. Most artists and performers consumed and borrowed culture without regard to racial origins. The recording of the Italian tenor Enrico Caruso enthralled Louis Armstrong; Meta Warrick Fuller drew inspiration from Auguste Rodin; white comedian W. C. Fields borrowed ideas from Bert Williams's performances; and "hillbilly" singers Lee and Austin Allen so closely mimicked black blues that their recording of "Bow Wow Blues" was issued as a "race record" (or, in other words, for a black audience). The technologies of radio, records, and film accelerated and deepened these musical and artistic exchanges across the race line.

As early as the turn of the century a few black artists had demonstrated that they could achieve "crossover" success with white audiences. The allure of gaining a white audience for Bert Williams and other black performers was not merely financial; Williams and his compatriots self-consciously sought to use their craft to subvert and revise invidious racial stereotypes. To demonstrate the humanity and complexity of African Americans through performance before white audiences, they insisted, was to make a critical contribution to dismantling the patterns of thought and behavior that sustained black oppression. At the same time, as the experience of Black Swan Records highlighted, black businessmen competed in a marketplace where racial boundaries were porous. Even while white-owned record executives eschewed the goals of racial uplift embraced by their black competitors and white record companies reinforced racial boundaries by segregating their recordings according to the race of their intended audience, white companies sometimes seemed as attuned to their black customers' tastes as Black Swan Records had been.

The challenges confronted by these early black entrepreneurs in the cultural marketplace presaged the struggles of their successors during the remainder of the century. Throughout the peak years of his career, Bert Williams had to continually consider which roles to undertake, which venues to perform in, and which audience to cater to. Answers to these questions had both practical consequences and broader political and cultural implications. At issue were the possibilities for personal freedom and expression in an age of commercialized leisure as well as for cultural expression grounded in community obligations and identity. In the end, black cultural entrepreneurs in the early twentieth century were unable to achieve the loftiest goal that they set for themselves. But they identified and grappled with the complex interrelationship of race, consumerism, and public life that would continue to vex Americans across the remainder of the twentieth century.

Even in the most promising settings and during the best of times, such as Chicago during the 1920s, a truly independent black economy or culture industry was, at best, a distant dream for black leaders and cultural entrepreneurs. Limited credit and opportunistic competition from better-financed white rivals, who selectively targeted the most lucrative portions of the black market, placed black cultural entrepreneurs at a clear disadvantage. Although black leaders proclaimed that popular culture was vital to both black collective identity and entrepreneurship, neither they nor black consumers had the resources to build and sustain an independent black cultural marketplace. But not even the most pessimistic champions of black popular culture anticipated the corrosive effects of the Great Depression on the opportunities for blacks in the entertainment industry.

The devastation of the Depression was quickly evident in the popular music industry, the domain of mass culture in which African Americans had made their greatest strides during the first two decades of the twentieth century. Opportunities for black performers, managers, songwriters, and club owners shrank markedly during the Great Depression. With the national unemployment rate reaching a quarter of all Americans, the music industry inevitably suffered severe contraction. Only 6 million records were sold in the United States during 1932, as compared to 128 million six years earlier. The record business, in other words, shrank by 96 percent between 1927 and 1932. Likewise, the production of phonographs fell from nearly a million a year in the late 1920s to a mere 40,000 in 1932. So severe was the downturn that RCA Victor, the largest record company in the nation, issued no new recordings in 1931. Meanwhile, the Edison Company, the pioneer of the technology, went into bankruptcy and Columbia sank into deep debt. The plethora of smaller labels that had pioneered recording and marketing blues, gospel, and jazz shrank to a handful. As a consequence of this extreme contraction of the record industry, record retailing changed drastically. During the 1920s, when record sales were robust, retailers had been willing to invest in large inventories. The nation had been awash in recordings of a remarkably wide array of African American musical genres. During the 1930s, in contrast, retailers could not afford large inventories of slow-selling records or obscure genres of music. Attentive to these market forces, the few surviving record companies developed marketing and retailing strategies to sell a smaller number of records quickly. This new sales strategy hinged on the swift turnover of a strictly limited retail stock of "hits."[58]

This hollowing out of the recording industry coincided with the consolidation of national radio networks during the late 1920s and early 1930s. Beginning with the formation of the National Broadcasting Corporation (NBC) in 1926, chains of radio stations across the country began to broadcast the same shows and music at the same time. As major radio companies raced to consolidate vast national networks with mass audiences, radio corporations began to prey on other enterprises that also catered to mass markets, including music publishing and recording. Thus, while General Electric was emerging as a powerhouse in radio it also used its new sound-recording technology to become a force in the film industry. RCA (Radio Corporation of America) not only owned NBC but also created RKO Pictures to establish a beachhead in Hollywood. These new "empires of sound" were eager to take advantage of their diverse media holdings to promote their stable of performers, and so RCA recording artists were likely to perform on NBC radio broadcasts and get screen time in RKO movies. Virtually all branches of the entertainment industry, including music publishing, record companies, radio broadcasting, and cinema, moved in the direction of increasing merger and monopolization.[59]

This consolidation of the entertainment industry substantially reduced the venues and opportunities that had made possible musical experimentation during the previous two decades, thereby substantially narrowing the opportunities for black artists and entrepreneurs. Black musicians would continue to secure record contracts during the 1930s, but white swing bands and crooners would dominate the charts during the decade. And the popularity of radio did little to advance the careers of most black musicians. During the 1930s and 1940s, black-themed programming was, for the most part, limited to separate radio segments sponsored by advertisers pitching products to black consumers. A few black musicians, such as Duke Ellington and Count Basie, were featured on national network programming, but otherwise the radio waves were the preserve of white musicians. Not surprisingly, black radio ownership lagged substantially behind whites because many blacks understandably elected not to spend precious money on radios if the broadcasters never offered content that interested them. Although black consumers could still seek out records by black artists, black entrepreneurs could not easily overcome the high barriers that the consolidated record and radio companies posed for any new entries into the entertainment industry.[60]

Yet even during the depths of the Depression, black innovators continued to emerge in those areas of the entertainment industry where the costs of entry remained low and white competitors were either flat-footed or nonexistent. Thomas Dorsey, who transformed the composition and distribution of black sacred music, was one of the most striking examples of continuing black cultural entrepreneurship during the 1930s. Born in 1899 and raised near Atlanta, he absorbed at an early age both traditional hymns and early blues and jazz. In 1916 he moved to Chicago. There, he undertook formal musical training, and, at the age of twenty-one, published his first song. With a growing reputation as a songwriter Dorsey also worked as a composer and arranger for music publishing companies and as a music coach for several record companies. In 1924 popular blues singer Ma Rainey chose him to lead her Wild Cats Jazz Band. Although still a young man in a rapidly changing industry, Dorsey grasped the importance of retaining control over his compositions. By doing so he ensured that when King Oliver and other artists recorded his songs, his royalties and fame grew apace. He enjoyed his greatest success beginning in 1928 when he and "Tampa Red" Whittaker recorded more than sixty records, including the bawdy blues, "It's Tight Like That." By the end of the decade, Dorsey had accompanied most of the famous blues performers of the era, including Big Bill Broonzy, Blind Lemon Jefferson, Memphis Minnie, and Victoria Spivey.[61]

Dorsey's success in the popular music industry of the 1920s was suggestive of the opportunities available to talented and ambitious black musicians, songwriters, and arrangers during the boom years of the decade. Like many of his contemporaries, from William Grant Still to Paul Robeson, Dorsey composed and performed music across genres. Thus, even while he was composing risqué blues, he wrote and performed sacred music. When he became director of music at New Hope Baptist Church in Chicago in 1931, he fused his jazz and blues vocabulary with the lyrical and musical traditions of sacred music. The result was a tremendously influential fusion of gospel choir music with the emotional and personal intensity of the blues.

Dorsey's immersion in all aspects of the popular music industry gave him an acute understanding of the industry's accelerating consolidation. Dorsey set about organizing the business of gospel music. He founded and then led for five decades the National Convention of Gospel Choirs and Choruses. In this role he exerted enormous influence over the performance traditions of black gospel music. He simultaneously directed his prodigious organizational and business acumen to publishing and marketing gospel music. Dismayed by the treatment that most songwriters experienced at the hands of established publishers, Dorsey opened the first major black gospel publishing company, Dorsey House of Music. But his ambitions extended beyond simply better treatment of composers. Prior to his venture, most religious music was disseminated under the auspices of the churches in which it emerged. Dorsey envisioned a consolidated publishing enterprise that served songwriters and consumers regardless of denominational affiliation. When he established his clearinghouse for black gospel compositions he created a black-run commercial realm within the larger, increasingly consolidated commercial music industry. His primary intent was to spread the gospel rather than maximize profits. He viewed the commercialization of gospel as one of the best means to introduce ecstatic gospel performance, a vital act of devotion, to a larger audience. Even so, by creating a publishing and marketing infrastructure for the music, Dorsey made a crucial contribution to the commercialization and cultural consolidation of the genre.

Dorsey's cumulative impact on American music is almost incalculable. He helped erode the categories of high and low culture by promoting the adoption of a soulful, bluesy style of gospel singing by large choirs and virtuoso church bands. He bridged the divide that had previously separated secular and religious music by familiarizing listeners with instrumentation more commonly associated with disreputable forms of popular music. Over time, both religious and secular audiences would grow accustomed to the combination of devotional themes with musical forms derived from the blues, jazz, and other genres of popular music. The robust commercial arena he created in turn facilitated black artistic creativity and entrepreneurship and nurtured a national community of gospel performers and consumers whose influence extended far beyond the black congregations where the music had first emerged.

Dorsey's rise as a gospel mogul during the 1930s was one measure of the tenacity of black cultural entrepreneurship even during the nation's worst economic calamity. Although the foothold that black songwriters, performers, and businessmen had secured in the entertainment industry shrank during the Depression, blacks did not return to the margins of popular culture that they had occupied decades earlier.

By the 1930s at least two generations of Americans had become accustomed to performances by black entertainers. The cumulative effect of these performances on collective memory should not be underestimated.[62] Just as horrific spectacles of black debasement, especially lynchings, skewed public debate about the "Negro problem," so too contrary performances of black artistry and skill undercut shibboleths of black barbarism. New technologies of mass culture, such as recordings, radio, and film, possessed a profound capacity to generate powerful memories, including memories that contested, sometimes in a dramatic and far-reaching manner, inherited prejudices. Even while many black film roles perpetuated invidious stereotypes, black performers such as Bill "Bojangles" Robinson and Hattie McDaniel demonstrated that even conventional roles as faithful retainers and mammies could be rendered with complexity and poignance.[63] Likewise, in his performances Louis Armstrong projected a combination of dignity, humility, virtuosity, and humanity that subverted caricatures of black musicality. Black athletics challenged inherited images of lazy, bumbling, timid, and simple-minded blacks. Indeed, virtually any public performance by a black in the arena of mass culture had the potential to transform commercialized recreation into a political act.

Both Jack Johnson, the world champion heavyweight boxer during the 1910s, and Paul Robeson, an outstanding collegiate athlete, understood the power and influence that athletes were accruing as physical recreation became simultaneously commercialized and professionalized. Almost certainly, Jack Johnson would have been a controversial figure regardless of how he conducted himself in public and private. A black champion was an intolerable affront to white racial superiority at a time of pervasive anxiety among whites about their race's perceived decline. Johnson knowingly courted notoriety and fame with his faux English accent, ostentatious dress, and oversized appetite for high living and flamboyant women. That many whites expressed outrage at Johnson's transgressions and glee at his eventual decline was predictable. But so, too, did some black politicos, editors, and religious leaders. Invested as they were in racial uplift based on the politics of respectability, they recoiled from Johnson's bravura performances in and out of the ring.[64] Paul Robeson's storied career as an undergraduate athlete at Rutgers was much more compatible with conventional notions of racial uplift. He was the embodiment of the idealized masculine specimen;

he was a brilliant student, a popular campus figure, a gifted artist, and a consummate athlete. Not surprisingly, Robeson became an icon of the New Negro movement and a fixture in the salons of the Harlem Renaissance. But Robeson elected the concert hall and the stage, rather than the sports field, as his preferred performance venues.[65] It fell to Joe Louis to demonstrate the full potential of athletic performance to confound received images of African Americans.

Louis was born in 1914 in the Black Belt of rural Alabama. After a run-in with the Ku Klux Klan, Louis's family joined the Great Migration and emigrated to Detroit. While still a teenager, Louis began to compete in amateur boxing. From the outset of his career, Louis displayed a preternatural understanding of the racial politics of both sports and business. Suspicious of white managers who he believed exploited black boxers while impeding their success, Louis sought out black managers. Although his managers proved no less self-interested than other boxing managers, they did carefully shape Louis's media image so that he avoided the disastrous notoriety that hobbled Jack Johnson's career. Specifically, they established a code of etiquette for Louis that enabled him to achieve respectability in the eyes of both whites and blacks. At a time when boxing, which had devolved into a sordid mixture of mediocre athletes, fixed fights, and organized crime, was in desperate need of a marketable hero, Louis was generally portrayed in the white media as a clean-living, modest, and even heroic person.[66]

Louis's remarkable success in the ring and his riveting fights with Max Schmeling, a German boxer and Nazi icon, transformed Louis into a national hero. Louis understood the burden he carried as black man and American boxer when he fought Schmeling. After President Franklin D. Roosevelt urged Louis to demonstrate the superiority of American values by defeating Schmeling, Louis concluded, "I had to get Schmeling good. I had my own personal reasons and the whole damned country was depending on me." African Americans had embraced Louis long before he became a national hero in the eyes of whites. Langston Hughes recalled, "Each time Joe Louis won a fight in those depression years, even before he became champion, thousands of colored Americans on relief or W.P.A., and poor, would throng out into the streets all across the land to march and cheer and yell and cry because of Joe's one-man triumphs. No one else in the United States has ever had such an effect on Negro emotions—or on mine. I marched and cheered and yelled and cried, too."[67] With his decisive thrashing of Schmeling in 1938, many white Americans joined Hughes and other African Americans in reveling in Louis's prowess.

Louis's accomplishments as a boxer, of course, did not immediately transform American race relations. Despite his fame and success, Louis was repeatedly reminded of the enduring power of racism. When he later served in the Army during World War II, he endured both segregation and periodic brushes with bigotry. And he would wage an exhausting struggle to desegregate the sport of golf in his declining years. Nevertheless, Louis's emergence as a national hero was an unprecedented development in American mass culture. Previously it was inconceivable that a black man, especially a black athlete, would be embraced as a national icon by whites.

When blacks in the early decades of the twentieth century battled to secure greater control over the production, content, and dissemination of mass culture, they advanced and anticipated many of the cultural contests of the twentieth century. They confronted the challenges of commercial culture that would confound both entrepreneurs and cultural activists for the remainder of the century. Efforts to explicitly harness black culture to the program of resisting white culture could, and sometimes were, undercut by the preferences of black consumers. Without question, mass culture promoted black identity, pride, and solidarity. But black participation in the creation of the nation's mass culture could not perform or replace the work that organized protest and political action could perform. In the end, the most profound development of the participation of blacks in the creation of the nation's mass culture was that the face of American culture was permanently transformed. No matter how often genteel bigots and virulent white supremacists agreed about the primacy of the nation's Anglo-Saxon culture, the ascendant popular culture of the twentieth century belied their claims. The nation had moved, irrevocably, far beyond blackface.

NOTES

1. David Nasaw, *Going Out: The Rise and Fall of Public Amusements* (New York: Basic Books, 1993), esp. 1–9; Kenneth W. Goings, *Mammy and Uncle Mose: Black Collectibles and American Stereotyping* (Bloomington: Indiana University Press, 1994). Scholars have offered varying definitions of "mass" and "popular" culture. For the purposes of this essay, mass culture and popular culture are synonymous. They refer to a set of cultural values and practices that arise from common exposure of a population to the same media, music, art, or leisure activities. Popular mass culture becomes possible only with rapid and nearly universal forms of communication, such as the telegraph, rural delivery mail services, radio, and, more recently, television. Popular culture, moreover, is a commercial culture, mass produced for

mass consumption. Because popular culture is rooted in the marketplace, its forms, creators, and audiences are constantly in flux. Thus, even while popular-culture performers and entrepreneurs typically seek out a broad spectrum of the public, new expressions of popular culture routinely originate from subcultures that previously were unknown to mainstream audiences. For a lucid introduction to the contentious debates surrounding popular culture and its definition, see John Storey, *Cultural Theory and Popular Culture: An Introduction* (Athens: University of Georgia Press, 2006).

2. The best survey of the debate over the "Negro problem" remains George M. Fredrickson's *The Black Image in the White Mind: The Debate on Afro-American Character and Destiny, 1817–1914* (New York: Harper & Row, 1971).

3. John W. Cell, *The Highest Stage of White Supremacy: The Origins of Segregation in South Africa and the American South* (New York: Cambridge University Press, 1982); and Rayford W. Logan, *The Negro in American Life and Thought: The Nadir, 1877–1901* (New York: Collier Books, 1965).

4. W. E. B. Du Bois, *The Souls of Black Folk* (1903; New York: Modern Library, 2003), 8.

5. Waldo E. Martin Jr., *No Coward Soldiers: Black Cultural Politics in Postwar America* (Cambridge: Harvard University Press, 2005), 3.

6. Lawrence W. Levine, *Highbrow/Lowbrow: The Emergence of Cultural Hierarchy in America* (Cambridge: Harvard University Press, 1988).

7. The interlocking ideas of culture and civilization are deftly discussed in Gail Bederman, *Manliness and Civilization: A Cultural History of Gender and Race in the United States, 1880–1917* (Chicago: University of Chicago Press, 1995); and Daniel J. Singal, "Towards a Definition of American Modernism," in *Modernist Culture in America*, ed. Daniel J. Singal (Belmont, Calif.: Wadsworth Pub. Co., 1991).

8. The boundaries between "high" and "low" culture were never secure. For example, at the beginning of the nineteenth century Shakespeare's plays were popular with both elite and popular audiences. Yet even while snippets of Shakespeare were familiar to and regularly performed before all classes of Americans, the great Shakespearean interpreters of the day in the United States were exclusively white and were accorded the status of cultural lions. See Lawrence W. Levine, "William Shakespeare and the American People: A Study in Cultural Transformation," *American Historical Review* 89 (February 1984): 34–66.

9. Aldridge's career is surveyed in Errol G. Hill and James V. Hatch, *A History of African American Theatre* (New York: Cambridge University Press, 2003), 40–47.

10. W. Fitzhugh Brundage, "Meta Warrick's 1907 'Negro Tableaux' and (Re)Presenting African American Historical Memory," *Journal of American History* 89 (March 2003): 1368–400.

11. Meta Warrick Fuller to Freeman Murray, April 5, 1915, Freeman H. M. Murray Papers (Moorland-Spingarn Research Center, Howard University, Washington D.C.); Kirk Savage, *Standing Soldiers, Kneeling Slaves: Race, War, and Monument in Nineteenth-Century America* (Princeton University Press, 1997), 70; William Francis

O'Donnell, "Meta Vaux Warrick, Sculptor of Horrors," *World Today* 13 (November 1907): 1139–45.

12. Brundage, "Meta Warrick's 1907 'Negro Tableaux.'"

13. The two best accounts of Joplin's life are Edward A. Berlin, *King of Ragtime: Scott Joplin and His Era* (New York: Oxford University Press, 1994); and Susan Curtis, *Dancing to a Black Man's Tune: A Life of Scott Joplin* (Columbia: University of Missouri Press, 1994).

14. On Joplin, see Susan Curtis, "Black Creativity and Black Stereotype: Rethinking Twentieth-Century Popular Music in America" in this collection.

15. Lane's career and the glimpses it offers of interracial minstrel dancing are expertly traced in James W. Cook, "Dancing Across the Color Line," *Common-Place* 4 (October 2003), www.common-place.org/vol-04/no-01/cook/; and James W. Cook, "Master Jube, the King of All Dancers! A Story of Stardom and Struggle from the Dawn of the Transatlantic Culture Industry," *Discourses in Dance* 3 (2006): 7–20.

16. For a concise and thoughtful account of the cakewalk's cultural significance in turn-of-the-century American culture, see James Gilbert, *Whose Fair? Experience, Memory, and the History of the Great St. Louis Exposition* (Chicago: University of Chicago Press, 2009), 146–52.

17. On the rage for "authentic" black performance, see David Krasner, "The Real Thing" in this collection. On Overton Walker see David Krasner, "Rewriting the Body: Aida Overton Walker and the Social Formation of Cakewalking," *Theatre Survey* 37 (November 1996): 66–92; Richard Newman, "'The Brightest Star': Aida Overton Walker in the Age of Ragtime and the Cakewalk," in *Prospects: An Annual of American Cultural Studies* 18 (New York: Cambridge University Press, 1993), 464–81.

18. Quoted in Jayna Brown, *Babylon Girls: Black Women Performers and the Shaping of the Modern* (Durham: Duke University Press, 2008), 182.

19. On Overton Walker's *Salome* dance, see Brown, *Babylon Girls*, 181–84; Susan A. Glenn, *Female Spectacle: The Theatrical Roots of Modern Feminism* (Cambridge: Harvard University Press, 2000), 112–18; David Krasner, *A Beautiful Pageant: African American Theatre, Drama, and Performance in the Harlem Renaissance, 1910–1927* (New York: Palgrave, 2002) 63–70.

20. Gayle Murchison, "'Dean of Afro-American Composers' or 'Harlem Renaissance Man': The New Negro and the Musical Poetics of William Grant Still," in *William Grant Still: A Study in Contradictions*, ed. Catherine Parsons Smith (Berkeley: University of California Press, 2000), 39–93; Catherine Parsons Smith, *William Grant Still* (Urbana: University of Illinois Press, 2008).

21. Evelyn Brooks Higginbotham, *Righteous Discontent: The Women's Movement in the Black Baptist Church, 1880–1920* (Cambridge: Harvard University Press, 1993), chap. 7.

22. "What the Concert-Goer Says of the 'The Negro Music Journal,'" *Negro Music Journal* 1 (October 1902): 28.

23. See, for example, Frederick Jerome Taylor, "Black Musicians in the *Philadelphia Tribune*," *Black Perspective in Music* 18 (1990): 129.

24. The travels of the Black Patti Troubadours are traced in Lynn Abbott and Doug Seroff, *Out of Sight: The Rise of African American Popular Music, 188-1895* (Jackson: University Press of Mississippi, 2002), 89, 162, 284, 351, 438–39; and Abbott and Seroff, *Ragged But Right: Black Traveling Shows, "Coon Songs," and the Dark Pathway to Blues and Jazz* (Jackson: University Press of Mississippi, 2007), 38–44. On the Whitman Sisters, see Nadine George-Graves, *The Royalty of Negro Vaudeville: The Whitman Sisters and the Negotiation of Race, Gender and Class in African-American Theatre, 1900-1940* (New York: St. Martin's Press, 2000).

25. Wilson Jeremiah Moses, *The Golden Age of Black Nationalism, 1850-1925* (1978; New York: Oxford University Press, 1988), 255. See, in general, Moses, *Golden Age*, 220–71; Clare Corbould, *Becoming African Americans: Black Public Life in Harlem, 1919-1939* (Cambridge: Harvard University Press, 2009), esp. 18–87; Mary G. Rolinson, *Grassroots Garveyism: The Universal Negro Improvement Association in the Rural South, 1920-1927* (Chapel Hill: University of North Carolina Press, 2007), esp. 72–130.

26. On Du Bois's aesthetics, see Robert Gooding-Williams, "Du Bois, Politics, Aesthetics: An Introduction," *Public Culture* 17 (Spring 2005): 203–15; Ronald A. T. Judy, "The New Black Aesthetic and W. E. B. Du Bois, or Hepheastrus Limping," *Massachusetts Review* 35 (Summer 1994): 251–73; Ross Posnock, *Color and Culture: Black Writers and the Making of the Modern Intellectual* (Cambridge: Harvard University Press, 1998), 111–45; David Levering Lewis, *W. E. B. Du Bois: Biography of a Race, 1868-1919* (New York: Henry Holt, 1993), 127–39, 441–43; David Levering Lewis, *W. E. B. Du Bois: The Fight for Equality and the American Century, 1919-1963* (New York: Henry Holt, 2000), 174–82.

27. W. E. B. Du Bois, "Criteria of Negro Art," *Crisis* 32 (October 1926): 292. For other relevant pronouncements by Du Bois on art, see "Negro Art," *Crisis* 22 (June 1921): 55; and "Books," *Crisis* 33 (December 1926): 81–82.

28. Alain Locke, "Foreword" and "The New Negro," in *The New Negro*, ed. Alain Locke (1925; New York: Atheneum, 1975), xv-xvii, 3–16; Krasner, *A Beautiful Pageant*, 138–52; Posnock, *Color and Culture*, 111–45.

29. Tera W. Hunter, *To 'Joy My Freedom: Southern Black Women's Lives and Labors after the Civil War* (Cambridge: Harvard University Press, 1997), 168–86; Kathy Peiss, *Cheap Amusements: Working Women and Leisure in New York City, 1880 to 1920* (Philadelphia: Temple University Press, 1985), 88–114; Gregory A. Waller, *Main Street Amusements: Movies and Commercial Entertainment in a Southern City, 1896-1930* (Washington, D.C.: Smithsonian Institution Press, 1995), 168–70.

30. Two foundational works in the transformation of American attitudes toward leisure are Roy Rosenzweig, *Eight Hours for What We Will: Workers and Leisure in an Industrial City, 1870-1920* (Cambridge: Cambridge University Press, 1985); and Warren Susman, *Culture as History: The Transformation of American Society in the Twentieth Century* (New York: Pantheon, 1985), 271–86.

31. Kathy Peiss, *Hope in a Jar: The Making of America's Beauty Culture* (New York: Henry Holt, 1999), 94. On Walker's career and marketing strategies, see

Davarian L. Baldwin, *Chicago's New Negroes: Modernity, the Great Migration, and Black Urban Life* (Chapel Hill: University of North Carolina Press, 2007), 53–91; Julia Kirk Blackwelder, *Styling Jim Crow: African American Beauty Training During Segregation* (College Station, Tex.: Texas A&M University Press, 2003), 34–63; A'Leila Perry Bundles, *On Her Own Ground: The Life and Times of Madam C. J. Walker* (New York: Scribner, 2001); and Beverly Lowry, *Her Dream of Dreams: The Rise and Triumph of Madam C. J. Walker* (New York: Knopf, 2003).

32. Robert Higgs, *Competition and Coercion: Blacks in the American Economy, 1865–1914* (Chicago: University of Chicago Press, 1977), 117.

33. On Williams's and Micheaux's travels, see Eric Ledell Smith, *Bert Williams: A Biography of the Pioneer Black Comedian* (Jefferson, N.C.: McFarland & Co., 1992), 1–48; Patrick McGilligan, *Oscar Micheaux: The Great and Only: The Life of America's First Black Filmmaker* (New York: Harper Collins, 2007), esp. 1–107. Valuable starting places in the vast literature on the Great Migration are Peter Gottlieb, *Making Their Way: Southern Blacks' Migration to Pittsburgh, 1916–1930* (Urbana: University of Illinois Press, 1987); James Grossman, *Land of Hope: Chicago, Black Southerners and the Great Migration* (Chicago: University of Chicago Press, 1989); and Louis M. Kyriakoudes, *The Social Origins of the Urban South: Race, Gender, and Migration in Nashville and Middle Tennessee, 1890–1930* (Chapel Hill: University of North Carolina Press, 2003).

34. James N. Gregory, *The Southern Diaspora: How the Great Migrations of Black and White Southerners Transformed America* (Chapel Hill: University of North Carolina Press, 2007), esp. 153–236.

35. David Robertson, *W. C. Handy: The Life and Times of the Man Who Made the Blues* (New York: Knopf, 2009), esp. 52–73; Elijah Wald, *Escaping the Delta: Robert Johnson and the Invention of the Blues* (New York: Amistad, 2004), 98–99.

36. The plight of black education is surveyed in James D. Anderson, *The Education of Blacks in the South, 1860–1935* (Chapel Hill: University of North Carolina Press, 1988); Louis R. Harlan, *Separate and Unequal: Public School Campaigns and Racism in the Southern Seaboard States, 1901–1915* (1958; New York: Atheneum, 1968); Leon F. Litwack, *Trouble in Mind: Black Southerners in the Age of Jim Crow* (New York: Knopf, 1998), 52–113; Robert A. Margo, *Race and Schooling in the South, 1880–1950: An Economic History* (Chicago: University of Chicago Press, 1990)

37. Ralph L. Crowder, *John Edward Bruce: Politician, Journalist, and Self-Trained Historian of the African Diaspora* (New York: New York University Press, 2004), 5–48; John Edward Bruce, *The Black Sleuth*, ed. John Cullen Gruesser (Boston: Northeastern University Press, 2002).

38. James Weldon Johnson, *Along This Way: The Autobiography of James Weldon Johnson* (1933; New York: Penguin Books, 1990), 3–156.

39. For provocative discussions of the relation of "folk" music and the technologies of commercial, commodified popular music, see John Minton, *78 Blues: Folksongs and Phonographs in the American South* (Jackson: University Press of Mississippi, 2008); William Howland Kenney, *Recorded Music in American Life: The*

Phonograph and Popular Memory, 1890–1945 (New York: Oxford University Press, 1999), 3–22.

40. W. C. Handy, *Father of the Blues: An Autobiography*, ed. Arna Bontemps (New York: Macmillan, 1941).

41. Camille F. Forbes, *Introducing Bert Williams: Burnt Cork, Broadway, and the Story of America's First Black Star* (New York: Basic Civitas Books, 2008), 167–252; and Geoffrey C. Ward, *Unforgivable Blackness: The Rise and Fall of Jack Johnson* (New York: Knopf, 2004); esp. 188–224.

42. The careers of these multitalented black performers is skillfully described in Thomas Riis's "Crossing Boundaries: Black Musicians Who Defied Musical Genres" in this collection.

43. Thomas L. Morgan and William Barlow, *From Cakewalks to Concert Halls: An Illustrated History of African American Popular Music from 1895 to 1930* (Washington, D.C.: Elliott & Clark, 1992), 101–3, 121–23.

44. Samuel Charters and Leonard Kunstadt, *Jazz: A History of the New York Scene* (Garden City, N.Y.: Doubleday, 1962), 73; Hildred Roach, *Black American Music: Past and Present* (Malabar, Fla.: Krieger Publishing, 1992), 53; Henry T. Sampson, *The Ghost Walks: A Chronological History of Blacks in Show Business, 1865–1910* (Metuchen, N.J.: Scarecrow Press, 1988), 321; Wayne D. Shirley, "The House of Melody: A List of Publications of the Gotham-Attucks Company at the Library of Congress," *Black Perspective in Music* 15 (Spring 1987): 79–112.

45. Tim Brooks, *Lost Sounds: Blacks and the Birth of the Recording Industry, 1890–1919* (Urbana: University of Illinois Press, 2004), 13–72.

46. Reid Badger, *A Life in Ragtime: A Biography of James Reese Europe* (New York: Oxford University Press, 1995), 90–91, 236; Brooks, *Lost Sounds*; Kenney, *Recorded Music*, 110–12.

47. Andre Millard, *America on Record: A History of Recorded Sound*, 2nd ed. (Cambridge: Cambridge University Press, 2005), 65–95; Kenney, *Recorded Music*, 114–16.

48. W. E. B. Du Bois, "Phonograph Records," *Crisis* 21 (Feb. 1921): 152; on Black Swan Records, see David Suisman, "Co-Workers in the Kingdom of Culture: Black Swan Records and the Political Economy of African American Music," *Journal of American History* 91 (March 2004): 1295–324; Ted Vincent, "The Social Context of Black Swan Records," *Living Blues* 20 (May-June 1989): 34–40.

49. Suisman, "Co-Workers in the Kingdom of Culture": 1307–9.

50. Kenney, *Recorded Music*, 111; Suisman, "Co-Workers in the Kingdom of Culture": 1317–18.

51. Black entertainers during the nineteenth century had already encountered many of the challenges that confronted their successors at the dawn of the twentieth century. My larger point is not that the predicament that black artists and impresarios faced was new, but that its scale was magnified by the technologies and popularity of mass culture in the early twentieth century. On the nineteenth-century antecedents for the dilemma of the cultural marketplace, see Cook, "Master Juba."

52. The performance spaces and traditions of jazz and blues are deftly analyzed by Kathy J. Ogren, *The Jazz Revolution: Twenties America and the Meaning of Jazz* (New York: Oxford University Press, 1989), 11–86.

53. For an especially cogent treatment of black public space, commerce, and popular culture, see Baldwin, *Chicago's New Negroes*, 21–52.

54. Baldwin, *Chicago's New Negroes*, 26, 47, 100, 103; Jessie Carney Smith, "James T. Gibson," in *Encyclopedia of African American Business*, ed. Jessie Carney Smith (Westport, Conn.: Greenwood Press, 2006), 340–43; Waller, *Main Street Amusements*, 170–79.

55. On Dudley, see Krasner, *A Beautiful Pageant*, 270–80. See also Anthony Hill, *Pages from the Harlem Renaissance: A Chronicle of Performance* (New York: Peter Lang, 1996), 69–71; and George-Graves, *Royalty of Negro Vaudeville*, 103–9, 131–32. John T. Gibson's career as a theater magnate in Philadelphia parallels that of Dudley in many regards. See Taylor, "Black Musicians," 127–40.

56. Jim Haskins, *The Cotton Club* (New York: Random House, 1977), chap. 2–3.

57. William Howland Kenney, *Chicago Jazz: A Cultural History 1904–1930* (New York: Oxford University Press, 1993), 123–25; Taylor, "Black Musicians," 128.

58. Kenney, *Recorded Music in American Life*, 158–81; Millard, *America on Record*, chap. 8.

59. David W. Stowe, *Swing Changes: Big-Band Jazz in New Deal America* (Cambridge: Harvard University Press, 1998), 94–120.

60. Stowe, *Swing Changes*, 121–29; Kenney, *Recorded Music in American Life*, 109–34.

61. The essential starting point for Dorsey's life is Michael W. Harris, *The Rise of Gospel Blues: The Music of Thomas Andrew Dorsey in the Urban Church* (New York: Oxford University Press, 1992).

62. Amy Wood, *Lynching and Spectacle: Witnessing Racial Violence in America, 1890–1940* (Chapel Hill: University of North Carolina Press, 2009).

63. Donald Bogle, *Toms, Coons, Mulattoes, Mammies, and Bucks: An Interpretative History of Blacks in American Films*, 4th ed. (New York: Continuum, 2002), 35–100.

64. Gail Bederman, *Manliness and Civilization: A Cultural History of Gender and Race in the United States, 1880–1917* (Chicago: University of Chicago Press, 1995), chap. 1; Ward, *Unforgivable Blackness*.

65. Martin Duberman, *Paul Robeson: A Biography* (1988; New York: New Press, 2005), esp. 19–30. See also Baldwin, *Chicago's New Negroes*, 221, 223.

66. See Lewis A. Erenberg, "More than a Prizefight: Joe Louis, Max Schmeling, and the Transnational Politics of Boxing" in this collection; and Lewis A. Erenberg, *The Greatest Fight of Our Generation: Louis vs. Schmeling* (New York: Oxford University Press, 2006), esp. 7–70.

67. Langston Hughes, *Autobiography*, vol. 14 of *The Collected Works of Langston Hughes*, ed. Joseph McLaren (Columbia: University of Missouri Press, 2002), 307.

first coda

Representations of Blackness in Nineteenth-Century Culture

The boisterous popular culture of the nineteenth century and the technological innovations of the age generated antecedents for the mass culture of the twentieth century. Among the most enduring and potent legacies of the nineteenth century were a storehouse of visual representations of blackness. These two essays provide contrasting images of blackness that coexisted during the century. John Stauffer explores black abolitionists' faith in and use of images, especially photography, to transform themselves from object to subject. He emphasizes the correlation between the ascendant technology of photography and the transformation in black self-representation. Frederick Douglass especially grasped the emancipatory potential of photography, and he used it skillfully to control his popular image. In the aftermath of the Civil War and certainly by the beginning of the twentieth century, both the novelty and potential of photography seemingly had waned. W. E. B. Du Bois displayed much less optimism about its capacity to refashion the black identity. The evolving expectations of photography's potential among blacks would presage blacks' experiences with many of the subsequent technologies of popular culture during the late nineteenth and early twentieth centuries.

Stauffer's excavation of blacks' experimentation with photography should be placed against the backdrop of the popularity of blackface minstrelsy during the nineteenth century. Stephanie Dunson's essay reveals how minstrelsy transformed the very image of blacks by rendering "real" blacks invisible. The extraordinary popularity of minstrelsy, like the popularity of photography, was a manifestation of the nation's accelerating industrial revolution. The proliferation of mass-produced sheet music brought the imagery and sounds of minstrelsy into middle-class parlors. Minstrelsy, at its heart, was an expression of white fantasies and fears, but ersatz black bodies — actually, whites embodying blacks — became the vehicle for the acting out of the fantasies and fears. Thus, one of the signal challenges for all blacks, and most acutely black entertainers, was to assert authority over the depiction of their bodies in American culture. Only a few blacks succeeded in making any headway in this crucial task before the rise of the brilliant duo of Bert Williams and George Walker at the century's close. As Dunson explains, the success of Williams and Walker was suggestive of an accelerating shift in the representation of blacks in popular culture.

Black Misrepresentation in Nineteenth-Century Sheet Music Illustration

STEPHANIE DUNSON

To appreciate the challenges and expectations that African American entertainers had to contend with in the early era of twentieth-century mass culture, we must initially turn our attention back to the antebellum decades that saw the rise of the blackface minstrel tradition—when white men in black face paint entertained northern audiences with songs and skits meant to represent black culture. In truth, no music played a more central role in nineteenth-century American culture than the melodies generated by blackface minstrelsy, from the 1820s, when individual blackface performers popularized routines that were meant to reproduce black dance and music for white northern audiences, to the end of the century, when Tin Pan Alley songwriters cranked out "coon songs" for consumers who took racial stereotypes for granted.[1]

But in positioning blackface minstrelsy as the historical backdrop for our larger consideration of African Americans and early mass culture, we must move beyond the protestations and maneuverings of scholars who characterize the tradition as something other than the "mere" practice of racial disparagement.[2] The erasure of black identity as a historical fact, perhaps even a psychological necessity, is a precondition for the American tradition of blackface minstrelsy. Thus disparagement lies in the cultural system of privileging representation over reality and in the systems of power and oppression that allow such privileging to become the standard. The matter is more profound than the mere question of racial disparagement as popular entertainment; at issue is the work that blackface performed in a society that essentially felt compelled to evict black people from their own skin and then allow pretenders to take up residency there. This is the requisite backdrop against which the national fascination for minstrelsy was performed and the cultural standard that African American performers in the early twentieth century were forced to accommodate.

Even if we wanted to, it would be impossible to reproduce the bombast and swagger that was the nineteenth-century minstrel show.[3] But the covers and content of nineteenth-century sheet music serve as a viable source for studying the evolution of the blackface tradition. Sheet music—printed music published for home performance—offers workable facsimiles of both the melodies and the images that were popularized on the minstrel stage. In truth, sheet music was to nineteenth-century America what music videos are in current society: a key medium for importing new music and trends into the middle-class home. The images from the cover art of sheet music provide visual reference points that parallel the blackface phenomenon as it existed on the stage: first obscuring and then misrepresenting black identity.

Minstrel man T. D. Rice is commonly credited with popularizing blackface performance in early nineteenth-century America; the unprecedented popularity of his Jim Crow routine (one he reportedly learned from a black street performer)[4] propelled him from obscurity to international fame almost overnight.[5] But the practice of white actors "blacking up" to imitate black characters had been regular practice for decades before Rice appeared on the scene—primarily because on American stages, black actors were not allowed to perform in white theatrical productions.[6] As a result, white actors in black face paint routinely stood in for black characters in productions staged by white theatrical companies; some white performers also used the black guise to add novelty to musical routines offered as entr'acte diversions. Also, although they were banned from performance in most proper theaters, free blacks who hoped to make money as entertainers could be observed on the street corners and in the market squares of practically every northern city. It should come as no surprise, then, that by the 1820s, blackface performance was a common feature on American stages. But Rice's performance as Jim Crow proved to be an unparalleled sensation.

There is no explanation for his unprecedented success that is more convincing than the most obvious one: that he was a gifted performer who happened upon the right material. But what was so right about his routine? What was it that made his performances so irresistible to his white audiences? In effect, what Rice brought to the stage was a particularly artful and novel imitation of what black street performers did—or perhaps more accurately, what white passersby thought they saw when they observed these black performers. Whether it was intended as mimicry or mockery, Rice moved with a fluency and facility that startled and enthralled the crowd. Rice's bold imitation seemed to bring the curious black body into view of white audiences without the troubling presence of an actual black person.[7] The performance also raised Rice's status as a performer to unequaled heights. Surely he was just the same performer who had danced and sang routines for years without notoriety before he came upon this particular manner of performance. But the fact that he could perhaps do it with such authority—in a way that seemed to capture the supposed mannerisms of *real* black people—elevated him from adequate to extraordinary and situated him as the main cultural phenomenon of his day.[8] What audiences saw in Rice's Jim Crow character (a clown, a folk artist, an object of desire, an object of scorn) and how they saw it (sympathetically, admiringly, enviously, disparagingly) is ultimately a matter of interpretation. What is more definite is what they were *not* seeing: legitimate black identity, autonomy, humanity.

But why should audiences of that era find the erasure of black identity so gratifying? And why would those purchasing sheet music to play in their parlors find the associated images so compelling? The answer lies in the increasingly exacting standards of nineteenth-century comportment. This was the era of the newly expanding middle class, the decades when the growing industrial revolution was bringing unrivaled wealth, status, and opportunity to a broader expanse of the American populace.[9] But with those gains came no modest amount of social anxiety. In an effort to distinguish themselves from the burgeoning middling classes, the established elite appeared to embrace a mindboggling array of behaviors and standards to measure social worth. As a result, those newly entering the middle class and those ambitious to position themselves higher still on the social ladder looked to assert their class worthiness through the observation of exacting and ever-changing standards of deportment. In this new climate of posturing and propriety, any individual's character might be measured by bodily carriage.[10] Journals and etiquette manuals revealed that there were very particular ways that proper men and women sat, walked, stood, ate, drank, and conversed—that there was a right and a wrong way to hold a fork, entertain guests, and address a member of the opposite sex.

In an era of what amounted to social hysteria over bodily alignment, the spirit of release occasioned by Rice's performances was electric. Here was a white man licensed only by black paint to stand before hundreds of viewers wiggling his hips, shaking his arms, ducking and weaving and jumping and hollering. In his songs he could brag about picking fights, bucking convention, and kissing "pretty yaller gals." What was enthralling was not Rice's impersonation of a black man but rather his employment of the blackened guise as a means of transgression. After all, if the thing that fascinated white audiences was truly black culture, they could have observed that firsthand in the routines of black players who commonly performed on the streets of northern cities. What Rice offered was both different and darker than that; it was the use of the black body as an excuse for expressing "baser" urges proper white society disallowed.[11] In the routines offered by Rice's closest contemporary, G. W. Dixon, white audiences found another form of release. Dixon's contribution to the minstrel tradition was the character Zip Coon— a blackface buffoon who delighted and amused white audiences with his absurd attempts to pass himself off as a refined gentleman.[12] For white audiences saddled with their own social insecurities, Zip Coon offered a figure they could laugh at and look down upon, whose failures at refinement outmeasured their own shortcomings, whose station on the lowest rung of the social ladder assured their own tenuous hold on propriety. In short, blackface performance as popularized by Rice and Dixon was gratifying because it provided two things middle-class Americans ached for: release and assurance.[13]

But these things came at the expense of black people in America. Denied access to the venues and audiences that fueled the minstrel phenomenon, black performers were generally powerless to counter or extend the misaligned characterizations that white actors were setting as the standard. The absorption of black identity into the fantasy of minstrel misrepresentation can be readily observed in the varied depictions of Rice on the covers of 1830s print music. Three covers offer a chronological progression that is striking. On each cover, the image is identified as Rice, both by name and by the classic pose that came to represent his famous dance routine. But the similarity of the pose held in each illustration is in sharp opposition to the increasingly abstract characterization of the actual figure. The first (fig. 2.1) offers a realistic depiction of Rice, as a white man in black face paint and wig. However, the second cover (fig. 2.2) clearly represents him as a black man—the broad nose and thick lips features that could not be fashioned from mere face paint. This alteration is significant in that it signals an important shift in perception—from Rice's routine offered as an imitation of black behavior to Rice's routine offered as a manifestation of black identity. The third cover (fig. 2.3) pushes from the view of Rice as embodying black identity to the actor's broad gestures fully *eclipsing* the black body—the black figure in the mind of white viewers becoming caricature, becoming cartoon.[14] These illustrations offer a visual equivalent of the erasure of black

(ABOVE LEFT) *Figure 2.1.* "*Jim Crow: The Celebrated Nigger Song*" (London: n.p., ca. 1830s). *Lester S. Levy Collection of Sheet Music, Sheridan Libraries of the Johns Hopkins University.*

(ABOVE RIGHT) *Figure 2.2.* "*The Original Jim Crow*" (New York: E. Riley, ca. 1830s). *Lester S. Levy Collection of Sheet Music, Sheridan Libraries of the Johns Hopkins University.*

(LEFT) *Figure 2.3.* "*Jim Crow*" (New York: Firth and Hall, ca. 1830s). *Lester S. Levy Collection of Sheet Music, Sheridan Libraries of the Johns Hopkins University.*

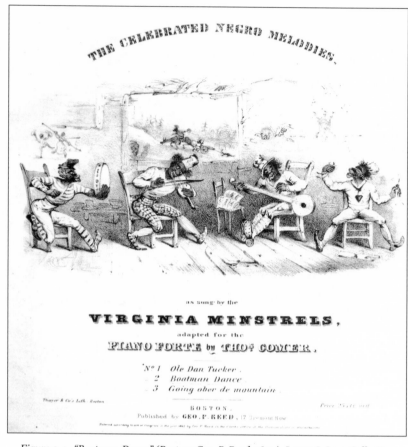

Figure 2.4. "Boatman Dance" (Boston: Geo. P. Reed, 1843). Lester S. Levy Collection of Sheet Music, Sheridan Libraries of the Johns Hopkins University.

identity that came to be the standard of the blackface tradition: black identity first imitated, then co-opted, and ultimately evicted for the entertainment and gratification of white audiences. (See fig. 2.4.)[15]

The changing nature of blackface performance in the years after Rice and Dixon appeared on the scene bears this out. Initially a modestly playful diversion, minstrel performance throughout the 1830s was increasingly marked by loud and bawdy material. We might imagine a cross between a rowdy rock concert (complete with mosh pit and raucous behavior) and a wildly boisterous sporting event (on the order of World Federation Wrestling); there, crowds of young white men drunk on the elixir of democracy (and sometimes just plain drunk) were whipped into a frenzy by blackened minstrel men who performed the black body as a site for the transgression of standards of propriety whites were generally expected to observe.

By the late 1830s, the medium of blackface minstrelsy had devolved into a loud and reckless affair, in part because of the rollicking nature of the music and material, and in part because of the audience reaction such material elicited. In truth, at this point in American history, live performance of every sort was characterized by a degree of audience participation that we now would find astonishing. For instance, immediately after a favorite moment in a play, theatergoers might demand that the actors repeat the scene (sometimes multiple times) for their enjoyment. Or an audience member might shout out the name of a popular tune in the middle of a theatrical production and expect the actors to stop the scene to perform the song. But at blackface performances, audiences were particularly vocal, rowdy, even violent. If they did not like a performance, they might threaten the performers or shower the stage with all manner of detritus; if they enjoyed the show, they might rush upon the stage in large numbers to more closely witness (and more closely identify with) the outrageous antics of the minstrel player. Skilled minstrels knew how to play to the passions of the crowd by improvising in response to cries from the audiences, commonly layering their songs with double entendres and offering sexual gestures meant to play up the racier possibilities of the material.[16]

Surprisingly, the raucous attitudes of the minstrel stage were not a deterrent to the sales of minstrel sheet music. After all, in the otherwise staid context of the parlor, music with a bit of dash and daring was a welcome departure, *if* it could be presented with some measure of restraint.[17] That was achieved in the 1840s through a clever adjustment in the representation of minstrel performers in sheet music cover art. (See fig. 2.5.) Increasingly minstrel music was finessed into the brocade confines of the parlor behind covers that offered images of upstanding, well-groomed white performers along with the grotesque black characters they portrayed. Dignified white figures mediated the threat that their grotesque characters potentially posed to the decorum of the parlor. The upright gents presented an element of elegance, of prestige, even as they perpetuated base parodies of black identity. Cover illustrations seem to present dapper entertainers as gentlemen callers, politely awaiting introduction into the refined space of the family parlor, or as handsome escorts adding legitimacy to the spectacle commonly associated with the blackface performance. The white figures ushered the rollicking minstrel show into the intimate confines of the

Figure 2.5. J. Sanford, "Walk Along John" (Boston: Keith's Music Publishing House, 1844). Lester S. Levy Collection of Sheet Music, Sheridan Libraries of the Johns Hopkins University.

American home, the potentially threatening atmosphere of the minstrel theater neutralized even as the gaudy misrepresentations remained intact.

In this form, sheet music proved the ideal vehicle for early minstrel troupes—quartets and quintets of minstrel men who together were performing what was by the mid-1840s becoming the standard formula of the fully realized minstrel show: a full evening of minstrel songs, skits, and comic speeches. By broadening the venue of blackface, performers such as the Virginia Minstrels and other troupes of so-called Ethiopian Delineators provided white audiences with a wide screen for the projection of their wildest fantasies and deepest fears about themselves and, by extension, the black population. Songs idealized the plight of southern slaves, stump speeches made a mockery of free blacks in the North, skits parodied black family relationships, and the punctuating walkabout to the merry strains of "Lucy Long" closed the show with a finale "rich in dark fun."[18] The shows themselves were so entertaining, the players so skilled, and the music so engaging that few cared that by commandeering the black body, the performers were introducing—even calcifying—countless racial stereotypes. It was cultural slander offered as harmless fun, unanswered and unchecked by actual black performers (commonly banned from performing in northern theaters) who might challenge and counter the parodies of black culture and identity popularized by white actors and embraced by white audiences.

Stage pantomime and cover design aside, the music itself fueled the fascination with blackface minstrelsy throughout the antebellum era. Early minstrel men such as Rice and Dixon leveraged their talents upon the claim that they were in essence recreating the authentic musical customs of the southern slave for the enlightenment and entertainment of northern audiences. And some performers did indeed take their early instruction in the songs and syncopation of black folk music from southern slaves and free blacks. For these few white performers, black culture was reflected in the method and the music they brought to their early performances;[19] but the majority had neither time, temperament, nor inclination to immerse themselves into black culture for the sake of authenticity. And they readily discovered that true authenticity was not necessary to convince northern audiences. If a song was played with "appropriate" syncopation and abandon, audiences could easily be persuaded that they were hearing something new and exotic: the "authentic music" of actual black slaves.[20] Ultimately, the material performed by blackface pretenders was given more credence as a marker of what was supposed to be black culture and identity than the corporeal fact of black people who populated northern cities and served as slaves in the South.

The pervasive popularity of the songs and relative ease of the arrangements made the material almost irresistible to those trying to make appealing music in the parlor. In truth the connection between the stage and the parlor to some extent was assured not by the musical arrangement but rather by the front covers placed on the music; arrangements that offered little that was substantively innovative could be made to seem exotic mainly on the basis of the association with minstrel scenes.[21] For women in particular and others in the parlor who in the early years of the minstrel show would have had no direct experience of the songs as actually performed by professional minstrels, it did not take much more than superficial elements to make the music seem accurate enough.

In performance and in print, the first era of the blackface tradition constituted a cumulative denial of the corporeal fact of black identity. White performers appropriated the black body for use as a screen upon which to defy the social behaviors antebellum standards of propriety demanded of the class-conscious populace of the North. An evolving middle class looked to minstrel sheet music at their parlor pianos to assuage their social insecurity and to add a degree of "fun" to evenings that were otherwise rather staid and starchy affairs. Whether intentional or not, the messages of antebellum minstrel sheet music helped to drive into the psyche of Americans the idea that blacks were foolish, hypersexual, and (unless carefully monitored) dangerous.[22] In antebellum sheet music and on the minstrel stage, the blackface tradition had offered an endless stream of images of blacks as buffoons, as careless and carefree braggarts, as wanton women, as hot-tempered, ill-tempered, and intemperate lovers, as thieves, and as fops. Repeatedly presented as incapable of maintaining even the most basic standards of decorum and dignity, comic black caricatures amused parlor-dwelling Americans and eased middle-class uncertainty by marking the woeful extremes of social failure. Unchecked and unchallenged for decades, these images informed and influenced attitudes about black identity by importing devastatingly racist ideology into the American home in the guise of harmless entertainment.

This becomes markedly apparent in the years after the Civil War, particularly in the North, when white Americans struggled to reconcile their assumptions and misconceptions with the behavior and attitudes of blacks living among them in urban centers in increasingly large numbers. The results are evident in postbellum perceptions of blacks; for black performers to have any hope of success on the stage, they were generally obliged to embody the established racial stereotypes—to, in essence perform their own invisibility. Restricted by the warped perceptions of white audiences, black performers stepped into the vacant spaces of their own bodies, their true selves, in essence, rendered invisible by audiences who refused to see them as other than the cartoon shapes their white predecessors had invented. Following conventions that generally demanded that even African American performers blacken their skin with face paint, black entertainers found that, aside from talent, their success depended on self ridicule and their ability to assure their white audience of the validity of their own stereotypes.[23] White audiences did not want to see black culture as it actually was and were generally not empathetic toward or interested in black issues and identity. What they wanted were "real coon shows" that reinforced their nostalgia for absurdly simplistic images of blacks generated decade after decade on the antebellum minstrel stage.[24]

By degrees black performers were able to infuse more humanity into their own representations, but not without cost and compromise. The struggle presents itself pointedly on sheet music covers throughout the late nineteenth century and well into the twentieth. By the end of the Civil War, the standard for representing blacks in practically all forms of entertainment media was firmly anchored in caricature established by the minstrel tradition. The degree and regularity of racial caricature on sheet music covers receded somewhat in the years directly after the war. But the cultural backlash that followed Reconstruction saw the nation's anxiety and unease with black citizens play out in vicious and visceral ways on the covers of "comic" coon songs that gained popularity throughout the last quarter of the nineteenth century.

Nowhere does the trend present itself more fluidly than on the covers of sheet music written by African American songsmiths and performers in the 1870s and 1880s. African Americans Dan Lewis, Sam Lucas, and James Bland were the three most popular and prolific composer/performers of that era. But each was also limited to performing and producing material consistent with the racial stereotypes then fully accepted by larger white American society; and as continued to be the case for black performers throughout the late nineteenth and early twentieth centuries, black performers had scant control of how they were depicted on the covers of the songs they composed and popularized. For instance, in his three most popular songs, Lewis writes of one black character who denies a child ("It Don't Belong to Me"), another who abandons his dying mother to go carousing with his friends ("A Mother's Request"), and a third who is a hero to his black community primarily because he supplies them with watermelons ("Mose Cart Dem Melons Down"). The shared cover for Lewis's songs is configured like those of antebellum minstrel songs popularized by white performers, such as E. P. Christy (fig. 2.6). But here (fig. 2.7) the tableau form previously filled by more fanciful and stylized illustrations is filled with more "realistically" rendered images that are, ironically, "authenticated" by Lewis's own portrait. A graduate of Howard University, James Bland came to be touted as "The World's Greatest Minstrel Man" while a member of the internationally acclaimed Haverly's Genuine Colored Minstrels. Although many of his compositions were both masterful and memorable, he found his greatest success with songs such as "O Dem Golden Slippers" and "Carry Me Back to Old Virginny," melodies that capitalized on (and capitulated to) the American fascination with plantation nostalgia. On sheet music covers (fig. 2.8), his handsome and refined portrait does little to neutralize the broad racial caricatures that crowd the cover. Many considered Sam Lucas to be one of the most celebrated theatrical actors of his age; in his portrayal of the central role in *Uncle Tom's Cabin* he was, in fact, one of the first African American actors to perform with an otherwise all-white theatrical company.[25] And although sheet music of songs he wrote for *Uncle Tom's Cabin* occasionally present him with dignity (fig. 2.9), it is respect extended less to the performer than to the venerated character he portrays. And even as a respected actor, he could not escape the draw to pen such songs as "De Coon Dat Had De Razor" (fig. 2.10). In what almost seems a direct erasure of the restraint afforded him as Uncle Tom, on the cover of this song Lucas appears only in name, the illustration otherwise given over entirely to the blade-wielding brute decried in the title.

Although it may well be argued that each of these artists brought their own individual craft and charisma to bear in their performances, cultural limitations girded their talents into roles and material that, in the eyes of a benighted white mainstream, strongly reflected stereotypes from the minstrel tradition. In essence, by the end of the nineteenth century, racial blackness and the performative parody of blackface were probably more seamlessly merged in American popular culture than ever before.[26]

Still the efforts of the first generation of black performers in the postbellum era ultimately did serve as leverage for African American performers in the early modern period. Even as the minstrel show receded in popularity, individual black performers found the opportunity to "perfect" the coon routines that were showcased among the varied acts offered in vaudeville.

Figure 2.6. E. P. Christy and C. D. Abbott, "Rosa Dear" (New York: Jaques and Brother, 1847). Lester S. Levy Collection of Sheet Music, Sheridan Libraries of the Johns Hopkins University.

Of course, the central appeal of the coon song was its reflection of racial stereotype. But the individual performance of material gave performers such as Bert Williams and George Walker access not only to broader audiences but also the chance to offer more nuanced interpretations of the types they performed. One of the most famous examples is the routine Williams created for the song "Nobody," which he wrote with Alex Rogers for *Abysinnia*, one of the first African American musicals to find success on Broadway. By 1906, when Williams first began performing the song as part of his regular routine, he was already one of the most celebrated performers in the Ziegfeld Follies.[27] Having garnered initial acclaim with his partner, Walker, Williams found increasing popularity with his impeccable comic timing and an ability to counter humor and pathos that anticipated the work of Charlie Chaplin and Buster Keaton. His acclaim with the Follies, however, was no measure of his acceptance among his white peers; by his own account, Williams managed best by going directly from his dressing room to

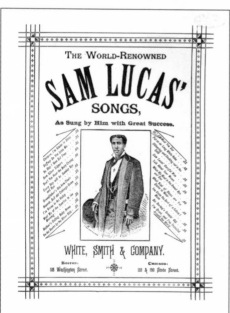

(ABOVE LEFT) *Figure 2.7. Dan Lewis,*
"It Don't Belong To Me" (Boston: White, Smith,
and Co., 1881). Lester S. Levy Collection of Sheet
Music, Sheridan Libraries of the Johns Hopkins
University.

(ABOVE RIGHT) *Figure 2.8. James Bland,*
"In the Evening by the Moonlight" (New York:
Benjamin W. Hitchcock, ca. 1880). Lester S. Levy
Collection of Sheet Music, Sheridan Libraries
of the Johns Hopkins University.

(LEFT) *Figure 2.9. Sam Lucas, "Oh I'll*
Meet You Dar" (Boston: White, Smith, and Co.,
ca. 1880). Lester S. Levy Collection of Sheet
Music, Sheridan Libraries of the Johns Hopkins
University.

Figure 2.10. Sam Lucas,
"De Coon Dat Had De
Razor" (Boston: White,
Smith, and Co., ca. 1885).
Lester S. Levy Collection
of Sheet Music, Sheridan
Libraries of the Johns
Hopkins University.

the stage and back to his dressing room with as little interaction with the other players as possible. A profoundly gifted but deeply isolated performer, Williams was once described by comedian W. C. Fields as "the funniest man I ever saw, and the saddest man I ever knew."[28] His professional isolation was not wasted in his performance of what quickly became his signature song:

> When life is full of clouds and rain,
> And I am filled with nothin' and pain,
> Who soothes my thumping, bumping brain?
> ... Nobody.
>
> When winter comes with snow and sleet,
> And me with hunger and cold feet,
> Who says, "Here's two bits, go and eat"?
> ... Nobody.

Black Misrepresentation **59**

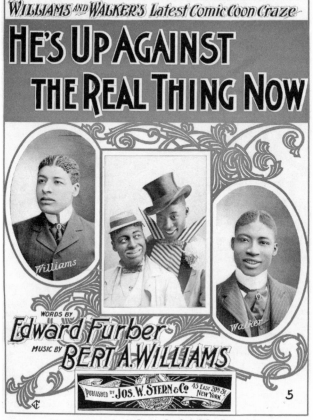

Figure 2.11. Edward
Furber and Bert A.
Williams, "He's Up
Against the Real Thing
Now" (New York: Jos. W.
Stern, and Co., ca. 1898).
Lester S. Levy Collection
of Sheet Music, Sheridan
Libraries of the Johns
Hopkins University.

I ain't never done nothin' to Nobody.
I ain't never got nothin' from Nobody, no time.
And until I get somethin' from somebody, sometime,
I don't intend to do nothin' for Nobody, no time.

On the stage, audiences ostensibly saw what audiences had seen for decades: a character in blackface paint stuck at the lowest rung of the social ladder. But as reinvented by Williams, the figure was not a caricature. Comical, yes, but not a buffoon. Destined to fail, perhaps, but not because of his own failings. Entertaining, always, but also surprisingly tragic. On stage, Williams performed the song almost as a recitation, a soliloquy. If this was a stereotype, it was one rendered with such intimacy and tenderness that its otherness dissolved into profound humanity. Williams's effectiveness in his performance of the song had less to do with appearing pathetic as it had to be with appearing fully human—a man with a beating heart, a perceptive mind, and social awareness. In that way, Williams presented the world with a subversive figure, an augur of change in the ways that African Americans were beginning to present and perceive themselves in popular culture.

Of course, Williams also had to suffer the racist depictions and stereotypical images commonly associated with sheet music design in the early twentieth century. But even in print publication, he and other popular black performers were beginning to challenge the status quo at any opportunity. Perhaps the earliest example of this is the cover of a song Williams popularized with Walker as early as 1898, "He's Up Against the Real Thing Now" (fig. 2.11). The lyrics describe various scenes where men who believe they're the best are brought low when confronted with "the real thing"—unexpected figures who turn out to be better, stronger, and more deserving of respect. Aside from the lyrics, the title alone—particularly written and presented by African American performers—seems to confront and challenge black character types previously formed by the wants and whims of white audiences and white performers. The cover design is also a visual assertion of this idea. Positioned at the center is a photo of Williams and Walker in comic guise. But that central picture is flanked by individual photos of the *real* men who *play* the roles: Williams, dignified and refined, and Walker, handsome and composed. The actors are not tucked away or dwarfed by racial caricature. Rather, they beam assertively, even triumphantly, policing the periphery of their comic selves—characters they have inherited, but characterizations they control.

NOTES

1. For a more complete account of the evolution of blackface minstrelsy in America, see Annemarie Bean, James V. Hatch, and Brooks McNamara, eds., *Inside the Minstrel Mask: Readings in Nineteenth-Century Blackface Minstrelsy* (Hanover, N.H.: Wesleyan University Press, 1996); W. T. Lhamon Jr., *Raising Cain: Blackface Performance from Jim Crow to Hip Hop* (Cambridge: Harvard University Press, 1998); and William J. Mahar, *Behind the Burnt Cork Mask: Early Blackface Minstrelsy and Antebellum American Popular Culture* (Urbana: University of Illinois Press, 1999).

2. I share W. T. Lhamon's concern about scholarship on the blackface tradition that only addresses racism in minstrelsy "by emphasizing its presence, then moving on to discuss the form's other—even its counter—aspects." Lhamon, *Raising Cain*, 6.

3. Direct accounts of such raucous and low entertainment as early minstrel performance are hard to come by; respectable papers generally did not comment on blackface performance until the more acceptable minstrel show gained broader cultural acceptance in the mid-1840s. But a visual representation exists in a playbill in the collection of the New-York Historical Society. The illustration shows minstrel sensation T. D. Rice dancing amid a throng of rowdy audience members who have rushed the stage. The caption reads, "American Theatre Bowery New York: View of the Stage on the Fifty-seventh Night of Mr. T. D. Rice of Kentucky in His Original and Celebrated Extravaganza of JIM CROW on Which Occasion Every Department of the House Was Thronged to an Excess Unprecedented in the Records of Theatrical Attraction. New York 25th November 1833." (A reprint of the illustration can be found on page 125 of Eric Lott, *Love and Theft: Blackface Minstrelsy and the Working Class* [New York: Oxford University Press, 1993].) It's also telling that once respectable papers did start promoting and reviewing minstrel shows in later years, promoters sought to allay concerns about the medium's prior bad reputation: e.g., "All business is concluded at a reasonable hour. . . . Every representation . . . is chaste, moral and free from vulgarity and all objectionable allusions. No improper person (male or female) admitted. . . . FRONT SEATS RESERVED FOR LADIES. . . . Gentlemen are most respectfully requested not to beat time with their feet." Jon W. Finson, *The Voices That Are Gone: Themes in Nineteenth-Century American Popular Song* (New York: Oxford University Press, 1994) 187; Harvard Theatre Collection, minstrel box on White's bill.

4. "As [Rice] sauntered along one of the main thoroughfares of Cincinnati, as has been written, his attention was suddenly arrested by a voice ringing clear and full above the street, and giving utterance, in an unmistakable dialect to the refrain of ['Jim Crow']. . . . [Rice reportedly thought,] might not 'Jim Crow' and a black face tickle the fancy of pit and circle . . . ? Out of the suggestion leaped the determination; and so it chanced that the casual hearing of a song trolled by a negro stage-driver, lolling lazily on the box of his vehicle, gave origin to a school of music destined to excel in popularity all others." Robert P. Nevin, "Stephen C. Foster and Negro Minstrelsy," *Atlantic Monthly* 20 (1867): 608–9.

5. As James Kennard Jr., recounted in an 1845 article, "Who Are Our National Poets," "[Mr. Thomas Rice] accordingly learned their poetry, music, and dancing, blacked his face, and made his fortune by giving the world his counterfeit presentment. . . . From the nobility and gentry, down to the lowest chimney-sweep in Great Britain, and from the member of Congress, down the youngest apprentice of schoolboy in America, it was all: 'Turn about and wheel about, and do just so, / And every time I turn about I jump Jim Crow.'" James Kennard Jr., *Selections from the Writings of James Kennard, Jr., with a Sketch of His Life and Character* (Boston: William D. Tickner, 1948), 107–8.

6. See Dale Cockrell, *Demons of Disorder: Early Blackface Minstrels and Their World* (Cambridge: Cambridge University Press, 1997), 13–29.

7. See Lott, *Love and Theft*, 111–35.

8. For the most complete and compelling account of Rice's Jim Crow routine, see W. T. Lhamon Jr., *Jump Jim Crow: Lost Plays, Lyrics, and Street Prose of the First Atlantic Popular Culture* (Cambridge: Harvard University Press, 2003), 1–92.

9. See Richard L. Bushman, *The Refinement of America: Persons, Houses, Cities* (New York: Random House, 1993), 402–47.

10. The definitive text on the role of etiquette and deportment in nineteenth-century America is John F. Kasson, *Rudeness and Civility: Manners in Nineteenth-Century Urban America* (New York: Hill and Wang, 1990).

11. The bawdy nature of this early era of blackface cannot be overstated; in fact, the increasingly vulgar nature of minstrelsy in the 1830s turned blackface performances into shows no "proper" lady would attend. Minstrel performers played to the baser urges of their primarily male, working-class audiences by asserting a degree of raunchiness that we would now find shocking. The possibility for raciness is suggested in the thinly veiled double entendre of such early minstrel songs as "Coal Black Rose": "[Stay] a little, Sambo; I [come] soon / As I make a fire in [the] backroom / . . . Make haste, Rose, [lovely] dear / I froze [stiff] as a poker [standing] here." (I've standardized the dialect here for the sake of clarity.) Lhamon, *Jump Jim Crow*, 94–95.

12. Mahar, *Behind the Burnt Cork Mask*, 203–9.

13. Bushman, *Refinement of America*, 438.

14. The relative quality of the image in fig. 1 might be attributed to the fact that this article of sheet music was produced in London, where the music publishing industry was more firmly established and the printing presses were technically superior to the equipment available in early nineteenth-century America. But given that comparable American sheet music covers featuring white characters offered more realistic depictions, I argue that the devolution of the black characters demonstrated in figs. 2 and 3 is less the result of inferior equipment as it is a reflection of American attitudes about what the figure signified.

15. The Virginia Minstrels were the originators of the fully realized minstrel show—that is, a complete evening's entertainment of minstrel songs, comic routines, and skits offered by a troupe of players (rather than by a single performer). It is in this form that minstrelsy eventually reached the mainstream in the 1840s and beyond, as performers and promoters "cleaned up their acts" in an effort to draw more respectable people (including women and children) to increase their revenues. But this 1843 cover still suggests the kind of raucous attitudes associated with the earlier era of the blackface tradition. Note how here the sexuality that characterized early live performance finds its visual counterpart in the cocked fist of the first figure, phallic positioning of the banjo played by the third figure, and the broadly spread legs of the fourth.

16. See Richard Butsch, *The Making of American Audiences: From Stage to Television, 1750–1990* (New York: Cambridge University Press, 2000), 5–6.

17. For more on the evolution and influence of parlor culture in nineteenth-century America, see Katherine C. Grier, *Culture and Comfort: Parlor Making and*

Middle-Class Identity, 1850–1930 (Washington, D.C.: Smithsonian Institution Press, 1988).

18. The phrase "rich in dark fun" has come to be a catchphrase in characterizing attitudes about the minstrel show in antebellum America. It is a variation of a quote attributed to British actor Charles Mathews; having come upon the idea of featuring the imitation of a black man in his one-man show "A Trip to America" (1822), he is said to have exclaimed, "I shall be rich in black fun." Walter Blair, "Charles Mathews and His 'A Trip to America,'" *Prospects* 2 (1977): 2.

19. Through the late 1820s and 1830s, a white performer's ability to play the banjo could itself stand as proof of his direct exposure to black culture. The prototype for what would become the banjo was the banjar—an instrument that came directly out of slave culture. Originally made simply of rudimentary materials, the banjar was modeled after any of a range of African stringed instruments. In its many makeshift forms, the instrument was commonly played in a style that white Americans generally found mystifying (i.e., a percussive downward striking of the strings rather than conventional upward plucking); indeed, throughout the eighteenth century and well into the nineteenth, many believed that the instrument that was coming to be known as the banjo could only be mastered by slaves and members of the African race. So as late as the 1840s, it could be argued that any white man who could play the banjo in the so-called clawhammer style had necessarily learned to play from a black person, thus assuring some sustained exposure to black folk-music forms. Indeed, the first banjo instruction book was not published until 1851, *The Complete Preceptor for the Banjo*, by Elias Howe (a.k.a. Gumbo Chaff). Joseph Weidlich, ed., *Minstrel Banjo: Briggs' Banjo Instructor* (Anaheim Hills, Calif.: Centerstream Publishing, 1997), 4. Also see Philip F. Gura and James F. Bollman, *America's Instrument: The Banjo in the Nineteenth Century* (Chapel Hill: University of North Carolina Press, 1999).

20. A striking example of this is the popular minstrel song "Old Joe." The chorus lyrics ("Old Joe kickin' up a hind and a foe; / And a yellow gal kickin' up a hind Old Joe") are attached to a melody that is little more than the tune "Twinkle, Twinkle Little Star"—a fact that, drawn into the exotic minstrel setting and styling of the song, few nineteenth-century audiences noticed. *The Early Minstrel Show* (New World Records, 1988).

21. As music historian Nicholas Tawa characterizes the scene in the mid-nineteenth-century parlor, "The more up-to-date children pranced about in imitation of minstrel men and mouthed their dialect ditties. Young men and women sent forth popular songs depicting the various stage of love, or they danced. If a piano was in the parlor, young people clustered around it for amusement if not for courtship. . . . The best way to restrain the more urgent amorous feelings was through the comings-together in a parlor, where music might act as a safety valve, while married adults monitored conditions nearby." Nicholas E. Tawa, *High-Minded and Low Down: Music in the Lives of Americans, 1800–1861* (Boston: Northeastern University Press, 2000), 163.

22. Fighting among slaves is a common theme in antebellum minstrel music. The

second verse of "Cudjos Wild Hunt" (1843) offers a good example: "Dem niggers for sartain are gwan for to fight / See dar! dat big nigger dere frashing, / Dey squash his big head, and dey sarve him right, / And Cudjo his Banjo is smashing."

23. See Henry T. Sampson, *Blacks in Blackface: A Source Book on Early Black Musical Shows* (Lanham, Md.: Scarecrow Press, 1980); and Ike Simond, *Old Slack's Reminiscence and Pocket History of the Colored Profession from 1865 to 1891* (Bowling Green, Ohio: Popular Press, 1974).

24. For a demonstration of this nostalgia, we need not look any further than one of the most visible figures of the era, Mark Twain. Although famously liberal for his time and generally progressive in views on race, he apparently had no qualms and felt no conflict in proudly proclaiming his nostalgia for "the real nigger show—the genuine nigger show, the extravagant nigger show." Mark Twain, *The Autobiography of Mark Twain*, ed. Charles Neider (1917; New York: Harper Perennial Classics, 2000), 76. For historical and cultural contextualization of Twain's attitudes toward the minstrel show, see Henry B. Wonham, "'I Want a Real Coon': Mark Twain and Late Nineteenth-Century Ethnic Caricature," *American Literature* 72, no. 1 (2000): 117–52.

25. See Robert C. Toll, *Blacking Up: The Minstrel Show in Nineteenth-Century America* (New York: Oxford University Press, 1974), 217–18.

26. Given the general social and political conditions for African Americans at the turn of the century, this should come as no surprise. Reflecting back on the period in *Black Manhattan*, James Weldon Johnson writes, "The status of the Negro as a citizen had been steadily declining for twenty-five years; and at the opening of the twentieth century his civil state was, in some respects, worse than at the close of the Civil War. . . . The general spirit of the race was one of hopelessness or acquiescence. The only way to survival seemed along the road of sheer opportunism and of conformity." James Weldon Johnson, *Black Manhattan* (New York: Knopf, 1930), 127–28.

27. For a complete account of the life of Williams, see Camille F. Forbes, *Introducing Bert Williams: Burnt Cork, Broadway, and the Story of America's First Black Star* (New York: Basic Civitas Books, 2008).

28. Ibid., 298.

Creating an Image in Black

The Power of Abolition Pictures

JOHN STAUFFER

"One picture is worth ten thousand words," the adman Frederick R. Barnard said in *Printer's Ink Magazine* in 1927. His quip has of course become an adman's proverb. Indeed, Barnard may have only given authorship to a saying that had already been around for decades. Admen were not the first group to champion the use of pictures as a means to sell their wares. Abolitionists had done much the same thing. They, like advertisers, relied on images to sell ideas of the good society. But the *source* of their desire was much different: they sought to end slavery and racism and transform the means of production, rather than generate demand and fuel consumption.[1]

Reformers in America and Europe became enraptured with the power of the picture beginning around 1830, once changes in lithography and line drawings had enabled large-scale mass production of images in newspapers and magazines.[2] Their enemies—the politicians and gatekeepers of the existing order—felt so threatened by their images that they tried to censor them.[3] When the young William Lloyd Garrison began publishing *The Liberator* in 1831, what most offended southerners were the images— particularly the masthead, which depicted a slave auction in front of the nation's Capitol, the flag of liberty atop its dome, a whipping post in its plaza, and in the foreground a grieving slave family at auction and a discarded Indian treaty (fig. 3.1). Vice President John C. Calhoun, an ardent proslavery advocate, was so outraged by the image that he attempted, unsuccessfully, to ban newspapers with "pictorial representations" of slavery from the mails. Abolitionist texts were tolerable, in his mind, but not images.[4]

Abolitionists relied heavily on the power of pictures in their reform work. Their desire to transform themselves and their world fueled their interest in images, for images helped to make visible the contrast between their dreams of reform and the sinful present.[5]

Black abolitionists were particularly invested in the power of images.

Figure 3.1. The Liberator *masthead, 1830s. Widener Library, Harvard University.*

Some of the most prominent, from Frederick Douglass and William "Ethiop" Wilson to James McCune Smith, Sojourner Truth, and Harriet Jacobs, embraced the black image as an aid in their reform work. Their rise to public prominence from the mid-1840s through the 1860s paralleled the rise of visual culture, when Americans increasingly began to define themselves with images.[6] The twin rise of visual culture and black public personas is not coincidental; black abolitionists relied on images as a way to acquire a public voice, enter into the public sphere, and revise public opinion. Yet the ways in which they used, appropriated, and thought about visual images have been largely ignored.[7]

Most critics, when discussing African Americans and pictures, focus on how blacks have been objectified. They view the black image as part of the process of exploitation. To be in front of the camera lens, to have one's body represented, photographed, *taken*—symbolically if not literally—is to render that body powerless.[8] Gazing becomes a masculine, empowering (and "white") condition, while being seen is a feminine (and "black") one.[9]

Yet the process of visual representation is much more complicated. Robyn Wiegman has argued that in the twentieth century, the commodified appearance of the black body became a "representational sign for the democratizing process of U.S. Culture itself."[10] Little has been said about the ways in which black abolitionists sought, in effect, to objectify *themselves* as a source of power and as an aid in their reform work. From their perspective, the relation between subject, object, and power looks much different. They *wanted* to be objects rather than subjects—art objects, in particular— and at times wrote eloquently about the power of pictures. I want to explore the nature of this objectification.

Frederick Douglass relied as much on his image as on his voice and words to create his public persona. He photographed as well as wrote himself into public existence. He was also one of the most perceptive writers in the nineteenth century on the uses of visual images.[11]

Part of Douglass's fascination with images stemmed from his faith in "true" art as a social leveler. "True" art for him meant accurate and "authentic" images of blacks, rather than caricatures such as blackface minstrelsy. Through speeches, writings, and images, he sought to fashion himself as an art object, or performer, that would confer upon *both* his persona and his white perceivers the "gift of life," to borrow from Elaine Scarry, which would link them together and dissolve social barriers. The slave as "thing," or black man as object, acquired life and humanity when represented as an art object or performer. And the perceiver acquired new life by perceiving that thing as human.[12]

The representation of the black body as an objet d'art that could transform whites depended on *how* that body was represented. Douglass continually sought to control how he appeared in his portraits. In an 1849 review of *A Tribute for the Negro*, by the Quaker abolitionist Wilson Armistead, he praised the prose but attacked the imagery, including the engraving of himself. The engraver had probably cut the image of Douglass from Douglass's 1845 *Narrative of the Life of Frederick Douglass* (figs. 3.2–3.3), which had been cut from a painting. But the engraver for *A Tribute for the Negro* had added a smile without consulting Douglass, rendering him, as Douglass accused, with "a much more kindly and amiable expression than is generally thought to characterize the face of a fugitive slave" (fig. 3.4). Although he was no longer a fugitive slave, Douglass wanted the look of a defiant but respectable outsider. "Negroes can never have impartial portraits at the hands of white artists," he stated: "It seems to us next to impossible for white men to take likenesses of black men, without most grossly exaggerating their distinctive features. And the reason is obvious. Artists, like all other white persons, have adopted a theory respecting the distinctive features of Negro physiognomy." The vast majority of whites could not create "impartial" likenesses of African Americans (even though they might be

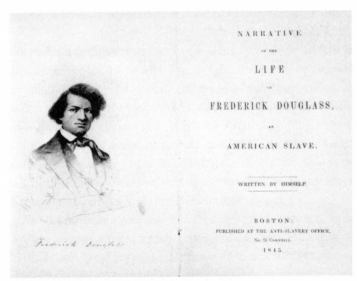

Figure 3.2. Frontispiece and title page of Frederick Douglass's Narrative of the Life of Frederick Douglass *(first American edition, 1845). Houghton Library, Harvard University.*

(ABOVE LEFT) *Figure 3.3. Unidentified artist,* Frederick Douglass, *oil on canvas, ca. 1845. National Portrait Gallery, Smithsonian Institution, Washington, D.C.*

(ABOVE RIGHT) *Figure 3.4. Unidentified artist,* Frederick Douglass, *engraving. From Wilson Armistead,* A Tribute for the Negro: Being a Vindication of the Moral, Intellectual, and Religious Capabilities of the Colored Portion of Mankind . . . *(Manchester: William Irwin, 1848), following p. 456. Widener Library, Harvard University.*

able to write about them impartially) because of their preconceived notions of what blacks looked like.[13]

Douglass was right: the vast majority of white artists degraded or dehumanized blacks when representing them. Most white Americans in the antebellum era believed that blacks were innately inferior, incapable of self-government, and thus unable to participate in civil society. They used pictures—though *not photography*—to show it. Scientists teamed up with artists to depict blacks as subhuman. One of the most popular scientific books of the antebellum era was heavily laden with images to further the authors' racist arguments. *Types of Mankind*, first published in 1854 by the respected ethnologists Josiah Nott and George Glidden, included numerous engravings that evoked a strong affinity between blacks and gorillas. The first printing of the book sold out immediately, and the second edition, published in 1855, included an engraving that compared heads and skulls of a "creole negro," a "young chimpanzee," and a *statue* of the white Apollo Belvidere (fig. 3.5). The image was meant to encapsulate their argument: blacks were more akin to apes than to humans. One did not need to be literate to understand their "scientific" claim.[14]

Even white abolitionists betrayed their paternalistic attitudes toward blacks when they depicted them. Probably the best-known white abolitionist image is that of the supplicating slave, pleading: "Am I Not a Man and a Brother?" It was created by the Quaker-led Society for Effecting the Abolition of the Slave Trade in London in 1787, which hired three designers to create an engraving for the society's use. Josiah Wedgwood, a British pottery maker and a member of the society, hired a designer from his Staffordshire factory to make a relief of the seal for a cameo (fig. 3.6). In a letter to Benjamin Franklin in 1788, Wedgwood said that he felt the image would help promote freedom and create an "epoch before unknown to the World." Franklin replied by saying that the effect of the image was "equal to that of the best written Pamphlet, in procuring favour to those oppressed People." The image would induce whites' sympathy for slaves, and its effect would be more immediate than a pamphlet.[15]

But the *nature* of whites' sympathy is telling: the slave is praying and kneeling, pleading to God *and to whites* for his freedom. The image highlights white abolitionists' belief that *they*, with God's help, would deliver freedom to slaves, rather than slaves liberating themselves. Black agency was not the central component of their visual and mental world.

The Wedgwood image was used throughout the British and American abolition movement and appeared on everything from snuffboxes, brace-

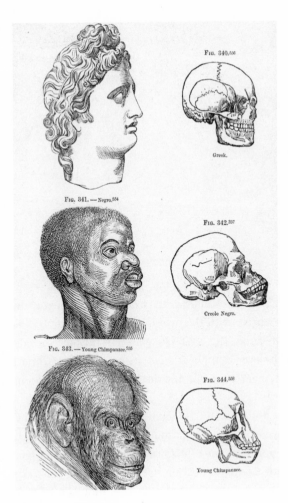

Figure 3.5. Apollo Belvidere, Negro, Young Chimpanzee, *engraving. From Josiah Nott and George Gliddon,* Types of Mankind: or, Ethnological Researches *(Philadelphia: Lippincott, Grambo, 1855). Widener Library, Harvard University.*

lets, and pins to stationery and broadsides. In 1837 a woodcut engraving of the image was included on a popular broadside above a poem by John Greenleaf Whittier, "Our Countrymen in Chains!" (fig. 3.7) The slave is now stronger; indeed, the size and tone of his muscles resemble those of a Greek god. He is much more capable of claiming his own freedom. But he remains kneeling, a servant and supplicant to God and whites. That white abolitionists saw themselves as blacks' deliverers betrayed their own sense of racial superiority. They doubted that blacks would be able to achieve their own freedom "without bloodshed," and the white abolition movement originated from the doctrine of nonviolence.[16]

Douglass revised the iconic image of the kneeling slave. In his 1853 *Autographs for Freedom*, a collection of abolitionist writings compiled with his

Figure 3.6. "Am I Not a Man and a Brother?," medallion, ca. 1787. W. E. B. Du Bois Institute, Harvard University.

friend and editor Julia Griffiths, he includes as the frontispiece an engraving of a slave kneeling before Christ, with the inscription, "He [Christ] Is Not Ashamed to Call Them Brethren" (fig. 3.8). Douglass's frontispiece avoids confusion about whom the slave is supplicating to: he kneels before Christ, who holds his hand. White men appear in the distant background, gazing on this scene of racial uplift.[17]

The slave auction was another icon of black degradation as well as the evils of slavery. Like the image of the supplicating slave, it stood for an epoch or system of beliefs—its power meant to inspire an age of emancipation. Garrison includes a vignette of a slave auction in the masthead of his *Liberator*. When Harriet Beecher Stowe published her best-selling novel, *Uncle Tom's Cabin* (1852), which became the most popular book in the nineteenth century save for the Bible, she included six engravings by Hammatt Billings to visualize her story; one of them is of the slave auction at "the court-house steps" of Washington, Kentucky, where Mr. Haley purchases three slaves (fig. 3.9). In this image, as in almost every other depiction of slave auctions, whites tower over blacks, as if to suggest that America would remain a white nation even after emancipation, which is what Stowe concludes at the end of her novel when she champions black colonization.[18]

Douglass's criticism of white artists helps to explain why he was so taken with photography: he thought that the *veracity* of the daguerreotype—the most popular form of photography in America from its invention in 1839 through the mid-1850s—prevented distortions of blacks that came from the

(LEFT) *Figure 3.8. G. H. Hayes, "He Is Not Ashamed to Call Them Brethren,"* frontispiece of Autographs for Freedom *(1853). Author's collection.*

(BELOW) *Figure 3.9. Hammatt Billings,* The Auction Sale, *engraving. From Harriet Beecher Stowe,* Uncle Tom's Cabin *(Boston: John P. Jewett and Company, 1852), following page 174. Widener Library, Harvard University.*

THE AUCTION SALE.   Page 174.

hands of white artists. He also knew that the vast majority of daguerreotypes (over 90 percent) took the form of portraits. The photograph, and accurate renditions or sympathetic engravings drawn from the photograph, became his medium of choice for representing himself visually.[19]

Douglass was so taken with daguerreotypy that he called Louis Daguerre, the inventor of the daguerreotype, "the great discoverer of modern times, to whom coming generations will award special homage." Because of Daguerre's invention, he said, "we have pictures, true pictures, of every object which can interest us." "Men of all conditions and classes," he added, "can now *see themselves as others see them and as they will be seen by those [who] shall come after them.* What was once the special and exclusive luxury of the rich and great—is now the privilege of all. The humblest servant girl may now possess a picture of herself such as the wealth of kings could not purchase fifty years ago."[20]

For Douglass, the daguerreotype contributed to an *authentic* picture-making process. In his mind, all humans sought *accurate* representations both of material reality and of an unseen spiritual world. This affinity for true pictures is what distinguished humans from animals: "Man is the only picture-making animal in the world. He alone of all the inhabitants of earth has the capacity and passion for pictures." Emphasizing the humanity of all humans was central to Douglass's reform vision, since all but the most radical of Americans defended inequality and racial hierarchies on the grounds that black slaves and their descendants were fundamentally different from other humans.

Douglass attacked racism not only by championing the "truthfulness" of the photograph, but also by stressing the picture-making proclivity of all humans. To make and appreciate pictures required imagination, and for this reason Douglass emphasized the superiority of imagination over reason. While "dogs and elephants are said to possess" the capacity for reason, he argued, only humans sought to recreate nature and portray both the "inside soul" and the "outside world" through such "artificial means" as the photograph. The power of the "imagination," he added, was "a sublime, prophetic, and all-creative power." Imagination could be used to create a public persona in the form of a photograph or engraving. It could also be used to usher in a new world of equality, without slavery and racism. The power of the imagination linked humans to "the Eternal sources of life and creation." It allowed them to appreciate pictures as *accurate* representations of some greater reality, and it helped them to realize their sublime ideals in an imperfect world. As Douglass aptly put it: "Poets, prophets, and reformers are all picture makers—and this ability is the secret of their power and of their achievements. They see what ought to be by the reflection of what is, and endeavor to remove the contradiction." Douglass considered himself all three: a poet (by which he meant "artist"), a prophet, and a reformer. He drew on divine sources to create sublime pictures of a new world of inter-racial equality. It was a millennial vision defined in nationalist terms.

Douglass went so far as to suggest that the "moral and social influence of pictures"—and "representation," more generally—were *more* important in shaping the nation than "the making of its laws." Art, in other words, was more important than politics for changing society. It is a remarkable state-ment, for Douglass always defined himself as an abolitionist and reformer, and throughout the 1850s and 1860s he was deeply committed to political action. But art was the engine of social change.[21]

Douglass highlights the power an authentic black image can have on a white subject in his only work of fiction, "The Heroic Slave" (1853). The nar-rative opens with Mr. Listwell, a white man, who chances upon Madison Washington, the black hero, talking to himself in the forest. Listwell is aptly named, for he can "listen well" to what blacks have to say, as Robert Stepto has shown. He stands at the edge of the forest, gazing at Washington with-out the latter's knowledge, and is utterly transformed by what he sees and hears. Washington's "soliloquy" rang "through the chambers of his soul, and vibrated through his entire frame." "From this hour," Listwell vows, "I am an abolitionist. I have seen enough and heard enough, and I shall go" home *"resolved* to atone for my past indifference to this ill-starred race." He treats Washington's performance as authentic, an accurate representation of his person.[22]

Listwell's capacity to "see well" surpasses his ability to listen well, for five years later, when he finally meets Washington, he recognizes him instantly. "Ever since that morning . . . you have seldom been absent from my mind." "From that hour, your face seemed to be daguerreotyped on my memory."[23]

Daguerreotyping a character was a common trope in abolitionist nar-ration. (Harriet Beecher Stowe "daguerreotype[s]" Uncle Tom "for [her] readers.")[24] It conveyed more than physical description or even photo-graphic memory, for a daguerreotype was thought to penetrate the per-ceiver's soul as well as his mind.[25]

Americans saw God's work in the daguerreotype. Douglass and his con-temporaries widely believed that daguerreotypes were "likenesses" in a reli-gious sense—part of the individual's essence, "a matter of spiritual similarity" rather than a mere "picture."[26] A daguerreotype, it was thought, contained part of the body and soul of the subject. It was a unique, one-of-a-kind, copper-plated object, covered with glass, whereas subsequent photographic forms such as *cartes de visite* were infinitely reproducible pieces of paper. Having Washington "daguerreotyped" on Listwell's memory connects the two men's souls, and they become equals and friends. Both men benefit from their friendship: Listwell gains his spiritual freedom by atoning for his sin of indifference to slavery; and Washington gains his physical freedom, with help from his friend.

Daguerreotyping a character reflected a level of authenticity that went beyond representation to include the essence of the referent. Although this faith in authenticity, not to mention the notion of spiritual essence, may seem curious to us today, it was widespread in antebellum America. Many theatergoers, for instance, treated actors on stage as the real thing, inseparable from the roles they played. Lawrence Levine describes the effects of this confusion between representation and reality. During a production of *Othello* in Albany, New York, a canal boatman interrupted the performance, and screamed at Iago, "You damned scoundrel, I would like to get hold of you after the show and wring your infernal neck."[27]

Sojourner Truth was possibly more famous for her *cartes de visite* images than for her actual presence in abolition meetings. Her carefully chosen portraits made her a familiar presence to millions of viewers (fig. 3.10). They depicted "a respectable, middle-class matron," as Nell Painter has summarized.[28] Truth's famous maxim that she included with her images, "I sell the shadow to support the substance," links her image [shadow] to her actual self [her substance], as well as to a growing consumer ethos. She wanted her image to be an extension of herself and her nation. Her yarn forms the contours of the eastern United States, with Florida's panhandle and Texas clearly visible. Her image thus presents her as a representative American woman, her piety and simplicity shaping the nation. Her maxim suggests that she wanted to extend the "aura" of the daguerreotype onto other forms of photography in order to preserve the link between image and reality, shadow and substance, without distortion.[29]

Abolitionist James McCune Smith believed, with Douglass, that an authentic black persona could be extremely effective in breaking down racial barriers. In 1855 he reviewed a performance of the singer Elizabeth Greenfield, known as the "Black Swan," at the Broadway Tabernacle, and con-

cluded that "*true* art is a social leveler, and thoroughly isocratic," or egalitarian. Greenfield's performance was so powerful that she collapsed racial barriers and created an integrated community in the Tabernacle: "Never was the Tabernacle so thoroughly speckled with mixed complexions; blind gentlemen sat side and side with dark ladies," and "colorblind" *white women* sat next to *black men.* Greenfield refused to succumb to "the requirements of American Prejudice"; instead of trying to hide her ancestry, she stood forth "simple and pure a black woman." For McCune Smith, Greenfield's stage presence reflected her true self.[30]

But McCune Smith also recognized the shortcomings of relying solely on a performative self to combat racism. "The colored man must do impracticable things before he is admitted to a place in society," he acknowledged in 1854. "He must speak like a [Frederick] Douglass, write like a[n Alexandre] Dumas, and sing like the Black Swan before he could be recognized as a human being." McCune Smith knew, too, that his own medium of choice, the essay, had limited popular appeal, especially compared with public speaking, photography, and stage performance. One reason for his comparative lack of popularity was that he rarely had his picture taken and was not a brilliant performer, and so did not stand ever present, as it were, before people's eyes.[31]

William Wilson, a colleague of McCune Smith and the Brooklyn correspondent of *Frederick Douglass' Paper*, used ekphrasis—representing visual objects with words—to create an "Afric-American Picture Gallery." Writing under the pseudonym "Ethiop" to emphasize his black persona, Wilson wrote a series of seven "papers" in 1859, describing twenty-six images in his picture gallery that summarized the social, political, and cultural conditions of America. "I always had a penchant for pictures," Ethiop confesses at the beginning of his series. "From a chit of a boy till now, my love for beautiful, or quaint, old pictures has been unquenched." In one of his "rambles" in search of pictures, he "stumbled over the Afric-American Picture Gallery," which became one of "my dearest retreats."[32]

Ethiop guides his readers through the various images, characters, and settings in his picture gallery. The images are emblems of black resistance and achievement: Haitian leader Toussaint L'Ouverture; a "Young Tom," who, unlike "Uncle Tom," is full of mischief and rebellion; the Underground Railroad; Phillis Wheatley; and a black artist-prophet who stands erect in the "Black Forest," a setting that affirms black identity.[33]

What is significant about Wilson's gallery is his attempt to transform writing into images for greater effect. A "true" picture, he argued, had a moral dimension that writing lacked. "Truth" and "beauty" stemmed from God; they illuminated America's present condition and pointed the way to a new age. For Wilson, Douglass, Truth, and McCune Smith, the authentic black image was a source of power: it brought new life to blacks and inspired whites to see the full humanity of blacks.[34]

While the authentic black image, or object, was a source of power, a black *viewer* had comparatively less power. Harriet Jacobs describes this lack of cultural capital. In *Incidents in the Life of a Slave Girl* (1861), she becomes a viewer behind a lens. For nearly seven years she hides from her captors in the attic of a house. The sensation she describes resembles that of being inside a camera obscura. While daguerreotypists draped themselves behind the camera, Jacobs sat inside her box, as it were, at the lens: "Countless were the nights that I sat late at the little loophole [the lens] scarcely large enough to give me a glimpse of one twinkling star. . . . Season after season, year after year, I peeped at my children's faces, and heard their sweet voices, with a heart yearning all the while to say, 'Your mother is here.'" As a viewer, Jacobs is ineffectual. At the same time, however, through her narration she objectifies herself for her readers, which, she hopes, will empower her and transform them into abolitionists. Like William Wilson, who creates pictures with words and includes himself in his gallery, Jacobs appears as both object and observer for her readers.[35]

The two most successful black daguerreotypists, James P. Ball and Augustus Washington, did not capitalize on the transformative power of art described by Douglass. Ball began photographing in Cincinnati in 1849 and opened a lavish studio on New Year's Day 1851, calling it "Ball's Great Daguerreian Gallery of the West." His studio was featured in Boston-based *Gleason's Pictorial Magazine*, which noted that he had nine men "superintending and executing the work of the establishment" (fig. 3.11). Frederick Douglass reprinted the article in his newspaper, along with a less detailed copy of the *Gleason's Pictorial* engraving. But despite Ball's lavish studio, he himself remained comparatively invisible. There is only one known portrait of him, as an old man living in Seattle, Washington (fig. 3.12). Although he treated daguerreotypy as both a business and an art, his business did not adequately harness the power of his artistic image to transform his society. In fact he was compelled to move numerous times, in part owing to whites who viewed him as a competitor and threat to white prosperity. Sometime in the 1870s Ball and his family left Cincinnati for Minneapolis. He worked as an itinerant photographer for a few years, and in 1888 moved further west, to Helena, Montana. In 1892 he moved to Seattle, Washington, and died in Hawaii in 1904. As a public persona he remained comparatively obscure.[36]

Even at the highpoint of his career in the 1850s, Ball downplayed his role as performer. In 1855 he published a fifty-six-page pamphlet entitled *Ball's Splendid Mammoth Pictorial Tour of the United States*, which was a history of the horrors of slavery from capture in Africa through the middle passage to American forms of bondage. The pamphlet had a pictorial counterpart: a panorama of fifty-three images, most of them painted by the black landscape painter Robert Duncanson. The panorama was exhibited in Ball's studio and also in Boston's Armory Hall in the spring of 1855. What is especially striking about Ball's pictorial history is that it represents a kind of photographic negative of William Wilson's Afric-American Picture Gallery. Whereas Wilson writes in the first person, presents himself as protagonist and artist, and emphasizes black resistance and achievement, Ball down-

(ABOVE) *Figure 3.11 S. C. Peirce,* Ball's Great Daguerrian Gallery of the West, *engraving. From* Gleason's Pictorial *(1853). Widener Library, Harvard University.*

(LEFT) *Figure 3.12. Unidentified photographer,* James P. Ball, *ca. 1892.*

Figure 3.13. Augustus
Washington, John Brown,
quarter-plate daguerreotype,
1847. National Portrait Gallery,
Smithsonian Institution,
Washington, D.C.

plays his identity as storyteller and depicts images of black oppression and
degradation. Ball's pamphlet is written in the third person; he divorces himself from the narrative except to emphasize his success as a businessman
who triumphed over poverty. His persona as an artist or objet d'art, in other
words, is downplayed.[37]

The black daguerreotypist Augustus Washington similarly downplayed
his persona as performer and art object. There are no known photographs
of him, despite his profession. He felt more comfortable writing about himself than photographing himself. He was an accomplished writer as well as
photographer. Educated at Oneida Institute, an integrated manual labor
school in upstate New York, he then briefly entered Dartmouth College, but
dropped out owing to lack of funds. He turned to daguerreotypy as a way
to make money and opened a studio in Hartford, Connecticut, in the mid-
1840s, in a building that was owned by a white abolitionist family.[38] His
most famous photograph is of John Brown in 1847 (fig. 3.13). In it Brown
holds a "Subterranean Pass Way" flag and is apparently pledging allegiance
to the cause of freedom. Brown had conceived the Subterranean Pass Way
as a militant alternative to the Underground Railroad. The scheme involved
a network of armed men that would extend from the Allegheny Mountains

to the Adirondacks for the purpose of raiding slave plantations and running fugitives north to Canada. The Subterranean Pass Way never got off the ground, though. It evolved into a much more grandiose scheme to raid the federal arsenal at Harpers Ferry, distribute arms to slaves, and incite a massive slave rebellion.[39]

Augustus Washington was a fervent abolitionist and friend of Brown. But he found little satisfaction as a daguerreotype businessman in a predominantly white society, even though Martin Delany, another black abolitionist, called Washington one of the most successful daguerreotypists in Hartford. Washington felt increasingly frustrated with the spread of slavery and the racial oppression that he faced every day. For many years he advocated "the plan of a separate State for colored Americans—not as a choice, but as a necessity." Washington believed that "it would be better for our manhood and intellect to be freemen by ourselves than political slaves with our oppressors". In 1853, with his daguerreotype business declining, he acted on his vision of a separate black state and emigrated to the black colony of Liberia, which had been established by the white-run American Colonization Society as a way to gradually rid the country of both slavery and blacks. Washington brought his daguerreotype equipment with him and photographed numerous emigrants, including Edward James Roye, who became a member of the Liberian Senate (fig. 3.14). Juxtaposed with the portrait of John Brown, it is a striking image: while John Brown pledges allegiance to the American ideal of interracial equality, Roye pledges allegiance to a separatist ideal of a black Liberia. As a viewer and photographer rather than a performer in front of the lens, Washington felt comparatively powerless at changing white perceptions and dissolving social barriers.[40]

After legal freedom came, Americans began to lose faith in the veracity and "aura" of the image and the value of authenticity. Nancy Armstrong notes that at the turn of the twentieth century Alfred Stieglitz "sought to liberate photography from its dependence on a material referent, and so renounce the very realism that had fostered its development as a popular medium." In his 1892 short story, "The Real Thing," Henry James has his protagonist, a popular illustrator, declare that he prefers "the *represented* subject over the *real* one," because "the *defect* of the *real* one was so apt to be a *lack* of representation": "I liked things that *appeared*; then one was sure. Whether they *were* or not was a subordinate and almost always a profitless question."[41]

This loss of faith in the "truthfulness" of the picture, and in the direct link

Figure 3.14. Augustus Washington, Edward James Roye, *daguerreotype, ca. 1857. Library of Congress.*

between image and material referent, was not limited to white artists. At the turn of the century, black reformers began embracing the trope of the "New Negro," which was "only a metaphor," as Henry Louis Gates has noted. It signified "a black person who lives at no place" and at no time, a fictive utopia. The New Negro was an image without a natural referent, as is suggested by the fantastic, collage figure of the *The New Negro* by Alan Freelon, which was published in 1928 in the *Carolina Magazine* (fig. 3.15). Indeed, in Freelon's collage the New Negro has become a female Christ, resurrected after her crucifixion in Calvary: in the background on the mountaintop are three crosses, and two crucified bodies hang from tree limbs.[42]

Booker T. Washington was, like Frederick Douglass, the most famous African American of his generation, relying as much on his image as on his voice and words to create his public persona. In the era of Jim Crow and lynching, he believed that an accurate, or authentic, representation of the black body could transform whites—by inspiring them to give money to educate blacks. And like Douglass, he rigorously tried to control the dissemination of his image, hiring a team of photographers to circulate his persona. But unlike Douglass, he never analyzed the role of photography as a cultural force. Significantly, he had lost faith in the "truthfulness" of the photographic image.

Figure 3.15. Alan Freelon, The New Negro. *From* Carolina Magazine *(1928).*

Washington's loss of faith in the veracity of photography is reflected by his changing views toward the medium. Early in his career, from the 1870s to the 1890s, he used photographs, "nearly always taken by white artists," to tell his story to whites and raise money for black education, as Michael Bieze has recently shown. During his mid-career, from the 1890s until around 1905, "he developed different messages in words and images for audiences along race lines." He sent those photographs taken by whites to white publications and those taken by blacks to black publications. During the last decade of his life, from 1906 to 1915, he "lost trust of white leadership, . . . gradually abandoned his efforts to appeal to northern white supporters," and presented himself to the black masses using "the cameras of black photographers." Whereas Douglass never lost faith in the veracity of the photograph, even those taken by whites, Washington effectively believed that the photographer controlled the meaning of the image, distorting the connection between representation and referent. Understandably, he followed Henry James in emphasizing appearance over the murky and "profitless" problems of reality.[43]

W. E. B. Du Bois was, like Douglass, profoundly influenced by the power of the image. And like William Wilson, he thought narratives should aspire to the condition of an image. In the opening pages of *The Souls of Black Folk*, Du Bois states his purpose: "I have sought here to *sketch*, in vague, uncertain outline, the spiritual world in which ten thousand Americans live and strive." But his spiritual world resembled the metaphor of the New Negro—it was a fragmented image, detached from its material referent. This fragmentation stemmed from a "vast veil," producing a double self and obscuring the link between black object and white perceiver that could give both subject and object new life.[44]

Du Bois had great faith in the power of the photograph to redeem the image of African Americans. In 1899 he helped create the Exhibit of American Negroes at the Paris Exposition of 1900. With over 50 million visitors, the Expo would become one of the major celebrations of the era, highlighting the nineteenth century's successes and the new century's faith in continued progress. The Negro Exhibit featured hundreds of photographs of African Americans and their institutions, chiefly from Georgia, the state with the largest nonwhite population. The images depicted blacks with dignity and respect, displaying their subjects' "delicate beauty [and] tone," as Du Bois noted. He hoped these photographs would offer a potent antidote to the slanderous opinions of whites who thought of blacks as savages and rapists incapable of self-government. And he characterized the exhibit in sociological terms: it was the "honest, straight-forward exhibit of a small nation of people, picturing their life and development without apology or gloss."[45]

But if Du Bois had great faith in the redemptive potential of photography, he had also lost faith in the medium's essential truthfulness. In a column entitled "Photography" in the *Crisis* a few years later, he argued that "the average white photographer does not know how to deal with colored skins, and having neither sense of their delicate beauty of tone nor will to learn, he makes a horrible botch of portraying them." Understandably, Du Bois used only the work of black photographers for the exhibit at the Paris Exhibition, much as Booker T. Washington hired only black photographers late in his career. Like the elder Washington, he believed that black photographers could create a "new visual language for 'reading' black subjects, an image of self-empowerment—a 'New Negro,'" according to Deborah Willis.[46]

And yet fifty years earlier, Frederick Douglass had also referred to photography as "a new visual language" that empowered African American subjects. Douglass's faith in photography offers a striking contrast to that of Washington and Du Bois. While Douglass saw photography as an antidote to white artists who "grossly exaggerated" blacks' "distinctive features,"

Washington and Du Bois believed that photography was as biased and in-authentic as other forms of representation; for them, there was no coherent link between image and referent. Du Bois's solution was to call for more "colored photographers" to correct the distortions by whites. In Paris these efforts largely failed, for very few white Americans witnessed the "small nation of people" standing ready to be citizens of the world. Similarly, when Washington turned to black photographers to disseminate his image to blacks late in his career, his persona among whites declined. Perhaps the endpoint of this obstruction between black image and white perceiver is Ralph Ellison's Invisible Man, who willfully *refuses* visibility as an act of re-sistance.[47]

Douglass, Truth, McCune Smith, and Wilson had embraced visibility cre-ated and seen by whites as an act of resistance and empowerment. They defined their spiritual selves through their material selves and saw their images as containing, if not their essence, at least an authentic representa-tion of it. But after Reconstruction, and especially at the dawn of the twen-tieth century, whites no longer treated black images as the real thing, much as the laws establishing black freedom lost much of their prescriptive power. It is profoundly ironic that authentic black representation, which sought to combat slavery, was itself dependent on slavery for its proliferation and strength. In one sense, you could say that slavery was a strange muse that fueled the power of the authentic black image—and black art more gen-erally—which in turn sought to vanquish slavery.[48] As a consumer society replaced a "slave republic," the black image, lacking a natural referent, lost much of its prescriptive power.

NOTES

1. *Printer's Ink Magazine*, March 10, 1927. Barnard was the National Advertis-ing Manager of Street Railways Advertising Company. The evolution of his maxim is fascinating; in a 1921 advertisement, Barnard opened with the quote, "One look is worth a thousand words," which, he said, came from "a famous Japanese philoso-pher." The slogan was a centerpiece of a campaign to sell advertising posters on street railways. By 1927 the slogan had been changed to, "One picture is worth ten thou-sand words," and now the attribution was a "chinese proverb." Barnard included a translation in Chinese to enhance the authenticity of his proverb. See *Printer's Ink Magazine*, December 8, 1921, 96–97; March 10, 1927, 114.

On the power of pictures in general, see Vicki Goldberg, *The Power of Photogra-phy: How Photographs Changed Our Lives* (New York: Abbeville Press, 1991); Michel

Melot, *The Art of Illustration* (New York: Skira, Rizzoli, 1984); and David Freedberg, *The Power of Images: Studies in the History and Theory of Response* (Chicago: University of Chicago Press, 1989), esp. chaps. 7, 5, 13, 15. Freedberg has a superb discussion of the "lifelike" quality and the "felt efficacy" of the image (157). On images and advertising see Jackson Lears, *Fables of Abundance: A Cultural History of Advertising in America* (New York: Basic Books, 1994); Stephen Fox, *The Mirror Makers: A History of American Advertising and Its Creators* (New York: Morrow, 1984); and William Leach, *Land of Desire: Merchants, Money, and the Rise of a New American Culture* (New York: Pantheon, 1993).

2. On the rise of visual culture, see Beatrice Farwell, *The Cult of Images: Baudelaire and the 19th-Century Media Explosion* (Santa Barbara: UCSB Art Museum, 1977); Patricia Anderson, *The Printed Image and the Transformation of Popular Culture, 1790–1860* (Oxford: Clarendon Press, 1991); Nancy Armstrong, *Fiction in the Age of Photography: The Legacy of British Realism* (Cambridge: Harvard University Press, 1999), 1–74; Geoffrey Batchen, *Burning with Desire: The Conception of Photography* (Cambridge: MIT Press, 1997), 54–103; John Tagg, *The Burden of Representation: Essays on Photographies and Histories* (Amherst: University of Massachusetts Press, 1988), 34–59; Eustelle Jussim, *Visual Communication and the Graphic Arts: Photographic Technologies in the Nineteenth Century* (New York: R. R. Bowker, 1974); Alan Trachtenberg, *Reading American Photographs: Images as History, Mathew Brady to Walker Evans* (New York: Hill and Wang, 1989), 3–20; Trachtenberg, "Photography: The Emergence of a Keyword," and Barbara McCandless, "The Portrait Studio and the Celebrity: Promoting the Art," in *Photography in Nineteenth-Century America*, ed. Martha A. Sandweiss (New York: Harry N. Abrams, 1991), 16–47, 48–75; Robert Taft, *Photography and the American Scene: A Social History, 1839–1889* (1938; reprint, New York: Dover, 1964), 46–166; John Stauffer, "Daguerreotyping the National Soul: The Portraits of Southworth and Hawes," *Prospects* 22 (1977): 69–107; Beaumont Newhall, *The History of Photography, from 1839 to the Present* (New York: Museum of Modern Art, 1988), 9–72; Michel Frizot, ed., *A New History of Photography* (Köln: Könemann, 1988), 9–89; Robin Kelsey and Blake Stimson, eds., *The Meaning of Photography* (Williamstown, Mass.: Sterling and Francine Clark Art Institute, 2008).

3. As an example of European reformers' use of images, when Louis-Philippe took the throne in France in 1830, he vowed to "free" the press from censorship, but freedom lasted only five years. He reestablished censorship by banning images, and only images: caricatures, which were deployed by the "cartoon press" to attack his regime. Political pamphlets were considered a "violation of opinion" and thus tolerable, but a caricature amounted to an "act of violence" that was deemed "too dangerous" to go unchecked. See Goldberg, *Power of Photography*, 7; Melot, *Art of Illustration*, 231.

4. Henry Mayer, *All On Fire: William Lloyd Garrison and the Abolition of Slavery* (New York: St. Martin's Press, 1998), 124–25. Mayer refers to Calhoun as "Senator Calhoun," but in 1831, when Garrison began publishing *The Liberator*, Calhoun was Jackson's vice president. While Garrison began publishing *The Liberator* on Janu-

ary 1, 1831, the illustrated masthead first appeared on April 23, 1831. In that issue Garrison briefly describes the "new head for the *Liberator*."

For other examples of American politicians taking offense at abolitionist imagery, see Jean Fagan Yellin, *Women and Sisters: The Antislavery Feminists in American Culture* (New Haven: Yale University Press, 1989), 3–26; and William Lee Miller, *Arguing About Slavery: The Great Battle in the United States Congress* (New York: Alfred Knopf, 1996), 96–97.

5. See John Stauffer, *The Black Hearts of Men: Radical Abolitionists and the Transformation of Race* (Cambridge: Harvard University Press, 2002), chap. 2; Carl Peterson, "19th Century Photographers and Related Activity in Madison County, New York," *Madison County Heritage* 23 (1998): 15–25; Alan Trachtenberg, "The Daguerreotype: American Icon," in *American Daguerreotypes from the Matthew R. Isenburg Collection* (New Haven: Yale University Art Gallery, 1989), 16; John Wood, "Silence and Slow Time: An Introduction to the Daguerreotype," and Alan Trachtenberg, "Mirror in the Marketplace: American Responses to the Daguerreotype, 1839–1851," in *The Daguerreotype: A Sesquicentennial Celebration*, ed. John Wood (Iowa City: University of Iowa Press, 1989), 1–29, 60–73; John Wood, "The American Portrait," *America and the Daguerreotype*, ed. John Wood (Iowa City: University of Iowa Press, 1991); Mary Panzer, *Mathew Brady and the Image of History* (Washington, D.C.: Smithsonian Institution Press, 1997), 23–38, 71–92; Tagg, *Burden of Representation*, 34–59.

6. Daguerreotype portraits proliferated beginning in the mid-1840s, and by the mid-1850s, with the development of new processes and techniques, Americans had their pictures taken at an unprecedented rate.

7. I discuss some of this in Stauffer, *Black Hearts of Men*, chap. 2. I have also been influenced by Leonard Cassuto, *The Inhuman Race: The Racial Grotesque in American Literature and Culture* (New York: Columbia University Press, 1997), chap. 3; W. J. T. Mitchell, *Picture Theory: Essays on Verbal and Visual Representation* (Chicago: University of Chicago Press, 1994), chaps. 5–6; Ann Fabian, *The Unvarnished Truth: Personal Narratives in Nineteenth-Century America* (Berkeley: University of California Press, 2000); Deborah Willis, ed., *Picturing Us: African-American Identity in Photography*; Yellin, *Women and Sisters*, 3–26; George Sullivan, *Black Artists in Photography, 1840–1940* (New York: Cobblehill Books, 1996), 1–57; David Morgan, *Protestants and Pictures: Religion, Visual Culture, and the Age of American Mass Production* (New York: Oxford University Press, 1999), 3–122; 305–48.

8. See for example Mary Niall Mitchell, "'Rosebloom and Pure White,' Or So It Seemed," *American Quarterly* 54, no. 3 (September 2002): 369–410; Shawn Michelle Smith, *American Archives: Gender, Race, and Class in Visual Culture* (Princeton: Princeton University Press, 1999); Saidiya V. Hartman, *Scenes of Subjection: Terror, Slavery, and Self-Making in Nineteenth-Century America* (New York: Oxford University Press, 1997); Susan Gubar, *Race Changes: White Skin, Black Face in American Culture* (New York: Oxford University Press, 1997); Nicholas Mirzoeff, ed., *Visual Culture Reader* (London: Routledge, 1998), 281–390; Laura Wexler, *Tender Violence:*

Domestic Visions in an Age of U.S. Imperialism (Chapel Hill: University of North Carolina Press, 2000), 52–93, 127–76; Shirley Samuels, "Miscegenated America: The Civil War," in *National Imaginaries, American Identities*, ed. Larry J. Reynolds and Gordon Hutner (Princeton: Princeton University Press, 2000), 141–58; Eric Lott, *Love and Theft: Blackface Minstrelsy and the American Working Class* (New York: Oxford University Press, 1993); and Albert Boime, *The Art of Exclusion: Representing Blacks in the Nineteenth Century* (London: Thames and Hudson, 1990).

There are a few exceptions to this tendency to focus on the visual exploitation of black abolitionists. See note 7 above; Maurice Wallace's excellent essay, "'Are We Men?': Prince Hall, Martin Delany, and the Masculine Ideal in Black Freemasonry, 1775–1865," in *National Imaginaries*, 182–210; Nell Irvin Painter, *Sojourner Truth: A Life, A Symbol* (New York: W. W. Norton, 1996), 185–99; Painter, "Representing Truth: Sojourner Truth's Knowing and Becoming Known," *Journal of American History* 81, no. 2 (September 1994): 461–92; Yellin, *Women and Sisters*, 3–28, 77–98.

I have also been influenced by a number of works concerning other periods or types of imagery that similarly avoid the tendency to dwell on black exploitation. See Orlando Patterson's superb *Rituals of Blood: Consequences of Slavery in Two American Centuries* (Washington, D.C.: Civitas, 1998), esp. 233–80; Marcus Wood's magnificent *Blind Memory: Visual Representations of Slavery in England and America, 1780–1865* (London: Routledge, 2000); Werner Sollors, *Neither Black Nor White Yet Both: Thematic Explorations of Interracial Literature* (New York: Oxford University Press, 1997), chaps. 1, 3–4, 7, 9–10; Linda Williams, *Playing the Race Card: Melodramas of Black and White From Uncle Tom to O. J. Simpson* (Princeton: Princeton University Press, 2001); Mark Seltzer, *Bodies and Machines* (New York: Routledge, 1992); and Bernard F. Reilly Jr., "The Art of the Antislavery Movement," in *Courage and Conscience: Black and White Abolitionists in Boston*, ed. Donald M. Jacobs (Bloomington: Indiana University Press, 1993), 47–72, though Reilly's essay focuses almost exclusively on white abolitionist art.

9. The idea of the male gaze originates with Laura Mulvey, "Visual Pleasure and Narrative Cinema," *Screen* 16, no. 3 (1975): 6–18. For one of the most recent, and much more nuanced permutations, see Armstrong, *Fiction in the Age of Photography*, 248–61.

10. Robyn Wiegman, "Black Bodies/American Commodities: Gender, Race and the Bourgeois Ideal in Contemporary Film," in *Unspeakable Images: Ethnicity and the American Cinema*, ed. Lester Friedman (Urbana: University of Illinois Press, 1991), 325.

11. I analyze Douglass's use of images in Stauffer, *Black Hearts of Men*, chap. 2; and "Race and Contemporary Photography: Willie Robert Middlebrook and the Legacy of Frederick Douglass," *21st: The Journal of Contemporary Photography: Culture and Criticism* 1 (1998): 55–60.

12. Elaine Scarry, *On Beauty and Being Just* (Princeton: Princeton University Press, 1999), 69, 90. Leonard Cassuto makes a related point about slave narratives: "Before they humanize themselves, slave narrators first objectify themselves: they

make themselves into grotesques. Fugitive slave narrators degrade themselves as a rhetorical pose." See Cassuto, *Inhuman Race*, 107. I focus not on the degradation but the sublimity of objectification. See my related article, "Frederick Douglass and the Aesthetics of Freedom," *Raritan* 25, no. 1 (Summer 2005): 114–36.

13. Douglass, quoted from Philip S. Foner, ed., *The Life and Writings of Frederick Douglass*, vol. 1 (New York: International Publishers, 1950), 379–80. This paragraph is revised from *Black Hearts of Men*, 50–51.

14. Stauffer, *Black Hearts of Men*, 53–55.

15. Hugh Honour, *The Image of the Black in Western Art, 4.1: From the American Revolution to World War I, Slaves and Liberators* (Cambridge: Harvard University Press, 1989), p. 62.

16. Honour, *Image of the Black in Western Art*, 4:1, 62–64; T. T., "A Dream," *The Liberator*, April 2, 1831; T. T., "Another Dream," *The Liberator*, April 30, 1831; James Brewer Stewart, "The Emergence of Racial Modernity and the Rise of the White North, 1790–1840," *Journal of the Early Republic* 18, no. 2 (Summer 1998): 181–89, 209–17; Dickson D. Bruce Jr., *The Origins of African American Literature* (Charlottesville: University Press of Virginia, 2001), 208–10; Bruce Dain, *A Hideous Monster of the Mind: American Race Theory in the Early Republic* (Cambridge, Mass.: Harvard University Press, 2002), 168–69; John Stauffer, "In the Shadow of a Dream: White Abolitionists and Race," Gilder Lehrman Center Fifth Annual International Conference, 2003, online at http://www.yale.edu/glc/events/race/schedule.htm.

17. *Autographs for Freedom* (Boston: John P. Jewett and Company, 1853), frontispiece. Douglass and Griffiths published a second volume of *Autographs for Freedom* in 1854. Both volumes were published to raise money for Douglass's newspaper, and the 1853 volume includes his novella, "The Heroic Slave."

18. Hammatt Billings's engraving and the description of the slave auction appears in chapter 12 of *Uncle Tom's Cabin*. Mr. Haley heard about it from an advertisement in a newspaper describing an "Executor's Sale" in which the slaves Hagar, John, Ben, Saul, Albert, and others would be sold "for the benefit of the creditors and heirs of the estate of James Blutchford, Esq." In 1853 Billings oversaw the "Illustrated Edition" of *Uncle Tom's Cabin*. With 117 new images, it was one of the first lavishly illustrated picture books, and it included three images of the slave auction. On Billings, see James F. O'Gorman, *Accomplished in All Departments of Art: Hammatt Billings of Boston, 1818–1874* (Amherst: University of Massachusetts Press, 1998). On the "Illustrated Edition" of *Uncle Tom's Cabin*, see the excellent website, "Uncle Tom's Cabin and American Culture," at the University of Virginia.

19. Stauffer, *Black Hearts of Men*, 51–52.

20. Douglass, "Pictures," holograph, n.d. [ca. late 1864], Frederick Douglass Papers, Library of Congress.

21. Quotations in the last three paragraphs are from ibid.; and Douglass, "Pictures and Progress," *The Frederick Douglass Papers*, series 1, vol. 3, ed. John Blassingame (New Haven: Yale University Press, 1985), 456. My analysis appears in different form in Stauffer, *Black Hearts of Men*, 51–52, 54.

22. Douglass, "Heroic Slave," in *Violence in the Black Imagination: Essays and Documents*, ed. Ronald T. Takaki (New York: Oxford University Press, 1993), 38, 41, 42; Robert Stepto, "Storytelling in Early Afro-American Fiction: Frederick Douglass' 'The Heroic Slave,'" *Georgia Review* 36 (1982): 355–68.

23. Douglass, "Heroic Slave," 45.

24. Harriet Beecher Stowe, *Uncle Tom's Cabin, or, Life Among the Lowly* (1852; reprint, New York: Penguin Books, 1986), 68.

25. Trachtenberg, *Reading American Photographs*, chap. 2; Trachtenberg, "Mirror in the Marketplace"; Floyd and Marion Rinhart, *The American Daguerreotype* (Athens: University of Georgia Press, 1981), 78.

26. W. J. T. Mitchell, *Iconology: Image, Text, Ideology* (Chicago: University of Chicago Press, 1986), 31.

27. Lawrence W. Levine, *Highbrow/Lowbrow: The Emergence of Cultural Hierarchy in America* (Cambridge: Harvard University Press, 1988), 29–30. I witnessed a similar faith in the power of authenticity when I saw *The Passion of Christ* at a theater with a number of apparently devout Christians, who broke down and wept throughout the film. It was as though the film was not so much a representation, but contained the essence of their spiritual and historical reality.

28. Painter, *Sojourner Truth*, 187.

29. On the "aura" of an image, see Walter Benjamin, "The Work of Art in the Age of Mechanical Reproduction," in *Illuminations: Essays and Reflections* (New York: Schocken Books, 1968), 221–24.

30. James McCune Smith, "The Black Swan," *Frederick Douglass' Paper*, March 9, 1855. McCune Smith's article has been reprinted in John Stauffer, ed., *The Works of James McCune Smith, Black Intellectual and Abolitionist* (New York: Oxford University Press, 2006), 119–22.

31. McCune Smith, quoted in John Blassingame, ed., *The Frederick Douglass Papers*, 1:3 (New Haven: Yale University Press, 1985), 74.

32. Ethiop, "Afric-American Picture Gallery," *Anglo-African Magazine* (1859; reprint, New York: Arno Press, 1968), 52.

33. Ibid., 53–55, 88–90, 100–103, 174–77, 216–18.

34. Ibid., 87, 88, 174, 175, 176, 324.

35. Harriet A. Jacobs, *Incidents in the Life of a Slave Girl, Written by Herself*, ed. Jean Fagan Yellin (Cambridge: Harvard University Press, 1987), 148.

36. Deborah Willis, ed., *J. P. Ball: Daguerrean and Studio Photographer* (New York: Garland Publishing, 1993), xi–xix; Esther Hall Mumford, *Seattle's Black Victorians, 1852–1901* (Seattle: Ananse Press, 1980), 81. The copy of *Seattle's Black Victorians* at Harvard's Widener Library includes an errata insert stating that the Ball family moved to Seattle in 1892.

37. Willis, *J. P. Ball*, xi, xv–xix, 243–52, 290–99. In her journal Charlotte Forten describes her visit to Ball's "Panorama" in Boston, which she liked "very much." See Brenda Stevenson, ed., *The Journals of Charlotte Forten Grimké* (New York: Oxford University Press, 1988), 135.

38. Ann M. Shumard, *A Durable Memento: Portraits by Augustus Washington, African American Daguerreotypist* (Washington, D.C.: National Portrait Gallery, Smithsonian Institution, 2000), 1–24; Wilson Jeremiah Moses, ed., *Liberian Dreams: Back-to-Africa Narratives from the 1850s* (University Park: The Pennsylvania State University Press, 1998), ix–xxxiv, 179–224.

39. Stauffer, *Black Hearts of Men*, 170–72; Shumard, *Durable Memento*, 4.

40. Augustus Washington, "Thoughts on the American Colonization Society, 1851," in Moses, *Liberian Dreams*, 187. See also Shumard, *Durable Memento*.

41. Armstrong, *Fiction in the Age of Photography*, 248–49; Henry James, "The Real Thing," in *The Complete Tales of Henry James*, vol. 8, 1891–1892, ed. Leon Edel (Philadelphia: J. B. Lippincott, 1962), 237; Miles Orvell, *The Real Thing: Imitation and Authenticity in American Culture, 1880–1940* (Chapel Hill: University of North Carolina Press, 1989), 122–23; Stauffer, "Daguerreotyping the National Soul," 100.

42. Henry Louis Gates Jr., "The Trope of a New Negro and the Reconstruction of the Image of the Black," in *The New American Studies*, ed. Philip Fisher (Berkeley: University of California Press, 1991) 322, 325; Gates, "The Face and Voice of Blackness," *Facing History: The Black Image in American Art, 1710–1940*, ed. Guy C. McElroy (Washington, D.C.: Corcoran Gallery of Art, 1990), xxxi–xxxix.

43. Michael Bieze, *Booker T. Washington and the Art of Self-Representation* (New York: Peter Lang, 2008), 1–6, 15–31, 53–82, quotations from 1–2, 17, 220. According to Bieze, Washington lost faith in white leaders following an incident at Fort Brown in Brownsville, Texas, in which black soldiers were dishonorably discharged without trial stemming from charges that they had shot at local white residents. Washington asked President Theodore Roosevelt, who had invited him to the White House for a state dinner, for a more rigorous investigation before reaching a decision. This time Roosevelt ignored him "and Washington knew his days as privileged advisor to the presidency were numbered" (220).

44. W. E. B. Du Bois, *The Souls of Black Folk* (1903; reprint, New York: Penguin Books, 1989), 1, 4.

45. David Levering Lewis and Deborah Willis, *A Small Nation of People: W. E. B. Du Bois and African American Portraits of Progress* (New York: Amistad, 2003), 13–78, quotations from Du Bois on 39, 51. On Du Bois and photography, see Shawn Michelle Smith, *Photography on the Color Line: W. E. B. Du Bois, Race, and Visual Culture* (Durham: Duke University Press, 2004).

46. W. E. B. Du Bois, "Photography," *Crisis* 26, no. 6 (October 1923): 247–48 (quoted); Lewis and Willis, *A Small Nation of People*, 51–52, quotation from Willis on 52.

47. Douglass quoted in Foner, *Life and Writings of Frederick Douglass*, 1:379–80; Du Bois, "Photography"; Lewis and Willis, *A Small Nation of People*, 48; Bieze, *Booker T. Washington and the Art of Self-Representation*, 1–2, 84–107, 118–21. See also Mitchell, *Picture Theory*, 163.

48. Gates, "Trope of a New Negro," 321. Gates notes that between 1867 and 1876, "black people published as books only two novels. Between 1895 and 1925, however,

black writers published at least sixty-four novels. While the historical period known as Reconstruction seems to have been characterized by a dramatic upsurge of energy in the American body politic, the corpus of black literature and art, on the other hand, enjoyed not such apparent vitalization. . . . Once redemption had established itself as a new form of enslavement for blacks, blacks regained a public voice, louder and more strident than it had been even during slavery" (321).

second coda

The Marketplace for Black Performance

David Krasner charts the important role that black performers played in the advent of "realism" in American popular culture. That dance provided the opening for black performers to contribute to cultural innovation was a testament to the newfound popularity of social dance in the United States. Before the late nineteenth century, social dancing was circumscribed to specific settings. It was reserved chiefly for private functions, such as formal balls, or for disreputable dance halls where prostitution and gambling took place. But starting with the cakewalk, a lengthening list of new dances attracted ever-increasing numbers of Americans onto the dance floor. By the end of the first decade of the new century, even casual observers recognized the transformation in the popularity of dance. "The decade between 1910 and 1920," one observer wrote, "can be identified primarily as the period in which America went dance mad." This new popularity of social dance signaled a significant development in American life. It transformed how audiences listened to music; it redirected the composition and performance of popular music; and it altered the public spaces where Americans experienced music. This new departure in American popular dance was bound up in the popularity of ragtime and other dance-suited music.

Like ragtime, the dance craze of the early twentieth century was a consequence of cultural cross-fertilization. While the formal elements of European dance were relaxed to adapt to syncopated dance rhythms, the improvisational elements of African American dance were simultaneously formalized to adjust to the more regular rhythms of dance music. For whites eager to master the new dances, "real" black performers, as opposed to whites masquerading in blackface, acquired new prestige and career opportunities. The appeal of black dancers and dance mirrored the enthusiasm for the "real" and "authentic" that became pronounced in an era of mass production. Black performers, as Krasner points out, were not only beneficiaries but also instigators of these cultural developments.

In her essay on the music that propelled the dance craze, Susan Curtis highlights the changes in tastes and technology that made black musical forms not only acceptable but ascendant in popular culture. She underscores the importance of black popular music in propelling the shift from the Victorian ethos to a modern consumer culture. That this shift provoked howls of outrage from critics of the new cultural forms is hardly surprising. But the evolution of ragtime and the popular music industry, Curtis reminds us, also disappointed the very black composers and performers who were its originators. They discovered that ragtime's cultural associations—with hedonism and leisure—precluded adequate recognition or compensation for their cultural and business innovations. Perhaps no musician of the era more fully exemplified this simultaneous elevation and marginalization than Scott Joplin.

Tom Riis reveals the "boundary jumping" that was pervasive in music during the era. Directing our gaze beyond the bright lights of the nation's urban centers, Riis recovers the world of black entertainers who were jacks of all trades, handling snakes one minute, singing soprano the next, and cakewalking a moment later. Riis not only demonstrates that there were literally thousands of these now-nameless performers but also that at least some of them were unapologetic about their craft. These musicians and performers took advantage of any opening to secure a foothold in the emergent popular culture industry of the age.

Davarian Baldwin's essay shifts the focus to black Chicagoans' role as consumers of popular culture. He enables us to see the diversity of actors in the cosmopolitan cultural spaces that grew in Chicago in the wake of the Great Migration. Rather than a monolithic "community of consumption," the South Side of Chicago was home to a diverse array of consumers. Most important, popular culture emerged as one of the most important forums for debates over public behavior, community values, and modernity among both long-time residents and newcomers. In short, popular culture was a realm in which black Chicagoans debated and contested diverse ideas of race and community. At the center of this debate were the recent migrants from the Deep South, whom Baldwin restores to their proper place as catalysts of modern mass culture.

Like Baldwin, John Giggie draws our attention to how blacks participated in the consumer marketplace and the meanings they attached to their consumption. From our contemporary vantage point in a mature consumer society, it may be difficult to imagine a time when consuming mass-produced goods was not second nature but rather something that had to learned. As

Giggie demonstrates, southern blacks had ample reasons to be wary of the market; they, after all, had been commodities themselves before the Civil War and were frequently its victims during the Jim Crow era. Moreover, black consumerism had to be reconciled with black spiritual values. Ministers, he explains, played a crucial role in stoking, channeling, and legitimating the consumer desires of their congregations. To do so complemented the ministers' efforts to promote modernity, respectability, and wealth accumulation among their flock. Thus, when black ministers hawked records of their sermons and other domestic commodities, they helped fashion an enduring alternative black culture of consumption that acknowledged the imperatives of faith as well as those of the market.

The Real Thing

DAVID KRASNER

I'm the real thing
I dance and sing.
—AIDA OVERTON WALKER,
"I Wants to Be an Actor Lady"
(1903)

"We finally decided that as white men with blackfaces were billing themselves 'coons,'" wrote the performer George Walker of the Williams and
Walker Theatrical Company in 1906, "Williams and Walker would do well
to bill themselves the 'Two Real Coons,' and so we did."[1] Walker and his
partner, Bert Williams, did indeed "do well," becoming the dominant black
theatrical company from 1899 to 1909. Their productions of *In Dahomey*,
(1902–5), *Abyssinia* (1905–7), and *Bandanna Land* (1907–9) were among
the most bankable musical vaudeville shows on Broadway.[2] At the peak of
their career, George Walker reported the company's payroll at $2,300 per
week, making them one of the most successful companies of the time.[3] *In
Dahomey* attained success in London during its 1903 tour, and the company maintained successful engagements from there.[4] Capitalizing on the
"coon song" craze, Williams and Walker appropriated the term "coon" and
applied it to their show. The script for *Two Real Coons* has been lost, but the
idea of being the "real coons" was not lost on black performers. Williams
and Walker, and their friend and rival Robert "Bob" Cole and his company,
Cole and Johnson, displayed throughout their writings and actions an acute
awareness of the "real" as a cultural signifier and marketing tool.

For Williams and Walker and Cole and Johnson, interest in the real
as a commercial device made it possible to break mainstream show business's color barrier. The real enticed white audiences because realism was
in vogue. For the educated white bourgeoisie of the late nineteenth century,
historian T. J. Jackson Lears contends, "authentic experience of any sort

99

seemed ever more elusive; life seemed increasingly confined to the airless parlor of material comfort and moral complacency. Many yearned to smash the glass and breathe freely—to experience 'real life' in all its intensity."[5] Being quite cognizant of this fact, black performers sought to contrast their "realness" with white imitation. White minstrelsy's "seeming counterfeit," Eric Lott's coinage describing a "contradictory popular construction that was not so much true or false as more or less pleasurable or politically effi-cacious in the culture that braced it,"[6] was dissolving. Although blackface would be revived in Hollywood from the 1920s to the 1940s, by the turn of the century America's interest in racial "counterfeiting" waned, replaced by an obsession with the real. The "real thing"—to co-opt the period's jar-gon—signified what Miles Orvell calls the "tension between imitation and authenticity," which "has been a key constituent in American culture since the Industrial Revolution and assumes critical importance in the shift from the nineteenth to the twentieth centuries that we have called—in all its en-compassing multiplicity—modernism." Orvell adds that the emphasis on realism eventuated popular productions that "catered increasingly to a taste for lifelike imitation that floated easily over the border between life and art. It was an excess of such theatrical representation—which might include everything from real food eaten on stage to real horses used to enact battle scenes"—that reflected "the taste for realism in literature."[7] When black per-formers created "life and art" by putting on the "coon" mask and attaching the term "real" to it, they complicated (and contributed to) the semiotics of realism in American culture.

Following Toni Morrison's call for a "re-interpretation of the American canon,"[8] I hope to show that African American performers played a critical role in defining American culture at the turn of the century. Emphasis on realism in America at the time was certainly broad, but the significance of black performers' contributions to this cultural event has largely gone un-noticed. Black performers are rarely mentioned in studies of how American realism took root.[9] This disparity is due at least in part to the negative value judgment labeling realism retrograde. Such condemnation is exemplified by Amy Kaplan, who remarks that from "a progressive force exposing the conditions of industrial society, realism has turned into a conservative force whose very act of exposure reveals its complicity with structures of power."[10] I shall argue, however, that realism by black performers was a tactic used to dismantle the structures of power.

Not all black performers opposed what was then the status quo; in fact, the use of the blackface mask by black performers perpetuated the accepted stereotype. But some performers, especially George Walker's wife, Aida Overton Walker, skillfully manipulated the prevailing reality and in doing so contributed to the creation of a revised American realism. She countered hegemonic and racist depictions by exploiting the desire for the real among whites. The notion of "authenticity" displayed in her cakewalking dance deserves recognition as an imaginative and constructive employment of cultural paradigms.

In this essay I will attempt to shed light on Walker's role in shaping American culture. First I will provide background by accounting for how the real came to be a cultural signifier and marketing tactic. Then I will examine Walker's success in marketing herself as the "real" cakewalker. Walker contributed significantly to an enduring strategy that has come to be known in contemporary parlance as "crossover appeal." The goal here is to locate and analyze some of the roots of this appeal.

The new "realism" at the turn of the century was paradoxical in its appeal to both what was real and what was not. The theatrical companies of Williams and Walker and Cole and Johnson were black, but the fixture of the stage "coon" that they embodied was a theatricalized portrayal made commonplace by nonblack actors. Minstrelsy was the nineteenth-century white performer's attempt to create a slippery reality superficially related at best to black culture. By the end of the nineteenth century black performers had to adopt the stage convention—especially the debasing yet indispensable use of blackface makeup—in order to attract audiences demanding minstrel traditions. To function successfully, even to survive, black performers had to don blackface and satisfy white expectations of black buffoonery. While pandering to their audiences, black performers negotiated ways of undermining the derogatory image.[11] Still the price was high, given the perpetuation of the blackface stereotype even among those who found it offensive. As a result of this complex mixture of the real and unreal, of complicity in stereotyping and subverting it, African American performers not only joined in the creation of a new "realism" in American art and culture, they were a force in making realism a major component of American aesthetics. However much this realism might be unreal—even surreal—it does not detract from their cultural contributions.

For black performers, the real was commodified in order to lead the challenge against minstrel theater. At a time when African Americans had been denied participation in a growing economy, blacks sold one of the few commodities they owned: "realness." Like the Buffalo Bill Wild West shows of the 1890s, blacks jumped on the bandwagon of the "authenticity" phenomena while exploiting the euphoria over realness. Buffalo Bill Cody had enticed the masses with his extravaganza replete with "real" cowboys and Indians, rodeo, and reenactments of battle scenes onstage that recreated the adventures of the Great Plains. Most of all, Cody advertised the productions as not merely Wild West shows, but as resurrections of the Wild West itself. Cody and his producing partner, Nate Salsbury, realized that audiences would pay to see dramatized portrayals of the "real" West, provided that what passed for real was a carefully chosen performance that concealed much of the truth.[12] Following Cody's success Salsbury produced another "reality" show, *Black America*, a reenactment of the plantation that opened in Brooklyn in 1895.[13] Although it was hardly as successful as his Wild West endeavor, Salsbury followed the same promotional strategy: resurrect the "real." Savvy marketers took advantage of the "authentic" by turning entertainment into big business and the real into something appealing. Thomas Postlewait writes that "both entertainment and advertising learned how to deliver the hyperreal, the domain of desires."[14] Producers Salsbury, P. T. Barnum, B. F. Keith, Florenz Ziegfeld, the Shubert brothers, and the Frohman brothers, along with film moguls Samuel Goldwyn and the rising department store empires of Walgreens, Woolworth's, Macy's, Jordan Marsh, Marshall Field's, and the Sears, Roebuck and Montgomery Ward catalogues, created visual splendor and commercial spectacle that merged theater and the marketplace during the Gilded Age. Robert Ogden, Wanamaker's partner and superintendent of the New York department store, put it best when in 1897 he said, "I have no doubt whatever that the high priests of art would sneer at the statement that art in advertising is art for humanity's sake; but, nevertheless, such is the case, and humanity benefits by the art that is expended upon advertising, and the benefits include the artist himself and the audience to which he appeals." Jettisoning "art for art's sake," he averred: "art belongs to commerce; it must be connected with practical things."[15] Black performers appear to have heeded this advice by merging art and commerce.

The advent of marketing and realism was fortuitous, and black performers made the most of it. Remarking on Williams and Walker's performance of *A Lucky Coon* during its first tour of England in 1899, the Washington, D.C., *Colored American* reported that "Williams & Walker are the only two 'real coons' (as they facetiously style themselves) who ever had the honor of appearing before royalty while in Europe."[16] Williams and Walker and Cole and Johnson advertised the "fact" that they were "coons"—albeit coyly. "I attribute our success to our knowledge that to please an audience we must give them the real negro character," wrote George Walker around 1906. "We know that when we try to act like white folks, the public won't have us; there are enough bad white actors now."[17] The complicated mapping of racial identity and authenticity suggests many vantage points from which to explain its popularity. Black actors and producers, like other theatrical and business people, were obsessive self-publicists. They were favorably disposed to commercialization of realness, even going so far as to invent stories about it. George Walker, for example, extolled the skills of his partner, Bert Williams, and his use of blackface by comparing Williams to white comedians: "Black-faced white comedians used to make themselves look as ridiculous as they could when portraying a 'darky' character." The "one fatal result" of such performances, he claimed, "was that they imitated the white performers in their make-up as 'darkies.'" In other words, for Walker, whites were replicating other whites, creating characters having no connection to black realty. Bert Williams, however, "is the first man that I know of our race to attempt to delineate a 'darky' in a perfectly natural way, and I think much of his success is due to this fact."[18] Williams, according to Walker, was able to avoid white minstrelsy because he was "original and natural," a turn of phrase apropos of the era's cultural lexicon. The paradox of acting "in a perfectly natural way" while donning blackface is hardly an expression of "reality." It is show business hyperbole and a form of masking. Trying to find some primordially authentic, natural identity through representation is, as Plato cautioned in Book X of *The Republic*, a tenuous illusion at best. However, the success of Williams and Walker did not go unnoticed. R. C. Murray, incorporating the period's emphasis on racial uplift, wrote in the *Colored American Magazine* in 1905 that "Williams and Walker have pulled up as they have mounted, hundreds of their kind, and have demonstrated in a most convincing manner, both the persevering ability of the colored actor and the shallow crust of American prejudice."[19] The use of the real and the natural by Walker and others cannot be easily dismissed; as a tool for the promotion of racial equality, it served to establish a presence in the mainstream marketplace. The depiction of realism as one-sidedly conservative simplifies the picture and suppresses the contributions by African Americans. The story of African American contributions to American realism is complex and involved, taking place as it does amid the turbulent transformation of turn-of-the-century modernism and the ever-evolving confluence of American race relations. For better or worse, the ideas and strategies begun by George Walker, Bert Williams, Bob Cole, and Aida Overton Walker remain relevant but are yet to be fully appreciated or understood.

Marketing the Real, Selling the Race

The complex interconnection of authenticity, race, and commodification at the turn of the century converges at its focal point in American modernism. The transition from Victorianism (ca. 1870s–1880s) to modernism provided a threshold through which black performers could cross, yet it also brought with it considerable humility. Such was the case of the performer Ernest Hogan, who produced his 1895 vaudeville show *All Coons Look Alike to Me* by marketing the lead song of the same title. According to a 1930 retrospective on Hogan in the *Baltimore Afro-American*, "All Coons Look Alike to Me" had "a beautiful melody, as many who recall the song will attest, and while the words were quite innocuous the title became a byword and an epithet of derision, and Hogan never forgot it."[20] The 1895 song and show likely influenced the decision of Williams and Walker to title their shows *A Lucky Coon* and *Two Real Coons* (from 1900 onward they dropped "coon" from their titles). Regrettably the term "coon" had market value; Bob Cole's 1898 *A Trip to Coontown*, for instance, evoked a show that used the "coon" vocabulary and continued a stage convention. In *The Last Darky*, Louis Chude-Sokei observes that for Williams and Walker (as well as other performers) "the African American stereotype had been filtered through many generations of white impersonation; only their own racial authenticity could be used as an edge in the 'mimic warfare' of vaudeville."[21] The turf for this warfare was theater, where the authentic and the real would be exploited for tactical advantage.

The idea of African Americans "selling" themselves as performers is hardly new. "Selling blackness," Harry J. Elam reminds us, "conjures images of the auction block and black bodies sold to the highest white bidder. In the arena of slavery, the auction block compelled restricted, distorted performances of blackness where any display of black agency raised concerns, and blackness became understood only in terms of white desire and black economic utility."[22] Despite the deplorable conditions of slavery and its aftermath, the dynamics of theater has historically highlighted the conflict between a performer's desire for agency on the one hand and an audience's insistence on convention on the other. Elam is correct, however, insofar as blacks often sought ways of asserting their self-determination even as audiences impelled them to act in a reified manner. Whites, writes Ellis Cashmore, "having material, if not moral, power sufficient to dictate the ebb and flow of plantation life, would have had the ability to impose certain conditions." As these conditions evolved in the early twentieth century, Cashmore says, "Blacks may have been consciously playing the roles whites had created for them; they may also have been manipulating images for expedient purposes."[23]

This was evident in the use of blackface by black performers. The mask of blackface minstrelsy was so embedded into the American psyche that any vaudeville show, black or white, without a "coon" mask was sure to fail (Spike Lee's film *Bamboozled* makes this point well). Black performers at the turn of the century were aware of the legacy of minstrelsy and realized that they lived a conflicting "double consciousness" where desire and demands were often at odds. I have noted elsewhere that "performing within a prescribed framework established by whites in blackface, black performers had to negotiate between representations of self, and representations of blackness fixed in the minds of audiences accustomed to white caricatures. Black performers were keenly aware of this paradox, which created a complex, and often contradictory, relationship between performance and representation."[24] This Du Boisian double consciousness was summoned up in Franz Fanon's observation that despite his desire to assert his selfhood he was "an object in the midst of other objects." The dual consciousness has also been described in a proverb Bernard Bell's grandfather was fond of reciting: "Got one mind fuh white folks to see, 'nother fuh what I know's me."[25]

The late nineteenth century coincided with two significant events impacting black entertainment: the end of Reconstruction and the legalization of Jim Crow segregation. Both conditions resulted in economic hardship for African Americans. Blacks, influenced by Booker T. Washington's self-help agenda, rallied to combat poverty through labor and a sense of self-sufficiency. Many black performers were enthusiastic followers of Washington, who advocated economic advancement through manual labor.[26] According to Washington, once economic parity was achieved, other benefits such as educational equality would accrue. In his famous 1895 Atlanta Exposition address, Washington urged blacks to "cast down your buckets where you are," i.e., create business and economic opportunities despite obstacles. "Our greatest danger," he said, "is that in the great leap from slavery to freedom we may overlook the fact that the masses of us are to live by the productions of our hands, and fail to keep in mind that we shall prosper in proportion as we learn to dignify and glorify common labor, and put brains and skill into the common occupation of life; shall prosper in proportion as we learn to draw the line between the superficial and the substantial, the ornamental gewgaws of life and the useful."[27] Historian Sven Beckert remarks that, for Washington, freedom "rested on economic power." To remain free, Beckert maintains, "people of African heritage had to become part of the global capitalist economy, of 'civilization' in Washington's words, while retaining their ability to provide for themselves independently."[28] Washington's separation of the utilitarian and the frivolous would subsequently impact black performers. Furthermore, his emphasis on capitalism and useful productivity was, I believe, at the root of the decision to use the term "coon" despite its negative connotation.

African American actors realized that their best chance of theatrical mainstream commercial success rested on two principles: talent and marketing. Talent they had in abundance; but the marketing of and for black theater had by this time been hardwired into America's psyche. Minstrelsy's stereotypic caricature produced a seemingly endless parade of white actors who stepped into the gestures of an American minstrel archetype—T. D. Rice's Jim Crow caricature is famous for this—portraying recognizable and derogatory features. During the nineteenth century white actors in blackface were an accepted artifice; this theatrical convention endured in the public's imagination even through the twentieth century. How to free black theater from white control became the circumambient concern of African American performers. However, early twentieth-century performers had experienced what many performers encounter even now: a perceived need to appeal to white audiences. With such acquiescence came financial success, despite the objection of African Americans who were strongly opposed to the images of minstrel derogation and superficial disport.

Amid the heady times of venture capitalism that arose in the late 1890s, black performers were caught in a bind: they needed to advertise to succeed, but they also needed to assuage fears of middle-class blacks who considered their work an abetting of racism. Additionally, the appearance of department stores fed a burgeoning consumerism that had found its way into world's fairs, hotels and museums, film, magazines, and tourism.[29] Turn-of-the-century industrialization resulted in nearly everyone across the political spectrum and up and down the economic ladder embracing free-market credos. Commercialization was transforming economies, and they in turn were transforming the world. A "deep-going change in the capitalist mode of production and exchange," writes Martin J. Sklar, "represented a new stage in the development of market society."[30] The pace of industrialization accelerated, notably in the rapid spread of mass production, oil refineries, pipelines, retail chains, bigger and faster railroads, and the emerging telephone system. Following the depression of 1893 to 1896, the economy continued to grow, with the next two decades experiencing an unprecedented upsurge. The unemployment rate remained close to 4 percent, and per capita income rose nearly 2.5 percent a year from 1896 to the beginning of World War I. Overall, from the late nineteenth century to the end of World War I, within one generation, Americans' average standard of living had jumped by nearly two-thirds.[31]

America boasted of being the "land of opportunity," where success was available for the ambitious and plucky. Entrepreneurs reported rising like the phoenix from nothing to become powerful kings of industry. Gilded Age rapacity encouraged individuals to seize upon any available opportunity, and many made their fortunes. The "theology of the free market," writes political scientist James E. Block, demanded the "moral liberty" of individuals to pursue goals and pioneer invention.[32] This resulted in a literature replete with "how-to" books and articles embracing the "self-made man." "Every man for himself, and the Devil take the hindermost," noted social scientist David Wells in 1875.[33] The nation's industrial revolution—indeed explosion—led to a growth in new methods of distribution, which in turn led to an increase in marketing. Individual liberty in a free-market system combined with the reorganization of market forces resulted in a new middle class. The idea of advertising one's goods—in the Sears catalog, for example—had a profound impact on the American way of life. As people made their mark in the hurly-burly of capitalism, the consequences of this excitement was evidenced by the boom in manifestos and pamphlets urging individuals to "get up and go." "Life is *action*," wrote William Mathews in his 1878 book, *Getting on in the World: Hints of Success in Life*. "Money is power," added Russell H. Conwell in his 1890 book, *Acres of Diamonds: How Men and Women May Become Rich*, and the key to success was said to be within one's grasp: "Your wealth is close to the spot where you sit to read these pages; perhaps within your fingers' reach. . . . Not far from you now is all the wealth your heart should desire, and more than you will ever need."[34] Inventiveness, diligence, and fortitude were terms of the new zeitgeist. Railway transportation rushed goods across the nation; new inventions fostered overnight wealth; and captains of industry such as the Vanderbilts, the Rockefellers, and J. P. Morgan became worthy of youthful emulation. These were new business leaders whose endurance and plentitude brought with them a sense of adventure. Wilbur F. Crafts, in his popular 1883 book, *Successful Men of Today and What They Say of Success*, announced that "'sticktoitiveness' is often mentioned as the essential condition of success."[35] Passivity was shunned, and laziness was deemed immoral; only those who took the initiative would reap the rewards. "Don't *wait* for your opportunity. *Make it*," urged Orison Swett Marden in his book, *Pushing to the Front: Or, Success Under Difficulties*: "The giants of the race have been men of con-centration, who have struck sledge-hammer blows in one place until they have accomplished their purpose. The successful men of to-day are men of single and intense purpose."[36] Amid this euphoric rush to wealth, marketing strategies abounded.

Like everyone else, blacks wanted their rightful share. However, the door to opportunity was not only shut, it was slammed shut. In its 1896 *Plessy v. Ferguson* decision the Supreme Court ruled that "separate but equal" facili-ties were constitutional, thereby allowing institutions and individuals to institute racial segregation unimpeded. This decision had enormous con-sequences, none more devastating than its economic impact on the black community. Social historian Nikhil Pal Singh has commented that racism "operates at the level of market activity and so-called private life, where blacks have been prevented both formally and informally from acting as proprietors of their own capacities, sellers of their labor-power, and sensu-ous participants with exchange relations."[37] By law blacks were prevented in many instances from acting as entrepreneurs of their own inventiveness and brokers of their own labor. As business expanded in virtually every corner of the marketplace, blacks were largely relegated to sideline observers. Outside of their own communities African Americans could work only in prescribed professions, usually menial and servile vocations. With little or no involve-ment in the means of production, and few opportunities for imaginative self-employment in business, blacks were locked into "their place." Frustra-tions began to mount not merely because of restrictions, but also because American business was growing at a fever pitch. The timing of the Supreme Court ruling on segregation could not have been worse, for it not only cre-ated second-class citizenship, it effectively cut off blacks from the era's ex-hilarating possibilities. Poverty is devastating, but poverty amid seemingly boundless wealth is cruelly ironic in a so-called free-market society.

Competitiveness required selling. If blacks were to be denied the right to sell commodities, they were left to sell themselves. It was a déjà vu of slavery, but this time the item was marked and polished by its "realness." But merely selling the "real coon" would not be sufficient to overcome white hegemony in the theater. The "realness" had to be transferable; in other words, whites not only had to observe "real" blackness, they had to experience it as well. "Blackness" had to be made marketable, a species not only in the showcase window (or on the auction block), but something a buyer might sensuously "adorn." The product had to be felt, bejeweled, and experienced; it had to be tactile as well as visual. The mode of exchange was performance; what would be marketed would be teaching whites how to "be black." Blacks sold authenticity using rhetoric, gesture, and conviction—blackness in the body itself and not just the mere surface greasepaint of blackface. Reality had to be invented, but it also had to conform to real body language, movement, and performance. Whites would have to purchase blackness from those best equipped to sell it—"real" black performers.

Black performers, Aida Overton Walker in particular, capitalized on what Thorstein Veblen famously called "conspicuous consumption." In his well-known 1899 book, *The Theory of the Leisure Class*, Veblen illuminated the sort of portal through which black performers might enter as successful "investors." According to Veblen, the turn of the century created a need for people not merely to acquire wealth but to display it ostentatiously. "In order to gain and to hold the esteem of men," he said, "it is not sufficient merely to possess wealth or power. The wealth or power must be put in evidence, for esteem is awarded only on evidence."[38] The wealthy sought ways to demonstrate their social status; the cakewalk, a dance that Walker taught to whites, became a signifier of Veblen's conspicuous consumption. Walker emerged as the principal cakewalking teacher. Acting "primitive"—a catchphrase of the era—by way of cakewalking became one of the cultural artifacts being collected by the West. Co-opting the vogue of primitivism (Cubism is the well-known example), the movement toward collectibles and acquisition fell in line with the "realness" whites associated with primitive societies. Like Cubism, cakewalking was therefore marked by its primitive imbrication, which elevated its cachet. If whites could learn the cakewalk, they could learn the "performance of blackness," the bodily gestures that displayed their conspicuous consumption. If real blackness was something desirable (albeit at a safe distance), and if blacks were the original cake-walkers—as Will Marion Cook's 1898 musical, *Clorindy, the Origins of the Cakewalk*, attested—then whites could demonstrate their ability to display blackness through cakewalking. But to be successful at this, whites had to learn it from someone "authentic." Taking cakewalking lessons from Aida Overton Walker was therefore de rigueur for the upstart wealthy as well as the blue bloods. Walker did for the cakewalk dance what William Cody's Buffalo Bill show did for the Wild West—capitalizing on and literally selling a wish to experience something "essential" about a certain culture. As we will shortly observe, cakewalking was a conglomerate dance of mixed origins and hardly the result of a singular or linear development. But this mattered little in the rhetorical strategy of selling the cakewalk; what mattered to its promoters were consumers eager to demonstrate their status and sellers deftly marketing the product.

Cakewalking to the Real Thing

The most popular cakewalk dancer in the United States during the turn of the century, Aida Overton Walker (1880–1914) was described by Sterling Brown as "the most talented Negro soubrette and dancer of her time."[39] Five years after her death, Howe Alexander eulogized her work as "the apogee of dancing done by Colored dancers." Her dance, he said, "had the power to dilate the vision and stretch the imagination."[40] In 1914 *Variety* reported that she was "easily the foremost Afro-American stage artist"; and sixteen years after her death James Weldon Johnson crowned her "beyond comparison the brightest star among women in the Negro stage of the period; and it is a question whether or not she has since been surpassed."[41] According to her biographer, Richard Newman, Walker's "life changed" when in 1898 Stella Wiley, a performer and occasional dance partner to Bob Cole, "invited her to pose dancing the cakewalk for an American Tobacco Company trade-card photograph."[42] Walker joined George Walker (whom she would marry in 1899), Bert Williams, and Wiley, becoming the company's leading choreographer and actress. When Williams and Walker performed *In Dahomey* in London in 1903, Constance Beerbohm reported in the *London Tatler* that in "*In Dahomey* at the Shaftesbury Theatre we are nightly seeing real negroes dancing real calk-walk and noting the grace and true inwardness of the dance."[43] Beerbohm's emphasis on "real Negroes" and "real calk-walk" was part of a cultural interest in the real that spotlighted the popular American dance. However, the notion of "realness" was also part of a designed strategy that worked on behalf of the performers. A brief history of the cakewalk confirms how Walker in many ways marketed its "realness."

Walker was not the first African American to popularize the cakewalk among whites. Dora Dean danced it during the 1890s in Europe, and the composer Will Marion Cook's Broadway musical *Clorindy, the Origins of the Cakewalk* certainly contributed to the dance's popularity. What Walker did was advance the cakewalk as a kind of "myth." She branded her insignia on cakewalking: over time her appropriation of the dance became more elaborate and ambitious, and her emphasis on grace and ease was her signature on the dance itself. Its commodity value was the "authenticity" she lent to the cakewalk—hers was the "true" knowledge of a genuine black

Figure 4.1. George and Aida Overton Walker performing a dance in their production of Bandanna Land. *Schomburg Center for Research in Black Culture, SC-CN-82-0029.*

dance having African roots. Like Buffalo Bill's "cowboy," the image of cakewalk dancing loomed large in popular imagination, even if the actual era of both the cakewalk and the cowboy was fleeting. The "real" cowboy endured merely two decades, and the popularity of the cakewalk lasted at most two decades. The cakewalk's influence coincided with interest in ragtime from the 1890s to its decline around 1910. What remained was the association of "cakewalk" as something that can be accomplished with ease. Although difficult to confirm, the popular expression "it's a cakewalk" is likely credited to Aida Overton Walker.

The news of Walker's cakewalking success in the 1903 London production of *In Dahomey* led to a desire by New York elite to absorb it from "the real thing." An interview of Walker titled "Cakewalk Society" reported that the "New York 400"—an elite social group—has "fallen under [the] spell of the willowy dance" and that Walker "leads young women in the mazy steps." The article went on to say that Walker, "a well-known colored actress, has taken the '400' by storm by her graceful dancing and under her graceful leadership society has taken up the cakewalk until it is the perfect rage."[44] The emphasis here and elsewhere was on Walker's trademark "grace." She had conducted several interviews on the subject of cakewalking in which she portrayed the dance as intertwined with race, authenticity, and social acceptability. The operative word she stressed was *grace*. When asked why African Americans are adept at cakewalking, she replied: "The negroes are not pessimists; there is no expression of sadness in their countenances, even in repose. . . . Think of moonlight nights and pine knots and tallow dips of lives untouched by the hardness of toil, for I tell you there was sunshine in the hearts of those who first danced the cakewalk." Her response was designed to draw a compelling picture of lightness and joy, but it was also meant to create a backdrop of authenticity. Relating the history of cakewalking, she describes its ease and charm: "In the old times there was more of what the original cakewalker called 'dignity.' It was more of a walk, less of a dance. The African race is a graceful people. It thrums banjoes with a flourish, and even when it has to do with pickaxes it gives those implements a long and graceful swing. That grace is inborn." Emphasizing this "grace" as innate, she asserted her authenticity and improved her marketability. She added that "society, which is now learning the cakewalk, has had the advantage of years of training by the best masters of dancing and of the bodily graces." Placing herself front and center as *the* cakewalker, she went on to define the dance:

> The cakewalk is a dance peculiar to our people. Its steps, however, are of American origin, whatever the original idea may have been. The tempo is often that of the two-step and the march. . . . But that is only the mathematics of it. . . . Remember that the cakewalk in itself is an expression of joy, of freedom from toil, of solitary making. There, too, bear in mind that there are other purposes. It is necessary to impress the judges with the gracefulness of the cakewalker in order to win the prize. . . . Because each dancer desires to attract to himself or herself the most graceful partner, for the judges make up their decisions upon

the appearance of a man and woman cakewalking together. . . . Don't
you see how necessary it is for the dancers to be not only as graceful
as they can, but also to convey an idea by their expression that they are
delighted with the chance of dancing together. Therefore, I say, don't
forget the eyes. . . . In fact, a little flirtation—just a little flirtation—is
a prime requisite.[45]

In evidence here is the explanation of the cakewalk's origination and
its history as a symbol of grace and sexual charm. Walker's cool aloofness
beneath the crowd-pleasing charm, the caginess behind the exaggerated
sangfroid, and the mask covering the self-promotion was what she had to
do: white star actors knew the mainstream press would fan their legends;
Walker and her cohorts had to stump for themselves. But more than these
ideas of elegance and self-promotion, Walker's notion of improvisation and
creative impulse went a long way in establishing an aesthetic even while
capitalizing on perceived "traditions." The dance, as Walker explained it, was
always evolving. The evolving idea was part of a strategy that Paul Gilroy
calls "black diaspora styles," the process of performance "emphasized by
their radically unfinished form—a characteristic which marks them indel-
ibly as the products of slavery."[46] Walker kept the description of the dance
"in fashion" by stressing its slave tradition and evolutionary contours: "Be
happy, for the original cakewalkers were glad at the light of the moon when
their work was done." But she also folded in a nuanced style. In describing
the actual steps of the dance, Walker stressed flirtation and charm, emphasizing the cakewalk's dulcet attributes:

As far as the actual execution of the steps is concerned many persons
may surpass their instructors in time. If, however, they do not remember to show by the expression of their faces that they are interested
and happy, I do not believe that any amount of fancy steps will make
up for such a defect. . . . The cakewalk is characteristic of a race, and
in order to understand it and appreciate it and to become adept in it,
it is necessary to keep your mind on the judges, your partner and especially upon what the cakewalk really is—a gala dance.[47]

By commodifying the cultural authenticity of the cakewalk ("characteristic of a race"), Walker, as I have noted elsewhere, "cloaked the origins of her
choreographic ideas and signified on the basic ideas of a semantics of authenticity."[48] The origins of the cakewalk are inchoate at best; Terry Waldo
suggests that the cakewalk originated "with slaves who dressed up in 'high

fashion' and mimicked the formal dances of their masters. Their caricatures were picked up by white performers and used in the grand finale of
the minstrel show." African Americans "performing in the black-stereotype
mold of the white minstrel shows picked up the dance. By the time the ragtime era began in 1896, the cakewalk was being performed by blacks imitating whites who were imitating blacks who were imitating whites."[49] The
comedic hall of mirrors that is the cakewalk appears to undermine Walker's
view that the dance expresses a "characteristic of a race." However, Walker's
description of cakewalking is best conceived of as a bricolage of influences
and modifications, an understanding that signifies the dance as a subcul-
tural invention. According to Dick Hebdige, such bricolage "is basically the
way in which commodities are *used* in subculture which mark the subculture off from more orthodox cultural formations."[50] Walker exploited many
clichés, in particular those associated with the "origins of the cakewalk" as
an essentialized construction. But she did so out of necessity. She capitalized on the aggressive "go-for-it" rhetoric of her time, selling what she had
at her disposal. Furthermore, white Americans frequently depicted African
Americans as bound to their "original" state, as people fixed and without
history. The cakewalk, like African American culture more generally, was
perceived as frozen in time. Its gestures and movements were alleged to
be a source of authenticity from its inception. Thus, for Walker, the cakewalk represented a link to a "primitive" past. According to Brooke Baldwin, "the cakewalk can be identified as an Afro-American folk form with
roots in African music through its traits of syncopation and suspended beat,
polyrhythmic structure, signifying, improvisation, and responsoriality. All
combine to make it a genuinely black cultural product, which is exactly
why whites, from the beginning, attempted to co-opt and stereotype it."[51]
Baldwin's description is correct up to a point. It does not take into account
that the cakewalk itself was of dubious origins. Its hybrid form had in fact
many influences. According to Roscoe Lewis in *The Negro in Virginia*, the
cakewalk "has been ascribed to African tribal celebrations."[52] There can be
little doubt that it evolved from African dance traditions, especially the "ring
shout"; however, as it was absorbed in the American vernacular, it became
a common festive dance in which slaves imitated their masters. "The slaves
would assemble en masse—dressed in their Sunday best. . . . Masters and
mistresses would be there, one of whom would award the prize for the best
'cuttin' of the figgers.' Sometimes the mistress of the big house would donate
a prize cake." (It is likely that this last detail that gave rise to the dance's
name.) Marshall Sterns contends that during slavery, couples "promenaded

(LEFT) *Figure 4.2. Portrait of Aida Overton Walker, ca. 1911. Schomburg Center for Research in Black Culture, SC-CN-85-0158.*

(ABOVE) *Figure 4.3. Aida Overton Walker as Salome, drawing by Moe Zayas. From* New York World, *August 30, 1908, Metropolitan Section, p. 2.*

grandly with a high kickstep, waving canes, doffing hats, and bowing low." Vaudeville performer Tom Fletcher makes the interesting claim that the cakewalk was originally a processional dance called "the chalkline-walk" or "walk-around," developed "from a 'Prize-Walk' from the days of slavery, generally at get-togethers on the plantation."[53] But once it was picked up by white minstrel performers, its steps were modified. When blacks copied minstrel whites, who imitated plantation blacks, who were sarcastically mimicking their white masters, details of the dance's origins go up for grabs. Walker finessed the dance's meaning and maximized its market value. She catered to the demands of her white students but asserted her control over its distribution.

Despite success, black performers faced another problem. The widespread popularity of the cakewalk and the intense condemnation of it elicited public debate. Some "New Negro" progressives campaigned against it, believing that it promoted open sexuality and folderol (Washington's frowned-upon "gewgaw") and recalled memories of a painful past. One 1897 editorial from the *Indianapolis Freeman* maintained that the "good people of this country have nothing in common with cake walks," because "the great crime attached to cake walks is the resurrection of supposed obsolete manners . . . and if there is anything that gets close to the modern Negro, it is the reminder of past associations and tribulations."[54] The fear of losing control owing to the dance's seductive powers prompted the *Cleveland Gazette* to report disapprovingly that "some of our best girls, even some who sing in the Baptist church choir, I regret exceedingly to say, were roped in and took part in the disgraceful affair."[55] In an article entitled "Rag-Time Music and Calk Walks," the front page of the *Chicago Broad Ax* called the "two above named past-times disgusting—ridiculously disgusting!" Why, the paper inquired, should "mothers of refinement and proper training allow their young, pliable, easily impressed daughters to indulge in any such devilment and monkey shines is a mystery to the writer, who would far prefer washing her daughter's face and following her to the cemetery to see her going to hell" as the result of "dancing cake-walks, indulging in rag-time music, and other such deviltry."[56] In *The Negro in Etiquette*, E. M. Woods was even more critical: "The cake walk is really a negro product. Nevertheless, its more prominent features are 'monkey shines,' coarse, clownish jokes, and many ludicrous didos akin to the funny mule in the circus." He added sarcastically: "The more zealous votaries of the cake-waking fad, hold that it teaches naturalness and gracefulness. This is not denied; nor is it altogether affirmed. For one may be a natural fool or an artificial fool."[57] One of the strongest condemnations came in an 1898 *Freeman* editorial: "As representative of the colored race I desire to enter my protest against the 'cake walk' which is now becoming a fad among some colored people, encouraged by whites. . . . The whites go to these exhibitions of buffoonery to laugh at and ridicule the monkified contortions of the principal actors." The editorial concludes: "I insist that the cake walk is beneath the dignity of the better class of 'the race,' and that it brings them into ridicule and contempt . . . and so should be frowned down by the better class of colored people."[58] The acidulous critique resulted from the belief that it possessed sexual overtones and gimcracks that contradicted appropriate moral standards. But criticism in a broader sense can be viewed as part of the backlash against modernity traceable to the early 1900s. This period experienced a reaction to progress, defended creationism over encroaching Darwinism, and favored what Ferdinand Tönnies called *Gemeinschaft* (community), with its emphasis on trust, kinship, social bonding, and pastoral values, over *Gesell-schaft* (civil society), with its emphasis on business, competition, market orientation, urbanity, and ruthlessness.[59]

Walker, as I have suggested, "hoped to mollify middle-class blacks suspicious of cakewalking, and, simultaneously, to make cakewalking acceptable to that part of white society interested in transgressing racial boundaries. If black society had cast a shadow of doubt over cakewalking, Walker attempted to allay its fears that cakewalking was representative of racial stereotyping; and as white elite society wanted to learn about black dance, Walker emerged as cakewalking's popular practitioner."[60] Balancing propriety and salesmanship, she defended herself and her career: "Colored people on the stage have been given very little consideration by our colored writers and critics; perhaps they have considered them unworthy of the attention, or perhaps it has just been a matter of oversight." She added—keeping Booker T. Washington's emphasis on discipline and work ethic in mind— that the stage was a viable avenue for black women and "decent" labor. Her rearguard action in African American newspapers was an effort to justify her work: "In the past the profession which I am now following may have merited severe criticism, but like every other calling or profession, the Stage has improved with time, and I am proud to say that there are many clever, honest and well deserving men and women of other races in color in professional life who will compare favorably with men and woman of other races in the profession or other professions." She argued that "when white people refuse to classify, in dealing with us, we get highly indignant and say we should not all be judged alike, and yet we often fail to classify and make distinctions when judging ourselves. . . . Some of our so-called society people regard the Stage as a place to be ashamed of. Whenever it is my good fortune to meet such persons, I sympathize with them for I know they are ignorant as to what is really being done in their own behalf by members of their race on the Stage." Walker added:

> In this age we are all fighting the one problem—that is the color problem! I venture to think and dare to state that our profession does more toward the alleviation of color prejudice than any other profession among colored people. . . . As individuals we must strive all we can to show that we are as capable as white people. In all other walks of life when colored people have had fair play, they have proved their ability, those before the lights must do their part for the cause. . . . Our people are capable and with advantages they will succeed.[61]

But black people, as Walker knew well, did not enjoy "fair play." Consequently, the cakewalk had to be transformed to suit her agenda. If the "real" cakewalk could be turned into the mythical embodiment of "primitive Africa," then Walker would have to give the British and Americans what they wanted: a dance with "genuine" African roots. Walker stepped into the center of the cakewalk craze as the "authentic" dancer with legitimate credentials. The fact that the cakewalk was a hybrid did not deter her from promoting the "real thing." The fault line between truth and invention was artfully joined by Walker in her approach to the cakewalk dance. She had created a process by which, in anthropologist Michael Taussig's words, the real is "really made up."[62] Walker maneuvered the tight space between accusations of degrading stereotype and promoting a cultural touchstone. Her footing was surest when she articulated the importance of women as professionals. Examining market strategies of Walker's dancing the "original" cakewalk reveals a complex and ingenious use of the real to circumvent racist obstacles and establish her company's success. Julia Kristeva contends that the "true-real" of modernity "relativizes the notion of truth, and, while maintaining it, often presents it to us in an extremely attractive way."[63] Walker, too, relativized an authenticity that, as the above endeavors to show, fit several demands.

The popularity of cakewalking during its heyday epitomizes much of what black popular culture has utilized in selling the real now. At the beginning of the twentieth century, writes Karen Sotiropoulos, "black popular artists sold white Americans on the idea that black style was the very essence of cool."[64] If dancing the cakewalk was "cool," Walker's method was to sell the "real cool," anticipating what has come to be called "ghetto fabulous." According to John L. Jackson,

> To be ghetto fabulous is to embrace a sense of self utterly irreducible to one's assumed location at the residential and spatial bottom of national or international pecking order. Ghetto fabulousness takes the quantified assumptions of localizing marginality and transforms them into a qualitatively different kind of lived experience, a way of traversing the socio-spatial margin that privileges personal and intimate privatizations over market-based instrumentality of social scientists, government agencies, and economic modeling.

Ghetto fabulous, Jackson adds, "is not simply a depressing enslavement to designer clothes—foolish ghetto residents living beyond their means in authentic Versace, Prada, or even Burberry fashion." Rather, it "epitomizes a consumerism and commercialism that revels in knock-offs and wears them, sincerely, against the grain of societal expectations," yielding "the underside of the global to challenge its own confinement, to declare the social margins quite central to the people who live there, even as they struggle for more access to a global mainstream."[65] The cakewalk was "ghetto fabulous" because it characterized an underground localized economy and promoted a marginalized "authenticity." It came from the "spatial bottom," represented conspicuous consumerism much like knock-off clothes are "slumming-it" commodities of today, and declared its marginal status as central to those living with it. Cakewalking was, furthermore, "real" at the moment it was exchanged; it existed partly in what had occurred before, and partly in Walker's imagination, but it was concretized when it was sold on the open market—when it was *actually danced*—while Walker's authenticity lent it currency. When whites donned the countenance of cakewalking and followed Walker's instructions, they were ipso facto "real" cakewalkers. Its realism was not based on a reified past but an active and evolving present orchestrated by Walker. It was the "real thing" in the same way as fashion is authenticated. Fashion is itself a shill game, but is nonetheless real in its empirical actions and material existence. It is a testament to Walker's insight that she had the wherewithal to envision the cakewalk in a social context in ways that we take for granted now. Walker's ken as entrepreneur and actress allowed her to accomplish what she did, and perhaps more astonishingly, when she did it.

NOTES

1. George Walker, "The Real Coons," *Theatre Magazine* 6 (1906), 224.

2. Their early shows were *Senegambian Carnival* (1898), *Two Real Coons* (1898), *A Lucky Coon* (1899), *4-11-44* (1899), *The Policy Players* (1899–1900) and *Sons of Ham* (1900–1902). For statistical records of the shows, see Edward Mapp, *Directory of Blacks in the Performing Arts* (Metuchen, N.J.: Scarecrow Press, 1978); and Bernard L. Peterson, *Profiles of African American Stage Performers and Theatre People, 1816–1960* (Westport, Conn.: Greenwood Press, 2001).

3. George Walker, "Bert and Me and Them," *New York Age*, December 24, 1908, 4.

4. See Thomas Riis, *Just Before Jazz: Black Musical Theatre in New York, 1890–1915* (Washington, D.C.: Smithsonian Institution Press, 1989); Allen Woll, *Black Musical Theatre: From Coontown to Dreamgirls* (Baton Rouge: Louisiana State University Press, 1989); Errol Hill, "New Vistas: Plays, Spectacles, Musicals, and Opera,"

in *A History of African American Theatre*, ed. Errol Hill and James V. Hatch (Cambridge: Cambridge University Press, 2003), 135–85; and Jeffrey Green, "In Dahomey in London in 1903," *Black Perspective in Music* 11, no. 1 (Spring 1983): 22–40.

5. T. J. Jackson Lears, *No Place of Grace: Antimodernism and the Transformation of American Culture, 1880–1920* (Chicago: University of Chicago Press, 1983), 5.

6. Eric Lott, *Love and Theft: Blackface Minstrelsy and the American Working Class* (New York: Oxford University Press, 1993), 110.

7. Miles Orvell, *The Real Thing: Imitation and Authenticity in American Culture, 1880–1940* (Chapel Hill: University of North Carolina Press, 1989), xvi, 34.

8. Toni Morrison, "Unspeakable Things Unspoken: The Afro-American Presence in American Literature," *Michigan Quarterly Review* 28, no. 1 (1989): 11.

9. One fine exception is Kenneth W. Warren, *Black and White Strangers: Race and American Literary Realism* (Chicago: University of Chicago Press, 1993).

10. Amy Kaplan, *The Social Construction of American Realism* (Chicago: University of Chicago Press, 1988), 1.

11. See David Krasner, *Resistance, Parody, and Double Consciousness in African American Theatre, 1895–1910* (New York: St. Martin's Press, 1997); and Karen Sotiropoulos, *Staging Race: Black Performers in Turn of the Century America* (Cambridge: Harvard University Press, 2006) for a history of their resistance to racism.

12. See Louis S. Warren, *Buffalo Bill's America: William Cody and the Wild West Show* (New York: Knopf, 2005); Larry McMurtry, *The Colonel and Kittle Missie: Buffalo Bill, Annie Oakley, and the Beginning of Superstardom in America* (New York: Simon & Schuster, 2005); and Robert W. Rydell and Rob Kroes, *Buffalo Bill in Bologna: The Americanization of the World, 1869–1922* (Chicago: University of Chicago Press, 2005).

13. See Barbara Webb, "Authentic Possibilities: Plantation Performance of the 1890s," *Theatre Journal* 56, no. 1 (March 2004): 63–82.

14. Thomas Postlewait, "The Hieroglyphic Stage: American Theatre and Society, Post–Civil War to 1945," in vol. 2 of *The Cambridge History of American Theatre, 1870–1945*, ed. Don B. Wilmeth and Christopher Bigsby (Cambridge: Cambridge University Press, 1999), 161.

15. Robert Ogden, "Advertising Art," May 15, 1898; quoted in William Leach, *Land of Desire: Merchants, Power, and the Rise of a New American Culture* (New York: Vintage, 1993), 52.

16. "Williams and Walker Coming," *Colored American* (Washington, D.C.), May 6, 1899, 2.

17. George Walker, "Colored Actor Tells the Story of His Life from Kansas to Abyssinia," undated clipping circa 1906 (the date of the *Abyssinia*'s production), from the Williams & Walker clipping file, Billy Rose Theatre Collection, New York Public Library for the Performing Arts at Lincoln Center, New York, N.Y. (hereafter Billy Rose Theatre Collection).

18. Walker, "The Negro on the American Stage," 566.

19. R. C. Murray, "Williams and Walker, Comedians," *Colored American Magazine*, September 1905, 496.

20. *Baltimore Afro-American*, August 16, 1930, 9.

21. Louis Chude-Sokei, *The Last Darky: Bert Williams, Black-on-Black Modernity, and the African Diaspora* (Durham: Duke University Press, 2006), 124.

22. Harry J. Elam Jr., "Change Clothes and Go: A Postscript to Postblackness," in *Black Cultural Traffic: Crossroads in Global Performance and Popular Culture*, ed. Harry J. Elam Jr. and Kennell Jackson (Ann Arbor: University of Michigan Press, 2005), 379.

23. Ellis Cashmore, *The Black Cultural Industry* (London: Routledge, 1997), 28, 29.

24. Krasner, *Resistance, Parody, and Double Consciousness*, 9.

25. Franz Fanon, *Black Skin, White Masks*, trans. Charles Lam Markmann (New York: Grove, 1967), 109; Bernard W. Bell, *The Afro-American Novel and Its Tradition* (Amherst: University of Massachusetts Press, 1987), xi.

26. See a report on the Williams & Walker Glee Club, a musical group sponsored by Williams and Walker for the promotion of classical music. The glee club performed before Washington at his Tuskegee Institute. "Washington, Williams and Walker," *New York Age*, August 3, 1905, 4.

27. Booker T. Washington, "Atlanta Exposition Address," 1895, in *African-American Social and Political Thought, 1850–1920*, ed. Howard Brotz (New Brunswick, N.J.: Transaction Press, 1993), 357.

28. Sven Beckert, "From Tuskegee to Togo: The Problem of Freedom in the Empire of Cotton," *Journal of American History* 92, no. 2 (September 2005): 508.

29. See Leach, *Land of Desire*; Richard Ohmann, *Selling Culture: Magazines, Markets, and Class at the Turn of the Century* (London: Verso, 1996); Kathy Peiss, *Cheap Amusements: Working Women and Leisure in Turn-of-the-Century New York* (Philadelphia: Temple University Press, 1986); Richard W. Fox and T. J. Jackson Lears, eds., *The Culture of Consumption: Critical Essays in American History, 1880–1980* (New York: Pantheon, 1983); Elizabeth and Stuart Ewen, *Channels of Desire: Mass Images and the Shaping of American Consciousness* (Minneapolis: University of Minnesota Press, 1992); Robert Rydell, *All the World's A Fair: Visions of Empire at American International Expositions, 1876–1916* (Chicago: University of Chicago Press, 1987); and Alan Trachtenberg, *The Incorporation of America: Culture and Society in the Gilded Age* (New York: Hill and Wang, 1982).

30. Martin J. Sklar, *The United States as a Developing Country: Studies in U. S. History in the Progressive Era and the 1920s* (Cambridge: Cambridge University Press, 1992), 21.

31. Benjamin M. Friedman, *The Moral Consequences of Economic Growth* (New York: Knopf, 2005), 132.

32. James E. Block, *A Nation of Agents: The American Path to a Modern Self and Society* (Cambridge: Harvard University Press, 2002), 481.

33. David A. Wells, "Influence of the Production and Distribution of Wealth on Social Development," *Journal of Social Science* 8 (May 1876): 5 (paper delivered in 1875).

34. William Matthews, *Getting on in the World: Hints of Success in Life* (Chicago: S. C. Griggs, 1878), 125; Russell H. Conwell, *Acres of Diamonds: How Men and Women May Become Rich* (Philadelphia: John Y. Huber, 1890), 22.

35. Wilbur F. Crafts, *Successful Men of Today and What They Say of Success* (New York: Funk & Wagnalls, 1883), 146.

36. Orison Swett Marden, *Pushing to the Front: Or, Success Under Difficulties* (New York: Thomas Y. Crowell, 1894), 23, 109.

37. Nikhil Pal Singh, *Black Is a Country: Race and the Unfinished Struggle for Democracy* (Cambridge: Harvard University Press, 2004), 26.

38. Thorstein Veblen, *The Theory of the Leisure Class* (1899; reprint, New York: Dover, 1994), 24.

39. Sterling A. Brown, "The Negro on the Stage" (1940), unpublished study, *The Negro in American Culture*, Carnegie-Myrdal Study, Schomburg Center for Research in Black Culture, New York, 37.

40. Howe Alexander, "How Dancing Studs the Pages of History," *Half-Century Magazine*, 7, no. 2 (August 1919): 16.

41. *Variety*, October 17, 1914, 13; James Weldon Johnson, *Black Manhattan* (1930; reprint, New York: Arno Press, 1968), 107.

42. Richard Newman, "'The Brightest Star': Aida Overton Walker in the Age of Ragtime and Cakewalk," in *Words Like Freedom: Essays on African-American Culture and History* (West Cornwall, Conn.: Locust Hill Press, 1996), 57.

43. Constance Beerbohm, "The 'Cake-walk' and How to Dance It," *London Tatler*, July 1, 1903, 13.

44. Undated clipping, Williams & Walker file, Billy Rose Theatre Collection.

45. Undated clipping, c. 1903, Williams & Walker file, Billy Rose Theatre Collection.

46. Paul Gilroy, *The Black Atlantic: Modernity and Double Consciousness* (Cambridge: Harvard University Press, 1993), 105.

47. Undated clipping, c. 1903, Williams & Walker file, Billy Rose Theatre Collection.

48. Krasner, *Resistance, Parody, and Double Consciousness*, 95.

49. Terry Waldo, *This Is Ragtime* (1976; reprint, New York: Da Capo Press, 1991), 25.

50. Dick Hebdige, *Subculture: The Meaning of Style* (London: Routledge, 1979), 103.

51. Brooke Baldwin, "The Cakewalk: A Study in Stereotype and Reality," *Journal of Social History* 15 (1981): 213.

52. Quoted in Sterling Stuckey, *Slave Culture: Nationalist Theory & the Foundations of Black America* (New York: Oxford University Press, 1987), 95.

53. Virginia Writers' Project, *The Negro in Virginia* (New York: Hasting House,

1940), 89; quoted in Lynne Fauley Emery, *Black Dance in the United States from 1619 to 1970* (New York: Dance Horizons, 1980), 91; Marshall Sterns, *Jazz Dance: The Story of American Vaudeville Dance* (London: Macmillan, 1964), 116; Tom Fletcher, *100 Years of the Negro in Show Business* (New York: De Capo Press, 1984), 103.

54. "That Cake Walk," *Indianapolis Freeman*, January 9, 1897, 4.

55. "New Castle Pa, News," *Cleveland Gazette*, November 19, 1898, 2.

56. "Rag-time Music and Cake Walks," *Chicago Broad Ax*, January 20, 1900, 1.

57. E. M. Woods, *The Negro In Etiquette: A Novelty* (St. Louis: Buxton & Skinner, 1899), 131.

58. *Indianapolis Freeman*, February 2, 1898, 4.

59. Ferdinand Tönnies, *Community and Civil Society*, trans. Josh Harris and Margaret Hollis (1887; reprint, Cambridge: Cambridge University Press, 2001).

60. Krasner, *Resistance, Parody, and Double Consciousness*, 76.

61. Aida Overton Walker, "Colored Men and Women on the Stage," *Colored American Magazine*, October 1905, 571–75.

62. Michael Taussig, *Mimesis and Alterity: A Particular History of the Senses* (London: Routledge, 1993), xiii-xix.

63. Julia Kristeva, "The True-Real," trans. Seán Hand, in *The Kristeva Reader*, ed. Tori Moi (Oxford: Blackwell, 1986), 221.

64. Sotiropoulos, *Staging Race*, 237.

65. John L. Jackson Jr., *Real Black: Adventures in Racial Sincerity* (Chicago: University of Chicago Press, 2005), 59–60.

Black Creativity and Black Stereotype

Rethinking Twentieth-Century Popular Music in America

SUSAN CURTIS

In 1900, the *Etude*, a magazine devoted to articles about music and musical performance, lambasted "the insane craze for 'rag-time' music" that was then sweeping the country. It editorialized:

> The counters of the music stores are loaded with this virulent poison which, in the form of a malarious epidemic, is finding its way into the homes and brains of the youth to such an extent as to arouse one's suspicion of their sanity. The pools of slush through which the composers of some of these songs have dragged their questionable rimes are rank enough to stifle the nostrils of decency, and yet young men and ladies of the best standing daily roll around their tongues in gluttonous delight the most nauseating twaddle about "hot town," "warm babies" and "blear-eyed coons" armed with "blood-letting razors"—some of them set to double-jointed, jumping jack airs that fairly twist the ears of an educated musician from their anchorage. Some of these songs are so maudlin in sentiment and rhythm as to make the themes they express fairly stagger in the drunkenness of their exaggerations. They are a plague to both music and musicians and a stench to refinement.[1]

The *Etude* was not alone in its denunciation of ragtime music. The *Negro Music Journal* likewise registered concern about the "real harm" such music was doing to the moral fiber and musical standards of Americans at the dawn of the new century. "It is an evil music," the editor insisted, "that has crept into the homes and hearts of our American people regardless of race, and must be wiped out as other bad and dangerous epidemics have been exterminated."[2] Frank Damrosch, director of the Institute of Musical Arts, compared ragtime tunes to pimples: "They come and go. They are impurities in the musical system which must be got rid of before it can be considered clean."[3] Others denounced the music as "vulgar," "evil," "barbaric," and "perturbing."[4] But their diatribes fell on many ragtime-deafened ears—for this music took the nation by storm at the beginning of the twentieth century.

Still, the intensity of the opposition to and critique of ragtime music is telling and historically significant. Its alarmist language of epidemic, insanity, vulgarity, and outright evil alerts us a century later to a powerful sense of urgency felt by these critics. They recognized something that in the intervening decades has been lost to us in our misty-eyed nostalgia for this old-fashioned musical form. They saw ragtime as nothing less than a revolution that turned upside down the mainstays of late nineteenth-century American culture. When I use the term "revolution," I am not implying a liberation of oppressed people—at least, not exactly. But I do see the emergence of ragtime music as part of a major transformation in how people lived and thought that liberated them from cultural imperatives and impossible ideals that were being undermined every day as U.S. society embraced an increasingly urban, industrial future.

Angry denunciations like those made by the *Etude* and the *Negro Music Journal* cast ragtime music as a form of entertainment that had arisen from the underside of American culture—an evil that surely would soon pass. The very shrillness of such attacks, however, reveals their concern about the extent to which Americans had taken to this new popular music. Indeed, as scholarship in more recent decades has shown, ragtime gave way to jazz in the late 1910s and served as the foundation for popular American music in the following decades.[5] Moreover, ragtime's heyday coincided with the emergence of the modern popular music industry, which took advantage of national networks of communication and commercial distribution, technologies related to the reproduction of sound, the unprecedented affordability of pianos, and newly established sites of leisure such as amusement parks, cabarets, and dancehalls to stimulate and satisfy the desire for the latest musical hit. It is also clear that ragtime was part of what John Higham has called the "re-orientation" of American culture at the turn of the century, when Victorianism lost its stranglehold on the national imagination.[6]

I have suggested elsewhere that the ragtime craze was fundamental to this cultural shift.[7] Here I wish to make explicit the connections between ragtime and the establishment of the popular music industry in twentieth-century America, and at the same time to restore the central role played by African Americans in the process. For what was understood at the dawn of the century—namely, that African American composers, performers, and musical traditions provided the creative impetus for ragtime—faded rather quickly as white artists, performers, and publishers jumped on the ragtime bandwagon and took credit for crafting the quintessential American popular music. As James Weldon Johnson saw it in the mid-1920s, "before the Negro succeeded fully in establishing his title as creator of his secular music the form was taken away from him and made national instead of racial." Johnson's assertion indicates yet another instance of what Eric Lott calls "love and theft."[8]

I am interested, however, in more than recovering our memory of men and women whose creativity gave ragtime its shape and appeal, because the uses to which this music was put were not what its African American progenitors imagined. Ragtime, the popular music industry, and the cultural reorientation that they initiated and of which they were products were all tied inextricably to the establishing and policing of the color line at the dawn of the twentieth century. The amnesia surrounding the role of African American musicians and performers in instantiating this lucrative business arises, I argue, from capitalizing on the yearning for carefree exuberance ascribed to African Americans even as African Americans themselves were derided for their inherent inability to compete in modern America.[9] The psychological "wages of whiteness," as W. E. B. Du Bois called the benefits that accrued to white people, paid cultural dividends that included acceptance of wage labor in exchange for sufficient time and money to participate in leisure activities—including those associated with popular music—that offered ways to express personality, define one's identity, and cultivate social bonds of one's own choosing outside of the workplace. The willingness of men and women to consume this music, believing that it provided escape from the strictures of an unfulfilling set of cultural values and imperatives, fueled the demand for popular entertainment that grounded the fledgling music industry.

The emergence of the popular music industry in the 1890s was the result of both a cultural rebellion against Victorianism and deteriorating race relations. This period is, of course, remembered as the "nadir" for African Americans—a low point, indeed, when record numbers of lynchings made for "strange fruit" hanging from southern trees, disfranchisement debarred most black voters from the polls, racial discrimination consigned workers of color to the lowest paid and most menial jobs, and *Plessy v. Ferguson* legalized Jim Crow segregation all across the land. It was also an era of "class warfare," which exploded into violent confrontations between workers and the armed henchmen of their employers. The march of Coxey's Army to the nation's capital, seeking redress for widespread unemployment, signaled an unresolved tension between the nineteenth-century Protestant work ethic and industrial labor. White men's fascination with bodybuilders and escape artists arose, according to John F. Kasson, from feelings of helplessness and entrapment in unfulfilling jobs and work regimens. "New Women" and national fads, enabled by national marketing and mass communication, contributed as well to a general overhauling of the dominant culture.[10]

In the past couple of decades, scholarship on the emergence of consumer culture, of which the music industry was a part, has focused on ideals, values, and institutions appealing to white people. White businesses and advertisers with a national reach enjoyed a privileged position in this emerging culture because they gained ready access to periodicals, daily newspapers, publishing houses, and other sites of cultural production where their vision for the "good life" could be disseminated. It is important to note the existence and importance of other cultures of consumption, particularly those appealing to African American clients and readers. As Davarian Baldwin and Adam Green have shown, African American cultural leaders, businesses, and intellectuals made use of advertising and mass-marketing strategies to create race consciousness and to offer advice of particular interest to readers of color.[11] Without diminishing the significance of this site of consumer-oriented cultural work, the focus of this essay is on the broad-based, white-dominated consumer culture whose creators imagined its audience in racially exclusive terms. For it is in this cultural space that questions of race were implicitly rather than explicitly articulated.

Indeed, within the dominant (white) consumer culture and in the scholarship that has examined it, the crumbling of Victorian values and the intensification of race-based discrimination and oppression have been seen as coincidental but not implicated in one another. That is, when the subject is ragtime, African Americans and their experience of exclusion play central explanatory roles. But when the subject is the transition from Victorian culture to consumer culture, race relations enter the discussion, at best, in a minor way.[12] I believe the two interpretations are inextricably bound together, and institutions such as the popular music industry, which took shape in that era, are integral parts of both stories. As a form of amusement, popular music accompanied and demanded a consumerist ethos, that is, a willingness to purchase the latest novelty available for sale, either directly in the form of sheet music and, later, recordings, or indirectly in dancehalls, cabarets, vaudeville, and, later, moving pictures. Consumerism sprang in part from the rejection of abstemiousness and self-control and through products or experiences that delivered the feeling of freedom. Unlike political activists struggling for justice, economic opportunity, social and civil equality, and workers' rights, who sought freedom by challenging the economic, social, and political structures that bound the majority to drudgery for the opulence of a few, culture workers and purveyors of popular music envisioned a different kind of freedom. They challenged the rules that governed economic and social life. The freedom they envisioned left intact wage labor and a gap between the leisure class and working poor—the "millionaires" and "tramps," as Populists put it—but rewrote the meaning of work as a means to an end rather than a noble end in itself, and the desired object was expressive self-definition. The self to be defined and expressed was the one squelched by time discipline and self-control—a forbidden self whose form and behavior had first to be imagined. As these inchoate yearnings surfaced, the simultaneous marginalizing and demonizing of African Americans supplied the details for the white imagination. African Americans were vilified for their childlike irresponsibility, their insatiable sexual appetite, and their resort to thievery and violence; and the allure of shirking work, abandoning sexual repression, and striking out at the privileged drew eager consumers to music by and about African Americans.

Thus ragtime, the earliest form of popular music in the modern era, gained an enthusiastic following at the very moment when the cultural crisis came to a head in the 1890s and when the color line was being both drawn and vigilantly patrolled. At this very moment Americans began eagerly "dancing to a Black man's tune"—making the products of the African American cultural imagination the basis for popular American music and crowning Scott Joplin the King of Ragtime. Joplin, whose life perfectly frames this period of change when nineteenth-century Victorian culture and liberal individualism gave way to modern, consumer culture and the corporation and when African Americans reached the nadir, helps us see how these two narratives are intertwined in the making of the popular music industry.

The Cradle of Ragtime

Joplin was born in 1868 near present-day Texarkana in the midst of ratification of the Fourteenth Amendment to the Constitution. He died on April Fool's Day, 1917, days before the United States entered the First World War.[13] Between these two landmark moments the national culture underwent a sea change in no small part because of music Joplin and his contemporaries produced. As a teenager in the 1880s, Joplin embarked on a career as an itinerant musician working, presumably, in the riverfront districts of towns and cities located on the Mississippi. His travels took him to Chicago in 1893, the year of the World's Columbian Exposition, and as far away as Syracuse, New York, where in 1895 he published two songs, *A Picture of Her Face* and *Please Say You Will*, neither one of which hinted at the ragtime innovations that would soon follow. It was not until he settled in Sedalia, Missouri, that he began writing music that would propel him to popularity. There, in Sedalia, Joplin became known as the "King of Ragtime," and in 1899 his "Maple Leaf Rag" became a hit in the region and eventually across the nation.[14]

It was not merely Joplin's success, however, that made Missouri the cradle of ragtime, nor was it the presence of such talented musicians and composers as Tom Turpin, Louis Chauvin, Sam Patterson, James Scott, and Arthur Marshall, as important as these men were to the development of ragtime. According to Joplin, he and other black musicians had been playing this distinctive style of music for years, long before white audiences took notice of it in the early 1890s. Other forces—post-Reconstruction economic changes and accompanying demographic shifts—were beginning to rock cities and towns such as Sedalia. In the 1890s, Sedalia, like a lot of communities, experienced rapid economic development thanks to transportation systems that linked them to other centers of exchange and industrial production. Sedalia had become an important railhead in Missouri after serving as an early terminus of the famed cattle drives from Texas in the late 1860s.[15] Because of the constant rail traffic, Sedalians witnessed an influx of strangers, new ideas, consumer goods, and business activity, all of which eroded the barriers that had contributed to the community's relative isolation. Sedalia supported a thriving entertainment district where Joplin and other entertainers could find steady work. Their customers were people who sought release, comfort, and diversion from the business of making a living, and their presence in these "upholstered sewers," as Arthur Marshall described the nightspots, suggests both the desire and opportunity to escape from staid Victorian ways.[16]

While these social and economic patterns could be seen in many communities, Sedalia's particular history played an important role in the emergence of ragtime. As a former slave state, Missouri was home to thousands of African Americans, and in the aftermath of civil war, hundreds of African American laborers migrated to the city from other parts of the state as well as from former Confederate states. Sedalia's founder, George R. Smith, set aside a section of the city for black settlement, and by the 1890s, about 1,500 African Americans lived and worked in Sedalia. Smith also founded the George R. Smith College for Negroes, where Joplin enrolled in music courses at the urging of friends who collaborated with him, shared favorite riffs, and performed his avant-garde compositions in local clubs, at dances, on railroad excursions, on regional tours, and in street fairs.[17] Even before Joplin's arrival, a lively community of African American musicians and entertainers played music by night and worked in the city by day. Although Joplin had formed various musical groups as an itinerant, he had a ready-made cohort in the Queen City Band in Sedalia. The community nourished Joplin's creative spirit, and he, in turn, assumed the role of teacher and mentor to younger black musicians. Ultimately, knowledge of musical notation allowed Joplin to do what many of his friends could not—commit his complicated rhythms accurately to the printed page.[18]

When we hear Joplin's and other composers' ragtime music today, we associate it with the "Gay Nineties"—the happy-go-lucky music of a by-gone simpler time. But that view and the name "Gay Nineties" do not accurately reflect what was going on in places such as Sedalia at the turn of the century. The very economic growth and transportation networks that contributed to Sedalia's emergence as a regional center of social, cultural, and business activity also drew Sedalians into new forms of work organization and into national markets that were both alien and fragile. Working people—on the shop floor, in mines, and in offices—experienced palpable and disturbing changes in their everyday lives. Craftsmen could not keep pace with factories mass producing goods more quickly and less expensively. People working in Sedalia's railroad shops and factories faced strict time discipline and long hours and often were squeezed by the intense competition among the captains of industry, who cut wages in the hope of gaining the edge on their economic rivals. Working men and women lived precariously from one payday to the next, ever uncertain if the twelve-hour workdays would provide subsistence. Among Missouri's coal miners, for example, only one out of every ten found that they could support a family free of debt. Labor militancy ensued. The Strike of 1877, which threatened to explode into a general strike in St. Louis, was but the first in a series of post–Civil War upheavals. Railroad workers in and around Sedalia defied Jay Gould in 1885 and 1886, "defending a way of life," as Michael Cassity has suggested. In 1894, Coxey's Army of unemployed men traveled through Missouri en route to the nation's capital and commandeered local trains to carry them on their way.

While some workers may have resolved, like Upton Sinclair's fictional Jurgis Rudkus, to "work harder," for many others, the motto of the eight-hour day movement—"eight hours for work, eight hours for sleep, and eight hours for what we will"—made more sense.[19]

Perhaps most important of all, working men and women were increasingly frustrated by what they saw as a failed social system. That is, according to the mantra of the nineteenth century, hard work and self-control were supposed to bring success and happiness. But increasingly they did not. In short, the cultural ideals were not fulfilled by actual experience—and anger, militancy, and a desire to rewrite the social contract followed.

By the 1890s, however, it was not just wage laborers who were concerned. The situation in the American countryside was not much better, as the intensity of the Populist movement in the early 1890s eloquently testifies. Frustrated with their dependence on railroads, distant markets, speculation on their commodities, and agricultural processors, with an inflexible monetary system and with serious inequities in their society, farmers who supported the People's Party voiced their desire for political and economic change. Their plaint, like that of many other working people in the so-called Gay Nineties, contained anger over the fact that the laboring classes in an industrializing economy seemed unable to reap just rewards for their hard work.[20]

When the stock market crashed in 1893, followed by several years of sustained economic depression, the middle class felt the pinch, too.[21] Rising taxes and the loss of homes led many to take part in "taxpayer revolts." Widespread unemployment affected the life chances of many in the middle class—indeed, the promise of a better life for one's children was no longer guaranteed, as families saw the next generation slip from the ranks of the middle class.[22] In Sedalia, Charles, Pearl, and Joseph Minter were forced to close the doors of their dry-goods business in January of 1893. A month later, the Osborns quit the grocery business because of hard times. J. B. Murphy followed them into bankruptcy, and others, still operating in Sedalia's downtown business district, sold their wares at drastically reduced prices in the hope of riding out the economic storm. A small army of vagrants wandered the streets in the vain search for work—there were too many men for the available jobs and too many men to jail for vagrancy. Even the *Sedalia Bazoo*, the newspaper that reported one financial disaster after another, suspended publication in August. In its last issue, the *Bazoo* reported: "Hard times seem to have struck railroad work in earnest, judging from cuts being made in wages and employees."[23] In Sedalia, as in communities large and small across the United States, it was no longer a given that hard work and thrift would bring comfort. The crisis of the 1890s cast serious doubt on Americans' core beliefs.

It was in this context that ragtime gained a hearing among white Americans. For African Americans, the music contained familiar, complex rhythms and harmonies, varieties of which they had heard in many parts of the South. Alexander Ford, one of Joplin's contemporaries in Texarkana, claimed that Joplin had been playing some of the strains of "Maple Leaf Rag" way back in the 1880s, long before he wrote it down.[24] But African Americans alone, though ragtime's initial creators, did not propel this music into the national limelight. The men and women who first heard and liked ragtime music in the 1890s were those who frequented brothels and nightspots such as Sedalia's Maple Leaf Club, where the working class of both races unwound after excruciatingly long days of work. They would have been the ones who knew Joplin as "The Entertainer." But it was the white middle class that bought the sheet music, ten-cents-on-the-dollar pianos, and, later, player pianos, piano rolls, and recordings that made the entertainment industry into a big business. In Sedalia, respectable families commissioned black bands to play for their dances and practiced cakewalk moves to the sound of ragtime music.[25] To them, ragtime was *not* familiar. It was both exotic and a tad scandalous. When Scott Joplin was interviewed in 1913 by Lester Walton of the *New York Age*, he insisted: "There has been ragtime music in America ever since the Negro race has been here, but the white people took no notice of it until about twenty years ago."[26] That would have been 1893, when the economic depression sent hundreds of thousands of white Americans into unemployment lines and bankruptcy courts, and toward a quest for a more meaningful culture.

In this artistic and cultural context, white Americans first heard what would become ragtime music, and it spoke to them with profound power. The syncopated rhythm defied the usual order and regularity of three-quarter-time waltzes and dreamy ballads and the four-four time of marches and hymns. The steady beat of the left hand echoed the rhythm of factory, machine, and train, but the unexpected accents by the right hand, as well as the fast-paced melodies, announced a refusal to be contained by that steadiness. Ragtime's rhythmic exuberance, as performed by African American itinerants in places such as Chicago and in tenderloin districts of other American cities, invited the casting off of restraint; joy, uninhibited emotion, and lively dancing seemed natural. Ragtime songs contained lyrics that told of an unfamiliar life beyond the boundaries of Victorian respectability—a world where sheer love of fun and sensuality were seductively accessible.

When Joplin met John Stark, a white music store owner in Sedalia, his musical compositions became grist for Stark's publishing mill and helped the businessman take advantage of both economies of scale and the public's demand for hot music. Stark mass-produced sheet music and sold it for ten cents a copy to a public strapped for cash in the midst of the 1890s depression. After Joplin's smash hit of 1899, "Maple Leaf Rag," Stark moved his family and business to St. Louis, where he could tap into a much larger market. He employed cutting-edge consumer-oriented strategies—making a celebrity of Joplin, brand naming, inspiring desire for the latest hit, and advertising directly to consumers. Stark audaciously proclaimed Joplin the "King of Ragtime" after the initial, experimental short-run of "Maple Leaf Rag" had sold out, a title that stuck almost immediately. By the 1910s, Stark would print on the back page of "Maple Leaf Rag" an advertisement for "Kismet Rag": "It is needless to say anything of the writer of 'Maple Leaf,' 'Cascades,' 'Sunflower,' or 'Entertainer.' You know him." Stark also printed excerpts from Joplin compositions as advertisements on copies of other pieces to tantalize buyers to "Try This on Your Piano." And he took advantage of mass circulation periodicals like *Ragtime Review* to advertise his wares.[27]

Stark's promotion of Joplin had limits, of course, because of the oppressive racial climate in the United States. Stark touted Joplin's rags as a hybrid of classical and black elements, but he balked at the composer's efforts to produce serious pieces such as the *Ragtime Ballet* in 1902, and his two operas—*A Guest of Honor* (1903) and *Treemonisha* (1911). He also refused to include photographs of Joplin or references to the African American origins of ragtime in his local ads—pushing instead the benefits of wholesome family entertainment made possible by a piano in the parlor. Although not as blatantly racist as Carl Hoffman, who published Joplin's "Original Rag" in 1899 with an insulting image of a rag picker to illustrate the cover, Stark— and, for that matter, other publishing houses of the day—frequently made use of stereotyped caricatures of African Americans to elicit a sense of superiority in white consumers and to permit the socially forbidden participation in the lascivious, expressive, and illicit ways associated with black life.

African American music in this sense authorized white desire. Changes brought on by industrialization and the ensuing depression had created tensions between the sexes that the emerging culture in general, and ragtime in particular, were called upon to heal. In 1894, a new newspaper appeared in Sedalia. *Rosa Pearle's Paper* contained commentary that reveals this aspect of the cultural revolution. In one of the first issues, a column on "The Woman of To-Day" characterized her as intelligent, independent, conscious of style, and no longer bound to traditions of the past. It reflected a new reality in Sedalia as more women had to find employment outside of the home in order to supplement their husband's wages and as more young women pursued educational opportunities that could lead to economic independence from men. The same issue also explored what it meant to be "up-do-date" in Sedalia in 1894. The article contained two lists of questions, one that might have been asked in the past and one that must be asked today. While the "out-of-date" reader was asked, "What does your wife say to your going to the theatre?" and "Does your wife approve of your smoking?" the "up-to-date" reader had to consider, "What do you say to your daughters going to the theatre?" and "Do you approve of your wife smoking?"[28]

Changed relationships between men and women, including more open sexual expression, were also bound up in ragtime music. Sydney Brown's lyrics for "Maple Leaf Rag," for example, tell the story of a poor man from Virginia who was transformed by the music:

> I dropp'd into de swellest ball, The great exclusive it,
> But my face was dead agin me and my trousers didn't fit.
> But when Maple Leaf was started my timidity departed.
> I lost my trepidation, you could taste de admiration.
>
> Go 'way man I can hypnotize dis nation,
> Shake de earth's foundation wid de Maple Leaf Rag!
>
> De men were struck wid jealousy. De razors 'gan to flash.
> But de ladies gathered 'round me for I'd sholy made a mash.
> De finest belle she sent a boy to call a coach and four.
> We road around a season till we both were lost to reason
>
> Go 'way man I can hypnotize dis nation,
> Shake de earth's foundation wid de Maple Leaf Rag!

Other popular ragtime songs from the period were even more direct. "Hello, Ma Baby!" (1899), for example, exclaimed:

Hello, mah Baby!
Hello, mah Honey!
Hello, mah Ragtime Gal!
Send me a kiss by wire;
Baby, my heart's on fire.
If you refuse me, Honey you'll lose me.
Then you'll be left alone.
So, Baby, telephone and tell me I'm your own.

in the saga of "Louie" and "Flossie" in 1904 in the famous "Meet Me in St. Louie, Louie"—Flossie's note to her husband explained her absence from the flat by having gone to the Louisiana Purchase Exposition.

Don't tell me the lights are shining anywhere but there.
We will dance the Hoochie Coochie
I will be your Tootsie-Wootsie
If you meet me in St. Louie, Louie
Meet me at the Fair!

Such songs as these offered broad hints about the need to cut through the cloying respectability of Victorian courtship and marriage. Ragtime shook the foundations of propriety, setting hearts on fire and prompting passionate, unchaperoned coach rides and hootchy-kootchy dancing.

Other forms of popular entertainment registered the change in attitude toward sexuality. In 1892, for example, a production of *The Spider and the Fly*, which, as the name suggests, traded in the seduction and destruction of innocent women, was roundly condemned as immoral. Sedalians were advised by local newspaper editors to avoid the show. A mere seven years later, the same show was advertised as "a gorgeous spectacular extravaganza," complete with a "beautiful array of forty pretty girls . . . [opera], comedy, and vaudeville." Amazingly, the show, once denounced by Sedalia's leaders, was scheduled to appear on a Sunday afternoon and evening.[29] At roughly the same time, local young people began sitting out a few dances in order to embrace without having to "gallop a mile or two for a hug or two."[30] The appearance of *Rosa Pearle's Paper* in 1894 attests to the fact that even a seemingly sleepy town such as Sedalia needed a new moral compass.

For white fans of ragtime and participants in the cultural revolution, African American music, the carnivalesque world of places such as Coney Island, and popular shows, with their hints of naughty behavior—all made possible by a rapidly expanding entertainment industry—helped reconcile the tensions between the work ethic and modern social and economic conditions. In important ways, work became a means to another end—a world of expressiveness, fun, and leisure available through consuming.[31] While labor activists and social movements did not cease their efforts to radically reorganize American social life, these cultural developments made modern working conditions at least a bit more palatable.

American Culture and the Color Line

By the 1910s much of the controversy surrounding ragtime had given way to a general embrace of it as quintessentially American music. In 1913 Natalie Curtis observed, "Our children dance, our people sing, even our soldiers march to 'ragtime,' which is fast becoming a national 'Pied Piper' to whose rhythm the whole country moves." Hiram K. Moderwell touted ragtime as "American exactly as skyscrapers are American" in the pages of the *New Republic*, to which one reader, A. Walter Kramer, responded, "Ragtime is American and no one can prove that it is not. It expresses something that we feel."[32] While one could still find grumpy dismissals of the music as immoral and lowbrow, ragtime by and large was accepted as America's most popular music. Moreover, in these years, Americans considered it common knowledge that the music had originated with American Negroes. Music dictionaries as well as popular commentaries identified it as a distinct contribution made by African Americans to the nation's culture.[33] Thus, insofar as the popular music industry was built on the foundation of ragtime, African American musical motifs, creativity, and performance styles played key roles in the cultural transition from Victorian culture to consumerism.

Such a straightforward connection, however, obscures a complicated relationship between black creativity and cultural change. Black composers and performers surely did seek popularity and acceptance, but not all intended to create popular music, with all that this term connoted. Joplin nurtured serious aspirations to write opera and ballet. While John Stark eagerly published his two-steps, marches, waltzes, and slow drags, he drew the line at Joplin's more ambitious works. Will Marion Cook, Bob Cole, J. Rosamond Johnson, Bert Williams, and James Reese Europe, who enjoyed success as composers and/or performers, had studied music at places such as the Oberlin Conservatory, the New England Conservatory, and the National Conservatory of Music or had attended or graduated from respected institutions of higher learning. They, too, had reason to hope for recognition as cultivated gentlemen composers and professional musicians whose works made art from the raw materials of African American culture. But they are not remembered for serious art music. Instead, when they are remembered at all, it is for their work for the musical comedy stage or, in the case of Europe, as the man who provided the best musical accompaniment for Irene and Vernon Castle's pathbreaking dances.[34]

The confinement of these African American musicians to popular performance venues had everything to do with the color line, even though the demand for cakewalk music and "coon songs" created opportunities for African Americans as full-time professional entertainers. They performed in vaudeville and in musical comedies. They placed their compositions with some of the leading publishers of popular sheet music on Tin Pan Alley in New York—the hub of the burgeoning popular music industry. Indeed, Ernest Hogan, who called himself the "Unbleached American," wrote one of the most popular coon songs of the 1890s—"All Coons Look Alike to Me." Although shortly before his untimely death in 1909 he purportedly told Lester Walton of the *New York Age* that he deeply regretted having written the song, Hogan recognized that it had enabled him to develop his professional career.[35]

The coon song craze of the 1890s traded in the worst of racial stereotyping. Sloth, violence, lust, and irresponsibility, these songs insisted, characterized the American Negro. While prejudice against African Americans and the belief in the fundamental inferiority of the race long predated this popular cultural phenomenon, the growing influence of popular music in the national marketplace helped standardize the stereotypical profile of black Americans. The widespread acceptance of race-based difference stiffened the determination to prevent the social mixing of white and black in the United States. The "strange career of Jim Crow" took off in the very decades when black or black-inspired music swept the nation.[36]

The danger posed by petty theft, sexual promiscuity, and laziness brought swift, harsh punishment at the hands of both the lynch mob and the legal system. Just when Joplin's "Maple Leaf Rag" was gaining a national audience, the Maple Leaf Club, a black social organization in Sedalia, drew increasing attention from the police force. It was held responsible for "the deterioration of the morals" on Main Street and was identified with the "bawdy element" in town. The Maple Leaf Club was shut down, but white-owned nightspots, serving up the same forms of diversion, remained open.[37] In Missouri, like many other states in the union, policing the color line took more dramatic forms than closing down a dancehall. The segregation of public schools began legally and in earnest in 1889 with a law passed by the legislature and enforced rigorously. In Sedalia the proposed location for the school for African American children was so far from the black neighborhood that it effectively denied many of those children access to formal education. African Americans faced lynch mobs increasingly after 1889—indeed, the rise in violence against black Missourians became so alarming that in 1892 prominent African Americans in St. Louis, including former U.S. minister to Liberia J. Milton Turner, called for a national day of "humiliation, fasting and prayer," hoping to shame their countrymen into renouncing such crime. Black Sedalians organized the Grand United Brethren of Equal Rights and Justice in 1895 "to prevent so far as possible the hanging (lynching) of negroes [sic]." Conditions for African Americans in Missouri continued to deteriorate in the early twentieth century, a period in which the white population increased by 6.5 percent, while the African American population declined by 2.3 percent, due mostly to unhealthful neighborhoods, dangerous occupations, and migration away from the state.[38]

The alleged behavior for which African Americans were punished bore a striking resemblance to the "freedom" for which fans of popular music longed and that protesters against the industrial order acted out. Greater familiarity between the sexes, implied in songs such as "Hello Ma Baby" and "Maple Leaf Rag", provided liberation from Victorian decorum, but it brought police action against the "bawdy element" in places such as the Maple Leaf Club. The fanciful images of blacks avoiding work on sheet music covers like the one for "A Tennessee Tantalizer" appealed to laboring people struggling to limit the working day to eight hours, but it also justified paying African Americans lower wages, offering them fewer educational opportunities, and forcing appearances in court for vagrancy.[39] Even the resort to knives and guns, while actionable if undertaken by African Americans, was lionized when the actor was a westerner meting out swift "justice," a labor activist defending a way of life, or the modern detective about whom hundreds of dime novels were written.

Eventually both African Americans and white commentators articulated the way that popular music traded in stereotype to advance (white) cultural liberation. In his autobiography, James Weldon Johnson described how whites used their perceptions of African Americans to serve their own ends: "On occasion, I have been amazed and amused watching white people dancing to a Negro band in a Harlem cabaret; attempting to throw off the crusts and layers of inhibitions laid on by sophisticated civilization; striving to yield to the feel and experience of abandon; seeking to recapture a taste of primitive joy in life and living; trying to work their way back into that jungle which was the original Garden of Eden; in a word, doing their best to pass for colored."[40] Similarly, Isaac Goldberg identified the centrality of African Americans' symbolic character in the rise and popularity of Tin Pan Alley: "The Negro is the symbol of our uninhibited expression, of our uninhibited action. He is our catharsis. He is the disguise behind which we may, for a releasing moment, rejoin that part of ourselves which we have sacrificed to civilization."[41]

By the 1910s, music publishers eagerly published songs and compositions by African American musicians, but as Lester Walton reported in the *New York Age*, they discouraged black musicians from spending time in their offices, complaining that having too many "spades" around hurt business.[42] In other words, the popular music industry in America rose from the ashes of Victorian culture *and* from the lynch mob's flames. It played a major role in rewriting the cultural rules for modern America *and* in maintaining the color line.

To appreciate the full contribution of African Americans to the modern music industry, however, it is imperative to peel back one more layer. Popular music helped legitimate white privilege, but for African Americans, the burgeoning industries devoted to popular entertainment provided opportunities to publish original compositions. Ernest Hogan's unfortunately titled "All Coons Look Alike to Me" set the presses rolling for hundreds of other writers of coon songs in the 1890s. Hogan enlisted talented lyricists to contribute to a production called *Rufus Rastus* in 1905, and as his circle of contacts widened, he recommended other black performers—notably Bert Williams and George Walker—for stage work. Between 1900 and 1910, Bob Cole and J. Rosamond Johnson wrote more than 150 songs, many of which were picked up and promoted by white vaudeville performers. Among their most well-known songs were "Under the Bamboo Tree" and "The Congo Love Song," but dozens of others enjoyed popularity in the early years of the twentieth century. Another unsung pioneer of popular music, Tom Turpin, not only is credited with publishing the first recognizable ragtime composition, "The Harlem Rag," in 1896, but also with mentoring and encouraging other African American musicians. A number of black performers—today, largely forgotten—rode the crest of this wave of interest in black comedy and performance style. They organized performance troupes and found receptive audiences in small towns and large cities across the nation. Like Joplin, many of them hit the vaudeville circuit and played to racially segregated audiences. Bert Williams and George Walker formed one of the most successful musical comedy teams of the era, and after Walker's death in 1911, Williams joined Florenz Ziegfeld's famous Follies. Aida Overton Walker introduced cakewalk dancing in the United States and in Europe. Hogan toured the United States with the Smart Set Company and Europe with a group called the Tennessee Students.[43]

These musicians and performers were clearly not on the margins of the musical world but rather were central to the sounds, motifs, rhythms, and melodies that formed the core products of the industry. Whether they knew it or not, audiences who turned out for performances by popular singers such as May Irwin heard music and lyrics that sprang from African American artistic genius. Indeed, an effort by Lester Walton to form a black-owned music publishing house in the late 1910s failed because African American musicians and songwriters enjoyed greater exposure by selling their work to well-established white publishers.[44]

Playing to biracial audiences posed a challenge, trying to please those on the main floor as well as those in the balcony. But embedded in the creative works of these pioneering musicians and performers were jokes and critical commentary that spoke to the gallery in ways not understood by most whites in the audience. The fact that performers such as Bert Williams used burnt cork meant that in a wily way, African American performers were poking fun at white people trying to perform blackness. While whites in the crowd howled at their antics, the black performers themselves were critiquing the society that routinely denied people of color their rights as citizens. Joplin's *A Guest of Honor* was intended more earnestly as a musical celebration of Booker T. Washington's dinner with Theodore Roosevelt at the White House, an event lambasted in many parts of the country. Others, in the guise of slapstick comedy, gave voice to political fantasy. One of Joplin's friends in St. Louis, Joe Jordan, wrote "Oh, Say Wouldn't It Be a Dream" for Ernest Hogan's *Rufus Rastus* show:

If I could blow a horn and lead a circus band,
Say Wouldn't it be a dream,
If coons could only rule this great United Land,
Say wouldn't it be a dream.
We'd make Bert Williams President and Walker would be Vice,
Joe Walcott for the Senate, where he'd cut a lot of ice;
Affairs of state they'd settle with a pair of poker dice;
Oh, say wouldn't it be a dream.

Other shows such as Williams and Walker's *In Dahomey* and Bert Williams's *Mr. Lode of Koal* drew large audiences who reveled in the ragtime songs that accompanied many of the acts but who probably missed the engagement with serious political issues of the day such as imperialism, political corruption, and moral reform.[45]

White artists and composers caught on to and capitalized on the public craving for ragtime music and dance, and over the first couple of decades of the twentieth century, they churned out popular tunes and largely took credit for the genre. For more than fifty years after his death in 1917, Scott Joplin was erased from the memory banks of most Americans, as was Bert Williams, who in his lifetime was considered "the funniest man in America." With Irving Berlin and Louis Hirsch now writing America's favorite rags, ragtime itself was "whitened."[46] But by then, the cultural transition was more or less complete.

The critics whose diatribes opened this chapter recognized the radical potential of this music—its contribution to reorienting American culture in ways that would release hard-pressed men and women from demands that social conditions prevented them from meeting. But from our vantage a century later, it is also painfully clear that the liberation of Americans from Victorian individualism came at the expense of the lives and memories of the men and women who created it. Black creativity was crucial to the emergence of the popular music industry in the twentieth century, but that contribution was obscured because the talents and achievements of African American composers, songwriters, and performers contradicted the racial stereotyping on which the appeal of popular music rested. The birth of the modern music industry mirrored the tragedy captured in *Birth of a Nation*. The United States, struggling to remake itself at the dawn of the modern era, found inspiration for national unity and democracy in the oppression of African Americans on whose labor and resilience they had made their fortunes.

NOTES

1. "Musical Impurity," *Etude* 18 (January 1900): 16.

2. "Our Musical Condition," *Negro Music Journal* 1 (March 1903): 138.

3. "Dr. Damrosch Hits Ragtime," *Musical America* 18 (July 26, 1913): 7.

4. For other examples of opposition to ragtime, see H. E. Greene, "A Few Questions Answered," *Etude* 23 (June 1905): 243; "President Bars Ragtime," *New York Age*,

February 6, 1908, 10, col. 3; "Ragtime Causing Mental Ailments," *Musical America* 18 (July 15, 1913): 28; and C. Crozat, "Rag-Time," *Etude* 17 (August 1899): 256.

5. Burton W. Peretti, "Emerging from America's Underside: The Black Musician from Ragtime to Jazz," in *America's Musical Pulse: Popular Music in Twentieth-Century Society*, ed. Kenneth J. Bindas (Westport, Conn.: Praeger, 1992), 63–72; and Jeffrey Melnick, *A Right to Sing the Blues: African Americans, Jews, and American Popular Song* (Cambridge: Harvard University Press, 1999), 26–28.

6. Melnick, *A Right to Sing the Blues*; Craig Roell, "The Development of Tin Pan Alley," in Bindas, *America's Musical Pulse*, 113–21; and John Higham, "The Reorientation of American Culture in the 1890s," in *Writing American History* (Bloomington: Indiana University Press, 1972).

7. Susan Curtis, *Dancing to a Black Man's Tune: A Life of Scott Joplin* (Columbia: University of Missouri Press, 1994), 45–67. See also Shelley Fisher Fishkin, "Interrogating 'Whiteness,' Complicating 'Blackness': Remapping American Culture," *American Quarterly* 47 (September 1995): 455.

8. James Weldon Johnson, introduction, *The Second Book of Negro Spirituals* (New York: Viking Press, 1926), 16–17; and Eric Lott, *Love and Theft: Blackface Minstrelsy and the American Working Class* (New York: Oxford University Press, 1993).

9. In many respects, this argument relies on reasoning similar to that employed by Michael Rogin on the underlying psychological causes of Indian removal in the 1830s and by Paul Boyer and Stephen Nissenbaum in explaining the witchcraft hysteria in Salem, Massachusetts, in 1692. See Rogin, *Fathers and Children: Andrew Jackson and the Subjugation of the American Indian* (New York: Knopf, 1975); and Boyer and Nissenbaum, *Salem Possessed: The Social Origins of Witchcraft* (Cambridge: Harvard University Press, 1978).

10. John F. Kasson, *Houdini, Tarzan, and the Perfect Man: The White Male Body and the Challenge of Modernity in America* (New York: Hill & Wang, 2001).

11. Davarian Baldwin, *Chicago's New Negroes: Modernity, the Great Migration, and Black Urban Life* (Chapel Hill: University of North Carolina Press, 2007); and Adam Green, *Selling the Race: Culture, Community, and Black Chicago, 1940–1955* (Chicago: University of Chicago Press, 2007)

12. Beginning with Rudi Blesh and Harriet Janis, *They All Played Ragtime: The True Story of an American Music* (New York: Knopf, 1950), African American composers have appeared as key creators of ragtime music. See also Curtis, *Dancing to a Black Man's Tune*; and Peretti, "Emerging from America's Underside." On consumer culture, see Richard Wightman Fox and T. J. Jackson Lears, *The Culture of Consumption: Critical Essays in American History, 1880–1980* (New York: Pantheon Books, 1983); Gregory W. Bush, *Lord of Attention: Gerald Stanley Lee and the Crowd Metaphor in Industrializing America* (Amherst: University of Massachusetts Press, 1991); Susan Curtis, *A Consuming Faith: The Social Gospel and Modern American Culture* (Columbia: University of Missouri Press, 2001); and Daniel Horowitz, *The Morality of Spending: Attitudes toward the Consumer Society in America, 1875–1940* (Baltimore: Johns Hopkins University Press, 1985).

13. The Fourteenth Amendment was originally conceived as a constitutional guarantee of equal protection under the law and the right to due process. By the 1880s, however, it was used as a way to protect corporations, defining corporate entities as "persons." See William L. Richter, *The Army in Texas during Reconstruction* (College Station: Texas A & M University Press, 1987), 159–61; and James M. Smallwood, *Time of Hope, Time of Despair: Black Texans During Reconstruction* (Port Washington, N.Y.: Kennikat Press, 1981), 64.

14. For details of Joplin's biography, see Curtis, *Dancing to a Black Man's Tune*; Edward Berlin, *The King of Ragtime: Scott Joplin and His Era* (New York: Oxford University Press, 1994); and Rudi Blesh and Harriet Janis, *They All Played Ragtime* (New York: Oak Publications, 1971). For information about *A Picture of Her Face* and *Please Say You Will*, see Vera Brodsky Lawrence, ed., *The Collected Works of Scott Joplin* (New York: New York Public Library, 1971). Lawrence's work is an invaluable source for the sheet music itself and for the covers that illustrated Joplin's rags.

15. This brief sketch of Sedalia's history and development relies mostly on Michael Cassity, *Defending a Way of Life: An American Community in the Nineteenth Century* (Albany: State University of New York Press, 1989), 36–50; and to a much lesser degree on Mark A. McGruder, *History of Pettis County Missouri* (Topeka: Historical Publishing Co., 1919).

16. For Marshall's colorful phrase, see Curtis, *Dancing to a Black Man's Tune*, 74.

17. Lawrence, *Collected Works of Scott Joplin*, 2:273–83; and "Did You Know Ragtime Was Born in Sedalia?" *Sedalia Democrat*, June 29, 1947, 7, col. 3.

18. Edward A. Berlin, a musicologist and one of the foremost scholars of ragtime, has shown convincingly that some of the printed works associated with ragtime did not bear the signature marks of syncopation, but when compared to transcriptions of performances they must be considered part of the larger ragtime era. See Berlin, *Ragtime: A Musical and Cultural History* (Berkeley: University of California Press, 1980), 23.

19. The scholarship on the social and economic impact of industrialization is enormous. For a good overarching summary of the dramatic upheavals of the late nineteenth century, see Nell Irvin Painter, *Standing at Armageddon: The United States, 1877–1919* (New York: Norton, 1987). For an important study that traces the changing discourse on the meaning of work in the period, see Daniel Rodgers, *The Work Ethic in Industrial America, 1850–1920* (Chicago: University of Chicago Press, 1974). And for a first-rate example of how the changes could lead to conflict between the classes over the public spaces devoted to leisure, see Roy Rosenzweig, *Eight Hours or What We Will: Workers and Leisure in an Industrial City, 1870–1920* (New York: Cambridge University Press, 1983). The story of Pettis County railroad employees during the strikes of 1885 and 1886 is eloquently told in Cassity, *Defending a Way of Life*; and other protests against modernization by Missourians are discussed in David P. Thelen, *Paths of Resistance: Tradition and Dignity in Industrializing Missouri* (New York: Oxford University Press, 1986). The reference to the Missouri miners and the march of Coxey's Army through Missouri comes from Susan

Curtis Mernitz, "Church, Class, and Community: The Impact of Industrialization on Lexington, Missouri, 1870–1900" (M.A. thesis, University of Missouri, 1981).

20. For discussions of the anger and frustration underlying the populist movement of the 1890s, see Bruce Palmer, *"Man Over Money": The Southern Populist Critique of American Capitalism* (Chapel Hill: University of North Carolina Press, 1980); and Lawrence Goodwyn, *Democratic Promise: The Populist Movement in America* (New York: Oxford University Press, 1976).

21. There is, to my knowledge, no book-length treatment of the depression of 1893. Some of the best evidence of its severity and significance still remains in the primary sources. It often is discussed in the context of more complicated analyses of such developments as government regulation of big business, the consolidation of big business, the "long depression" of the late nineteenth century, or the business cycle. For discussions of the depression of 1893, see David P. Thelen, *The New Citizenship: Origins of Progressivism in Wisconsin, 1885–1900* (Columbia: University of Missouri Press, 1972), 55–85; Painter, *Standing at Armageddon*, 110–40; Robert L. Heilbroner, *The Economic Transformation of America* (New York: Harcourt Brace Jovanovich, 1977), 105–25; and Carlos A. Schwantes, *Coxey's Army: An American Odyssey* (Lincoln: University of Nebraska Press, 1985), 23–33.

22. Thelen, *The New Citizenship*, 55–85; and Stephan Thernstrom, *Poverty and Progress: Social Mobility in a Nineteenth-Century City* (Cambridge: Harvard University Press, 1964).

23. "Minter Bros. Assign," *Sedalia Bazoo*, January 9, 1893, 4, col. 3. Less than a week earlier, the Minters had advertised a "January Clearance Sale" in the *Sedalia Democrat*. "WE NEED MONEY!" their ad had proclaimed, but apparently, cash and solvency were not forthcoming. See their advertisement in the *Sedalia Democrat*, January 4, 1893, 1, col. 2–3. "Will Leave the City," *Sedalia Democrat*, February 8, 1893, 2, col. 4. For other failures, see "Sold at Auction," *Sedalia Bazoo*, February 2, 1893, 4, col. 5; and "A Surprising Failure," *Sedalia Bazoo*, May, 23, 1893, 3, col. 2. Frank B. Meyer advertised goods he acquired from J. B. Murphy in *Sedalia Democrat*, June 12, 1893, 4, col. 2–3; and he announced his summer sale in the *Sedalia Democrat*, July 20, 1893, 4, col. 2–4. In the same July issue of the *Sedalia Democrat*, the following companies also announced summer sales: Holcomb's "Great Discount Sale," 2, col. 5–7; Kraesel's "Grand Clearing Sale," 3, col. 4–6; St. Louis Clothing Company "Mid-Summer Clearing Out Sale," 3, col. 2–7; and notice that all insurance policies whose premiums had not been paid by July 20 would be considered "null and void," 3, col. 7. The August 10, 1893, edition of the *Sedalia Bazoo* was drastically reduced, and the reduction was explained on the editorial page as a cost-saving measure. The next day's edition was its last until November 20, 1893. The comment about railroad conditions appears on page 4, column 1 of the August 11, 1893, edition.

24. Ford is cited in James Haskins and Kathleen Benson, *Scott Joplin* (Garden City, N.Y.: Doubleday, 1978), 59–60.

25. Curtis, *Dancing to a Black Man's Tune*, 68–97.

26. "Theatrical Comment," *New York Age*, April 3, 1913, 6, col. 1–2.

27. For a more detailed discussion of the relationship between Stark and Joplin, see Curtis, *Dancing to a Black Man's Tune*, 98–128. Stark's dubbing Joplin as the "King of Ragtime Writers" was echoed by Val A. Reis Music Co. on a 1902 composition, "Weeping Willow," and by Victor Kremer Co.'s printing of "Palm Leaf Rag" of the same year. See also "The King of Rag-Time Composers is Scott Joplin, a Colored St. Louisan," *St. Louis Globe-Democrat*, June 7, 1902, Sporting Section, 5, col. 1–3; and "Scott Joplin a King," *Sedalia Times*, June 13, 1903, 1, col. 1–2.

28. "The Woman of To-Day," *Rosa Pearle's Paper*, June 16, 1894, 4, col. 3; "Questions: Out-of-Date and Up-to-Date," *Rose Pearle's Paper*, June 16, 1894, 6, col. 1.

29. Compare the notices for *The Spider and the Fly* in these two newspapers: *Sedalia Bazoo*, December 26, 1892, 2, col. 2; and *Sedalia Sentinel*, November 29, 1899, 4, col. 4.

30. "Society," *Sedalia Evening Sentinel*, June 9, 1899, 5. col. 2–4.

31. John Higham's essay, "The Reorientation of American Culture in the 1890s," in *Writing American History* (Bloomington: Indiana University Press, 1972) was an early effort to sort out the shift away from Victorian culture at the end of the nineteenth century. For other treatments, see John F. Kasson, *Amusing the Million: Coney Island at the Turn of the Century* (New York: Hill & Wang, 1978); Curtis, *Dancing to a Black Man's Tune*, 56–97; and Alan Trachtenberg, *The Incorporation of America: Culture and Society in the Gilded Age* (New York: Hill & Wang, 1982).

32. Natalie Curtis, "The Negro's Contribution to the Music of America: The Larger Opportunity of the Colored Man of Today," *Craftsman* 23 (March 1913): 660–69; Hiram K. Moderwell, "Ragtime," *New Republic* 4 (October 16, 1915): 284–86; and A. Walter Kramer, "Extols Ragtime Article," *New Republic* 5 (December 4, 1915): 122.

33. For examples of this view see Olin Downes, "An American Composer," *Musical Quarterly* 4 (January 1918): 28; Bessie Hanson, "Ragtime the American National Music," *Christensen's Ragtime Review* 1 (March 1915): 8; and H. E. Krehbiel, "The Distinctive Note in American Music," *Etude* 24 (March 1906): 108; and for official definitions of ragtime, see W. L. Hubbard et al., eds., *The American History and Encyclopedia of Music*, vol. 10 (New York: Irving Square, 1910); and J. A. Fuller Maitland, ed., *Grove's Dictionary of Music and Musicians* (New York: Macmillan, 1908), 4:16.

34. For a superb introduction to the many musical contributions made by Cook, Cole, Johnson, and Williams, see Thomas L. Riis, *Just before Jazz: Black Musical Theatre in New York, 1890–1915* (Washington, D.C.: Smithsonian Institution Press, 1989); and for Europe, see Reid Badger, *A Life in Ragtime: A Biography of James Reese Europe* (New York: Oxford University Press, 1995).

35. "Theatrical Comment," *New York Age*, March 30, 1911, 6, col. 1.

36. James H. Dormon, "Shaping the Popular Image of Post-Reconstruction American Blacks in the 'Coon Song' Phenomenon of the Gilded Age," *American Quarterly* 40 (December 1988): 450–71; C. Vann Woodward, *The Strange Career of Jim Crow* (New York: Oxford University Press, 1974).

37. "To Move the Tough Element," *Sedalia Evening Sentinel*, July 27, 1899, 1,

col. 3–4; "Clubs Must Close," *Sedalia Evening Democrat*, January 25, 1900, 1, col. 1; "Raided a Club," *Sedalia Evening Democrat*, January 29, 1900, 4, col. 4.

38. For a good treatment of race relations in Missouri in this period, see Lorenzo J. Greene, Gary R. Kremer, and Anthony F. Holland, *Missouri's Black Heritage* (St. Louis: Forum Press, 1980), 91–106. For the relocation of Sedalia's African American school, see "Colored People Protest," *Sedalia Capital*, August 24, 1895, 4, col. 6; and for the Grand United Brothers of Equal Rights and Justice, see "A New Order," *Sedalia Daily Capital*, June 27, 1895, 3, col. 3.

39. The cover can be viewed in Berlin, *Ragtime*, 124.

40. James Weldon Johnson, *Along This Way: The Autobiography of James Weldon Johnson* (New York: Viking Press, 1933), 328.

41. Isaac Goldberg, *Tin Pan Alley: A Chronicle of the American Popular Music Racket* (New York: John Day Company, 1930), 32.

42. "More Publishers Drawing Line," *New York Age*, February 9, 1911, 6, col. 1.

43. Riis, *Just Before Jazz*, 29–47; and Nathan B. Young, "The Father of the Jazz Age." In Gerald Early, ed., *Ain't But a Place: An Anthology of African American Writings about St. Louis* (St. Louis: Missouri Historical Society Press, 1998), 345–46.

44. For more information about Lester Walton's multifaceted role in African American performing arts, see Susan Curtis, *Colored Memories: A Biographer's Quest for the Elusive Lester A. Walton* (Columbia: University of Missouri Press, 2008).

45. Riis, *Just Before Jazz*; Karen Sotiropoulos, *Staging Race: Black Performers in Turn-of-the-Century America* (Cambridge: Harvard University Press, 2006); and Susan Curtis, *The First Black Actors on the Great White Way* (Columbia: University of Missouri Press, 1998).

46. Carl Van Vechten, "The Great American Composer: His Grandfathers Are the Present Writers of Our Popular Ragtime Songs," *Vanity Fair* 8 (April 1917): 75, 140.

Crossing Boundaries

Black Musicians Who Defied Musical Genres

THOMAS RIIS

The historian and realist philosopher Herbert Muller, in search of meaningful patterns in golden ages of past societies, once declared, "All human reality is in some sense a spiritual reality, since it perforce includes things which are not seen."[1] The reality of African American popular entertainment over the last two hundred years reflects a powerful spiritual need, a very basic human need, I would say—to be seen and heard—but this history is only barely visible and audible not at all in the mainstream historical record. Even the tip of the proverbial iceberg of African American entertainment has been deeply submerged in all but the most complete modern accounts.

The phrase "crossing boundaries" in my title is an inadequate metaphor for the near total interweaving of black musical styles by the end of the nineteenth century. The documentary tours de force of Lynn Abbott and Doug Seroff establish the essential connection among all categories of African American music of the period: folk and school trained, sacred and secular, recreational and professional.[2] By the 1890s, appreciation of African American music was widespread across race lines. White Kansans, for example, had ample opportunity to see rags performed by black piano professors years before Ben Harney put ragtime piano playing on the map in New York City in 1896.

The seven-year period before the infamous *Plessy v. Ferguson* Supreme Court ruling of May 1896 is especially interesting for what it represents. Now over a century gone, the era from 1889 to 1895 saw a culmination of developments from the immediate post-Emancipation period. The *Plessy* decision did not end all progress, but it was one factor in keeping certain developments and crossovers safely "out of sight."

The process of submerged boundary crossing and musical interweaving had begun long before even this time. I will share just one example from the pre-ragtime era. Laurence Hutton, in his fascinating book called *Curiosities of the American Stage* (1891), mentions the ballad opera character of Mungo, a comic servant redolent of commedia dell'arte in Bickerstaff and Dibdin's popular eighteenth-century London theater piece, *The Padlock* (premiered in 1768). The role was written for one John Moody, a former resident of Barbados and student of its local black dialect, but the role was eventually played by America's first great black tragedian, Ira Aldridge, world renowned for his portrayals of Shakespeare's Othello opposite Edmund Kean's Iago in the 1820s and 1830s.

Aldridge was a great boundary crosser, a world traveler, renowned wherever legitimate drama was played, and much more successful abroad than at home during slavery days in America. But what intrigues me most about the role of Mungo is the actual text he sings. It suggests more crossovers than we musicologists have yet been able to imagine:

Dear heart, what a terrible life I am led!
A dog has a better that's sheltered and fed.
    Night and day 'tis the same;
    My pain is deir game;
Me wish to de Lord me was dead!
    Whate'er's to be done
    Poor black must run
    Mungo here, Mungo dere,
    Mungo everywhere;
    Above and below,
    Sirrah, come; sirrah, go;
    Do so, and do so.
    Oh! Oh!
Me wish to de Lord me was dead![3]

If these lines sound familiar, you may recall similar sentiments, almost verbatim, from the singing mouth of Mozart and Da Ponte's servant character Leporello in the opera *Don Giovanni* (1791), "Notte, giorno, faticar," and again in the even more ubiquitous "Largo al factotum" patter aria ("Figaro, Figaro, Figaro . . .") in Rossini's *Barber of Seville* (1816). The span of years between the creation of Mungo and the death of Ira Aldridge in 1867 is only one year shy of a century. Eighty-two years later and we have Bugs Bunny's over-the-top classical allusion—still familiar to children of all ages—in the 1949 cartoon *Long-Haired Hare*. The same Rossini aria. Talk about crossing boundaries and defying genres!

Figure 6.1. Fisk Jubilee Singers, ca. 1880. The publications of Fisk University's world-traveling Jubilee Singers emphasized the dignity of African American musicians and their rapid accomplishments immediately after the end of slavery. This classic portrait conveys the nobility and grace of the group and stands in sharp contrast to contemporary depictions of blackface minstrels. From J. B. T. Marsh, The Story of the Jubilee Singers with Their Songs *(Boston: Houghton, 1880), frontispiece.*

But let us get down to cases in the later nineteenth century. During 1889 and 1890, heroic touring singing companies, without blackface, had succeeded the original singing students of Fisk University in great numbers. Jubilee singing by 1900 had been carried to every humanly occupied continent on the globe. So-called authentic minstrelsy, a revitalized vaudevillian product, often managed by black entrepreneurs and using many vernacular elements, had been spread widely and played to black audiences in black-managed and black-owned theaters. Women, as never before, were welcomed as singers, dancers, actors, and comedians on vaudeville, burlesque, and minstrel show stages.[4]

The most readily available avenue for an African American man to enter show business after the American Civil War was the minstrel show, a genre developed in the 1820s and standardized by the 1840s by white American males, urban northerners trained in English circuses and at popular fair amusements. Some claimed to have—though this is sometimes disputed— actual knowledge of slave entertainments. They certainly recognized an effective vehicle when they found it, and the formalized three-part minstrel show dominated the American comic stage for fifty years at least, until the 1890s, and has never faded completely from the scene despite high levels of opprobrium aimed at it from all directions since the 1940s.

Though sometimes retaining the lampblack or burnt cork facial makeup and grotesque physical antics, "authentic" minstrelsy of this period was concerned with other theatrical goals besides racial parody, masked entertainments of all kinds being susceptible to subversion by clever players throughout most of recorded history. We know something of black entertainment in its amazing variety from the over 150 actively publishing newspapers aimed at African American readers during the 1890s.[5] These papers were mainly weeklies, and the one most attentive to music and entertainment came, not surprisingly, out of the Midwest, the *Indianapolis Freeman*. "From its inception," the *Freeman* was intended to be "a National Illustrated Colored Newspaper," offering a "complete review of the doings of the colored people everywhere." To fulfill this grand ambition, the paper's editors deputized a vast array of correspondents, solicited subscriptions far and wide, and distributed their editions in "safe zones"—barber shops, pool halls, and other black business establishments—in cities large and small, North and South, sometimes at great personal risk to individuals in more isolated and racist enclaves.

Against this background, consider a quotation from a memoir written by career showman Tom Fletcher, whose life demonstrates the opportunities for crossing genre boundaries. Fletcher was born in 1872 and died in 1954 at the age of eighty-two, having just completed his autobiography, entitled, "One Hundred Years of the Negro in Show Business," close to the time of his death. Fortunately for our purposes, Fletcher lived during some of the most transformative years of American political, social, and entertainment history. He also enjoyed a largely healthy period of retirement when he took the opportunity to recollect his experiences, make reference to his scrapbooks and souvenirs, reminisce with his friends, and put his thoughts down on paper. This is not a polished literary history, but rather a lively and concrete account by a pragmatic optimist. Near the top of the first page he writes, "I shall tell what went on before I entered the show business and what went on after. I came along early enough to be called one of the pioneers, and I stuck with the theater or one of its branches all of my life from then until now. In order to give the facts I cannot afford to pull punches so I will have call a spade a spade. I am sure no one will be angry about the truth." A bit further along in his introduction, he declares,

All of us who were recruited to enter show business went into it with our eyes wide open. The objectives were, first, to make to help educate our younger ones, and second, to try to break down the ill feeling that existed toward the colored people. The Fisk Jubilee Singers were the first to carry the spiritual songs which were created from our very souls. The greatest trouble was in finding places to stay while in different cities where they appeared.

They did most of their concerts in schools and churches. With the Charles Hicks Georgia Minstrel Company, one of the earliest known all-colored companies, things were a little different. Hicks' outfit was a commercial proposition, and started out soon after the Civil War when bad feeling still ran high. The town halls and theaters were owned and operated by white people, many of whom had formerly owned slaves, so Hicks, who had a very good show, had very few places to play.

Along came Charles Callender, a white man who had been in the show-managing business. He found a great company of originals all tied up in one package, so he bought the Hicks show and enlarged it. New performers engaged were good singers and dancers and, with tutoring from others already with the show, they easily fitted into the picture. With Charles Callender as a white advance agent, things began to get better.[6]

I find this a fascinating statement on many counts. First, Fletcher begins with the Fisk Jubilee Singers—in the same place as the erudite W. E. B. Du Bois in *The Souls of Black Folk*—and identifies them as seminal figures and role models. Second, he presents the economic improvement and social "uplift" motives as primary—rather than taking aesthetic or expressive principles as his starting point. He includes the pithy and not insignificant observation that once postbellum commercial theatricals were open to black folks, performers discovered that "the town halls and theaters were owned and operated by white people, *many of whom had formerly owned slaves.*" That human beings and buildings are bracketed together as economic possessions, whether true or not in this instance, reveals a depth of understanding about how things worked in the real world, not to mention an entirely justifiable suspicion about the motives of owners in general. Third, while the words minstrel and minstrel company *are* used in this passage and later, they are not explained. The actual content of Fletcher's act or those of his predecessors, is not the focus at this point, nor is it very much the center of attention or concern throughout the book. Everybody *knew* what minstrel shows were—or thought they did.

A bit more background on Fletcher may illuminate this perspective. While dismissing certain gestures and expressions within the form, Fletcher stoutly *defends* the minstrel show, blackface and all, as having opened important and lucrative doors. He most certainly does *not* see himself as an apologist for racism—nor should we. More striking to me than his brief in favor of the minstrel man's art—of course it was a man's job for most of the nineteenth century—is the numerous variety of doors that he unhesitatingly walked through in the course of his career: he tells us in short order about his skills, as (1) a distributor of handbills, (2) boy soprano, (3) brightly costumed leader of the band, (4) sound recording artist, (5) bass drummer, (6) actor on stage, in early movies, and on television, (7) eccentric dancer, and (8) stand-up comedian (sans blackface). He was most definitely acquainted with dozens of fellow show people (both women and men) who practiced every imaginable activity on stage: bicycling, snake handling, body contortion, hoop rolling, fire eating, trapeze acrobatics, and slackwire walking. He knows and names friends and colleagues who were opera singers, dramatic readers, serious actors, and composers.

Fletcher was born in 1873 in Portsmouth, Ohio, a town about fifty miles downriver from Huntington, West Virginia, on the way to the Mississippi and the American Midwest. The Ohio-Mississippi-Missouri basin and cities that grew and flourished on the river banks therefore was his domain. From Topeka and Kansas City in the West to St. Louis, Louisville, Evansville, and Cincinnati in the East, and down to Memphis, the Delta region, and New Orleans, we see a triangle of land occupied by people consumed with change and movement. The cities and towns of this region were cradles of black popular entertainment from the 1870s to the 1890s. Way stations for legendary frontiersmen and river rats, here is also where we first encountered in earlier decades the intrepid longshoremen and keel-boat workers that we hear about in Dan Emmet's "Boatman Dance" (ca. 1850): "High row, the boatman row. / Floating down the river, on the *Ohio*." (It is important to recall that slaves and former slaves wanting a better life left Mississippi and Tennessee and fanned out in all directions—to Kansas and beyond in the West, to cities and states north of Ohio, and south to the Caribbean.)

Ike Simond, who, calling himself "Old Slack," also wrote a rare and valuable "reminiscence of the colored profession" in the generation before Fletcher, names just these urban locations as being most receptive and nurturing for his fellow entertainers. He pinpoints the 1870s as an especially

Figure 6.2. "Old Dan Emmit's Original Banjo Melodies," sheet music cover, 1843. Although all of the named performers in this banjo songbook were white, "minstrel" music was fundamentally defined as black because of its characteristic African instruments (tambourine, bones, banjo, and fiddle) and the dark-complected musicians who performed it. Note the odd juxtaposition of dancing jollity and contention with nature in the form of a hungry crocodile and a head-butting goat. Collections of the American Music Research Center, University of Colorado School of Music, Boulder, Colorado.

high time for the profession. A full generation before any rags were known or published Charles (a.k.a. Barney) Hicks became the most prominent black minstrel manager in the nation, leading his company on a three-year tour of Australia. "Authentic" minstrelsy was the point of departure from which other boundary crossing could take place.

As Fletcher interweaves his own story with the larger history of black "show business," participating in some of the most impressive black musical comedies of the first decade of the twentieth century and hobnobbing with the rich and famous, we come to realize that he represents a rather sizable pool of talent. As impressive as his career was—at times he even played leading roles and performed for four U.S. presidents—Fletcher was not a lone tall tree in a small forest.

The federal census conducted soon after Fletcher began his career in the late 1880s reports a total of 1,490 Negro "actors and showmen" in the United States. By 1910, in the wake of the phenomenally successful musical comedies headed by Bert Williams and George Walker, Ernest Hogan, and Bob Cole and J. Rosamond Johnson, the number of *full-time professional* African American show people was counted at 3,088. Most of these had their

Figure 6.3. "Ambolena Snow," sheet music cover, 1897. This illustration, originally part of a four-color newspaper supplement, presents the subject of the song with large lips and an apelike facial mask despite her fashionable dress, thus showing the grotesque images of blacks that emerged from the "coon" song craze. Collections of the American Music Research Center, University of Colorado School of Music, Boulder, Colorado.

start in local theatricals, concert companies, small-time vaudeville, minstrel acts, and medicine shows. But here we come back to the submerged iceberg—and indeed why all this genre mixing and boundary crossing was both possible and necessary. Not a surprise really.

No more than a half dozen African American names are to be found in Edward Le Roy Rice's extensive biography, *Monarchs of Minstrelsy*, published in 1911—6 versus 3,088 in the census. In this instance the failure to cross boundaries in another sense can only be laid at the feet of white chroniclers whose inability to credit African American initiative fostered this neglect.[7]

Looking at the careers of Tom Fletcher and Ike Simond and then turning to the impressive data sets contained in three relatively new and rich books paints a more complete picture.[8] The larger playing field—the boundaries crossed and the opportunities that Fletcher sought and achieved—come into clearer focus. Ragtime, beginning in the late 1890s, and commercial blues—that is, staged, urban blues performances, the child of ragtime songs, a.k.a. coon songs—during the 1910s and 1920s, were the two most important musical developments in our period. These phenomena were permanently grafted into our collective culture with the rise of nonmusical and unprecedented means of transportation and communication.

Trains could transport whole casts of musical comedy companies across hundreds of miles in a matter of hours, and steamships crossed oceans in a matter of days. If you built the theater in Omaha, in San Francisco, in Minneapolis, or in Macon—or in Paris or in Peking—the crowds and the shows would come; and contrary to what you might have heard, African American theater *owners* and *managers* were actively catering to their home audiences, especially in midwestern and southern cities.

In 1878, just five years or so after Tom Fletcher's birth, Thomas Edison first "bottled sound" as the saying goes. The new medium of recording offered an even more efficient and powerful way to communicate instantly with a much vaster audience than could be controlled by any small elite, whether they be publishers, theater managers, promoters, or tour impresarios of whatever race. The development of cheap recording playback machines and, later, radio (in the 1920s) moved attention away from the *face*— and onto the *sound* of the singer or speaker. For this reason alone, recording technology was revolutionary within the American entertainment industry as a whole, despite persistent and onerous racial barriers imposed on black entertainers in particular.

In this realm, another emblematic and pioneering figure is one George W. Johnson, undeservedly neglected even up to the present moment, but to whom Tim Brooks gives eloquent words in is his book *Lost Sounds*. Born in 1846, a slave in northern Virginia, Johnson as an adult made his way to the midtown New York neighborhood known as Hell's Kitchen and lived as a street singer blessed with an especially powerful *whistle*. Acquaintance with some early recording enthusiasts and entrepreneurs brought him opportunities to present his specialty to a wider audience. Among some 800 sound recordings made by African American artists between 1890 and 1920, two of the most successful and repeatedly imitated hits of the late 1890s were "The Whistling Coon" and "The Laughing Song," both written and performed by Johnson. His songs were sold as sheet music, on cylinder, and in vinyl versions in the tens of thousands, translated into German, French, and Swedish. They launched the careers of recording companies and other individual performers more conveniently placed to profit from his ideas than he was. Sadly, his career declined as rapidly as it had arisen. A star performer in 1899, known to all in the business regardless of race, by 1910 he had sunk deeply into debt and drink. He was dead by the age of sixty-seven in 1914.[9]

(Ike Simond, Tom Fletcher, and others flourished where George W. Johnson had not partly owing to the formation of entertainers' benevolent and social organizations among the most entrepreneurial African Americans in the business after 1900, which served to secure the friendship networks established on the road and provide old-age, sickness, and burial benefits. Sadly the familiar color line persisted. Some kinds of boundaries could not be crossed.)

Two often overlooked genres or spaces were the circus band and the so-called tent variety show, also known as "tented minstrelsy," (what Paul Oliver simply calls "road shows"), which grew most rapidly in the two decades *after Plessy v. Ferguson*. These two industries, while not employing African Americans exclusively in all regions of the country, were dominated by them in the mid-South and Southeast. Circus bands and tented road companies combined with full-fledged musical comedies, vaudeville, and movies that appeared in permanent theaters, opera houses, and civic halls, constitute the five principal genres open to black talent in the period up to the Great Depression. All of these forms of entertainment, but especially the first two, amounted to laboratories or workshops where skills could be developed and apprenticeships served by hardworking newcomers.

Circus band musicians often traveled as coherent units over many years even as the shows they appeared in formed and reformed around them: P. G. Lowery's Band and Minstrels appeared with the Hagenbeck and Wallace Circus and later with the Ringling Bros. James Wolfscale's Concert Band was associated with Barnum & Bailey. J. S. Riggers Annex Band was affiliated with the early Three-Ring Circus of Coop and Lentz in 1916. L. K. Baker's Band and Minstrels played with the Jess Willard-Buffalo Bill Wild West Show in 1917.[10]

The range and longevity of all-black-cast tent shows are even more impressive. Pat Chappelle's *A Rabbits's Foot Company*, out of Jacksonville, Florida, lasted from 1903 to 1920. The Florida Blossoms Company, originating in Tampa, Florida, and headed by R. S. Donaldson, lived from 1907 to 1928. The most spectacular of all the tent minstrel shows was the brainchild of musical comedy veteran Eph Williams and his "troubadours," "the original, famous, happy purveyors of mirth, music and song."[11] In 1911 Eph Williams and the Troubadours presented the show *Silas Green from New Orleans*. Retaining that title but changing the contents, much like a successful television series does nowadays, the Silas Green company rarely missed a seasonal tour, with new acts each year, from 1911 until 1940.

One of the strongest arguments in favor of completing the history of these neglected forms of entertainments is their exposure to large audiences of both black and white viewers outside of urban centers. The evidence is clear that while the southern shows were dominated by black entertainers, the audiences were biracial almost everywhere. Aspiring *white* performers had many opportunities to observe what black show people were all about. One cannot hope to write an accurate history without taking into account these rather large swaths of activity.[12]

My final point is something of a geographical postscript, but I think an important one. The rapid spread of jazz to Europe soon after its appearance in America has often been remarked upon and amounts to a historiographical commonplace of music literature. But the ground was laid for this phenomenon by the almost equally rapid dissemination of *ragtime and black popular dance* a decade or so beforehand—that is, in the 1890s. That the fad was assisted by live African Americans "on the ground" in Europe is less well known but equally deserving of attention. Again, the boundaries crossed are not only generic and racial ones but geographical as well.

Rather than compile what is a fairly substantial list of entertainers, I instead refer you to a fascinating book by Rainer Lotz, called simply *Black People: Entertainers of African Descent in Europe and Germany*, privately published by the author in 1997.[13] The material Lotz has documented includes many dozens of sound recordings and so is a good to partner with Tim Brooks's *Lost Sounds*, which deals only with U.S. records. British recording authority Howard Rye has observed that a "very high proportion of records made by African-American artists in the last decade of the 19th and the first decade of the 20th century were made in Europe"—I am not sure how this assertion relates to Brooks's figure of 800 recordings overall.

While listenable recordings are hard to come by, their previous existence is fairly well documented. Black performers were making records in Europe because, of course, they were already traveling in Europe—as separate acts or as part of larger companies. They were often heard by significant indigenous black populations who lived in most major European cities and port towns—we must not forget the various Africa-Europe links that go back for centuries as well as the legacy of nineteenth-century colonialism.

Der Artist, a German weekly trade paper for traveling artists, refers to more than one hundred black performers, mostly Americans, in Germany in 1896 alone.[14] Such active individuals as Arabella Fields, Seth Weeks, and Will Garland toured as far east as Budapest, Belgrade, Moscow, and St. Petersburg. One of the leading operatic mezzo-sopranos, musical comedy actors, and cakewalk dancers in turn-of-the-century African American theatricals and films was a New Orleans native named Belle Davis. Ms. Davis, a nearly exact contemporary of Tom Fletcher, frequently toured and recorded in Europe between 1899 and 1929. She remained in England during World War I, coming back to the United States in 1919 and then returning to France, where she died, having spent her last four years (1925–29) as the staff choreographer for a prestigious nightclub, the Casino de Paris.

From coon shouter to operatic diva, recording artist to nightclub dancer—one could hardly find a more diverse resume. But, as you now know, Belle Davis was not alone. There is still much more to be learned about black musicians who defied musical genres at the dawn of the twentieth century.

NOTES

1. Herbert J. Muller, *Uses of the Future* (Bloomington: Indiana University Press, [1970] 1974), 76.

2. Lynn Abbott and Doug Seroff, *Out of Sight: The Rise of African American Popular Music, 1889–1895* (Jackson: University Press of Mississippi, 2002); Lynn Abbott and Doug Seroff, *Ragged but Right: Black Traveling Shows, "Coon Songs," and the Dark Pathway to Blues and Jazz* (Jackson: University Press of Mississippi, 2007).

3. Laurence Hutton, *Curiosities of the American Stage* (New York: Harper & Brothers, 1891), 93; Eileen Southern, *The Music of Black Americans: A History*, 3rd ed. (New York: Norton, 1997), 120.

4. Abbott and Seroff, *Out of Sight*, xi.

5. Ibid, xii.

6. Tom Fletcher, *One Hundred Years of the Negro in Show Business* (New York: Burdge, 1954), xviii.

7. Edward Le Roy Rice, *Monarchs of Minstrelsy, From "Daddy" Rice to Date* (New York: Kenny Publishing Co., [1911]).

8. Tim Brooks, *Lost Sounds: Blacks and the Birth of the Recording Industry, 1890–1919* (Urbana: University of Illinois Press, 2004); Abbott and Seroff, *Out of Sight* and *Ragged but Right*.

9. Brooks, *Lost Sounds*, 49–72.

10. Abbott and Seroff, *Ragged But Right*, 369.

11. Ibid., 313.

12. Ibid., 335.

13. Rainer E. Lotz, *Black People: Entertainers of African Descent in Europe and Germany* (Bonn: Birgit Lotz Verlag, 1997).

14. Lotz, *Black People*, 21.

Our Newcomers to the City

The Great Migration and the Making of Modern Mass Culture

DAVARIAN L. BALDWIN

> The fundamental theme of New World African modernity is
> neither integration nor separation but rather migration and emigration.
> —CORNEL WEST, *Keeping Faith: Philosophy and Race in America* (1993)

Camp Meetings and Hog Pens in the City

By 1910 the *Chicago Defender* had already begun to sound the alarm about "a racial amusement problem." As proof of "boisterousness and defiance of public sentiment," the *Defender* described in great detail what it called an act of "Loud Talking in the Pekin." The Pekin, a nationally famous race theater, had begun to create "mixed bills"; integrating live acts with the emergent and relatively more affordable mass-cultural amusement of "moving pictures." Such mixed bills brought with them a more diversified audience and hence a more diversified approach to appropriate decorum in the theater. In this context, the *Defender* article protested, "some of our citizens who claim to be so refined and up-to-date certainly showed how they were raised. While the great Albini was trying to explain his work there was so much loud talking that he was forced to ask them to quit." The writer grumbled that the Pekin was "not a hog-pen; why not respect it?" He finally decided, "We rather think it is our newcomers to the city who think they are at a camp meeting."[1]

This complaint, appeal, even lament, within the space of a mass-cultural venue, is significant for a number of reasons. First, the "racial amusement problem" was placed squarely at the feet of "our newcomers" at least five years before the Great Migration significantly transformed Chicago's South Side landscape. This highlights how powerful even the specter of migrants was toward transforming visions of black community. Clearly in this *De-*

fender essay, the loud-talking atmosphere of "camp meeting[s]" and "hog pen[s]" represented a primitive racial past and its southland origins. Such a raucous atmosphere was positioned in direct contrast to the proclaimed refinement and "up-to-date" behavior of civil silence. Both theater refinement and silence were thought to articulate a modern racial urbanity in the northern present. Second, the writer compared such deviant acts in the Pekin with what they asserted would be appropriate silence by the "same people" at a white-owned "Illinois, Grand, or Lyric" theaters, which points to the growing investment placed in mass culture as a site for regulating public behavior and more specifically for staging race pride and respectability. Finally, the writer's description of such loud talking as a moment of "defiance" begins to shed light on the conscious ways black migrants would continue talking back to the screen and speaking out against established notions of "public sentiment" in the city.[2]

"Our newcomers to the city" most effectively demonstrate how struggles over popular amusements were central to competing visions of an American modernity. At the same time, the Great Migration directly influenced the development of U.S. mass culture, both its "representational strategies and its practices as a social space." This essay takes the convergence between black migration and mass culture, specifically but not exclusively in Chicago, as the point of focus. First, white anxiety about black mobility (and possible equality) shaped the very production genres, commercial brands, aesthetic tastes, and consumption styles of modern mass culture. Second, mass culture served as a major site where black residents—old settlers and newcomers—made themselves over as modern. The mass culture/migration nexus demonstrates how and why the mere notion of the black migrant alongside the actual migration experience is central to the making of American mass culture in the early twentieth century.[3]

At the same time, "Loud Talking" showcases more than simply the fact that migrants engaged in popular amusements, but allows us to more closely examine the terms on which the migration experience gave meaning to mass culture. This episode pushes us to pay more attention to the Great Migration experience as a "living archive," a conceptual framework that speaks back to the historian about how and why "loud talking" in theaters was identified as the defiant act of "newcomers" against "public sentiment." A "living archive" catalogues a repository of collective facts and experiences but also represents an epistemic community built on the less articulated imaginations and desires of a people. As much as many may hope, our analysis of the archive is not simple observation (letting the data speak for itself) but an interpretive process in search of the meaning systems that can help us reconstruct the world from which the archives speak. So in this study, the Great Migration experience becomes a living archive that can provide the "meaning system"—rules, norms, values, limits, geography (both actual and imagined), vocabulary (articulate and inarticulate), and fears—that gives us a framework for interpreting mass cultural products and practices within a particular moment. At the same time, the archives we engage are not suspended in time, crystallized in ink and parchment, waiting to simply be "read." Archives are living (different things jump out based on changing interests in the archive) and therefore require us to recognize the limits of our interpretive reach predicated on our present-day interests in selective shards of the past and at the same time demand that we fully engage the world of our "sources," listening to explicit texts and the profound silences, even when the worlds assembled don't perfectly conform to our interests. Pure meaning extraction can't happen, but a dynamic and honest conversation between the past and present can take place.

Case in point, a vast range of migration experiences—from Jim Crow conditions, sexual violence, and freedom dreams to "Up North" dreams deferred, class distinctions, and race pride strategies—were brought to the table of making and debating mass culture. To be sure, the Great Migration is not the only "living archive," the only meaning system, which could be accessed here. But the intimate relationship between this literal social movement and the modernization of mass culture provides a hopeful start for those looking for strategies to help extract meaning from culture. In the case of mass culture, the spectre of the Great Migration and the various interests that swirled around this undoubtedly seismic shift in population and expectation helps us better make sense of the *competing* meanings brought to bear on mass culture, sometimes contests of meaning over the same exact cultural product or concept.[4]

As a living archive, the Great Migration becomes a paradigm of possibilities (both lost and won) through which to engage, examine, and verify the contested yet deep mass-cultural significance of "loud-talking" newcomers to the city. For example, "Loud Talking" points to the growing racial significance of a place like the Pekin as white anxieties about the growing spectre of the Great Migration were expressed in the racial segregation of city-wide vice into black neighborhoods combined with the hypervisibility of black minstrel-like images in mainstream popular culture. For old settlers, "Loud Talking" confirmed white stereotypes and suggested that mass culture must be used to reform and discipline the growing black demographic into a respectable bloc of workers, consumers, voters, and parishioners. Finally, "Loud Talking" demonstrated how the general newcomer desires for self-worth, relatively clean work, and geographical mobility were not completely found in sharecropper shacks, voting booths, kitchenettes, or factory floors. Such desires, in the extreme, were equally pursued and expressed through theatrical personalities, nonfunctional fashions, up-tempo rhythms, and athletic contests within mass culture.

Few migrants have left us textual evidence about the intended meaning of their mass-cultural products and practices. But we can extract meaning (sometimes more) from what migrants *did* and how people responded, as much as from what migrants *said* they did within this realm. The Great Migration helped turn mass culture into a public sphere for discourse and debate across class lines, between old settlers and newcomers waging campaigns for citizenship, among consumers and reformers over the racial market, and between black and white leaders over power. In the end, the Great Migration must be understood as a loosely bracketed moment in time and place, but also as a living archive, a modern reimagining of the relationship between North and South; between local, national, and global; between popular and mass culture; race and civilization; between property, propriety, and competing visions of freedom.

Surely images and ideas about "blackness" shaped mass culture at its inception, but as the Great Migration transformed city spaces, legal restrictions and racial violence physically forced black residents to also live and work in the urban zones of commercialized vice and amusement that serviced the entire city. The convergence between migration and mass culture directly informed journalistic and social scientific conceptions of cultural deviance, dysfunction, and disorder. Here, general notions of deviance became almost exclusively linked to images and ideas about blackness, especially as citywide commercial amusements were rezoned to "Black Belt" communities. Such conditions brought white slummers to celebrate, modernist artists to cultivate, uplift reformers to castigate, and cultural workers to appropriate the supposedly unique "folk values" of the African in the city. The Negro "folk," and now their migrant progeny, were seen at one extreme as the "Negro problem . . . more of a formula than a human being" and at the other extreme as a "deep reserve" of "race genius . . . recharging the batteries of civilization with primitive new vigor." But, of course, amid this swirling cauldron of caricatures stood actual migrants. And in the end, the urban presence of migrants and their dreams of possibility forever altered the course and shape of mass culture and, in the process, American modernity.[5]

Mass-Culture Modernity

The national rise of culture industries created entire professions and classes driven by "mental" labor and hence played a significant role in the emergence and viability of mass culture. Outside of the labor produced by and for corporate and academic research laboratories, culture industries were primarily devoted to leisure and entertainment. By the late nineteenth century, the more stabilized distinctions between "high" and "low" culture were collapsing under the weight of the industrialized production of cultural entertainments and artifacts. Such industries drew from the relatively new technologies of moving pictures, recorded sound, broadcasting, and mass-spectator sports. The ideas and commodities from these media spheres were further advertised and exchanged through the accelerated commercial networks of train, ship, newspaper, and airwave. But it was the modern revolution in commercialized sight and sound after World War I that increasingly made cultural production, exchange, and interpretation relatively inexpensive, and hence more accessible to a wider variety of people and perspectives. The shift to cinemas, stadiums, music studios, and mass appeal posed a direct challenge to the Victorian-era authority of the written text, the museum, the formal theater, and their designated critics.[6]

African American images and cultural practices have been central to the origins, popularity, and forms of arguably every dominant mass-cultural medium in the history of American popular amusements. A racial imagination shaped the contours and content of "entertainment" from backyard battle royals and sexual violence to the national pageantry of the Kentucky Derby; from song sheets, food labels, and the black-before and white-after Social Darwinism of beauty advertisements to the minstrel space of coon songs, plantation shows, vaudeville stages, and early films. As all Americans turned to the mass-consumer marketplace it became an especially hopeful and harrowing site for a diversity of African Americans. The technologies of sound, celluloid, and print made representations of black humanity more affordable and portable. From another perspective, these media were more efficient at disseminating now mass-produced racist ideas across the globe.[7]

The 1893 World's Columbian Exposition in Chicago is perhaps the most axiomatic mass-cultural spectacle to capture the national sentiment about the changing racial landscape of U.S. cities. Here Anglo-American world supremacy was desired as much as declared in the language of science and the conventions of the carnival. Visual mediums of exhibition and film created a mediascape of utopian order in sharp contrast to the perceived chaos

of the actual city. The spatial arrangements of booths and exhibitions allowed theatergoers to experience the desired hierarchy of races by literally "descend[ing] the spiral of evolution." At one end the self-explanatory
White City housed achievements in Euro-American culture and technology,
serving as a model of racially pure civilization and order. In sharp contrast,
the "mongrel" Midway organized a motley collection of racially distinct
anthropological villages, where living ethnological displays were organized
as carnival amusement (mosques, native waiters, and hootchy-kootchy
dancers).[8]

Farthest from the White City stood the "savage races," best embodied in
what *Frank Leslie's Popular Monthly* deemed the "barbaric ugliness" of the
Dahomey village, where fairgoers were able to "easily detect many characteristics of the American Negro." Critics and observers went on to make direct links between the racial savagery found on display as a warning about
the rising tide of black migrants on the urban horizon. Harvard anthropologist and initial Midway organizer Frederic Putnam argued that "the negro
types at the fair . . . represented very fairly the barbarous or half-civilized
state of a people who are a numerous and rapidly increasing class of American citizens." In the end, these anthropological amusements, running from
white civilization down to black primitivism, offered social cues for ordering
and engaging the migration-era race relations soon to come.[9]

Only six years later, then colonel Theodore Roosevelt stood in Chicago's
elite Hamilton Club, preaching the apocalyptic gospel of "The Strenuous
Life" as remedy for a specifically white imperial manhood encumbered with
the effeminate etiquette and bodily restraint of the Victorian era. Local
recreations and amusements, including the Improved Order of Red Men,
the Boy Scouts, body building, amateur football, and the pastoral "pre-
serves" of "City Beautiful" parks and playgrounds were thought to prepare
white manhood for the rugged "burden" of a modern multiracial U.S. empire in the Caribbean and Asian Pacific abroad. Vigorous recreations were
also proposed to counter the dangerous lure of cultural miscegenation and
race-mixing found in urban dancehalls, taverns, and vaudeville theaters at
home.[10]

The shifting relationships between empire, cultural miscegenation, and
white civilization also gave the male heavyweight boxing champion new significance. As *the* staged symbol, the heavyweight championship embodied
the virile transition from Victorian to modern America. In fact, up until the
second decade of the twentieth century, heavyweight championship boxing
bouts remained strictly the preserve of European ethnic males. Such spec-

tacles became the quintessentially "staged conquest," a contrived display of controlled discipline over nonwhite impulses and people (with a guaranteed "white" victory nonetheless) in a decidedly multiracial American imperial and immigration context. However, such staged conquests are never entirely complete, especially when imperial subjects or nonwhite actors "do not voluntarily adopt their allotted role" of social subordination and inferiority.[11]

On the historic evening of July 4, 1910, Chicago resident Jack Johnson, touted as the "Negro's Deliverer," soundly defeated the "Great White Hope," Jim Jeffries. "In one swift blow," white supremacy was momentarily denied, pockets emptied, scientific theories challenged, and "far more interest was taken in the aftermath of the fight at Reno than in the observance of the national holiday." Black communities all over the country seized the opportunity to collectively talk back to Jim Crow America. Race revelers "shouted" at whites in their cars, jostled them on sidewalks, made "threats," and blocked traffic. In response, white observers set off arguably the first-ever nationwide race riots in U.S. history to repress the "disorderly celebration of Johnson's victory." But white violence was met by collective, even armed, black resistance. When white protesters could not win in the ring or on the streets they took to the courts, hoping to repress the cinematic circulation of the Johnson-Jeffries match. Congress had long refused to even consider a bill banning boxing films, but the mass exhibition and reproduction of Johnson's black racial superiority in the ring was just too much. Three weeks after the fight, a Congressional bill was passed prohibiting the interstate circulation of boxing films.[12]

To be sure, Jack Johnson's import far exceeded that of a black boxer. In fact, the unprecedented and astounding black occupation of "white" public space after the fight matched the frustratingly extravagant ways in which this country migrant from Galveston, Texas, lived his public life in Chicago. Johnson was a superior boxer with an extremely conscious self-presentation. His quick wit, expensive boy toys, and dandy persona directly transgressed the current social position of black migrants and, particularly, black men. Moreover, Johnson used mass culture to flaunt his desire for white women and celebrate their desire for him. Such interracial sexuality and sociability was ominously showcased in his controversial black-and-tan (racially mixed) saloon, the Café de Champion. In the Progressive Era imagination, Johnson symbolized all that was wrong with mass-cultural excess. Here, the recently liberated white flapper found amusement with the dark dandy. The "New Woman" was literally in bed with the New Negro.

In 1912, Johnson was consequently charged with violating the Mann Act—described as the trafficking of white women across state lines for immoral purposes. The "Negro's Deliverer" was forced abroad into exile amid the controversy. The intended goal of suppressing this spectacular public exhibition of black aggression, mobility, and sexuality was achieved.[13]

The "Johnson Affair" must be understood as a "prelude to the generalized reaction against the influx of African-Americans from the south" into U.S. urban centers. As a migrant and mass-cultural icon, Johnson publicly disrupted the racial order of white supremacy that had been imposed on boxing with his victory and acts of defiance. Mass culture was haunted by the epic nature of the "Johnson Affair." In fact, comments in the *Los Angeles Times* aimed at black celebrants after the Johnson-Jeffries fight foreshadowed prescriptions directed toward black migrants in cities only five years later: "Do not point your nose too high. Do not swell your chest too much. Do not boast too loudly. Do not be puffed up. Let not your ambition be inordinate or take a wrong direction. . . . Your place in the world is just what it was." Because of the mass exodus of black residents out of the South after 1915, most overlook the impact of this "advance guard of the Great Migration" five years earlier. While actual numbers remained small, by 1910 both New York and Chicago experienced a more than 40 percent increase in black populations. Therefore, the Jack Johnson spectacle symbolized a historic rupture only as part of a larger mass-cultural and migration challenge to romantic images of women in the home and black people on the plantation. It was far from coincidence that on the eve of the Great Migration, Johnson's films were banned, while D. W. Griffith was creating an epic moving picture of white racial redemption and black subordination.[14]

From production to promotion, Griffith's *The Birth of a Nation* was haunted by the specter of Jack Johnson and the expression of black power he represented. Most scholars concede that even with its new level of aesthetic beauty, technological mastery, and presidential endorsement, this 1915 epic retold the Civil War and especially the period of "Reconstruction as a Gothic horror tale haunted by black brutes." Yet few have recognized that *The Birth* was as much a cinematic history of the present, a tale of early twentieth-century urbanization and the future implications of the Great Migration. With the Great Migration on the horizon, *The Birth* represented Reconstruction as an apocalyptic end of days, with black savages and interloping white northern race traitors colonizing a plantation South. Such images of black insurgency and white impotence in the film were as much about the first three decades of the twentieth century as they were a revisionist history of Reconstruction. When Silas Lynch, the northern mulatto, tells his white female captive, "I will build an empire and you will be my queen," he crystallized the larger national anxieties about racial miscegenation in cities amid the Great Migration and U.S. imperial expansion into a multiracial western hemisphere. Soon after Lynch's pronouncement, aggressive black lust is put down via a triumphant rescue by the Ku Klux Klan. The final scene enacts Abraham Lincoln's failed bid to board black "citizens" on ships to be sent "back" to Africa. *The Birth* therefore was at least partially an instructional amusement, where the spectacle of evil blackness was used to help consolidate a motley crew of European immigrant "races" into a unified force of white nationalism amid the Great Migration. In the 1920s, the film was exhibited nationwide to help galvanize the northern urban renaissance of the KKK. In many ways, Griffith converted concerns about the racial, spatial, and cultural transformation of the urban landscape into a mass-cultural clarion call for white racial confidence amid a wartime world of growing racial uncertainty.[15]

World War I brought together the inextricably tied forces of capitalism and anticolonial resistance—abroad and at home—in ways that altered the social significance of U.S. mass culture. Black mass culture traveled the transnational routes of war, disseminating subtle messages of dissent along with the waves of black men charging abroad to once again prove militarily their national inclusion. James Reese Europe's 369th U.S. Infantry Band—the "Hell Fighters"—was known both for its bravery and also for being one of the first "exporters" of jazz to France during the war. When Europe released the song "How 'Ya Gonna Keep 'Em Down on the Farm (After They've Seen Paree?)," it was one of the biggest hits in 1919, while possibly confirming the fears of migration-era black assertiveness signaled in *The Birth of a Nation*. The song touched on the larger wartime implications of "bringing the boys into town," expressed through the millions of black people "quitting" the South during the Great Migration, followed by urban race riots throughout the Diaspora.[16]

From the start, mass culture revealed that the Great Migration was far more than a response to wartime labor shortages, but a conscious social movement struggling for a more perfect freedom against the post-Reconstruction angels of death. Lynching had become the country's most "Deadly Amusement," with white families bringing children and picnic baskets and hence helping to transform many a black southerner into a northern migrant. The Chicago Urban League confirmed, "after a lynching, colored people from that community will arrive in Chicago inside of two weeks." The link between migration and racial militancy was not lost on white America when nationally popular authors Madison Grant and Lothrop Stoddard respectively chronicled this period as *The Passing of the Great White Race* (1914) at the hands of *The Rising Tide of Color Against White World Supremacy* (1916). T. S. Eliot further eulogized this multiracial modernity as a *Waste Land* (1922). Others stormed the capital agitating for anti-immigration and antimiscegenation laws after pulp novels, comic strips, and vaudeville shows sensationalized white slaving, red scares, yellow perils, brown hordes, and Negro problems.[17]

Between 1910 and 1930, New York City's black population more than tripled, while Chicago's exploded from 44,130 to 233,903. In response, Chicago newspapers screamed "HALF A MILLION DARKIES" bring "PERIL TO HEALTH." Migrants were demonized as helpless peasant refugees ignorant of urban life, with a culture that needed adjustment, containment, and discipline. At the same time, James Reese Europe's song subtly predicted how black soldiers quickly "return[ed] fighting" alongside newcomers and old settlers in the struggle against longstanding white restrictions on black labor, leisure, and living. White angst and annoyance with a growing black presence exploded into what writer James Weldon Johnson termed the "Red Summer" of 1919, with over forty race-rioting "hot spots" as far away as Liverpool, England. Violence in Chicago was sparked when black teenager Eugene Williams was stoned to death for accidentally floating "across the imaginary" racial line and into "white water" at the 29th Street Beach. Violent battles erupted to maintain white order, making clear that contests over labor, living, and leisure spaces were central.[18]

Legal and extra-legal methods of black containment included the residential and employment segregation of restrictive covenants and labor racism, augmented by various expressions of racial violence. Concurrently, the national edict of Prohibition sounded not the end to drinking and dancing but an even stronger rezoning of urban-wide vice directly within the tight confines of black communities. This combustible force of social conditions turned urban Black Belts into the nation's "good-time" zones. The convergence between black community and spaces of vice helped further materialize the general assumption that not only did black people engage in amusements but that black culture was the embodiment of vice and leisure.[19]

As an example, Chicago's Black Belt and, in particular, its business and amusement district, "the Stroll," became the physical manifestation of general ideas about urban mass-cultural deviance, dysfunction, and disorganization. When the "Chicago School" of sociology built its basic theories of social relations, Ernest Burgess used the "excessive increase . . . of southern Negroes into northern cities since the war" as the "objective" standard by which to measure disturbance in the natural "metabolism" of urban order. The authoritative Chicago School's urban studies text, *The City*, scientifically justified the situating of urban vice districts in Black Belts because the Negro's "racial temperament" was perfectly suited for the world of leisure and urban amusements. Social scientific logic diagnosed the Negro as exhibiting an "interest and attachment to external, physical things rather than to subjective states and objects of introspection, in a disposition for expression rather than enterprise and action." With earlier struggles over white masculinity in mind, the manly Anglo-Saxon temperamental impulse toward enterprise and action was placed in sharp contrast to the Negro's "genial, sunny and social disposition," which tellingly codified them, "the lady among the races." In Chicago, the spatial fixity of the majority of Chicago's vice and amusement to the geographical location of the Black Belt's "Stroll" physically marked and conceptually mapped mass-cultural deviance as a Negro "trait."[20]

Fear of black culture, however, soon turned to fascination. White artists, intellectuals, and bohemians witnessed white-on-white violence on the World War I stage. Many were critical or anxious about the modern convergence between Western industrial civilization, imperial expansion, and white-on-white violence. The caricatured sights, sounds, and styles of Africa, and its American urban descendants, now embodied the romantic ideals of vitality, spirit, rhythm, and communalism; best embodied in the primitivism movement in art and culture. Here, the living artifacts of a premodern Africa were "found" in the sonic and social rituals of migrant life in jazz clubs, storefront churches, and work-gang songs. Such black primitive traces were excavated, exoticized, and then civilized through the "Western" forms of canvas, compositional notation, and written verse. Negro culture was also being idealized as an outsider "folk" alternative, critique, and "safety valve for modern machine-ridden and convention-bound society." The Negro became both trapped and "en vogue" as the essence of all that Western modernity was not.[21]

Yet in the general turn to black culture, even the most powerful modernist cultural critiques of U.S. imperialism and Western civilization were a tangled web of interracial solidarity and primitive fascination. Composers mined Negro spirituals as the therapeutic raw-source material for an "authentic" American music; Pablo Picasso lifted (up) African sculptural forms for Cubism; dancers and choreographers appropriated black bottom and shimmy moves alongside cakewalk and Charleston flares to create modern dance; and Alan Lomax built folklore studies on static imaginings of black southern folk culture. Later, minstrel shows, live remote jazz broadcasts, and the imagined blackface migrant folkways of *Amos n' Andy* proved the commercial viability of American airwaves. The Negro was thought to exist outside of civilization, to be the antithesis of productivity and industriousness. But in war's aftermath the perceived black primitivism of emotional excess and bodily release became a life-affirming elixir where before it had been a dangerous enticement.[22]

The physical compression of more black bodies into slim belts of urban space and concentrated vice helped construct black communities as foreign reserves that had been "discovered." The racial contours of the modern mass-cultural landscape powerfully reinforced the idea that white adventures "uptown" or to the South Side were rejuvenating colonial tours or African safaris in the city. Scholarly articles and amusement advertisements billed black urban spaces as "destinations" for those seeking primitive release and premodern pleasure through a "moral vacation" in the concrete "orgies of the jungle." Harlem was described as "A Strange, Exotic Island" of "primitive passion . . . in the Heart of New York." While another essay short-handed a night at Chicago's famous black-owned Pekin Theater as "lawless liquor, sensuous shimmy, solicitous sirens, wrangling waiters, all tints of the racial rainbow. . . . A brown girl sang. . . . Black men with white girls, white men with yellow girls, old, young, all filled with the abandon brought about by illicit whisky and liquor music." The *Chicago Tribune* even dubbed a nearby streetcar line the "African Central."[23]

The migration-era organization of vice and black life not only offered the chance to travel to another place, but allowed white tourists the chance to go *back* in time. A nostalgic longing for the Old South swept the nation in the 1920s; many black-and-tan clubs and brothels crafted caricatures of the "peaceful" race relations before the end of slavery precisely at the point when northern communities were confronting New Negro neighbors. Cotton Clubs and Plantation Cafés, with their primarily black performer and white audience dynamic, staged longings for colonial or plantation relations in the city. Actual colonial tours throughout an emerging U.S. empire were translated into the domestic variant of urban "slumming." Many disillusioned modernists characterized excursions into Black Belts as opportunities for the "joyous revolt from convention."[24]

At the same time, a legion of black cultural producers, critics, and reformers understood the "Negro vogue" as one of the few opportunities to seize mass culture and transform it into a vehicle for race pride, profit, and even politics. Black populations were rapidly growing in northern cities, and many churches remained suspicious of the dangerous lure of commercialized leisure. Secular and sacred leaders specifically targeted the "bad deportment" of "newcomers" within very public amusements for reinforcing an image of black primitivism and hence undermining racial respectability. In fact, after the race riots of 1919, some argued that the vulgar behaviors and southern ways migrants brought with them "like a disease," including the early "wild escapades" of Jack Johnson, spawned "the very beginning of race hatred."[25]

The structural realities of recreational racism forced those of the "better class" to be "mixed with the undesirable or [remain] at home in seclusion." Most leaders were therefore either truly hopeful or resigned to believe that segregated amusements and leisure spaces such as the Stroll might serve as "the right arm of the church." The disorderly life of migrants could be reformed into the base for a political bloc and consumer patronage. Perhaps the convergence between the white cultural investment in all things Negro and the concentration of all urban vice and amusement into Black Belts might provide the base for an organized alliance between black producers and consumers. Mass culture might serve as a means toward some control over black images and institutions, away from the overwhelming force of white patriarchy, patronage, and philanthropy.[26] The competing black and white interests that converged on race films, race records, race newspapers, race league baseball, and general race enterprises might become positions of strength.

For black leaders mass culture raised a whole new set of both possibilities and problems, but it was a space that could not be ignored. Instead of turning their backs on mass culture, community leaders sought to shape local culture industries in ways that expressed their personal aims and collective desires for the uplift of new migrants. For example, W. E. B. Du Bois remained hesitant about the unwieldy force of popular amusements, especially those that could be associated with the current "coon craze." At the turn of the twentieth century, Du Bois argued on one hand that "the 'submerged tenth'" of professional "gamblers and sharpers" had migrated to the city under the cover of popular amusements, including "gambling, excursions, balls, and cake walks." Once there, these amusement professionals preyed on the "ignorant and easily influenced" children of migrants who became "the feeders of the criminal class." On the other hand, Du Bois's support of race-record companies, pageants, and later consumer theories confirmed his vigorous campaign to rescue amusement from the complete dismissal of the church. He astutely observed that "if properly limited and directed . . . between repression and excess" any amusement could "be a positive gain to any society."[27]

Chicago film critic Jean Voltaire Smith perhaps expressed the amusement-reformer outlook best: "Long sermons against the movies, admonitions to stay away from them, seem to result in empty pews in the church and an augmented attendance at the picture show around the corner." Many be-grudgingly agreed with cultural critics Alain Locke and J. A. Rogers that black popular cultures, as "undeveloped . . . resources," had to be physically uplifted from their saloon, "wayside inn," and "original religious setting" to the literary salon, concert hall, and "cabaret of the better type." Here, the specter of migration and migrant culture helped link the space for per-formance ("original religious setting") with an aesthetic value ("undevel-oped"). Such presumptions defined the terms through which black culture could make the transition from "folk-form" to "art-form," from primitive to modern.[28]

The push to construct mass culture as a form of racial uplift and mi-grant reform also helped generate spaces of sociability for the "better class" through a range of popular amusements. The *Chicago Defender* emerged as the national race paper because it crusaded against injustice, coordinated the Great Migration north, contained one of the first freestanding enter-tainment sections, *and* republished notorious "Folks We Can Get Along Without" cartoons and "dos and don'ts" lists aimed primarily at the public-amusement behaviors of migrants. In *Defender* pages, bandleader and cul-tural critic Dave Peyton used his column, "The Musical Bunch," to demand that silent-film exhibitions become "high art" through a seamless coherency between "classical" musical accompaniments in service to the narrative of the film. He castigated the primarily migrant musicians in pit orchestras that jazzed up and parodied standard music scores or talked and shimmied in ways that distracted audiences or altered the meaning of the film. *De-fender* film critic D. Ireland Thomas's early title as "Theatrical Efficiency Ex-pert and Motion Picture Specialist" helps showcase the early link between the reform of theater spaces and the rise of film criticism. In this capacity, Thomas spilled as much ink on constant admonitions to throw out pea-cockers, lip slobberers, spooners, and other "disorderly" patrons as he did on criticizing actual film and theater productions.[29]

Within the Negro spirituals movement, the compositions of artists such as Robert Nathaniel Dett and Edward Boatner literally contained black folk music within the uplifting discipline of classically composed and notated form. Such an approach was almost like a wish fulfillment of the "better class" to aesthetically uplift the unruly "folk" and their "useless ways" of religious "singing, shouting and talking." Classically composed spirituals also offset the vogue in black primitivism, exhibited here through the white slumming obsession with touring black storefront and "Holy Ghost" oriented churches as a form of entertainment. In contrast, on the stages of 5,000-person churches, the choirs were reverent ensembles that demanded a certain kind of vocal and bodily control, distinct from the minstrel usage of spirituals. During service or at extended Sunday musicales, anthems by Mozart and Beethoven were mixed in with concretized Negro spirituals where the choir was restricted to the notes on the page and the commands of the director. The performance was a fixed, self-contained cultural product with little room for response or improvisation.[30]

Such an approach to musical respectability and racial uplift also found voice within black-owned race recording enterprises and their battle against the high volume of mass-produced "comic darky songs." For example, Black Swan Records was innovative in its attempts to offer more balance in the commercial circulation of black music that otherwise had no commercial outlet. Yet even the blues and ragtime in its catalogue were "oriented around middle-class standards of dignity, refinement, and self-restraint."[31] Various leaders, reformers, and entrepreneurs deployed a spectrum of strategies to shape mass culture along uplift lines, demonstrating that the use of the consumer marketplace was not solely determined by economic concerns.

In the highly capital-intensive sphere of race filmmaking, black artists and entrepreneurs attempted to more successfully blend popular appeal and uplifting content by inaugurating what I call the *uplift comedy* genre. Uplift comedies combined sensational entertainment with moral instruction to make the behaviors of laziness, indecency, and immodesty the subject of laughter and ridicule. The representations of urban black middle-class characters on the Stroll in William Foster's *The Railroad Porter* and *The Butler* served as counters to negative stereotypes by showing "the better side of the race on canvas." Within the genre, black butlers and porters are portrayed as the hardworking heroes, whereas grafters and men of leisure represent a warning to migrants about the dangers of urban life.[32]

Peter Jones's *The Troubles of Sambo and Dinah* was specifically noted as a film that could "awaken the consciences of men and women to do the right thing in life and . . . discourage drunkenness, dishonesty and licentiousness." Alongside their pioneering work in documentary filmmaking, Foster and Jones saw laughter as a powerful visual method for establishing racial respectability and migrant reform. America's first black radio program, Jack Cooper's *All Negro Hour*, followed suit in 1929 with its own uplift comedy *Luke and Timber*, chronicling the follies and foibles of two Chicago migrants. Other race companies, however, tended to focus on the genre of melodrama and avoid comedy altogether because it potentially reinforced the association between black performance and blackface minstrelsy.[33]

The Lincoln Motion Picture Company, based in Los Angeles, was financially backed by the city's black "better class," but their films were distributed nationally. In dramas including *The Realization of a Negro's Ambition, The Trooper of Troop K*, and *The Law of Nature*, Lincoln "chose the route of gentle persuasion in 'uplifting' films about honor and achievement, the rewards of good character, morality, and ambition, picturing strong, positive role models to strengthen race consciousness and identity." Set in the western frontier, Lincoln films "established a new type of black protagonist, a middle-class hero who believes in the puritan work ethic." The films channeled the combined ethos of Booker T. Washington and Theodore Roosevelt to provide a Romantic vision of wide-open spaces where man was able to confront and endure conflict and where eventually patience and hard work pay off.[34]

Finally, the world of sport highlighted battles over migrant reform waged at the fault line between professional and amateur athletics. The South Side's all-black Wabash YMCA became an especially acute site of "welfare capitalism" where, in exchange for financial support, social programs were developed to secure worker loyalty and productivity in Chicago's major industries. The Wabash Y hosted "efficiency clubs" and a series of industrial, Sunday School, and military sports leagues to showcase an ethos of amateur character development that ran counter to an emerging black embrace of the "American spirit" of winning at all costs, especially against white teams. Elite black players had begun to sell their skills to the highest bidder, as victorious professionalized teams became an alternative expression of race pride. In response, assistant supervisor of physical education for Chicago high schools Edward Delaporte outlined a telling distinction between amateur and professional sport that paralleled the various prescriptions aimed at migrant behavior. He argued that the distinction was not just a matter of payment but that "true amateurism stands for a high sense of . . . temperance" in behavior and participation "purely for the pleasure of the game," while "others" play for "victory, the prize or the plaudits of an audience."[35]

The rise of semiprofessional and professional play begins to shed light on newcomers who felt as oppressed by the limited guarantees of a reform-based puritan work ethic as they did by domestic surveillance and industrial dehumanization. In this particular case, amateurism represented a particular kind of censure on professional play as a viable source of leisure *and* labor. The Great Migration moment and the migrant critique of both a solely rights-based or work-ethic vision of freedom encouraged many people to turn to leisure spaces within the mass marketplace for more than moral reform. Both newcomers and old settlers in fact engaged the world of amusement to construct their own visions of a mass-cultural modernity that could express various desires for social autonomy and collective association sought in everyday life.

"The Negro Peasant Turns Cityward"?: The Migrant Image Outside the Northern Mind

Black migrants were a conscious group of individuals with a diversity of reasons for leaving the South. This diversity of southern and migration experiences informed the various urban life ways that emerged in northern cities like New York, St. Louis, Los Angeles, and Chicago. All along the path to northern cities, migrants were required to negotiate a rapidly changing world. The sometimes liberating, sometimes unsettling migration experience created an "in-between" space between an always-changing "ancestral" past and a racially restrictive northern industrial present. Sociologists, labor recruiters, and newspapers continually painted pictures of sharp contrast between the modern glitz and glamour of places such as Chicago and the bleak, primitive lifeworld available to a supposedly naïve mass of rural peasants turning cityward. Yet such depictions were far from the actual migrant experience. Only 25 percent of Chicago's migrants, for example, had been agricultural laborers. A significant number in the remaining 75 percent had between five and ten years of experience in southern cities and hence were familiar with urban conditions *before* they arrived in Chicago.[36]

Life chances might not have compared with the scale of possibility in a place like Chicago, but part of migrants' early engagement with the urban South and their motivation to move north included participation in commercialized leisure. Many black southerners visited Chicago in 1893 for the World's Columbian Exhibition, overcame Jim Crow shopping limitations with catalogue purchases from Chicago-based stores such as Sears and Roebuck and Montgomery Ward, and later bought automobiles and radios. By World War I, two-thirds of those who read about the Stroll in the *Chicago Defender* lived outside Chicago, while National Negro League baseball teams supported themselves during the off-season with frequent barnstorming trips south. The North may have offered images of cultural freedom, but it was southern dollars and desires that made northern black consumer culture so viable.[37]

Moreover, there was such a fundamental disconnect between the ideals of the American work ethic and the very real inequities African Americans faced in factories, unions, and schools in northern and southern cities. Many migrants therefore found consumer culture to be an important space where they could express individual desires and even collective forms of dissent against the urban industrial order. For example, reform and social scientific reports evaluated various Black Belt buffet flats and brothels near the Stroll as a social threat. But these spaces were also understood as an opportunity for women to leave "the low-wage, low-status domestic labor that left them vulnerable to sexual harassment" with little compensation. One Chicago buffet-flat prostitute added, "When I see the word *maid*—why, girl, let me tell you, it just runs through me! I think I'd sooner starve." Even beyond wages and well-being, the status of maid was collectively resisted because, as one woman stated, there was no "place to entertain your friends but the kitchen, and going in and out of the back doors. I hated all that. . . . They almost make you a slave." The subservient memory of "slavery" or slave-like labor was still fresh in migrants' heads, and many women in particular turned to commercial amusements to ensure that they would "never work in nobody's kitchen but my own anymore."[38]

The better class showcased the seemingly more uplifting and respectably enterprising activities on the daytime Stroll. But it was actually the interconnected and illicit nighttime world of "sporting" and entertainment that most profoundly displays how the Great Migration provided the shape, form, and economic base for U.S. mass culture. For example, at the turn of the twentieth century, various older lottery games were declared illegal throughout the country, thus paving the way for the stock market to become the dominant economic system of speculation. However, during the Great Migration and segregated urbanization, black immigrants from the Spanish- and English-speaking Caribbean and migrants from the deep South brought versions of "policy" or "numbers" (now legalized as state lotteries) to urban centers. The 1920s witnessed a reenergized interest in lottery gambling as a viable popular amusement and informal economy, particularly within socially marginalized communities.[39]

Despite legitimate criticisms, by the late 1920s and especially during the Depression, policy or numbers operators were considered race leaders because hard-earned dollars were recirculated back into the black community through an informal economy providing a relatively higher rate of return than the racially exclusive stock market game. In New York, St. Croix immigrant Casper Holstein helped fund Marcus Garvey's social movement, Alain Locke's *New Negro* anthology, and the *Opportunity* magazine writers' contest. Chicago policy kings John "Mushmouth" Johnson, Henry "Teenan" Jones, Robert Motts, William Bottoms, and Dan the "Embalmer" Jackson backed theaters, churches, athletes, newspapers, banks, and insurance companies. This informal economy also generally underwrote the city's famed jazz and blues culture and sponsored politicians who mediated relationships with police, judges, and reformers. Migrant nickels and dimes placed on numbers in Chicago specifically set the stage for the Pekin Theatre, the Dreamland Café, Jesse Binga's banking empire, Jack Cooper's radio show, and the race radical *Whip* newspaper. On a smaller scale, struggling black businesses such as beauty salons, barbershops, and lunch counters served as legal "fronts," benefiting from increased customer circulation. Religious figures developed the related economies of spiritual readings and dream book publications to convert social events and otherworldly premonitions into numerical, and hopefully economic, meaning. In the face of racist hiring and banking practices and Depression-era economic decline, "policy gambling" became a necessary mass-cultural evil for some and for others a rational option toward black employment, entrepreneurship, and entertainment in a racially exclusive economy.[40]

Clearly, spaces such as the Stroll were more than the repository for an innovative informal economy or a stretch of buildings, amusements, sidewalks, and signposts. These commercial/community spaces became the public showcase for black "expressive behavior." To stroll on the Stroll meant to take part in a moving theater where black people were staging new visions of "the race" in the particular ways they looked and were looked at within a structured space of local exhibition. For example, on any given weekend migrants with hard-earned leisure time jumped off the elevated at 35th and State, landing in the middle of the blazing neon glory of the Stroll. The street was packed with black revelers (and more than a few white participant-observers); the air filled with music, laughter, and tears. To be sure, the streets and theaters were often dingy and many times dangerous. Sometimes illicit wares were too alluring, hawkers too aggressive, pickpockets too quick, madams too mothering, and shows too bawdy. A week's wages could be lost in a weekend. Still, a veneer of freedom permeated the soul as the shroud of subservience was lifted to reveal extravagant displays of fast talk, fine clothes, and feeling good.[41]

As revelers dropped nickels and dimes on their saunter down the Stroll, they underwrote a new world of expressive possibility. Some first ducked into the Monogram, the New Grand Theater, or north to the famed Pekin Theatre to catch a jazz set, with a few moving pictures mixed in. Some lucky revelers avoided the threats of ushers to steal a few kisses with their sweethearts while hiding in the shadows of the rising and falling luminescence of the screen. Cinematic attractions competed with the halftime jazz dances, muscular confrontations, and all-star spectaculars that transformed ballrooms, boxing rings, and baseball diamonds into a combination gambling refuge, religious revival, political rally, and rave. Stepping out of a show, spectators could be quickly converted into saints by wandering into "church on the street," where singing women evangelists packaged preaching, praying, and praise into a momentary haven of heaven on earth with a blues backbeat. An almost-identical soundtrack lured the curious and capricious into a nightcap visit to one of the all-you-can-eat enticements at a buffet flat or rent party. Small fees and big soul food plates brought slow grind dancing, taboo sexual encounters, and secure shelter, both for alienated migrants and workers on the grueling "chitlin' circuit" of race entertainment.

Here, the physical acts of mass-cultural exhibition and expression were equally a matter of socio-aesthetic concern. Struggles over the appropriate or desirous form, style, and tenor of black bodies and ideas on city streets were unevenly but directly tied to contested notions of black freedom, community, and even national belonging. The nighttime Stroll, as a mass-cultural space, physically consolidated the promises and pitfalls of brothels and battle royals, ballrooms and buffet flats, storefronts and policy stations, kitchens and kitchenettes, the saunter and the shake, as a collectively combustible archive adding form and substance to modern U.S. mass culture in global cities.

The transitional dreams and demands crystallized in the Great Migration shaped the very representational strategies and aesthetic approaches of modern mass culture. Beauty culturists such as former migrant washerwoman Madam C. J. Walker industrialized and mass marketed the time-consuming ritual of doing hair, taking black bodies back from mammy images and domestic labors of subservience. This space of personal artifice amid collective acts of self-fashioning helped build a beauty-culture modernity for black women via new bodily presentations, professions, and even organized politics. Meanwhile, filmmaker Oscar Micheaux cinematically approximated the migration experience via quick-shuffling back stories, inconsistent and jarring cuts, and internal dreamscapes. His films literally act out the unsettling scenarios of racial miscegenation, passing, violence, and redemption so constantly the subjects of his largely migrant consumer audiences' lives. Whether *The Homesteader*, *Within Our Gates*, or *Body and Soul*, his cinematic pulp fictions overwhelmed viewers with the unsatisfactory twin poles of a hellish southern pastoral gothic and a deceptive northern concrete purgatory. Both landscapes were violently juxtaposed against the "wide-open" western frontier as the only possible racial Promised Land for the perpetual migrant within Micheaux's cinematic ideology.[42]

In addition, "Father of Gospel Music" Thomas A. Dorsey, along with a largely female corps of gospel music demonstrators, fused the sounds of nighttime Stroll barrelhouse trills and buffet-flat blue notes with daytime, up-south storefront praise rhythms and race records performance styles. The chorus/verse structure of Dorsey's compositions directly embedded call-and-response possibilities within his sacred blues songs. Innovations such as gaps in the seven-note scale and first-person narratives also offered migrant parishioners and musicians a new voice for speaking back to the urban anonymity of the factory, the kitchen, and the old-line church. Such newcomer approaches to sight and sound resonated with the black athletic style of reactionary improvisation built on the counterpunch defense of Jack Johnson, the Harlem Renaissance's speed-dribble adaptation, the spin-move misdirection found in football's Brown Bombers, and Chicago American Giant's base stealing and changeup pitching innovations forever transformed the speed and style of sport. Such improvisations were always a hybrid force of personal signature and Afro-Diasporic sporting traditions. At the same time, all of these electrifying sporting lifestyles (speeding up the game and focusing on defensive strategies) served as muscular commentary about the racially unequal application of "the rules" on both playing fields and Stroll street corners.[43]

At both conceptual and physical center, the Stroll became a social space where the migration experience widened and sharpened the spectrum of possibility found in mass-consumer culture. The significance of the Stroll for migrants was both intimately manifest and insatiably mythic, whether traversing its streets, perusing this playscape in the pages of the *Defender*, or circulating sonic speculations about its bright lights bolstered by rumor and big talk. When migrant musicians such as Duke Ellington took time to document their impressions of Chicago, it was on the Stroll where the meaning of the Great Migration and mass culture converged. Even before his arrival, Ellington heard "very romantic tales about the nightlife on the South Side . . . and the apparently broken-down neighborhoods where there were more good times than any place in the city." From both near and far, a collective sense of race pride emerged. The shared experience of racial violence, restrictive covenants, and workplace racism provided powerful connective tissue for connecting far-flung Black Belts toward thinking about a collective sense of modern blackness.[44]

At the same time, the mass marketplace did not simply determine the experiences of migrants within its realm. The epic experiences of black migration shaped the material inner workings of mainstream culture industries and the *meaning* of mass-cultural spaces such as the Stroll. Mass culture was, in fact, an expression of the Great Migration, a medium through which white cultural entrepreneurs, old settlers, and newcomers could organize and manifest their competing desires for ideal social relations through the very acts of production, circulation, and consumption in a postmigration world. Attention to migration and mass culture reveals how such newcomers were literally being worked by the dual social forces of urban intensity and indifference but simultaneously working through a transformed set of consumption habits, practices, and desires central to making mass culture modern.

NOTES

1. "Loud Talking in the Pekin," *Chicago Defender*, April 23, 1910.

2. Ibid.

3. See Jacqueline Stewart, *Migrating to the Movies: Cinema and Black Urban Modernity* (Berkeley: University of California Press, 2005), 3. Basic ideas in this essay emerge from Davarian Baldwin, *Chicago's New Negroes: Modernity, the Great Migration, and Black Urban Life* (Chapel Hill: University of North Carolina Press, 2007).

4. My formulation of a "living archive" as both empirical fact and epistemic community is, at this particular moment, informed by the critical historical insights and interrogations of Clifford Gertz, Michel Foucault, and Cedric Robinson. Gertz points out that what we call our data are really "our own constructions of other people's constructions of what they and their compatriots are up to" (9). Our data from the archive is itself suspended in webs of meaning, and therefore the analysis of the archive is not simple observation (letting the data speak for itself) but an interpretive process in search of the meaning systems that can help us reconstruct the world from which the archives speak. This meaning system resonates with Foucault's

notion of a "local character of criticism" that is not a "primitive empiricism," what he calls the "worst kind of theoretical impoverishment"; instead this local knowledge is "an autonomous non-centralized kind of theoretical production, one that is to say whose validity is not dependent on the approval of the established regimes of thought." This theoretical production is marked as a subjugated knowledge system made up of "historical contents that have been buried and disguised in a functionalist coherence or formal systemization" (81). Yet, in direct examination of racial regimes of thought, Robinson reminds us that the reading of subjugated knowledge as buried or disguised leads to a kind of "unitarianism" that does not fully examine the "coexistence of alternative, oppositional, or simply different relations of power" (xi). We must interrogate the history of racial regimes with their own "discernable origins and mechanisms of assembly" outside of their utility function for tracking the genealogies of dominant regimes of truth. It is not simply the rupture between knowledge systems that is vital to historical work, but the "archeological imprint of human agency," which "radically alienates the histories of racial regimes from their own claims of naturalism" (xiii). So, in this study, the Great Migration experience becomes a living archive that provides the webs of meaning that give us a framework for interpreting mass cultural products and practices. This is an archive of knowledge production that does not come into existence solely at the point of its subjugation but exists within its own social relations and is animated by the agency of migrants. See Clifford Geertz, "Thick Description: Toward an Interpretive Theory of Culture," in *The Interpretation of Cultures* (New York: Basic, 1973); Michel Foucault, "Two Lectures," *Power/Knowledge: Selected Interviews and Other Writings* (New York: Pantheon, 1980); and Cederic Robinson, *Forgeries of Memory and Meaning: Blacks and the Regimes of Race in American Theater and Film Before World War II* (Chapel Hill: University of North Carolina Press, 2007).

5. Alain Locke, ed. *The New Negro: Voices of the Harlem Renaissance* (New York: Albert and Charles Boni, 1925), 3, 6–7, 199, 224.

6. Michael Denning, *Mechanic Accents: Dime Novels and Working-Class Culture in America* (London: Verso, 1998); Lawrence Levine, *Highbrow/Lowbrow: The Emergence of Cultural Hierarchy in America* (Cambridge: Harvard University Press, 1990); T. J. Jackson Lears, *No Place of Grace: Antimodernism and the Transformation of American Culture, 1890–1920* (New York: Pantheon, 1981).

7. Monah Domash, *American Commodities in an Age of Empire* (New York: Routledge, 2006); Marilyn Kern-Foxworth, *Aunt Jemima, Uncle Ben, and Rastus: Blacks in Advertising, Yesterday, Today, and Tomorrow* (Westport, Conn.: Greenwood Press, 1994); Jan Pieterse, *White on Black: Images of Africa and Blacks in Western Popular Culture* (New Haven: Yale University Press, 1992); Jill Swenson, "African-Americans and Advertising: Race and Representation in U.S. History," *Communication Quarterly* 43, no. 3 (Summer 1996).

8. See "Through the Looking Glass," *Chicago Tribune*, November 1, 1893, 1. General discussions of the Columbian Exposition include Gail Bederman, *Manliness and Civilization: A Cultural History of Gender and Race in the United States, 1880–1917*

(Chicago: University of Chicago Press, 1995); James Gilbert, *Perfect Cities: Chicago's Utopias of 1893* (Chicago: University of Chicago Press, 1991); and Robert Rydell, *All the World's a Fair: Visions of Empire at American International Expositions, 1876–1916* (Chicago: University of Chicago Press, 1984).

9. See Denton J. Snyder, *World's Fair Studies* (Chicago: Sigma Publishing Co., 1895), 237; Edward B. McDowell, "The World's Fair Cosmopolis," *Frank Leslie's Popular Monthly* 36 (October 1893): 415; and *Oriental and Occidental Northern and Southern Portrait Types of the Midway Plaisance* (St. Louis: N. D. Thompson Publishing Co., 1894), all quoted in Rydell, *All the World's a Fair*, 65–66. Also see Robinson, *Forgeries of Memory and Meaning*, 72–77.

10. On Roosevelt, masculinity, and U.S. imperialism, see Kristin Hoganson, *Fighting For American Manhood: How Gender Politics Provoked the Spanish-American and Philippine-American Wars* (New Haven: Yale University Press, 1998); Donna Haraway, "Teddy Bear Patriarchy: Taxidermy in the Garden of Eden, New York City, 1908–36," in *Primate Visions: Gender, Race, and Nature in the World of Modern Science* (New York: Routledge, 1989); and Theodore Roosevelt, "The Strenuous Life," in *The Strenuous Life: Essays and Addresses* (1901; St. Clair Shores, Mich.: Scholarly Press, 1970). On recreation, reform, and masculinity, see Clifford Putney, *Muscular Christianity: Manhood and Sports in Protestant America, 1880–1920* (Cambridge: Harvard University Press, 2003); Thomas Winter, *Making Men, Making Class: The YMCA and Workingmen, 1877–1920* (Chicago: University of Chicago Press, 2002); and James Whorton, *Crusaders for Fitness: The History of American Health Reformers* (Princeton: Princeton University Press, 1982). For more on social development through parks and playgrounds, see Robin Bachin, *Building the South Side: Urban Space and Civic Culture in Chicago, 1890–1919* (Chicago: University of Chicago Press, 2003); David I. Macleod, *Building Character in the American Boy: The Boy Scouts, YMCA, and Their Forerunners, 1870–1920* (Madison: University of Wisconsin Press, 1983); and Dominick Cavallo, *Muscles and Morals: Organized Playgrounds and Urban Reform, 1880–1920* (Philadelphia: University of Pennsylvania Press, 1981).

11. Amy Kaplan, *The Anarchy of American Empire in the Making of U.S. Culture* (Cambridge: Harvard University Press, 2002), 116; Bederman, *Manliness and Civilization.*

12. For "one swift blow," see Finnis Farr, *Black Champion: The Life and Times of Jack Johnson* (London: Macmillan, 1965), 72. For significance of fight over the Fourth of July, see *Boston Globe*, July 5, 1910, 4. On the fight films, see Dan Streible, "Race and the Reception of Jack Johnson Fight Films," in *The Birth of Whiteness: Race and the Emergence of U.S. Cinema*, ed. Daniel Bernardi (New Brunswick: Rutgers University Press, 1996). Reports of black "aggression" were in every major white newspaper that carried multiple reports from various locations. Riots discussed in Gilmore, *Bad Nigger!* 59–73; and Randy Roberts, *Papa Jack: Jack Johnson and the Era of White Hopes* (New York: Free Press, 1983), 108–9. Notably, even before Johnson's defeat of Jeffries, white angst was wonderfully captured in the two cinematic parodies, *The Night I Fought Jack Johnson* (Vitagraph, 1913) and *Some White Hope*

(Vitagraph, 1915). See Thomas Cripps, *Slow Fade to Black: The Negro in American Film, 1900–1942* (Oxford: Oxford University Press, 1977).

13. The general Jack Johnson scholarship includes Jack Johnson, *Jack Johnson—In the Ring—And Out* (1927; New York: Citadel Press, 1992); reprinted as *Jack Johnson Is a Dandy: An Autobiography* (New York: Chelsea House Publishers, 1969); Farr, *Black Champion*; Gilmore, *Bad Nigger!*; Roberts, *Papa Jack*; Thomas Hietala, *The Fight of the Century: Jack Johnson, Joe Louis and the Struggle for Racial Equality* (Armonk, N.Y.: M. E. Sharpe, 2002); and Geoffrey Ward, *Unforgiveable Blackness: The Rise and Fall of Jack Johnson* (New York: Vintage, 2006). On the Mann Act controversy, see Kevin Mumford, *Interzones: Black/White Sex Districts in Chicago and New York in the Early Twentieth Century Culture* (New York: Columbia University Press, 1997); and Al-Tony Gilmore, "Jack Johnson and White Women: The National Impact," *Journal of Negro History* 58, no. 1 (January 1973).

14. Mumford, *Interzones*, 7; and *Los Angeles Times*, July 6, 1910. Before the fight, the *New York Times* lamented that if Johnson won, "thousands and thousands of his ignorant brothers will misinterpret his victory as justifying claims to much more than physical equality with their white neighbors." *New York Times*, July 2, 1910. Gilbert Osofsky, *Harlem: The Making of a Ghetto, Negro New York, 1890–1930* (New York: Harper and Row, 1963), 17. Migration shifts for New York and Chicago are 36,183 and 14,271 in 1890 to 91,709 and 44,103 in 1910, respectively.

15. Clyde Taylor, "The Re-birth of the Aesthetic in Cinema," reprinted in Bernardi, *The Birth of Whiteness*, 19; D. W. Griffith, *The Birth of a Nation* (1915; Image Entertainment, 1998); Everett Carter, "Cultural History Written with Lightning: The Significance of The Birth of a Nation (1915)," in *Hollywood as Historian*, ed. Peter C. Rollins (Lexington: University Press of Kentucky, 1983), 9–19; Larry May, "Apocalyptic Cinema: D. W. Griffith and the Aesthetics of Reform," in *Screening Out the Past: The Birth of Mass Culture and the Motion Picture Industry* (New York: Oxford University Press, 1980); Thomas Cripps, *Slow Fade to Black* (London: Oxford University Press, 1977). It's important to note that Thomas Dixon wrote the racist books *The Clansman* (1905) and *The Leopard's Spots* (1902), on which the film was based, after just resigning from his New York City church located in the middle of the urban vice and entertainment district, the Tenderloin. This vice area was also known as Black Bohemia—New York City's central African American community before Harlem. At the turn of the century, the racially mixed Tenderloin/Black Bohemia area had become the forced repository of black migrants coming from "Little Africa" in southern Manhattan en route to the final destination of Harlem. There is no evidence that Dixon was directly targeting black migrants, or black migration north in his work. Yet there is a very substantive connection, in his mind, between northern black freedom, southern black rebellion, and the specter of racial miscegenation. In response to the Atlanta riots, Dixon predicted, "bloody riots, far worse than that of Atlanta, would occur in New York or Chicago in the near future, because of the liberties the negro is allowed in the North." See Dixon, "Atlanta Views on Riots," *New York Times*, September 24, 1906. Thank you so much to my colleague Lynn Lyerly for these in-

sights on Dixon. Also see Kenneth T. Jackson, *The Ku Klux Klan in the City, 1915–1930* (New York: Ivan R. Dee, 1992).

16. "How Ya' Gonna Keep 'Em Down on the Farm?" *James Reese Europe's 369th U.S. Infantry "Hell Fighters" Band: The Complete Recordings* (Memphis: Memphis Archives, 1996); and Brent Edwards, *The Practice of Diaspora: Literature, Translation, and the Rise of Black Internationalism* (Cambridge: Harvard University Press, 2003), 306–7. See the link between World War I, capitalist expansion, and racial imperialism in Hubert Harrison, *When Africa Awakes: The 'Inside Story' of the Stirrings and Strivings of the New Negro in the Western World* (1920; Baltimore: Black Classic Press, 1997); and W. E. B. Du Bois, "The African Roots of War," *Atlantic Monthly* 115 (May 1915).

17. See Barbara Foley, *Spectres of 1919: Class and Nation in the Making of the New Negro* (Urbana: University of Illinois Press, 2003); Marc Gallichio, *The African American Encounter with Japan and China: Black Internationalism in Asia, 1895–1945* (Chapel Hill: University of North Carolina Press, 2000); Tracy Mishkin, *The Harlem and Irish Renaissance: Language, Identity, and Representation* (Gainesville: University Press of Florida, 1998); James Allen et al., *Without Sanctuary: Lynching Photography in America* (Santa Fe, N.M.: Twin Palms Publishers, 2000); Grace Hale, "Deadly Amusements: Spectacle Lynchings and Southern Whiteness, 1890–1940," in *Varieties of Southern History*, ed. Jon Salmond and Bruce Clayton (New York: Greenwood Press, 1996). A sampling of the Great Migration literature includes James Gregory, *The Southern Diaspora: How the Great Migrations of Black and White Southerners Transformed America* (Chapel Hill: University of North Carolina Press, 2007); Joe William Trotter, ed., *The Great Migration in Historical Perspective: New Dimensions of Race, Class and Gender* (Bloomington: Indiana University Press, 1991); James Grossman, *Land of Hope: Chicago, Black Southerners, and the Great Migration* (Chicago: University of Chicago Press, 1989). Also see Griffin, *Who Set You Flowin'?* 17; T. S. Elliot, "The Waste Land" (1922), in *The Complete Poems and Plays, 1909–1950* (New York: Harcourt and Brace, 1962); Lothrop Stoddard, *The Rising Tide of Color Against White World Supremacy* (New York: Charles Scribner's Sons, 1920); Madison Grant, *The Passing of the Great Race* (New York: Charles Scribner's Sons, 1916). On the various scares and perils, see Brian Donovan, *White Slave Crusades: Race, Gender, and Anti-Vice Activism, 1887–1917* (Urbana: University of Illinois Press, 2006); Mae Ngai, *Impossible Subjects: Illegal Aliens and the Making of Modern America* (Princeton: Princeton University Press, 2005); Susan Courtney, *Hollywood Fantasies of Miscegenation: Spectacular Narratives of Gender and Race* (Princeton: Princeton University Press, 2004); Theodore Kornweibel, *Seeing Red: Federal Campaigns Against Black Militancy, 1919–1925* (Bloomington: Indiana University Press, 1999); and Gina Marchetti, *Romance and the "Yellow Peril": Race, Sex, and Discursive Strategies in Hollywood Fiction* (Berkeley: University of California Press, 1994).

18. The actual growth of New York's black population is modestly estimated as rising from 91,709 to 327,706 between 1910 and 1930. See Osofsky, *Harlem*. Also

see Grossman, *Land of Hope*. On alarmist newspaper reports, see *Chicago Tribune*, May 15, 1917; and Chicago Commission on Race Relations (hereafter CCRR), *The Negro in Chicago* (Chicago: University of Chicago Press, 1922), 524, 529–30, and 532. While this line was evidently quite real, the "imaginary line" quote is from St. Clair Drake and Horace R. Cayton, *Black Metropolis: A Study of Negro Life in a Northern City* (Chicago: University of Chicago Press, 1945), 66. Also see William Tuttle, *Race Riot: Chicago in the Red Hot Summer of 1919* (New York: Antheneum, 1970).

19. The 1911 Vice Commission report made it very clear that Chicago vice had been purposefully rezoned to the black community. See Vice Commission of Chicago, *The Social Evil in Chicago: A Study of Existing Conditions* (Chicago: Vice Commission of the City of Chicago, 1911), 38; and Mumford, *Interzones*.

20. See Robert Park, Ernest Burgess, and Roderick McKenzie, eds., *The City* (Chicago: University of Chicago Press, 1925), 54–57; and Robert Park, *Race and Culture* (Glencoe, Ill.: Free Press, 1950), 208, 262–64, and 282. A critical race reading of "Chicago School" social thought comes from Davarian Baldwin, "Black Belts and Ivory Towers: The Place of Race in U.S. Social Thought, 1892–1948," *Critical Sociology* 30, no. 2 (2004); and Henry Yu, *Thinking Orientals: Migration, Contact and Exoticism in Modern America* (New York: Oxford University Press, 2001).

21. Locke, *The New Negro*, 217. On the mixed bag of racial primitivism, see Lewis Erenberg, *Steppin' Out: New York Nightlife and the Transformation of American Culture* (Westport, Conn.: Greenwood Press, 1981); David Levering Lewis, *When Harlem Was in Vogue* (New York: Oxford University Press, 1981); Osofsky, *Harlem*.

22. Charles Hamm, "Dvořák in America: Nationalism, Racism, and National Race," in *Putting Popular Music in its Place* (New York: Cambridge University Press, 1995); Jody Blake, *Le Tumulte Noir: Modernist Art and Popular Entertainment in Jazz-Age Paris, 1900–1930* (University Park: Pennsylvania State University Press, 2003); Susan Manning, *Modern Dance, Negro Dance: Race in Motion* (Minneapolis: University of Minnesota Press, 2006); Benjamin Filene, *Romancing the Folk: Memory and American Roots Music* (Chapel Hill: University of North Carolina Press, 2000); Derek Valliant, 'Sounds of Whiteness: Local Radio, Racial Formation, and Public Culture in Chicago, 1921–1935," *American Quarterly* 54 (March 2002).

23. See Mumford, *Interzones*, 31; Osofsky, *Harlem*, 186; CCRR, *The Negro in Chicago*, 323; and *Chicago Tribune*, March 5, 1917.

24. See Locke, *The New Negro*, 217; and Chad Heap, "'Slumming': Sexuality, Race, and Urban Commercial Leisure, 1900–1940," (Ph.D. diss., University of Chicago, 2000). The heightened reference to "touring" and to domestic Black Belts as "little Africas" resonated with growing U.S. imperial interest in the African Diaspora, including the military occupation of Haiti (1915), the Dominican Republic (1916), Cuba (1917), and the government-backed growth of the Firestone Plantation Company in Liberia (1926). See Mary Renda, *Taking Haiti: Military Occupation and the Culture of U.S. Imperialism, 1915–1940* (Chapel Hill: University of North Carolina Press, 2000). For discussions of the interwar nostalgia for the "Old South," see Glenda Gilmore, *Defying Dixie: The Radical Roots of Civil Rights* (New York:

Norton, 2008), 26–27. On the "plantation genre" in film, see Ed Guerrero, *Framing Blackness: The African American Image in Film* (Philadelphia: Temple University Press, 1993), chap. 1.

25. Various black criticisms of leisure and recreation are discussed in Anna Everett, *Returning the Gaze: A Geneology of Black Film Criticism, 1909–1949* (Durham: Duke University Press, 2001); Ida B. Wells-Barnett, *Crusade for Justice*, ed. Alfreda Duster (Chicago: University of Chicago Press, 1970), 293; Vice Commission of Chicago, *The Social Evil in Chicago*, 247–48; Anne Meis Knupfer, *Toward a Tenderer Humanity and a Nobler Womanhood: African American Women's Clubs in Turn-of-the-Century Chicago* (New York: New York University Press, 1996), 103 and 125–26. Bad deportment and newcomer quotes come from *Chicago Defender* and *Whip*, respectively, quoted in Grossman, *Land of Hope*, 152 and 155. See *Chicago Defender*, March 24, 1917; May 25, July 6, and September 14, 1918; and *Whip*, June 24 and September 20, 1919. Also see E. Franklin Frazier, *The Negro Family in Chicago* (Chicago: University of Chicago Press, 1932), 112.

26. See Charles Marshall, *Indianapolis Freeman*, February 7, 1920; and Karen Sotiropoulos, *Staging Race: Black Performers in Turn-of-the-Century America* (Cambridge: Harvard University Press, 2006), 76.

27. W. E. B. Du Bois, *The Philadelphia Negro: A Social Study* (1899; Philadelphia: University of Pennsylvania Press, 1996), 311–15 and 319; Du Bois, "The Problem of Amusement," *Southern Workman* 27 (September 1897), republished in Dan Green and Edward Driver, eds., *On Sociology and the Black Community* (Chicago: University of Chicago Press, 1978), 226. Du Bois even included the sacred migrant music of "gospel hymns" as dangerous, like a "suppressed terror," because they encouraged the "pythian madness" of ecstatic worship. See Du Bois, *The Souls of Black Folk* (1903; New York: Penguin Books, 1989), 155–57. Also see Paul Anderson, *Deep River: Music and Memory in Harlem Renaissance Thought* (Durham: Duke University Press, 2001); and Bernard Bell, "W. E. B. Du Bois's Struggle to Reconcile Folk and High Art," in *Critical Essays on W. E. B. Du Bois*, ed. William Andrews (Boston: G. K. Hall, 1985).

28. Jean Voltaire Smith, "Our Need for More Films," *Half Century Magazine*, April 1922, 8; and Locke, *The New Negro*, 223, 201, 207.

29. *Chicago Defender*, August 17 and November 23, 1918, and April 12, 19, 26 and May 3, 17, 1919; Albert Kreiling, "The Commercialization of the Black Press and the Rise of Race News in Chicago," in *Ruthless Criticism: New Perspectives in U.S. Communication History*, ed. William Solomon and Robert McChesney (Minneapolis: University of Minnesota Press, 1993); Kreiling, "The Rise of the Black Press in Chicago," *Journalism History* 4 (Winter 1977–78); Roi Ottley, *The Lonely Warrior: The Life and Times of Robert Abbott* (Chicago: Henry Regnery Co., 1955). On "Folks We Get Along Without" cartoons, see Shane White and Graham White, *Stylin': African American Expressive Culture from Its Beginnings to the Zoot Suit* (Ithaca: Cornell University Press, 1998), 230–33. For a sampling of Peyton's *Chicago Defender* column, "The Musical Bunch," see "Orchestras as Theater Assets," October 16, 1926;

"Picture House Orchestra," September 23, 1926; "Standard Music," June 5, 1926; and "Playing on the Job," January 22, 1926. Also see D. Ireland Thomas, *Chicago Defender*, July 25, 1927; April 11, 1925; August 9, 1924. Also see Mary Carbine, "The Finest Outside the Loop': Motion Picture Exhibition in Chicago's Black Metropolis, 1905–128," *Camera Obscura* 23 (1990).

30. See William S. Bradden, *Under Three Banners: An Autobiography* (Nashville: National Baptist Publishing Board, 1940), 249; quoted in Grossman, *Land of Hope*, 157. On spirituals, see Ronald Radano, "Denoting Difference: The Writing of the Slave Spirituals," *Critical Inquiry* 22 (Spring 1996): 506–44; Paul Allen Anderson, *Deep River: Music and Memory in Harlem Renaissance Thought* (Durham: Duke University Press, 2001); Jon Cruz, *Culture on the Margins: The Black Spiritual and the Rise of American Cultural Interpretation* (Princeton: Princeton University Press, 1999); and Harris Michael, *The Rise of Gospel Blues: The Music of Thomas Andrew Dorsey in the Urban Church* (New York: Oxford University Press, 1994). Also see Edward Boatner and Willa A. Townsend, comps. and eds., *Spirituals Triumphant Old and New* (Nashville: Sunday School Publishing Board, National Baptist Convention, 1927). Locke, "The Negro Spirituals," in *The New Negro*, 199–210; "Our Little Renaissance," in Charles S. Johnson, ed., *Ebony and Topaz: A Collecteana* (New York, 1927). Also see Du Bois, "On the Sorrow Songs," in *The Souls of Black Folk*.

31. On race records, see David Suisman, "Co-Workers in the Kingdom of Culture: Black Swan Records and the Political Economy of African American Music," *Journal of American History* 90, no. 4 (March 2004): 22 and 33. Also see Evelyn Brooks Higginbotham, "Rethinking Vernacular Culture: Black Religion and Race Records in the 1920s and 1930s," in *The House That Race Built, Black Americans, U.S. Terrain*, ed. Wahneema Lubiano (New York: Pantheon, 1997); and Paul Oliver, *Songsters and Saints: Vocal Traditions on Race Records* (New York: Cambridge University Press, 1984).

32. See "Foster's Movies Make Big Hit," *Chicago Defender*, July 26, 1913; Jacqueline Stewart, *Migrating to the Movies*; Davarian Baldwin, "Chicago Origins," in *African Americans in Cinema: The First Half Century* (CD-ROM), ed. Phyllis Klotman (Urbana: University of Illinois Press, 2003); and Pearl Bowser, "Pioneers of Black Documentary Film," in *Struggles For Representation: African American Documentary Film and Video*, ed. Phyllis Klotman (Bloomington: Indiana University Press, 1999).

33. See "Peter P. Jones Heads Moving Picture Company," *Chicago Defender*, June 13, 1914; On Jack Cooper and "race radio," see William Barlow, *Voice Over: The Making of Black Radio* (Philadelphia: Temple University Press, 1999); and Jack L. Cooper Files, Chicago Historical Society.

34. Bowser and Spence, *Writing Himself into History*, 90. Also see Stewart, *Migrating to the Movies*; Pearl Bowser, Jane Gaines, and Charles Musser, *Oscar Micheaux and His Circle* (Bloomington: Indiana University Press, 2001); Cripps, *Slow Fade to Black*; and George P. Johnson Collection, Special Collections, University of California, Los Angeles.

35. Lizabeth Cohen, "Contested Loyalty at the Workplace," in *Making a New Deal: Industrial Workers in Chicago, 1919–1939* (New York: Cambridge University Press, 1990); Grossman, *Land of Hope*, 200–203; George Cleveland Hall, "Sporting," *Chicago Defender*, December 6, 1913, 7; "Supervisor of High School Athletics Defines 'Amateurism,'" *Chicago Defender*, February 25, 1925, 11; and Henry R. Crawford, "Amateur Athletics vs. Professional," *Chicago Defender*, February 25, 1928, pt. 2, 9 and April 7, 1928, pt. 2, 11. Also see Gerald Gems, "Blocked Shot: The Development of Basketball in the African American Community of Chicago," *Journal of Sports History* (Summer 1995). Attempts at reform and middle-class distinction in particular can also be found squarely within the professional realm of sport. Frank Leland, manager and owner of the Leland Giants baseball team, formed the Leland Giants Baseball and Amusement Association (LGBAA) in 1907, which developed a sports amusement complex, the Chateau de Plaisance, at Auburn Park on 79th and Wentworth. The Chateau presented itself as a healthy, high-class, and tasteful alternative to the Stroll, with a location purposefully on the perimeter of the black community that required a relatively pricey "Electric Car ride," and was advertised as a place where the better class could interact "unmolested or annoyed" by their black social inferiors in confining city spaces.

36. The notion of "in-betweeness" is drawn from Griffin, *Who Set You Flowin'?* On migration patterns, see Marks, *Farewell—We're Good and Gone*, 37; CCRR, *The Negro in Chicago*, 95. Also see Louise Kennedy, *The Negro Peasant Turns Cityward: The Effects of Recent Migrations to Northern Centers* (New York: Columbia University Press, 1930).

37. Jack Temple Kirby, *Rural Worlds Lost: The American South, 1920–1960* (Baton Rouge: Louisiana State University Press, 1987); Reed, *All The World Is Here*. On *Defender* circulation, see Otley, *Lonely Warrior*, 87–88; Frederick Detweiler, *The Negro Press in the United States* (Chicago: University of Chicago Press, 1922), 6; and Grossman, *Land of Hope*, 74. Also see Robert Peterson, *Only the Ball Was White: A History of the Legendary Black Ball Players and All-Black Professional Teams* (New York: McGraw-Hill, 1984), 112.

38. Quoted in Wolcott, *Remaking Respectability*, 102; Drake and Cayton, *Black Metropolis*, 598 (emphasis in the original); and CCCR, *The Negro in Chicago*, 387. On prostitution, see Cynthia Blair, "Vicious Commerce: African American Women's Sex Work and the Transformation of Urban Space in Chicago, 1850–1915," (Ph.D. diss., Harvard University, 1999).

39. Ann Fabian, *Card Sharps, Dream Books, and Bucket Shops: Gambling in Nineteenth-Century America* (Ithaca: Cornell University Press, 1990).

40. Nathan Thompson, *Kings: The True Story of Chicago's Policy Kings and Numbers Racketeers: An Informal History* (Chicago: Bronzeville Press, 2003); Victoria Wolcott, "The Culture of the Informal Economy: Numbers Runners in Inter-War Black Detroit," *Radical History Review* 69 (1997); Irma Watkins-Owens, *Blood Relations: Caribbean Immigrants and the Harlem Community, 1900–1930* (Indianapolis: Indiana University Press, 1996); Mark Haller, "Policy Gambling, Entertainment

and the Emergence of Black Politics: Chicago from 1900 to 1940," *Journal of Social History* 4 (1991); Dempsey Travis, *An Autobiography of Black Jazz* (Chicago: Urban Research Institute, 1983); Drake and Cayton, *Black Metropolis*, 470–94.

41. About the act and art of strolling and Chicago's Stroll in particular, see Stewart, *Migrating to the Movies*, 10–11 and 132–38; and White and White, *Stylin'*, 228–34.

42. On beauty, see A'lelia Perry Bundles, *On Her Own Ground: The Life and Times of Madam C. J. Walker* (New York: Scribner, 2001); Julia Willett, *Permanent Waves: The Making of the American Beauty Shop* (New York: New York University Press, 2000); Kathy Peiss, *Hope in a Jar: The Making of America's Beauty Culture* (New York: Henry Holt, 1999); Gwendolyn Robinson, "Race, Class and Gender: A Transcultural, Theoretical, and Sociohistorical Analysis of Cosmetic Institutions and Practice to 1920," (Ph.D. diss., University of Illinois at Chicago, 1984); and Willie Morrow, *400 Years Without a Comb* (San Diego: Black Publishers, 1973). On film, see Stewart, *Migrating to the Movies*; Bowser, Gaines, and Musser, *Oscar Micheaux and His Circle*; Bowser and Spence, *Writing Himself into History*; Sampson, *Blacks in Black and White*; and Cripps, *Slow Fade to Black*.

43. On gospel music and its larger religious culture, see Wallace Best, *Passionately Human, No Less Divine: Religion and Culture in Black Chicago, 1915-1952* (Princeton: Princeton University Press, 2005); Jerma Jackson, *Singing in My Soul: Black Gospel Music in a Secular Age* (Chapel Hill: University of North Carolina Press, 2004); Harris, *The Rise of Gospel Blues*; and Anthony Heilbut, *The Gospel Sound: Good News and Bad Times* (Garden City, N.Y.: Anchor Press, 1975). On sports style, see my detailed discussion in Baldwin, *Chicago's New Negroes*, 224–32; "Black Style?" section in Michael Oriard, *King Football: Sport and Spectacle in the Golden Age of Radio and Newsreels, Movies and Magazines, The Weekly and the Daily Press* (Chapel Hill: University of North Carolina Press, 2001), 319–27; and Gena Caponi-Tabery, "Jump for Joy: Jump Blues, Dance, and Basketball in 1930s African America," in *Sports Matters: Race, Recreation and Culture*, ed. John Bloom and Michael Nevin Willard (New York: New York University Press, 2002).

44. Edward Kennedy Ellington, *Music Is My Mistress* (New York: DaCapo Press, 1973), 131.

Buying and Selling with God

African American Religion, Race Records, and the Emerging Culture of Mass Consumption in the South

JOHN M. GIGGIE

In 1928, Rev. J. M. Gates of Atlanta caught his friends, family, and especially his record company, Vocalion, by surprise. One of his first-ever recordings, a seventy-eight with the arresting title, "Death's Black Train Is Coming," began to fly off the shelves. Thousands of African Americans, mostly southern, were plunking down a dime or more to buy a copy of this story of moral decline described as a train ride to hell. They purchased, however, not a typical blues tune or a rendition of a slave spiritual but a sermon that this forty-four-year-old minister sang and chanted with background vocals provided by women drawn from his congregation, Mount Calvary Baptist Church, in Rock Dale Park. They often bought the record from Gates himself, who personally pitched it to congregations across the South, appeared in countless advertisements for it in black religious presses, and enlisted the aid of fellow black ministers and Baptist leaders to drum up sales. In the case of this record and the dozens that followed over the next twenty years, Gates swore that they were reasonably priced and of high quality and that much of his profit would directly support his own house of worship and other worthy black institutions.

Gates was one of the most famous of the scores of black southern preachers who recorded chanted sermons during their heyday of popularity, from the early 1920s until World War II. He, along with Rev. F. W. McGee and Rev. A. W. Nix, cut hundreds of seventy-eights that captured a preaching style common in southern congregations and marketed them through their religious communities. All of the major recording studios of the day, including, in addition to Vocalion, Victor, Bluebird, Okeh, and Gennet, tripped over themselves to sign these preachers in the hope that at least one of their records would sell. Many of them did, giving commercial voice to a particular form of black oral tradition and creating a recreational commodity of great interest to black southerners and particularly southern migrants to the urban centers of the Midwest and North, who loved to listen to the sounds of a religious world left behind.

Recorded sermons have certainly caught the eye of scholars, who typically lump them with other black sound recordings of the era and label them "race records." Most see them as a strand of the history of the early blues and a vital document preserving the hopes and anxieties of the black working class at the turn of the century.[1] Yet these recordings are equally important for the issues that they evoke about the emerging character of southern black consumption and its relationship to black religion. In particular, they raise the deceptively simple question of why they sold so well. The quick response, of course, is to say that black consumers wanted them because they sounded so good, were so new and exciting, and offered important spiritual messages. But there is a broader and more complex issue embedded in the act of African Americans purchasing a recorded sermon in the early 1900s—namely, why would blacks actually trust the consumer market to produce reliable and honestly priced goods, especially at a time when they typically experienced commercial transactions as dangerous, degrading, and dirty? Why would a people only a generation removed from slavery and for whom the experience of a being a commodity themselves was a painful, and for some, still-vivid memory have faith in the operations of the market?

The answer lies in the hidden cultural history embedded in the transaction itself. African Americans purchased records from Gates because of their earlier experience with consumption and the pivotal role that their preachers and faith played in it. In the decades before Vocalion recorded Gates, blacks in the South came to rely on their religion as a critical resource for information about the market and its products. Indeed, when Gates advertised his records in person and in print to fellow black Christians, he was performing a well-established ritual of consumption in the rural South with roots that stretched back nearly thirty years. In this ritual, preachers acted as mediators between the market and their congregants, assuring buyers that the market could work in their favor. They provided knowledge about commercial goods and their delivery as a way to provide fresh access to the market for fellow worshippers, to raise money for black institutions, and to earn a few pennies for themselves.

This essay seeks to show how changes in African American sacred life in the decades after the Civil War in the South eventually led blacks to trust religious leaders such as Reverend Gates to sell them goods and, more generally, to view the consumer market with a greater degree of expectation. It hopes to illuminate as well a critical early chapter in the larger story of modern black consumption. The tremendous growth of the national and southern consumer market after Reconstruction, while introducing novel ideas and practices about segregation to the South, also created unexpected opportunities for African Americans to explore new dimensions to their faiths. Building on customs that integrated religion, labor, and consumption, blacks slowly experimented with contemporary advertising schemes and marketing ploys to devise new religious customs. Adapting fashionable sales techniques, they invented fresh methods of raising money and public support for their rapidly growing churches, schools, and newspapers.[2] These innovations, in turn, shaped how freed blacks experienced the consumer market and, as Reverend Gates understood so well, established African American religion as a key arena for the selling and buying of domestic commodities such as his records.

As the consumer market slowly expanded in the South after Reconstruction, blacks sought greater power over how and where they spent their money, while whites strove to control that power. It was an ongoing battle that went to the heart of segregation's power to shape black behavior. African Americans usually could secure what they needed to live either at the commissary, at the general store, or, less frequently, from a commercial salesman. But securing simple consumer goods unrelated to work—such as books, bibles, lithographs, Sunday shoes, tablecloths, or a bit of lace—was a different matter. Blacks frequently lacked enough money or credit to purchase them. Even when they could afford such goods, they had to circumvent whites bent on preventing them from inspecting and acquiring them.

These barriers, however, did not mean that blacks were unaware of the rapidly expanding consumer market in the late nineteenth-century South; they still saw, read about, and heard about it. A few rural blacks, when they could, also entered the market, often with a little extra money to spend. Many agricultural workers strove to supplement their incomes by doing extra jobs on and off the farm. They took on short-term employment, especially during the periods of slow activity on the farm, such as the months between planting and harvesting.[3]

Nor was the desire and ability of rural southern blacks in the post-Reconstruction era to incorporate literary and consumer goods into their religion entirely new. Slaves, when allowed to make extra money for themselves, often had bought a new pair of shoes, a suit, or a dress to be worn to Sunday church services.[4] This braiding of the market and religion among bondspeople symbolized their grasp of the close links between liberty and consumption. Slaves yearned to sample and own consumer goods and transgress the cultural spaces where they were exchanged because such activities resonated with the thrill of emancipation. Their appetites as buyers reflected an understanding of political identity that loosely integrated the role of citizen and consumer: to be slaves no more included the freedom to buy what they wanted and could afford.[5] Freedom only intensified this link.

The market's role in southern black religion after the Civil War quickly thickened. The number of commercial stores in the southern states soared, making it easier for residents to learn about manufactured products. By 1900, for instance, each county in Arkansas and Mississippi averaged 144 stores, nearly all white-owned. Typically they were small businesses— saloons, barbershops, drug stores, and furniture shops—grouped in threes and fours in rural towns. The most important was the general store, where visitors viewed an expanding range of agricultural and consumer products.[6] One turn-of-the-century store in the Mississippi Delta sold "plows, harnesses, bridles, saddles, rolls of rope and barbed wire, and chains ranging in size from log chains to trace chains. . . . Inside were barrels of flour, molasses, and sugar, crates of sardines, salmon and potted meat, drums of coal oil, and other staples." Others stacked display cases with fancier goods, such as bolts of gingham cloth, belts with silver buckles, patent leather shoes, pearl-handled parasols, plumed bonnets, and mosquito netting.[7]

The increase in the number of southern stores and variety of domestic commodities during the late nineteenth century was the result of a series of broad shifts in the national and southern economies, especially in rural areas. From 1860 to 1890, agricultural employment rose nationally by one-half, while the total amount of newly tilled land increased by 431 million acres, helping to boost the yield on cotton, wheat, and corn by 150 percent by the century's end. This rising supply of raw materials helped to lower production costs and boost the total output of manufactured clothing and foods. The new products moved from the warehouse to the market faster and more easily because of the concomitant expansion of railroads. New policy directives created by the federal government contributed to the increase in the flow of goods and services, as well. The founding of the Federal Bureau of Public Roads in 1893 helped ensure the expansion and upkeep of roads and turnpikes. The U.S. Post Office greatly enhanced the widespread success of mail-order buying by implementing a one-cent advertisers' postcard in 1871, rural free delivery in 1898, which provided a new point of access to consumer goods for many blacks, and, finally, the national parcel post program in 1912.[8] The rise of rural agricultural newspapers kept the public up to date about the latest piece of farm equipment or home utensils, while a slow but steady rise in national rates of overall farm-family incomes from 1880 to 1920 made it more possible to buy such goods.

Improvements in the transportation system and the consumer economy caused a surge in the regional supply of peddlers, especially those who traveled by one-horse wagons. Frequently called "drummers" because of the shape of their wagons, they were a welcome sight to rural residents. A vital link to manufacturers in northern and southern cities, drummers, recalled one white woman, "carried an unbelievable assortment of merchandise—bed spreads, lace curtains, pillow cases, sheeting, towels, men's shirts, undershirts and drawers." She wrote that "thin cotton blankets, which kept a baby warmer than quilts, were sold along with outing yardage for boys' shirts and girls' underskirts, and cotton flannel for thick warm diapers." Sewing supplies for sale included needle and thread along with bits of "lace, embroidery, insertion, rickrack braid, and ribbons of various widths." What drummers lacked they usually could order through the mail. Drummers eventually competed for business with their occupational cousins, the "commercial traveler," whose ranks grew as the railroad penetrated the South more heavily. Compared to simple foot peddlers or drummers, commercial travelers usually offered a greater range of finished goods and manufactured products, such as curtains, frames, prints, medicines, and shoes. By the 1910s they were the dominant type of mobile merchant in the South.[9]

The growth of the consumer market in the rural South, however, did not mean that it was any more accessible for blacks. For them, the cultural spaces of the market became more humiliating and difficult to enter than before because southern whites worked feverishly to etch their vision of a racially stratified society onto the modernizing experience of consumption.[10] Motivating whites was a powerful fear that blacks, emboldened by new market opportunities, might mount specific forms of challenge to the ideology of white supremacy. The market, by furnishing an unprecedented range of domestic goods to all who lived in the South, theoretically presented blacks with the physical ingredients from which to formulate the appearance of a refined lifestyle that comported with white ideals. If blacks suddenly began to dress in sophisticated suits, fashionable hats, or well-heeled shoes, to decorate their churches with custom-made drapes or electric chandeliers, or to adorn their homes with elegant prints, pictures, or books, they undercut white efforts to establish an image of racial superiority based on the possession and display of distinctive consumer commodities.

To counter these pressures, white storeowners and customers embellished stock racist stereotypes by displaying new commercial advertisements and products that explicitly linked images of blackness to servility, social awkwardness, and filth. For example, wholesalers and manufacturers widely distributed trade cards, which were pocket-sized pieces of laminated cardboard with grotesque characterizations of African Americans. Published first in the 1870s and widely used until the 1920s, the cards pictured blacks as grinning servants and social buffoons aping the conventions of white middle-class society. Campaigns for soaps and other cleaning products conveyed their effectiveness and appeal for white shoppers by showing black people "washing away" their color. Starting about 1905 and continuing until the 1920s, advertisers commonly selected labels for their brands of household and personal goods that included the word "nigger," as in "Nigger Head Tobacco."[11]

These types of advertisements festooned white-owned southern general stores. They formed a visual backdrop against which whites stylized local customs of segregation that shaped much of the public experience of consumption for African Americans. White shop owners regularly forced blacks to enter through the back, sold them inferior products, refused them credit, and waited on them slowly if at all. Many storeowners were also local creditors, which simplified the task of closely watching and controlling what blacks purchased and reporting about it to nearby plantation bosses and white landowners.[12]

White mistreatment and surveillance of blacks while they shopped continued at a stricter level in plantation commissaries, which, like general stores, also featured racialized advertisements. After picking cotton, for instance, it was common for sharecroppers to bring their sacks to the local plantation gin, where they received a small slip of paper with a sample of the cotton affixed to it. At this point, the croppers' sample was graded, priced, and recorded in the account book. Then the entire amount of picked cotton was stored. On settlement day, the croppers went to the landowner's office, presented the slips of paper indicating the value of their cotton, earned a credit against their debt, and received cash for amounts beyond what they owed. But even if sharecroppers were fortunate enough to earn money above their debts, landowners insisted that workers spend it at the plantation commissary, where the latest consumer items were routinely kept from them.[13] Drummers theoretically promised relief from this spectacle of observation and restraint, but in practice they rarely offered a wider or fairer selection of goods or more generous terms of credit to blacks.

In the rural South's growing consumer economy at the turn of the century, therefore, blackness was relentlessly experienced as a limit to commodity experimentation and accumulation. Whatever the mode of shopping or consuming, blacks regularly confronted the embarrassment and peril of being overcharged, ignored, refused credit, and sold shoddy goods. Race was the most obvious and fundamental factor that influenced the contours of economic exchange for African Americans; it directly affected what products they bought, what they paid for them, and what terms of credit they were offered. Some blacks fared better than others, of course. Black doctors, dentists, clerics, merchants, and teachers living in larger towns and cities stood a decent chance that, because of their status and income, a white merchant might attend to their needs.[14] But even then the hope of fair treatment usually went unfulfilled.

Despite the racial discrimination they faced in the market, black Baptists and Methodists in the South persisted in demanding ever greater entry to it. Much of their interest, of course, was historical: African Americans from across the South traditionally sought to extend their liberty and livelihood by buying and selling consumer goods. But it also reflected an amplification of a long-standing habit of combining the shifting rhythms of economic and spiritual life. Throughout the first decades of freedom, black Baptists and Methodists liberally mixed the patterns and pressures of agricultural and commercial life into many of their religious practices. These practices lacked any extensive use of manufactured goods or marketing schemes, which is not surprising given the state of the southern consumer market before 1900. Yet they signified a popular willingness among blacks in braiding the spiritual with the economic, a characteristic that underlay blacks' future efforts to combine the commodities of the market with their sacred lives.

For example, rural southern blacks made decisions about when to conduct religious celebrations and gatherings based on the crop schedule. Experienced clergy typically planned revivals and denominational conferences with one eye trained on the farmers' calendar, carefully choosing the end of the harvest season in the fall as the ideal time. It was only then that rural agricultural workers had a little time and extra cash on hand. Evangelists and missionaries foolish enough to ignore this agricultural cycle of work typically failed to raise as much money or to save as many souls as they wanted.[15]

On a more literal level, African Americans frequently integrated the physical elements of their labor as farmers and sharecroppers directly into their sacred lives. When crops were poor and cash was scarce, blacks in Arkansas built churches from whatever resources were at hand. In 1892, founding members of the Zion Wheel Baptist Church outside of Little Rock put up a rough-and-tumble church made of tree limbs and discarded lumber. It sat in the middle of the cotton field that they tilled.[16] During the busy weeks of planting season, it was common for farmers to use every available structure for storage, including their churches. The sight of cattle feed and cotton seed scattered about the pulpit initially puzzled Reverend J. W. E. Bradley when he began to preach in churches throughout Mississippi in June 1895. He recalled, I "went to the church and to my surprise I beheld on one side about 200 bundles of fodder, in another about three loads of hay and around the pulpit about 100 bushels of cotton seed."[17] Bradley soon learned that this was a common way that southern blacks mixed the competing demands of church and work during the early summer in cotton-growing areas.

This popular habit of loosely combining the imperatives of economic life with the demands of spiritual life underlay the growing interest in the consumer market in the late 1800s. Starting in the late 1870s, black Baptists and Methodists slowly started to expand their local networks of religiously based institutions by constructing new houses of worship and, often for the first time, primary schools, district associations, women's conventions, Sunday schools, newspapers, presses, and pastors' and young people's "unions."[18] Yet the survival of these institutions required a steady supply of care and cash, prompting many black ministers and laypeople to consider how they might profit from the growing southern consumer market by adopting versions of its advertising tactics and peddling some of its goods. These innovations eventually made it possible for preachers to sell commodities such as race records to their followers.

Fortunately, the new denominational networks developed structurally in ways that facilitated solving some of the financial challenges that they raised. Many of the new schools and associations were tightly clustered in neighborhoods or small towns, met frequently, were part of larger district and state conventions whose delegates gathered as regularly as every two weeks, and published minutes, proceedings, newspapers, and pamphlets.

As a result, black Baptists and Methodists saw, heard from, read about, met, and corresponded with each other in greater and more intimate detail than ever before. In effect, they created and participated in nexuses of modern communication that were crucial contexts for the flow of information about the market: through them, African American consumer desire and demand partly took shape and circulated through the South. Equally important, entrepreneurial black church leaders tapped these connections to promote and sell manufactured goods whose proceeds promised to fund part of the expense of their expanding list of denominational institutions.

Although most Baptists and Methodists strongly endorsed their new institutions, they struggled to find the extra money to stabilize them. As an early strategy of shoring up their denominational associations, church officials simply ordered ministers and congregants to sacrifice financially. In 1878, African Methodist Episcopal (AME) elders alerted their southern clerics "that they will not be able to get their licenses renewed if they do not take the CHRISTIAN RECORDER and read it."[19] Several years later African Americans from the all-black Upper Mississippi Conference of the Methodist Episcopal (ME) Church gave money both to their local college, Rust, based in Holly Springs, Mississippi, and to their regional newspaper, the *Southwest Christian Advocate*, in accordance with a new resolution. It read that "the future prosperity of the Church depends on the development of the whole man, head, hand, and heart," and that "we as a Conference rejoice in the success of establishing institutions of higher learning in the Southern States. . . . [and] work for the interest of that grand and noble cause."[20] As a result, churches organized special events such as "Rust Day," when congregants offered special prayers for the success of the college and took up a collection whose final tally was publicly reported at the annual state conference the following winter.[21]

Simply demanding more money from clerics and congregants, however, tended to fall short as a strategy of fundraising. Most black religious newspapers founded in the late nineteenth century failed. Typical was the story of the *South-East Advocate*, the short-lived newspaper of the Southeastern Baptist District Association in Arkansas. As reported by the district's president, Reverend Bailey, "this paper was doing fairly well and was keeping the people informed about the work of the District, but a great many of the subscribers got behind and the editor of the paper began to cry out for help but failed to get relief."[22]

Like the denominational newspapers, schools and colleges struggled. In 1880 a group of Baptist preachers from eastern Arkansas formed the Pastor's Union in the hope of building a seminary and university that would be called Helena and based in the Delta town of the same name. But poor fundraising apparently doomed the project from the start.[23] The educational institutions that succeeded often did so only by the narrowest of margins. In April 1895 Arkansas Baptist College, which was the legacy of Helena University, teetered on the verge of collapse and shut its doors for several months because its executive board failed "to raise sufficient means to supplement the tuition and meet the demands of the Institute." It reopened only when it had enough cash on hand to cover its operating expenses.[24]

With the dark cloud of economic ruin hanging over many of their religious institutions, black religious leaders were under continuous strain to find new ways to bring in money. At times they successfully appealed to sympathetic white churches and religious organizations for small amounts of aid and material assistance. For example, when the black Baptist Richard Boyd worked to open the doors of his National Baptist Publishing House in 1896, he begged his white counterparts with the American Baptist Publishing Society to loan him printing and book plates; when they turned him down for fear of increased competition in the selling of religious literature, he quickly appealed to another white organization, the Southern Baptist Convention, and got what he wanted.[25] Still, blacks, regardless of their denomination, could never completely depend on a steady stream of aid from white benefactors. To ensure the health and longevity of their institutions, they were forced to rely primarily on their own wherewithal.

The unending need for raising more money and rallying greater levels of public enthusiasm for their new spiritual associations and networks eventually pushed black Baptists and Methodists to explore the expanding consumer market for assistance. This is not to imply that it was the only reason. Blacks certainly turned to the market as a cultural site to experience a sense of liberty through acts of consumption, boost entrepreneurial activity, as in starting a general store or advertising a new business, and sell and buy personal goods. These causes, however, were generally not religious ones. The requirement to support the development of denominational schools, newspapers, and presses was, and it led blacks to experiment widely with ways of integrating the market into their daily spiritual lives that produced revenue and fired public support. Such integration involved, at the most basic level, further familiarizing blacks with the language of modern market transactions and establishing religious leaders as trusted guides to them.

In one of the earliest instances of blacks selectively borrowing from the consumer economy for the specific purpose of sustaining their religious networks, blacks created a new type of fundraising tactic. To raise cash for Arkansas Baptist College following its near collapse in 1895, the board of trustees, composed almost entirely of Baptist ministers, adopted a language of credit and debt as part of their public appeals. They publicly likened their campaigns to attempts by a private business to increase its cash assets by incorporating itself and selling stock to the public. This technique of selling "shares" in the college had been tried several years earlier, but tentatively and with little fanfare. It had been, though, at least partly successful in winning some donations: members of the Arkansas Baptist Sunday School Convention passed a resolution in early 1886 that authorized the treasurer to "purchase five shares of stock in the Arkansas Baptist College."[26] But now, facing mounting bills and living at a time of greater public knowledge about the market and its financing mechanisms, the trustees confidently invited every black Baptist church across the state to join their "Stockholders' Association" by purchasing "shares" at the cost of fifty dollars each. "Stockholders," they advertised, enjoyed the privilege of attending yearly meetings to discuss the financial health of the college. Those churches unable to make a lump-sum payment of fifty dollars could elect to use the "installment plan" and enjoy the benefit of spreading the payments out over several months.

The trustees assumed correctly that many black Baptists were familiar with popular commercial ideas about structuring debt, but they badly misjudged how their audience would interpret them. Potential donors, probably influenced by the financial depression of 1893 and 1894, believed that the sudden selling of stock by the trustees indicated that the college was on slippery footing, and so they quickly snapped their wallets shut. Trustees responded immediately by assuring local leaders that just the opposite was true: the stock was "benevolent and not speculative." They hastily clarified that "the 'shares' simply means so many units of responsibility for the launching of a first-class Baptist College, and the investments were bread 'cast upon the waters to come back after many days'—not in the form of cash dividends; b[ut] 'dividends' [of] character and religious leadership."[27]

The strategies employed by the trustees of Arkansas Baptist College were ultimately successful. Many church leaders soon became full-fledged stockholders, which allowed the school to open on schedule.[28] Other groups soon followed suit. When the leaders of the Southeastern District Baptist Association in Arkansas decided to build their school in 1897, they recruited individuals and churches to become members of a fledgling "Stockholders' Association." They met their goal of raising $20,000 by selling "shares of $30 each, which was to be paid by installments of $6 a year."[29] Similarly, in

1900, black Baptists from Pine Bluff, Arkansas, successfully raised money for a grade school based on what they called the "joint stock plan." The ministers were the "trustees," while churches and congregants were the "stockholders" of the Pine Bluff Normal School. Shares were sold at $25 each, and, according to a report on the school, "a sufficient number of shares was subscribed and paid for to encourage the leaders in organizing and starting that school."[30]

More commonly, black religious leaders, especially those who were college presidents and newspaper editors, increasingly raised money by treating their constituents as consumers who donated only when given something tangible in return. The Trustees for Arkansas Baptist College awarded a free student scholarship to every church, Sunday school convention, and women's association that contributed at least fifty dollars.[31] Other black spiritual leaders began rewarding financial supporters and active workers with small, mass-produced items sometimes marked with identifiable emblems of African American religion or history. In 1896, editors of the *Southwestern Christian Advocate* gave new subscribers a free set of communion implements; two years later, they offered a calendar that recalled their Methodist heritage by featuring a different scene each month from the life of John Wesley.[32] During subscription drives, editors presented the most industrious agents with a new Epworth organ or "fine $75 Mead Bicycle."[33] Similarly, in 1895, the presiding elders and pastors of the ME Church sold pictures of Frederick Douglass for one dollar to raise money for Rust University.[34] And, in 1896, men and women scanning the *Baptist Vanguard* learned that a new, leather-bound Bible could be theirs for free if they subscribed.[35] Or, if they preferred, they could receive an "Emancipation Chart," a two-foot-high reproduction of the Emancipation Proclamation framed by winged angels and a series of elaborate sketches of blacks progressing from slavery to freedom.[36]

By patronizing their religious leaders and newspapers, blacks began to discover and gain access to a narrow range of consumer goods. Even more important, they saw that an act of consumption performed through a black religious institution carried distinctive racial and political meaning. In these examples, black men and women witnessed how their financial support for a beloved cause brought new products into their homes—products that were otherwise difficult, if not impossible, to obtain—and which, in their physical makeup (as in the case of the stylized reproduction of the Emancipation Proclamation), often represented a proud moment in their history.

This defining of market behavior as a collaborative statement about religious and racial identification took sharper form as black newspapers began to advise readers about how to minimize the problem of racism experienced in the marketplace. Increasingly, editors served as guides to the politics of shopping by alerting readers about merchants who treated blacks unfairly because of their skin color. In 1894, church leaders listed on the masthead of the *Baptist Vanguard* urged constituents to avoid reading any white Arkansas newspaper or patronizing its advertisers if it failed to oppose lynching or the recent expulsion of local blacks from the ranks of postal employees.[37] Likewise, editors at the *Arkansas Mansion*, an independent black newspaper published off and on during the 1880s and 1890s in Little Rock, consistently encouraged their audience to avoid patronizing white businessmen who flatly refused to advertise with them. "In canvassing among the merchants, we find it as a rule, very difficult to secure advertisements," opened an editorial entitled "To the Colored People of Little Rock" in October 1883 and repeated in nearly identical fashion in subsequent editions for years to come, with only the names of the black-balled commercial establishments changing. "The merchants' plea is that the colored people are too ignorant to be guided by advertisements." To prove such ideas wrong and to punish their authors, the editors exhorted readers to shop only at the white-owned stores whose proprietors advertised in their paper. "For the next thirty days patronize Gus Blass & Co, M M Cohn & Co., Ottenheimer Bros., M. Stern for dry goods, etc. and every body else whose name appears in the *Mansion*."[38] Whether these calls for protest became actual boycotts that successfully changed the behavior of white merchants is unknown but probably unlikely.[39] Nevertheless, the editorials enabled black religious organizations to provide an alternate source of knowledge about the market to their readers.

More important, ministers and editors of black religious presses established themselves as trusted brokers of the marketplace for blacks by transforming sections of their newspapers into abbreviated mail-order catalogues. They guaranteed the quality and fair price of most items advertised in their pages and guaranteed the buyer's full satisfaction with a money-back guarantee. Sometimes they even promised to secure fair terms of credit backed by the manufacturer. Interested readers mailed back an order with payment to the editors, who then contacted the wholesaler or manufacturer, arranged for delivery via an itinerant minister or the postal service, and sometimes pocketed a small commission on the sale.

Leading the way were the editors at the *Southwestern Christian Advocate*, who, taking advantage of their publishing house being based in New

Orleans as well as their close ties to the white leaders of the ME Church, forged a series of relationships with local and national white manufacturers interested in finding new avenues to reach black consumers. They openly pitched their press as one of the most sensible and economical ways to shop. Subscribers learned that they could buy a twelve-volume encyclopedia at half off the normal price and with no shipping cost if they placed an order through the newspaper.[40] If they wanted a new bell for their church, they could entrust their order to an editor who worked closely with a maker in New Orleans.[41] To quell any apprehensions about buying an item advertised through their paper, editors inserted a comforting pledge: "Our readers will please bear in mind that every organ, piano, bell or book purchased through us, helps to swell the profits of the Book Concern; and, further more, we can and do give purchasers better articles at lower prices than if sent elsewhere."[42] One 1894 offer, which simultaneously underscored the newspaper's role as a purveyor of domestic commodities and reminded readers that items purchased through the paper helped it to survive and supported the overall cause of black Methodism, offered a Singer Sewer machine at a steeply discounted price with the word "Advocate" boldly stenciled in big white letters on both sides of its metal casing.[43]

In these examples, black newspaper editors offered a fresh opportunity for their constituents simultaneously to participate in the consumer economy and to shore up the financial future of their spiritual organizations. Yet some took a more personal interest in selling and turned their pastoral visits into occasions both to save souls and to sell a narrow range of literary and consumer goods usually produced by northern white manufacturers. These preachers who also served as peddlers to black communities were forerunners to ministers like Gates who would sell their own records. They helped create the public identity of the black minister as a reliable broker of information about the market.

The phenomenon of black preachers serving as peddlers in the late nineteenth century was not entirely new. Northern black churches had had them for decades. During Reconstruction, white religious groups, along with northern white manufacturers of a wide range of products, sought quick access to the new market for literary and consumer goods represented by freed people. They struck upon the strategy of employing blacks to sell to other blacks, assuming that African Americans with little experience with the consumer market would feel more comfortable learning about it from a member of their own race. In the South, the American Baptist Publication Society regularly hired local blacks as salesmen.[44] Its black agents earned money by organizing Sunday schools, inspecting existing ones, and supplying and selling materials to teachers and students.[45] This company heavily solicited African American salesmen through advertisements that ran in denominational publications, including the published minutes of the Arkansas Baptist Sunday school conventions.[46] Other white firms, both religious and strictly commercial, did too. The *Southwestern Christian Advocate* published entreaties for black agents who would sell an array of goods for a wide range of publishers and manufacturers, including *A Manual for Family Worship and Home Teaching*, distributed by Hunt & Eaton of New York City; Plating Dynamo, a jewelry-making device, crafted in Columbus, Ohio, by an organization of the same name; and Epworth Organs and Pianos, produced and assembled in Chicago.[47]

When recruiting black agents, white manufacturers prized black ministers above any other. The Union Book and Bible House of Philadelphia and the John Hertel Company of Chicago solicited preachers across the South, offering them a small commission of a few cents for every bible and religious storybook sold.[48] Companies like these viewed African American religious leaders as uniquely positioned to advise members of their race about matters of consumption.[49] Black ministers, because of their status as religious leaders sworn to lead an honest, virtuous, and God-fearing life, enjoyed an unmatched level of public confidence among African Americans. After the mid-1880s, they also traveled for free or at a greatly reduced rate on the railroad as well, making them more mobile and better able to visit plantations and rural towns than most black travelers.

One southern minister who peddled religious goods was Reverend James H. Hoke, an Arkansas Baptist and the general missionary for the state. In 1895, he scoured the South for converts, subscribers to the *Baptist Vanguard*, and donors to Arkansas Baptist College. Although Hoke was disappointed with the fruits of his labors, it was not for want of effort. By his own account, he covered 1,270 miles, visited forty-one churches, preached fifty-six sermons, delivered twenty-five lectures, attended twenty prayer meetings, and organized six Sunday Schools and one church. Despite his grumbling, he raised $106.70 and sold hundreds of single issues of the *Baptist Vanguard*, several six-month and yearlong subscriptions to the newspaper, and, most significantly, one hundred "Bibles, Testaments & Books."[50]

Ministers representing religious weeklies usually peddled items in addition to religious tracts and disciplinary manuals. Reverend Henry Bullock, a Colored Methodist Episcopal missionary and an editor with the *Christian Index* in the late 1890s, was a salesperson who dutifully attended to blacks curious about new manufactured products. Whether working on the road or at his desk, he fielded questions about the value and price of different market items and filled orders for those advertised in his paper. In a letter titled "From the Agent to the Church," Bullock told readers that "many of the patrons write to me for goods we do not carry, and we feel it our duty to get it for them. . . . We have a force of nice workmen and think we can give satisfaction."[51]

Importantly, some black editors and ministers grabbed at the chance to work as salesmen not only for the sake of helping their congregants but also themselves by earning small commissions. Southern ministers, who regularly served without payment for months at a time because their congregations or denominational conferences were too poor to pay them, were always on the lookout for ways to make a spare dollar. Black pastors in northwestern Mississippi traditionally made only a "small salary" and were forced to "farm or do other work" in order to live.[52] Patrick Thompson, chronicling the institutional history of his Baptist faith in Mississippi in 1890, fretted that the paltry sums paid to ministers imperiled the religious health of all local blacks. He spotlighted a fiery speech given at an unspecified Mississippi Baptist Convention by Reverend G. W. Gayles, who argued that "when ministers are better supported and cared for we will have better churches and congregations."[53]

In addition to black ministers and newspaper editors, black church women contributed to the public construction of African American spiritual leaders as reliable agents of the market. They also developed a commercial role for themselves as peddlers of consumer goods, though of a far more restricted nature than did ministers. They were typically presidents of women's associations and young people's unions as well as the wives of ministers, all prominent social roles that defined them as responsible public figures and brought them into close contact with a wide range of churchgoers. They worked mostly as literary agents for northern white religious organizations eager to promote Christianity among African American southerners and visited local black homes and churches in search of customers. As was the case with white southern women who performed similar labors among whites in the South, they earned few, if any, pennies for their labor: they often gave away their printed materials or, when they did sell a book of prayers or a yearlong magazine subscription, returned all of the proceeds to the publisher or distributor.[54]

Susie Bailey of Pine Bluff, Arkansas, was an African American colporteur for the American Women's Baptist Home Missionary Society (AWBHMS), a white-run institution based in Nashville, Tennessee, dedicated to spreading the Baptist religion among southern African Americans and other poor groups. Bailey was the wife of Reverend Isaac G. Bailey, the president of Southeastern Baptist District Association in Arkansas, and a leader of local Baptist women's associations. At the turn of the twentieth century, she teamed up with Joanna P. Moore, a white employee of AWBHMS then living in Little Rock, to distribute Bibles and other religious literature to blacks. Bailey, with Moore's help, quickly became a leading female agent in the region. Many blacks wrote to her for assistance in learning about a new publication or securing a favorite book for themselves, their families, or their church group. "I have had a number of persons who want the 'Little Hand Full of Truth,'" wrote Mrs. S. Bagley of Mars Hill, Arkansas, to Bailey in August 1901, referencing an AWBHMS publication. "Mrs. Bailey[,] if you have any on hand I would be glad to get them—as many as one dozen. . . . If you have them let me know and I will send for them at once."[55] When she did not have what her customers wanted, Bailey turned to Moore. "We have received your letter, asking for fifty Bibles," acknowledged Moore to a request made to her by Bailey in September 1906. "I have ordered them. Sent [to] you from Phil[adelphia] because the Bible we get from them is a much larger type than those at the Nat[ional] Pub[lication] Board."[56]

The enlarging scope and size of the consumer market was an important if restricted resource for black Baptists and Methodists desperately in need of ways of supporting their multiplying churches and associations in the South during the decades after Reconstruction. Their efforts marked a new stage in the development of their sacred lives. In it, religious leaders and institutions played a more aggressive role as intermediaries between the market and black consumers and nurtured a form of consumption that stamped the act of buying and selling with special significance in their struggle to build spiritual organizations during segregation. To be sure, they rarely sold goods other than small domestic commodities and never became a competitive alternative to the more customary sites of southern commerce. Yet these black preachers, editors, presses, and churches created a distinctive character of African American consumption that persisted for generations, in which religious leaders successfully counseled their followers about what they should buy, for what purpose, and from which seller.

It is this historical character of black consumption that helped make possible the commercial achievement of Rev. J. M. Gates and his peers who cut and sold recordings of their chanted sermons to their followers. Even as they pitched a new product and technology, their success depended on following well-established, older practices of buying and selling in the black community. They capitalized on the long intermingling of black religion and commerce that defined them and the products that they sold as mostly trustworthy.

In the end, it should surprise us little that Gates drew successfully on his spiritual authority to sell his songs to great effect. He was, after all, following a proven if limited pattern of success. What is perhaps more curious is that Gates did not try to market other types of goods. That he and his peers basically confined their labors to selling records serves as an important reminder about the limits of religion and commerce to cooperate and form a broad avenue connecting black southerners and the market. It was never the case that African American ministers or presses delivered a wide variety of goods or were completely trusted by their congregants. Church-goers regularly sounded notes of caution and confusion over the degree to which they could place their faith in preachers who also worked as peddlers, especially when their products were expensive and of dubious quality. Still, it is significant to realize that blacks, when formulating modern habits of consumption, drew upon their faith not only to think about the nature of the market and its spiritual worth but occasionally to slip by its racial gates and handle, inspect, and even purchase some of its goods.

NOTES

1. James H. Cone, *The Spirituals and the Blues: An Interpretation* (1972; Mary-knoll, N.Y.: Orbis Books, 1991), 9–20; Jeff Todd Titon, *Early Downhome Blues: A Musical and Cultural Analysis* (Urbana: University of Illinois Press, 1977), 205, 210; Bill C. Malone and David Stricklin, *Southern Music/American Music* (Lexington: University Press of Kentucky, 1979), 106, 124, 132, 133; Evelyn Brooks Higginbotham, "Rethinking Vernacular Culture: Black Religion and Race Records it the 1920 and 1930s," in *The House that Race Built: Black Americans, U.S. Terrain,* ed. Wahneema Lubianao (New York: Pantheon, 1997), 157–77; Adam Gussow, *Seems Like Murder in Here: Southern Violence and the Blues Tradition* (Chicago: University of Chicago Press, 2002), 1–17, who offers a solid theoretical introduction to the study of the blues and black music generally; Teresa L. Reed, *The Holy Profane: Religion in Black Popular Music* (Lexington: University Press of Kentucky, 2003), 89–113, 114–17; Jerma Jackson, *Singing in My Soul: Black Gospel Music in the a Secular Age* (Chapel Hill: University of North Carolina Press, 2004), 8–27.

2. On the symbiotic role between religion and commercial culture, see R. Law-

rence Moore, "Religion, Secularization, and the Shaping of the Culture Industry in Antebellum America," *American Quarterly* 41 (1989): 216–42; Moore, *Selling God: American Religion in the Marketplace of Culture* (New York: Oxford University Press, 1994); Leigh Eric Schmidt, *Consumer Rites: The Buying and Selling of American Holidays* (Princeton: Princeton University Press, 1995); and Diane Winston, *Red Hot and Righteous: The Urban Religion of the Salvation Army* (Cambridge: Harvard University Press, 1999). On the spread of evangelical Christianity through commercial techniques and networks, see Frank Lambert, "'Pedlar in Divinity': George Whitefield and the Great Awakening, 1737–1745," *Journal of American History* 77 (December 1990): 812–37; Lambert, *"Peddler in Divinity": George Whitefield and the Transatlantic Revivals, 1737–1770* (Princeton: Princeton University Press, 1994); and Harry Stout, *The Divine Dramatist: George Whitefield and the Rise of Modern Evangelism* (Grand Rapids, Mich.: William B. Eerdmans Publishing Company, 1991).

3. John Willis, *Forgotten Time: The Yazoo-Mississippi Delta after the Civil War* (Charlottesville: University of Virginia Press), 63, 255n48.

4. Albert J. Raboteau, *Slave Religion: The "Invisible Institution" in the Antebellum South* (New York: Oxford University Press, 1978), 223.

5. These roles are often presented as analytically distinct or even oppositional, with citizens rejecting luxury as a threat to civic virtue and consumers seeking cultural value and personal satisfaction in a world of material goods. But blacks living after Reconstruction in the Delta combined these roles and defined citizenship partly as the opportunity to access the market freely and consume its goods according to their own standards. See Lizabeth Cohen, *A Consumers' Republic: The Politics of Mass Consumption in Postwar America* (New York: Alfred A. Knopf, 2003), 8–9, on the African American intersection of citizen and consumers; and Cohen, *Making a New Deal: Industrial Workers in Chicago, 1919–1939* (Cambridge: Cambridge University Press, 1990), 148–56, on black uses of the consumer market as a challenge to racism.

6. Edward Ayers, *The Promise of the New South: Life After Reconstruction* (New York: Oxford University Press, 1992), 81–104; statistics from 81–83. See also Susan Atherton Hanson, "Home Sweet Home: Industrialization's Impact on Rural Southern Households, 1865–1925" (Ph.D. diss., University of Maryland, 1986), esp. chap. 3; Thomas D. Clark, *Pills, Petticoats, and Plows: The Southern Country Store* (Indianapolis: Bobbs-Merrill, 1944); LeGette Blythe, *William Henry Belk: Merchant of the South* (Chapel Hill: University of North Carolina Press, 1950).

7. Ruby Shepeard Hicks, *The Song of the Delta* (Jackson, Miss.: Howick House, 1976), 11.

8. Thomas J. Schlereth, "Country Stores, County Fairs, and Mail-Order Catalogues: Consumption in Rural America," in *Consuming Visions: Accumulation and Display of Goods in America, 1880–1920*, ed. by Simon J. Bronner (New York: W. W. Norton, 1989), 339–75. On blacks and their use of mail order, see Ted Ownby, *American Dreams in Mississippi: Consumers, Poverty, Culture, 1830–1998* (Chapel Hill:

University of North Carolina Press, 1999), 75; Grace Hale, *Making Whiteness: The Culture of Segregation in the South, 1890–1950* (New York: Pantheon, 1998), 176–79.

9. On the specific descriptions of drummers and traveling salesmen in Mississippi, see Hicks, *The Song of the Delta*, 105–6. On the history of commercial salesmen, see Timothy B. Spears, *100 Years on the Road: The Traveling Salesman in American Culture* (New Haven: Yale University Press, 1995), 2, 6–13, 197–99.

10. Cohen, *A Consumers' Republic*, 42–43; Hale, *Making Whiteness*, 169–70; Ownby, *American Dreams in Mississippi*, 72–73.

11. Hale, *Making Whiteness*, 152–53, 155–59, 160–61; Patricia A. Turner, *Ceramic Uncles and Celluloid Mammies: Black Images and Their Influence on Culture* (New York: Anchor Books, 1994), 45–59; Kenneth W. Goings, *Mammy and Uncle Mose: Black Collectibles and American Stereotyping* (Bloomington: Indiana University Press, 1994), 28–31; Robert Jay, *The Trade Card in Nineteenth-Century America* (Columbia: University of Missouri Press, 1987).

12. Ayers, *Promise of the New South*, 81–103; Clark, *Pills, Petticoats, and Plows*, 55–59; Hale, *Making Whiteness*, 171–75.

13. Nan Woodruff, *American Congo: The African American Freedom Struggle in the Delta* (Cambridge: Harvard University Press, 2004), 24–28; Ownby, *American Dreams in Mississippi*, 67–73, 83.

14. Janet Sharp Hermann, *The Pursuit of a Dream* (New York: Oxford University Press, 1981), 219–46; *The Leading Afro-Americans of Vicksburg, Miss. Their Enterprises, Churches, Schools, and Lodges and Societies* (Vicksburg, Miss.: Biographia Publishing Co., 1908), 1–8. Mississippi Department of History and Archives, Jackson, Miss.

15. J. E. Knox, "Trip Notes," *Baptist Vanguard* (hereafter *BV*), June 15, 1894. Campaigning for the same cause a year earlier, Reverend Joseph Booker of Little Rock, Arkansas, met with the same fate as Reverend Knox. During a fundraising trip through central Arkansas, he lodged at the home of Mr. and Mrs. H. B. Bennet in Marianna. Booker wrote in a letter to the *Baptist Vanguard* that even though these black farmers were financially well-off, they refused to give money and instead "pledged to help us on the building only when they gather up the crop." J. P. Booker, "Trip Notes," *BV*, September 29, 1893.

16. "Zion Wheel, Baptist." Box 418. F. 33, "National Baptist Convention of America." See also "St. Matthew Baptist Church." Box 417, F. 29, "Missionary Baptist." Works Project Administration Records, Historical Records Survey, Special Collections, University of Arkansas at Fayetteville.

17. J. W. E. Bradley, "Starkville Mission," *Christian Index* (hereafter *CI*), June 29, 1895.

18. In this context, "union" was a term synonymous with religious organization or group.

19. Rev. J. B. Webb, "Encouragement," *CI*, December 5, 1878.

20. *Journal of the Second Session of the Upper Mississippi Annual Conference of the Methodist Episcopal Church, Held at Columbus, Mississippi, February 3–8, 1892*

(Columbus, Miss.: Excelsior Book and Job Printing Establishment, 1892), 18, 20. J. B. Cain Archives, Millsaps College, Jackson, Miss. (hereafter Cain Archives).

21. *Journal of the Ninth Session of the Upper Mississippi Annual Conference of the Methodist Episcopal Church, Held at West Point, Miss., January 11 to 16, 189[9]* (Jackson, Miss.: Press of the Mississippi Sentinel, [1899]), 37. Cain Archives. Black Baptists in Memphis and throughout western Tennessee also held an "education day" every July, when preachers held services to collect donations and to pray for the expansion of one of their regional colleges, Roger Williams College in Knoxville. *Proceedings of the Third Annual Session of the Educational Missionary And Sunday-School Convention of Tennessee Held with the Mt. Zion Baptist Church, Knoxville, Tenn., 8–11, A.D. 1890* (Nashville, Tenn.: Tribune Pub. Co. Print, 1890), 16, in microfilm edition, *State Conventions and General Associations of the Nashville, Tennessee, Area Affiliated with Various National Baptist Conventions, 1865–1929*. Tennessee State Library and Archives, Nashville, Tenn.

22. Rev. Isaac Bailey, "Moderator's Report," typescript, November 3, 1909. Box 4. F. 23. Bailey-Thurman Papers, Special Collections, Emory University, Atlanta, Ga. (hereafter Bailey-Thurman Papers). Few of the approximately forty-one black religious newspapers founded between 1880 and 1897 across Mississippi, for example, lasted very long. Nearly every one collapsed within twenty-four months of publishing their first edition. Success rates were no better in Arkansas; only the *Baptist Vanguard*, the voice of the state's black Baptists, survived more than three years.

23. *Minutes of the Proceedings of the Pastors' Union of Arkansas, Mississippi, and Tennessee Held at Helena, Arkansas, March 3, 4, 5, and 6. A.D. 1881* (Little Rock: Dean Adams, 1881), esp. 11. *African-American Baptist Associations–Arkansas. 1867–1951," Records of Annual Reports, Minutes, and other Publications of Selected African-American Baptist Associations, and other Organizations 1867–1951*, microfilm, reel 2, Arkansas Historical Commission, Little Rock, Ark. (hereafter AHC).

24. John Franklin Clark, *A Brief History of Negro Baptists in Arkansas* (Pine Bluff: n.p., 1940), 57–58.

25. Sally McMillan, *To Raise Up the South: Sunday Schools in Black and White Churches, 1865–1915* (Baton Rouge: Louisiana State University Press, 2001), 113–14, 190–91.

26. *Minutes and Statistics of the Third Annual Session of the Arkansas Baptist Sunday School Convention Held at the Centennial Baptist Church, Helena, Ark., on the 10, 11, and 12 Days of June, 1886* (Helena: Golden Epoch and Job Print, 1886), 7. "African-American Baptist Associations–Arkansas. 1867–1951," *Records of Annual Reports, Minutes, and other Publications of Selected African-American Baptist Associations and other Organizations, 1867–1951*, microfilm, reel 2, AHC.

27. *Catalogue of Arkansas Baptist College, 1915–1916,* (Little Rock: Baptist Vanguard, 1916), 26–27. AHC.

28. For an example of churches buying shares, see *History of Phillips, Lee and Monroe County Missionary Baptist District Association*, 22. On stockholder meetings, see, "The Stockholders," *BV*, April 19, 1895. In a similar tactic that also borrowed

terms from the market, the Phillips, Lee and Monroe County District Association, in an effort to fill the coffers of Arkansas Baptist College in 1892, urged every house of worship in its province to hold "self-denial week," when supporters foreswore "some of the luxuries of life" for seven days and donated the extra money to their denominational school. "General Church Rally for the Benefit of Arkansas Baptist College," *BV*, April 27, 1894. "Self-Denial Week," *BV*, March 25, 1897.

29. L. W. Blue, *History of the Southeast District Baptist Association of Arkansas* (n.p., 1903). Box 4. F. 46. Bailey-Thurman Papers.

30. "Pine Bluff Ministerial Institute," *Pine Bluff Weekly Herald*, January 27, 1900.

31. *Catalogue of Arkansas Baptist College, 1915–1916*, 41. Eventually scholarships were given to any individual or institution that gave at least $15 to the college.

32. Subscription advertisement featuring communion implements, *Southwestern Christian Advocate* (hereafter *SWCA*), April 21, 1896. Subscription advertisement featuring calendar, *SWCA*, November 28, 1895.

33. Advertisement, "Prizes . . . Prizes," *SWCA*, September 23, 1897. See also "Further Inducements," *SWCA*, November 23, 1893.

34. J. C. Hartzell, "Our Southern District Campaign," *SWCA*, June 27, 1895.

35. Subscription advertisement featuring bible, *BV*, July 30, 1896, and October 8, 1896. In earlier years, editors offered new subscribers a copy of *Webster's Dictionary* for one dollar. "Do You Want a Dictionary," *BV*, February 16, 1893.

36. Subscription advertisement featuring "Emancipation Chart," *BV*, April 6, 1896.

37. Editorial, "The Press and the Colored People," *BV*, July 14, 1894.

38. Editorial, "To the Colored People of Little Rock," *Arkansas Mansion*, October 20, 1883. See also entries for November 10, 1883, and February 9, 1894.

39. On the limits of black boycotts to change the culture of segregation in the early 1900s, see August Meier and Elliot Rudwick, "The Boycott Movement Against Jim Crow Streetcars in the South, 1900–1906," *Journal of American History* 55 (March 1969): 756–76.

40. Advertisement for Chamber's American Encyclopedia, *SWCA*, July 20, 1893.

41. Advertisement for Church Bell, *SWCA*, October 29, 1891.

42. Editorial announcement, *SWCA*, June 20, 1895.

43. Advertisement for Singer Sewing Machine, *SWCA*, April 12, 1894.

44. Paul Harvey, "Richard Henry Boyd: Black Business in the Jim Crow South," in *Portraits of African American Life Since 1865*, ed. Nina Mjagkih (Wilmington, Del.: Scholarly Resources, 2003), 56.

45. McMillan, *To Raise Up the South*, 32–43.

46. *Eleventh Anniversary of the Arkansas Baptist Sunday School Convention Held with the Second Baptist Church, Helena, Ark., June 18, 19, and 20[, 1891]* (Little Rock: Baptist College Print Job), 11; in "African-American Baptist Associations–Arkansas. 1867–1951," *Records of Annual Reports, Minutes, and other Publications of Selected African-American Baptist Associations and other Organizations, 1867–1951*, microfilm, reel 2, *AHC*.

47. January 4, 1894; January 11, 1894; January 18, 1894; January 25, 1894; January 5, 1894; January 30, 1896, *SWCA*.

48. Henry T. and Mary Ann Harris Papers, no. 4360, Box 1, Series 3, F. 8, Southern Historical Collection, University of North Carolina, Chapel Hill.

49. McMillan, *To Raise Up the South*, 26–31: Harvey, *Redeeming the South*, 20–22.

50. J. H. Hoke, "From the Field," *BV*, April 19, 1895. For a short biography of Hoke, see Clark, *History of Negro Baptists in Arkansas*, 43. See also J. E. Knox, "Trip Notes," *BV*, June 15, 1894.

51. H. Bullock, "From the Agent to the Entire Church," *CI*, August 20, 1898. See also "Wynne District [Arkansas]," *CI*, January 11, 1892. Earlier in 1885 Reverend E. Cottrell, a bishop with the CME church and an agent for the *Christian Index*, sold more than just religious literature. He offered his customers a chance to subscribe to the newspaper and to buy "a large lot of Milk for babes and Children's bread . . . at a reduced rate." All proceeds benefited the CME Church. E. Cottrell, "Price List of Books for The Agent," *CI*, November 1, 1885.

52. "Tunica County," 26. RG 60, V. 415, F. "Churches - Tunica County," Works Project Administration Records, Historical Records Survey, Mississippi Department of History and Archives, Jackson; W. E. B. Du Bois, *The Negro Church* (Atlanta: Atlanta University Press. 1903), 60.

53. Patrick Thompson, *The History of the Negro Baptists in Mississippi* (Jackson, Miss.: R. W. Bailey Publishing Co., 1898), 170. Thompson failed to give the year of the Mississippi Baptist Convention at which Rev. Gayles spoke, but it had to have been sometime prior to 1890, when the convention was disestablished. Most likely the year was during the late 1880s, when the topic of preachers' income first became a popular one.

54. *Price List of Hope, Bibles, Fireside School Books, Etc.* (Nashville: np, nd). Box 1. F. 4. Bailey-Thurman Papers. On southern women working as literary agents, see McMillan, *To Raise Up the South*, 118.

55. S. Bagley to Susie Bailey, August 14, 1901. Box 1. F. 6. Bailey-Thurman Papers. See also Joanna P. Moore to Susie Bailey, May 13, 1896; and Eva Button to Susie Bailey, February 26, 1897. Box 1. Folder 5. Bailey-Thurman Papers.

56. Joanna P. Moore to Susie Bailey, September 18, 1906; Susie Bailey to Sister [Joanna] Moore, July 19, 1907. Box 1. F. 7. Bailey-Thurman Papers.

third coda

The Meanings and Uses of Popular Culture

Robert Jackson traces the challenges that Oscar Micheaux and other black filmmakers faced during the transitional period in the development of the most influential form of mass culture during the twentieth century. As the focus of filmmaking shifted from one-reel silent spectacles to the multi-reel epics of the 1920s, Micheaux and his counterparts provided black audiences with films made from an unmistakably black perspective. Whether intentionally or not, Micheaux's films stood in stark contrast to those of white directors, especially D. W. Griffith. In his landmark film *Birth of a Nation*, Griffith had wed spectacle and melodrama to compel viewers to accept his white supremacist narrative. Micheaux, according to Jackson, fused both sentimental forms and modernist techniques in his films, thereby enabling him to hone narratives of considerable complexity and ambiguity. This complexity and ambiguity was unsettling to censors. W. E. B. Du Bois's metaphor of "double consciousness" must have taken on special meaning for Micheaux; he had to at once cater to the tastes and enthusiasms of his black audiences while anticipating the objections of white censors in Virginia and elsewhere.

Like the films of Micheaux, the blues defied the familiar and comfortable, at least for whites, cultural categories deemed appropriate for black expression. Riddled with contradictions, the blues exalted individualism even while the music itself was quickly sucked into the vortex of the ascendant popular culture industry. Just as many anxious whites overlooked the ambiguities and complexities in Micheaux's films, so too many whites misunderstood the message of the blues. But they could not mistake the insistence on black autonomy and individualism that ran through the blues. Grace Hale stresses the conscious artifice of the blues, both as a musical form and as an adopted lifestyle. Her point is not that the blues were somehow contrived or artificial but rather were the product of design and desire.

They were not an archaic tradition but instead a distinctly modern innovation that was commercialized in its infancy.

Hale also directs our attention to the enormous contribution of women singers to the popularity of the blues. It was Ma Rainey, Mamie Smith, Bessie Smith, Virginia Spivey, and their peers who sold the records that filled the coffers of Black Swan, Columbia, Okeh, and the other record companies of the era. For these women, who were often migrants from the backwoods and small towns of the South, the blues offered more than an occupation, it also was the vehicle to fashion a new identity, an identity that exploited artifice, illusion, and what Hale calls the "precariousness of identity." Their black audiences, thrown together by migration and oppression, understood only too well this precariousness.

While Micheaux's films and the blues of Ethel Waters gave voice to a black counter-memory forged in slavery and the era of Jim Crow, the enthusiasm for Haiti evidenced by blacks during the 1920s and 1930s bespoke a broader, transnational black counter-memory. Haiti's appeal, Claire Corbould explains, was manifold; it was the first black republic; it was a symbol of black defiance, it was the victim of American imperialism, and it was rife with cultural traditions that American blacks found both exotic and mesmerizing.

The cultural politics that inspired the celebration of all things Haitian were ambitious. Black Americans hoped to end the occupation of the island republic while at the same time demonstrating the centrality of black heritage to democracy and modernity. To move Haiti from the periphery of white and black American imaginations was a tall order; Hollywood movies depicted the black nation as a bedlam of primitivism, and history books were usually silent about the revolutionary import of the nation's founding. But the embrace of Haiti during the 1920s and 1930s tapped into a rich vein of black memory that had run through the newspaper columns of John Edwards Bruce (a.k.a. Bruce Grit), the Broadway plays of Bert Williams and George Walker, and of course the extravagant cultural movement that was Marcus Garvey's Universal Negro Improvement Association. But, as Corbould explains, dislodging deeply rooted stereotypes of Haiti and Haitian culture was almost impossible. Nevertheless the cultural embrace of Haiti yoked the arts to the anti-imperialist cause and presaged the anticolonial politics that would blossom after World War II.

The Secret Life of Oscar Micheaux

Race Films, Contested Histories, and Modern American Culture

ROBERT JACKSON

The year 1884 is hardly remembered as an important one in the history of cinema. Indeed, Edison's kinetoscope, widely considered the starting point for commercial motion pictures, was still a decade off.[1] For historians of American culture, 1884 recalls less the dancing of celluloid images onscreen than the gliding of a makeshift raft down the Mississippi River. *Adventures of Huckleberry Finn*, Mark Twain's masterpiece of that year, chronicled the journey of its title character and the escaped slave Jim away from their hamlet in northern Missouri into the heart of the South, where their interracial bond—and indeed, the very character of their shared humanity—would face, and survive, severe trials. If things had been different, however, if Huck and Jim had not missed a key left turn at Cairo, Illinois, they would have come to a small town called Metropolis a few miles up the Ohio River. There in Metropolis, in 1884, Oscar Micheaux was born, one of eleven children of former slaves. Micheaux's parents could identify both with the world of slavery Twain described and with Jim's eagerness for freedom; determined to see their children take advantage of opportunities denied to themselves a generation earlier in the South, Calvin and Bell Micheaux had settled in Metropolis largely because of the town's schools. At the nexus of slave memory and the promise of modernity, Micheaux matured in an American society that was itself in the midst of profound changes. From such beginnings along the border of North and South, Micheaux would go on to become the foremost African American filmmaker of the first half of the twentieth century. Producing more than a film a year between 1919 and 1940 (and a final film, *The Betrayal*, in 1948, three years before his death), Micheaux was exceptional among blacks in cinema during his time, and his career gave shape to a larger body of "race films"—perhaps as many as 500 produced by blacks from 1910 to 1950, most of them not extant today—that marked the burgeoning motion picture industry with a significant African American presence.

To ground Oscar Micheaux in the imaginative topography of *Huck Finn* is more than merely a facile gesture to establish the filmmaker's presence on a map of American popular culture. It is instead a reminder that Micheaux's roots are a good deal deeper and more complex than much recent film studies scholarship, which has produced an admirable literature on Micheaux in recent years, has revealed.[2] Certainly some of the power of Micheaux's humane 1920 film *Within Our Gates*, which I will discuss at greater length below, arises from its brilliant and timely rebuttal of D. W. Griffith's racist 1915 epic *The Birth of a Nation*. And Micheaux represents a most valuable figure for film scholars to consider during the three decades of his career, particularly in order to counterpoint his struggles and achievements as a black independent with the developments of an increasingly studio-driven mainstream American film industry.[3] But 1884, a seemingly prehistoric date in these contexts, still demands attention. Micheaux was born amid the initial consolidation of southern Jim Crow practices in the wake of Reconstruction, anticipating the larger accident that his entire lifetime almost exactly coincided with the segregation era in U.S. history.[4] As a youth, Micheaux's experience was informed both by blacks' memory of recent slave life and by the seismic social shifts of the Gilded Age that were transforming America's regional identities: the rise of the industrializing and corporatizing "New South," harbinger of modern consumer culture; the Great Migration of African Americans to northern and largely urban destinations, as well as their movements from rural areas to urban centers within the South; the rise and fall of Populism, an insurgent political movement pitting North, South, and West in uneasy alliances and rivalries; the disturbing creep of southern lynching and the clarion call of early jazz.[5] Decades later Micheaux would address all of these concerns in his work. The South of Micheaux's cultural roots during these late nineteenth-century years, popularly viewed as, in H. L. Mencken's notorious appraisal, "a vast plain of mediocrity, stupidity, lethargy, almost of dead silence," was in actuality a region of enormous ferment, an active and improvisational space both grounded in the traditional folk cultures of the earlier decades of the nineteenth century and invested in the culture of modernity that would soon triumph in the twentieth.[6] Mark Twain's literary return to the slave era—he set *Huck Finn* around 1845—reflected an impulse not to emulate but to satirize the nostalgic antebellum pastoral tradition that underlay the white assumptions of black inferiority so necessary to the modern culture of segregation. Micheaux's own ambitious vision of racial uplift, the ideological basis of his filmic representations of black and white Americans, would remain in debt to this Gilded Age legacy, and to a black cultural memory forged by slavery and emancipation. As *Within Our Gates* reveals, Micheaux understood that the New Negro of the Jazz Age—a figure whose heroic service in World War I and urban sophistication in the decade after 1918 suggested the imminence of a more forward-looking vision of American race relations—would still have to contend with the happy darky of the plantation, a mass-produced figure looming up at every turn in the popular culture of white America. And to the greatest extent that his idiosyncratic and complex vision, limited production and distribution resources, and the apprehensive eyes of censors allowed, he projected a passionate response to this ongoing crisis of modern black identity.

Transitional Blackness

While blacks had been captured on film since the beginnings of the medium, independent African American filmmaking did not emerge until the years between 1907 and 1917, which film scholars have come to call cinema's "transitional era." Despite some concerns with the assumptions behind this label, scholars generally agree that this more discrete period within the silent era was marked by a set of enormously important developments both on movie screens and in the institutions that produced, exhibited, and regulated films.[7] The transition in question carried the medium from its early investment in the storefront nickelodeon to an incipient "classical" cinema by the late 1910s, and thus represents a vitally important period for the medium's consolidation. Among the key elements of the transitional era were the move from what Tom Gunning has called "the cinema of attractions" to "the cinema of narrative integration"; the shift from one-reel films, usually less than fifteen minutes long, to feature films of five or more reels in length; the rise of standardized mass production and the studio model; the creation of the star system; and the anxious moves by both state and private powers to censor and otherwise regulate the upstart medium.[8] By the time the Great War ended in 1918, motion pictures had become something quite different than what they had been just a few years earlier. Early race films reflected many of the narrative and technical innovations of this era.

William A. Foster, a producer based in Chicago, was active by the early 1910s in his operation of the Foster Photoplay Company. His two-reel comedy *The Railroad Porter* (1913) was perhaps the earliest film produced by an

African American.[9] Others followed hard on his heels. Founded by a prominent photographer who worked for the *Chicago Defender* in addition to doing freelance work, the Peter P. Jones Film Company of Chicago specialized in short documentary films, feeding African Americans' gnawing hunger to see themselves portrayed onscreen without the gall of caricature or stereotype. The documentary impulse so explicit in Jones's racially uplifting newsreel films would emerge in subtler ways in the fictional films of others, addressing contemporary social issues and recent historical events. An early film of the Johnson brothers — George ran a booking office in Omaha, while Noble, who himself performed a multiethnic variety of roles in Hollywood films of the day, ran their Los Angeles–based studio on a tight budget — offers an apt example of this trend. The Johnsons' Lincoln Motion Picture Company enjoyed an immediate success with *The Trooper of Troop K* (1916), a reenactment that wove fictional narrative lines into realistic portrayal (including some actual ex-troopers) of the African American Tenth Cavalry's engagement at the 1916 Battle of Carrizal in Mexico.

Prominent black newspapers around the country—*Chicago Defender*, *Pittsburgh Courier*, *New York Age*, *St. Louis Argus*, *Norfolk Journal and Guide*, *Louisville News*, and others, which constitute one of the best surviving sources of information about race films—diligently reported on the scores of new black film production companies and their products. Most of these companies, like the films they produced, did not survive long. The obvious risks inherent in the film industry—from high production expenses to the unpredictable movie-going habits of audiences—were exacerbated for black filmmakers, who generally struggled to find sufficient financing and distribution resources. During both parts of the process, production and exhibition, blackness was a liability. Humiliating segregation ordinances relegated black viewers to upper balconies sometimes called the "crow's nest" or "buzzard's roost," placing them at distant or disorienting angles from the screen, and otherwise served to discourage their attendance at white-owned theaters.[10] At other times special viewings known as "midnight rambles" would be offered to blacks, though on a much less frequent basis—and at the late hours suggested by the label—than viewings for whites. The perhaps one hundred black-owned or black-operated theaters, which ran the gamut from rough-and-ready storefront theaters to luxurious movie palaces, invited a more inclusive but certainly much smaller audience, effectively setting an upper limit on the profitability of individual films. Segregation could also punish black filmmakers in more openly punitive ways. In some southern locales, laws prohibited black theater ownership altogether, in order to prevent competition with whites. And the cuts demanded by suspicious or openly frightened censors, to whom I will return later, were demonstrably unkindest toward race films.

In a field so competitively populated by young black filmmaking outfits, and amid the countless deterring manifestations of segregation, Oscar Micheaux's career looks all the more remarkable. His ability to produce films quickly and cheaply became the stuff of legend, and his sometimes sketchy business practices helped him stay afloat even as he earned a few disgruntled detractors. The resilience he displayed as he far outlasted most other blacks in film may have come not just from his early formation in Metropolis, but in a place that would seem even more unlikely to produce such a figure: South Dakota. As a young Pullman porter riding trains out of Chicago, Micheaux had been attracted to the frontier West, and eventually purchased and worked a small farm for a short time. This experience was mined for an autobiographical novel (his third book in five years, which he self-published and sold door to door) called *The Homesteader* (1917). Micheaux preserved a lifelong fondness for his prairie years, advocating the virtues of frontier life with a curious rhetorical blend of Horace Greeley and Booker T. Washington; and his films often posited the big sky and empire building of the West as a healthy alternative for blacks to the crude, violent racism of the South and the moral dissolution and institutional racism of northern cities.

Micheaux's South Dakota sojourn ultimately brought him to the world of film. For when George Johnson of the Lincoln Motion Picture Company sought to buy the film rights to *The Homesteader*, Micheaux demanded that he himself oversee production of the movie. Understandably, Johnson demurred. And so, with no more training than he had received before presenting himself as a farmer and a novelist, Micheaux set out to film his own story. He raised the necessary financing from his neighbors out west, many of the same people who had purchased his books, and learned the craft of filmmaking on the job. In less than two years, on February 20, 1919, *The Homesteader* would premiere in Chicago. The eight-reel tale, melodramatically narrating a black homesteader's struggles to succeed in the West and to find happiness with the seemingly white girl he loves (she turns out, miraculously, to have black blood) despite the machinations of an unsupportive black community back in Chicago, was the first feature-length film produced by an African American. Despite such seemingly unpopular elements as a pervasive anti-urban sentiment and an open attack on the immorality and hypocrisy of black ministers (an obvious reference to Micheaux's detested father-in-law; Micheaux criticized religious figures routinely in his early films), the film enjoyed a strong run at the Vendome Theater on State Street, in the heart of Chicago's black entertainment district, and propelled Micheaux to favored status among the city's black elite.[11] His independence had paid off; and his confidence had grown.

No print of *The Homesteader* is known to exist today. Any close examination of Micheaux's early filmmaking style must be limited to three surviving silent films—*Within Our Gates* (1920), *The Symbol of the Unconquered* (1920), and *Body and Soul* (1925). While none of these surviving films can be considered definitive, particularly because censorship insured that different versions of a single film would be exhibited in different cities (shortening a Micheaux film by as much as two reels was not unusual), the existing prints afford an invaluable glimpse of the celluloid images on the other side of segregation statutes in state legal codes and promotional copy in black newspapers.

Revisionist Blackness

Within Our Gates, Micheaux's follow-up to *The Homesteader*, provides perhaps the most complete cinematic vision of black identity to be found in Micheaux's early films. Released less than a year after the notorious Red Summer of 1919, which saw scores of violent race riots in American cities, the film's elaborate treatment of lynching and rape gave it a historical urgency that formed an immediate part of its initial reception. Similarly, Micheaux's scenes of the lynching of innocent black tenant farmers recall the most famous film of the transitional era, D. W. Griffith's 1915 epic of southern Civil War and Reconstruction history, *The Birth of a Nation*. The question of whether or not Micheaux intended *Within Our Gates* as a rebuttal to Griffith's aggressively racist images of black lust and white virtue and heroism is perhaps an inevitable one; in the following comparison I hope to show the films' important commonalities as well as their divergences, particularly in their distinct visual styles.[12] But Micheaux made a far more ambitious historical claim in *Within Our Gates* than any critical comparison of the two films might bring to light. Beyond its articulate revision of the racist assumptions of *The Birth of a Nation*, *Within Our Gates* posited a chain of tradition in African American culture from slavery to the uncertain post–World War I present, a proven continuity of selfhood that could hold its own against both the unsettled trauma of the black past and the amnesiac mendacity of popular—that is, white—history. *Within Our Gates* did more than revise *The Birth of a Nation*'s Reconstruction; for black viewers, who already rejected Griffith's views, it invited a more comprehensive conversion, a renewed sense of black purpose, sophisticated enough for the Jazz Age 1920s but molded in the clay of the plantation.

As a native Kentuckian whose father had fought for the Confederacy, and as a young filmmaker who had produced a number of one-reel Civil War films with derivative racial codes (among some 500 short films he directed between 1903 and 1913), D. W. Griffith demonstrated the embeddedness of racist assumptions and practices in mainstream American cinema early in his career. Well before *The Birth of a Nation* captivated audiences with its epic narrative sweep and audacious scale of production, Griffith's style—focused on the primacy of the visual spectacle—had been formed.[13] It was in *The Birth of a Nation*, however, that this style served a more relentlessly racist agenda than ever before.

Griffith's emphasis on visuality in *The Birth of a Nation* demonstrated a larger historical and aesthetic reality: the cinema of attractions never simply gave way to the cinema of narrative integration during the transitional era. Instead, the two styles complemented one another in crucial ways. *The Birth of a Nation*'s length of more than two hours, reliance on several interwoven story lines, and assumption of its audience's familiarity with numerous events and periods in American history gave the film a strong narrative component. At the same time, though, Griffith's visual style routinely invoked the style of the earlier era, most particularly when emphasizing the importance of spectatorship. Indeed, the very process of viewing becomes a crucial element driving the narrative forward. And even as Griffith embodied the maturing technological possibilities of the young medium, his work relied most heavily on a vast reservoir of racial fear within his audience. This fear would be *The Birth of a Nation*'s most precious resource, and its most abundant product.

The utilization of fear was made explicit in the film's advertising campaign. Outside theaters in Los Angeles and New York, hooded Ku Klux Klan members on horseback promoted *The Birth of a Nation*'s local premieres in well-publicized episodes. Even before audiences found their seats inside, they encountered a stark image that anticipated the film's overall presentation of spectacle. Print advertising for the film also included prominent images of Klan riders in heroic action poses. In the film's narrative, Klan riders play a doubly intimidating role: primarily, of course, they intend to scare blacks into submission (both disarming and disfranchising them), to prevent intermarriage with white women, and to lynch those who dare to transgress racial prohibitions; and secondarily, the Klan's presence serves as a constant advertisement to whites of the need for such vigilance, and thus ensures the indefinite maintenance of white fears.

The Birth of a Nation's most notorious sequence catalyzes the race war that provides the film's climax. Gus, a black Union soldier policing the Reconstruction-era town of Piedmont, South Carolina, follows Flora, a young white woman who has gone sightseeing into the woods. Interrupting her idyll like a serpent in Eden, he proposes marriage. When she flees, Gus pursues her to the peak of a rocky cliff, from which Flora flings herself—fatally—rather than submitting to Gus's boundless lust. Intercut with this chase is the effort of Flora's brother, the young colonel Cameron, to rescue his innocent sister before it is too late. When she dies in his arms at the end of the dramatic sequence, it is impossible not to regard the remaining part of the story with anything but foreboding.

This sequence is a kind of primer on early cinema's investment in visuality, underscoring the institution's core values, inseparable here, of spectatorship and melodrama. Before being interrupted, Cameron's sister experiences great pleasure simply looking at the natural world around her; as her name implies none too subtly, Flora is at one with her surroundings. Close-up shots of a squirrel and her absorbed, childlike reaction suggest the naturalization and sentimentalization of her vision. At the same time, the girl is both viewer and object, as Gus eavesdrops on her in an insidious and sexually predatory way. Her feminized and naturally harmonious way of looking is fundamentally at odds with Gus's rapacious perspective. The young colonel himself relies on his own visual sense to follow the story, finding clues—items of clothing dropped during the chase—and finally overlooking the scene of his sister's death. His is finally the morally and cinematically authoritative perspective, the viewpoint with which Griffith's audience is intended to identify. And his outraged, distraught reaction as he cradles his dead sister—with a visage that expresses his temporary lack of vision, because of the sheer agony of the moment—leaves no doubt that his worst fears (and by extension, those of white viewers) have been realized.

White female virtue and innocence (little sister in the Edenic setting, looking innocently at nature); black corruption (Gus's eavesdropping); white male rigor, coming to the defense of the woman (Cameron's discovery of the trail of Gus's crime, and of his sister at the foot of the cliff): with these ways of looking Griffith uses the visual medium itself to argue for appropriate roles of race and gender in the Reconstruction South, as well as in the early twentieth-century United States in which the film is being exhibited.

To call such an agenda racist is to understate and oversimplify the fundamental operation of the visual style of the film. For Griffith seeks nothing less than to teach his audience a very specific way of looking at the world. *The Birth of a Nation* assumes a white viewer, it constructs its audience as white and identifies entirely with the plight of the Cameron family, and especially with the young colonel who will soon temper fear into courage to avenge his sister's death. The subsequent scene of domestic mourning, which appropriates the family hearth to illustrate the destructive effects of Reconstruction on white families, even includes a shot of loyal ex-slaves sobbing at Flora's death, sharing in the family's pain as though they themselves were blood relatives. Griffith contrasts these "faithful souls," as they are called in an intertitle, with Gus, whose lynching at the hands of the Klan is presented as a just punishment—and an authoritative visual spectacle—for his perverted visual perspective.[14]

The blacks in this world have set roles: toms and mammies content within the traditional white order of paternalism; mulattoes and bucks trying to destroy that order violently and sexually.[15] Griffith leaves no room for characters to express complex individual responses deviating from this rigidly racialized architecture. In doing so he effectively grafts the sentimental tradition onto a modern medium, utilizing melodrama's genre conventions to make demands on his viewers' emotions, and thus their fundamental social assumptions. Playing on the same fears of domestic trauma appropriated so effectively by the sentimental abolitionist masterpiece *Uncle Tom's Cabin* (1852)—the specter of the family being torn asunder and loved ones lost forever—*The Birth of a Nation* tries to scare its viewers into a white supremacist perspective.

It is difficult to say exactly what influence *The Birth of a Nation* had on African American filmmaking. Certainly it alarmed blacks in other areas of American life, including those in the fledgling National Association for the Advancement of Colored People (NAACP), which protested the film in print and public demonstrations. As one NAACP member wrote in a forty-seven-page pamphlet called "Fighting a Vicious Film: Protest against 'The Birth of a Nation'" in 1915: "It is three miles of filth. We believe this film teaches a propaganda for the purpose of so stirring up the people of the East and the West and the North that they would consent to allowing the Southern programme of disfranchisement, segregation and lynching of the Negro and finally to the repeal of the fourteenth and fifteenth Amendments to the Constitution."[16]

Did such sentiments fuel the efforts of blacks to create alternative portrayals of America's racial history in film? It is of course true that a significant number of black film companies came into being in 1915 and the several years afterward. Perhaps a more circumspect explanation for this timing, especially in view of the fact that blacks had been involved with filmmaking since at least 1909, would be to acknowledge that the fierce critique of *The Birth of a Nation* by blacks already quite familiar with the degrading racial caricatures of the overall body of American film served to reinvigorate their interest in providing alternative images of themselves.[17] Micheaux's work, no less than that of other early black filmmakers, showed his keen awareness of these high cultural stakes.

Like Griffith's epic, *Within Our Gates* tells several interconnected stories of southerners and northerners. Its protagonist is Sylvia Landry, a light-skinned black woman who teaches at the Piney Woods School for blacks in the Mississippi Delta. Seeing her vocation as part of the larger racial mission, Sylvia reflects Micheaux's philosophy of black uplift, which is squarely in the tradition of Booker T. Washington. When the school teeters on the verge of bankruptcy, she goes north to Boston to seek philanthropic aid (not surprisingly, Washington's preferred method of financing Tuskegee Institute in Alabama). By sheer chance, Sylvia meets and wins over the progressive dowager Mrs. Warwick (a visual evocation of the northeastern abolitionist), who generously contributes $50,000 — a full ten times more than is needed to save the school from insolvency. This donation represents an ideological victory as well as a crucially regional reconciliation, aligning Mrs. Warwick as a white northerner with the black South, and sundering her contact with Geraldine, a racist white southern woman who advises her not to buy into Sylvia's notions of black humanity and education. Mrs. Warwick's decision represents a crucial culmination in the central portion of the narrative, privileging not just Sylvia's progressive vision over Geraldine's repressive one, but also lending authority, as David A. Gerstner has convincingly argued, to Micheaux's preferred model of black masculinity. For by the time of Mrs. Warwick's decision, Sylvia has fallen in love with Dr. V. Vivian, a physician activist and proud intellectual "passionately engaged in social questions," as an early intertitle describes him. Contrasting his heroic pose is Geraldine's model of black manhood, the corrupt preacher Old Ned (another of Micheaux's hypocritical religious figures), who encourages blacks to accept their second-class citizenship and allows white men to insult him for sheer enjoyment. Cutting between Mrs. Warwick's deliberations and shots of Dr. Vivian and Old Ned, Micheaux visually suggests an important link between her financial investment and the male leadership that will dictate the direction of modern African American culture.[18]

But even more than this central portion, the concluding sequence of *Within Our Gates* contains an implicit rejoinder to the stunning visual racism of *The Birth of a Nation*, as well as a more general condemnation of the racial violence that prevailed in northern and southern cities after the conclusion of World War I. Micheaux explores both lynching and interracial rape from black perspectives, and leaves absolutely no doubt about where blame for these crimes should be assigned. He goes beyond this critique of Griffith to forge his own linkage of sentimental and modernist discourses. Particularly in the marriage of the northern Dr. Vivian, a progressive and understanding man who accepts the trauma and chaos of Sylvia's past, with the southern, past-haunted mulatto Sylvia, black citizenship and patriotism are defined in a progressive yet historically sensitive way.

In this elaborate sequence, Micheaux relies on a variety of visual methods. While most of the film occurs in real time, much of the last quarter is a flashback sequence recounting the harrowing events in Sylvia's life before her first trip north. Alma, a cousin whose jealousy had motivated her to sabotage Sylvia's prior love interest early in the film, makes amends by telling Dr. Vivian the truth about Sylvia's past. The latter's adopted parents, a black family in the Deep South, had been wrongfully accused of the murder of a cruel white landowner named Gridlestone—the actual killer was an embittered poor white tenant—and summarily lynched by a mob of bloodthirsty white men, women, and children. During this violence, Sylvia narrowly escaped rape at the hands of Gridlestone's brother when he discovered a scar on her shoulder revealing her to be his own daughter (from a "legitimate marriage" to a black woman, a bizarre intertitle reports).[19] Micheaux tells this backstory with the same technique of parallel editing that Griffith used to show the simultaneous actions of Gus's chasing Flora and Cameron's efforts to save her, and of the Klan's heroic ride to defeat the menacing black army in Piedmont. Cutting between the rape scene and the lynching bonfire, and occasionally returning to the framing perspective of Alma's narrative in the present moment, Micheaux achieves both a black subjectivity in the perspective of the crimes committed against innocent people, and a black authorial presence that orders this complex material in a familiar and manageable way. Micheaux also adds a critique of written accounts of the supposed crimes of lynching victims, cutting from printed lies in newspapers to a fictionalized version of Gridlestone's killing that imagines Sylvia's adopted father gleefully pulling the trigger. In so doing Micheaux not only discredits the mendacious language of newsprint but also calls attention to the manipulability of visual images. What is suspect here is not blackness—as Griffith would have it—but spectatorship itself.[20] Flora's squirrel in *The Birth of a Nation* has become Sylvia's scar in *Within Our Gates*, problematizing the viewer's identity rather than evasively sanitizing and sentimentalizing the entire field of vision.

Dr. Vivian's response to this harrowing tale becomes, then, the more or less "official" response Micheaux seeks from the film's audience, just as the young colonel's dazed expression as he holds the dying Flora, and his later resolve to bring Gus to justice, represent Griffith's authoritative response to racial trauma in *The Birth of a Nation*. Just as her biological father (the early, though anonymous, patron of Sylvia's schooling) had only belatedly recognized Sylvia by her scar, Dr. Vivian must "read" Sylvia (and her "misfortunes," as he rather obliquely calls them) to understand who she really is and guide her to new insights. Pounding his fist emphatically into his open hand at the conclusion of Alma's revelations, he is convinced more than ever that Sylvia will make, both at once, a good American and a good wife. Her tragic family history, the complexity and inescapability of her racial legacy, only serve to make her a more promising contributor to the uplift of the race and the nation as a whole.

In the film's closing scene, Dr. Vivian tries to convince Sylvia to adopt his perspective. His primary theme is patriotism. In a series of intertitles he says: "Be proud of our country, Sylvia. We should never forget what our people did in Cuba under Roosevelt's command. And at Carrizal in Mexico! And later in France, from Bruges to Chateau-Thierry, from Saint-Mihiel to the Alps! We were never immigrants. Be proud of our country, always! And you, Sylvia, have been thinking deeply about this, I know—but unfortunately your thoughts have been warped. In spite of your misfortunes, you will always be a patriot—and a tender wife. I love you!"[21] The black audience Micheaux addresses here, it seems, has earned its citizenship through service and suffering. Micheaux tries to marshal the resources of history for his own rhetorical agenda, to motivate an African American culture with a long memory of racial injustice toward constructive, uplifting ends.[22] His appeal to nationalism contains within it important implications for race- and gender-based identifications. Since Dr. Vivian's speech comes so soon after Alma's narrative of the violence in Sylvia's past, violence that clearly still has a strong sway over her psychological state, the speech takes on a more immanent meaning than it might otherwise. *Within Our Gates*, which had presented itself thus far as a migration narrative, a narrative of regional union between (black) South and (both black and white) North, and a revisionist racial narrative, now depends for its ultimate success on Sylvia's response to Dr. Vivian's speech. "And a little while later," the final intertitle announces anticlimactically, "we see that Sylvia understood that perhaps Dr. Vivian was right after all." In this moment the film becomes a conversion narrative as well as a liberation narrative. Sylvia sees the world with new eyes, and as a result she gains a measure of freedom from the haunting past. In a position comparable to Frederick Douglass, who predicated his freedom from bondage upon his empowering attainment of literacy in his slave narrative, Sylvia is finally educated by Dr. Vivian.[23] She and her beau come together with clasped hands in the final shot, looking out the window of his urban, bourgeois home, into the future, and gazing into one another's eyes in a visual tableau that evokes the next stop on their triumphant black ascension—the marriage altar.

Within the conventionality of this generic happy ending, however, Micheaux maintains considerable complexity and ambivalence. Sylvia's look of deep unease during Dr. Vivian's patriotic speech suggests her uphill struggle to overcome the fearful memories of her southern past. For the violence of that dark past, which has left her visibly and invisibly scarred, has migrated to Boston along with her. Micheaux acknowledges the gravity of this suffering in the present moment, only to sublimate it into a more generalized rhetoric of black aspiration and cultural nationalism. But on another level the film achieves something more complex, since it effectively draws attention to the constructed nature of history itself, both the grand narratives of nations and races and the individual experiences of ordinary African Americans. In this context the final scene between Dr. Vivian and Sylvia takes on greater meaning. For in visualizing the ability of black characters to discuss their pasts openly, to contemplate both the injustices and the achievements in their race's collective memory, and to arrive rationally at a constructive vision of their future, Micheaux makes a political statement that counters the assumptions of Griffith (and others with similar racial views) on a fundamental level. *The Birth of a Nation*'s argument, finally, is that blacks do not think consciously so much as act blindly according to an inner, bestial drive. *Within Our Gates*, after deriving a plausible alternative version of action and history, demonstrates otherwise. It is both the power of the images in Alma's confessional flashback narrative and the ability of intelligent individuals such as Dr. Vivian and Sylvia Landry to think through the meaning of such images that work to make the film's final statement on the extraordinary potential of modern black identity. Micheaux thus seems to resist the kind of totalizing and purifying rhetorical impulse behind Griffith's visual practice, providing instead a more open-ended—indeed, a more literate—reflection of his audience. Micheaux seems to have constructed his audience not just in racial terms—in contrast to, recall, Griffith's primary designation for his own audience as white, and as people to be intimidated with threatening images into adopting (or deepening) racist views. The conclusion of *Within Our Gates* offers, instead, compelling evidence that Micheaux viewed the audience for his race films as collaborative members of a creative enterprise, both on the screen and in the post–World War I America where blacks would have to draw themselves with greater sophistication and imagination than ever before.

Censored Blackness

Along with their mutual interest in the power of visual spectacle, D. W. Griffith and Oscar Micheaux both hated censorship. Griffith's faith in the wisdom of his white paternalism was so complete that even after the tumultuous reception of *The Birth of a Nation* in 1915 he failed to perceive how his film had savaged black identity and culture. Instead, he viewed himself as the primary victim of an exhibition system that failed to protect his freedom of expression. He wrote and self-published a fiery pamphlet called "The Rise and Fall of Free Speech in America," decrying the exceptional treatment of motion pictures and arguing that they were entitled to the same protections of free speech guaranteed by the Constitution of the United States. "The moving picture is simply the pictorial press," he wrote, lamenting censorship's distortion of "history" into "sugar-coated and false version of life's truths."[24] Invoking Thomas Jefferson's efforts to protect free speech in 1801, Griffith added: "The integrity of free speech and publication was not again attacked seriously in this country until the arrival of the motion picture, when this new art was seized by the powers of intolerance as an excuse for an assault on our liberties. . . . It is said that the motion picture tells its story more vividly than any other art. In other words, we are to be blamed for efficiency, for completeness. Is this justice? Is this common sense? We do not think so."[25] Righteous, or perhaps simply myopic, to the last, Griffith called his next film *Intolerance*. A cynic, or one too familiar with the ways of Hollywood, might be tempted to view "The Rise and Fall of Free Speech in America" as just another form of publicity for an upcoming film. But the single-mindedness of Griffith's vision, and the selective blindness, disturbingly common among white Americans in the midst of the segregation era, with which he perceived racial matters give his defense a more ingenuous quality.

Defending a re-release of *The Birth of a Nation* in Virginia against NAACP protests several decades later when the edifice of segregation was crumbling, an unsigned 1965 editorial for the *Richmond News-Leader* echoed Griffith's outrage. "History," the editorialist wrote, "in films as well as in books, must be re-written to fit the prevailing racial orthodoxy. The NAACP is projecting a new image for itself, that of public censor, telling the public what it should and should not see. *Birth of a Nation* must remain, in their view, a silent film."[26] Had this writer researched his or her subject more thoroughly, a different "history" might have revealed itself. The NAACP's censorship efforts were not part of any "new image," but had been a consistent part of the organization's work for many decades (owing in no small measure to the original release of *The Birth of a Nation* in 1915). More striking, however, was the editorialist's apparent lack of awareness that film censorship had been in practice by Virginia's own State Board of Censors without break since 1922, and that legal censorship had been used since its earliest days to maintain white supremacy in the Old Dominion.[27]

Much to his frustration, Oscar Micheaux would never be allowed to put the Virginia State Board of Censors totally out of his mind. As one of six states (and the only southern one) to create a censorship board by the early 1920s—more commonly, individual cities would take the lead in doing so—Virginia's official response to Micheaux's race films was of a piece with its larger administrative agenda, what J. Douglas Smith has brilliantly revealed as the "management" of race relations grounded in the assumptions of white paternalism and a strict (though less violent than in other parts of the South) racial etiquette.[28] "It may not be amiss here," wrote board chairman Evan R. Chesterman in his 1925 annual report to the governor, "to state that the members of the Board have scrutinized with peculiar care all films which touch upon the relations existing between whites and blacks. Every scene or subtitle calculated to produce friction between the races is eliminated."[29] Not bothering to define what material might "produce friction between the races," the board tended to reject in toto or demand major cuts to any film that did not promote what the board (and many white Virginians) believed were mutually satisfactory race relations between whites and blacks under segregation. "In a state where the best of feeling prevails between the two races," Chesterman wrote elsewhere in an unfavorable review, "it is always unwise to present, in any theatre or house of amusement, any entertainment which emphasizes race prejudice or suggests injustice to the coloured races."[30] Chesterman's revealing metaphor for the work of the censors—apt in a region devoted to gardening and overrun by kudzu—was that of the "pruning knife."[31] Micheaux's films, to say the least, kept the pruning knife quite busy.

Fortunately for Micheaux the Virginia State Board of Censors was not created until 1922, so his earliest films, including *Within Our Gates*, never came under its review. Chesterman's annual report of 1925 included an unusual passage noting the board's dealings with a single production company—Micheaux's—whose films had required an exceptional amount of time and attention. "One producing concern, a negro corporation," Chesterman wrote, "whose output is designed solely for colored houses, and whose actors, almost without exception, are colored people, has been severely disciplined on account of its infelicitous, not to say dangerous, treatment of the race question. Two of its pictures were condemned in toto, but subsequently were licensed after having undergone the elimination of hundreds of feet of film which included objectionable scenes and subtitles."[32] Even as Micheaux's films spoke to blacks in the seemingly innocuous terms of middle-class aspiration and nationalistic pride, Virginia's board tended to see in the images little more than blackness itself, and responded with characteristic vigor.

While Micheaux did manage to reedit several films and secure licenses for them in Virginia, the board remained manifestly apprehensive whenever dealing with his handiwork. The board's distaste for Micheaux's films emerged in a consistent pattern; reviews expressed, largely in the negative terms of confusion, fear, and censure, a sense of wonder at such images and stories. Sensing that such films addressed African American culture in sophisticated ways and transcended the racist stock character types of other black portrayals in early film, the board responded with anxiety. Indeed, a tone of genuine fear is unmistakable in some of Chesterman's writings. Upon learning that Micheaux had released *Birthright* (1924), an adaptation of the white novelist T. S. Stribling's 1922 novel, without bothering to submit it to the board for approval (the filmmaker probably knew it would be rejected), Chesterman wrote to the mayor of Norfolk to alert him to the possible presence of the film. Using language that suggests something of the perceived agency of motion pictures apart from human intention or control, Chesterman warned that "the film has been turned loose in Virginia without any recognition of our authority."[33] Chesterman cited other films, including

A Son of Satan (1924) and *The House Behind the Cedars* (1925), for their possible negative effects on viewers, quoting the state censorship statute's language prohibiting films that may "incite to crime."[34]

Micheaux generally sought to appease Chesterman and his colleagues and was willing to cut large sections from a film to win the board's approval. When confronted about releasing the unreviewed print of *Birthright*, Micheaux partially blamed some of his business partners and proceeded to appeal to the board's paternalism in seeking leniency for his offense. He added, by way of explanation: "As for me, I intended writing, telling you the truth as done above and make apology; but I was covering the south, riding in cinder ridden Jim Crow cars all night and was just so tired and distracted."[35] The board, wanting to end the episode's massive paper trail, fined him twenty-five dollars; there is no evidence that *Birthright* was ever licensed for exhibition in Virginia.

A letter to the board on March 13, 1925, which accompanied Micheaux's newly edited version of *The House Behind the Cedars*, noted the elimination of "the entire second reel which contains the parts to which you object." Responding to the board's judgment that the film might "incite to crime" its black viewers, Micheaux offered a dissent that was rare and unusually pointed in his correspondence: "I must also add that you are unduly alarmed as to how my race is likely to take even the discussion in the second reel. There has been but one picture that incited the colored people to riot, and that still does, that picture is the *Birth of a Nation*." Lest the board misconstrue the spirit of his remarks, Micheaux quickly added that the members of the Virginia board were "the most liberal minded Censors I had ever met—and I have met and know them all."[36]

Reading Micheaux's correspondence to the board, it is important to keep in mind that beyond the mixed rhetoric of victimization and self-reliance, of flattery and self-confidence, remained the goal of securing approval to exhibit his films. To recall that Virginia's was only one of scores of censorship boards in the United States, each with its own attitudes and demands, through which Micheaux's race films had to pass in order to make their way to movie screens, is to marvel at the seemingly inexhaustible energy with which he operated his business in the face of myriad unexpected obstacles. Producing an eight-reel film seems by comparison an almost pedestrian affair. Virginia's State Board of Censors was certainly not the only board worried about race, any more than twentieth-century America's Du Boisian "problem of the color line" was exclusively limited to the South.[37] In the workings of Virginia's board, however, can be traced a continuity of racial traditions, reaching well back into the days of slavery and gathering into a modernity of expert-managed race relations, resonant with that on display in a film such as *Within Our Gates*. The complex racial roles appropriated and performed by both sides—Chesterman and his colleagues as state officials, Micheaux as representative of the emergent tradition of African American cinema—speak as well to the board's continuing challenge of responding to the onward march of "high class Negro feature photoplays" in Virginia several decades before the end of segregation.[38]

Ultimately, though, Micheaux's very presence before Virginia's censors was a problem for which there could be no satisfying solution, a presence—like film itself—over which there could be no full authority, but only a kind of "unrelaxing vigilance," as one censor put it in 1925.[39] And such a problem, I think, hints at the profoundly underappreciated role of a southern-bred, migrating-and-remembering blackness in the life of modern American culture. For Virginia's censors, as for the many proponents of censorship elsewhere during the silent era, the medium of film itself represented something ominous and beyond control, far more alarming than oral or written language, or music, or still photography. The moving images seemed to exercise a power of agency altogether startling and often disturbing, regardless of their "morality" or their respect for current social codes. Perhaps more than in any other films they reviewed, Virginia's censors saw in Micheaux's films a casting into illusion and doubt of all symbols of stability in civil life—whiteness, state power, the containment of female sexuality, the paternalistic family unit. (This may not have been what black viewers saw, as Micheaux tried to explain in his correspondence, but the board never considered such distinctions.) In this sense Micheaux's menacing blackness was conflated with film itself: in the eyes of the censorship board, both represented media whose agency threatened to run amok in an otherwise healthy civilization; both required pruning. View the flickering, momentary image—the ghost in the machine, the "nigger in the woodpile"—then register its astonishing backstory: that an African American in Jim Crow Virginia could so consummately personify, in these cultural connotations, the dominant aesthetic form of twentieth-century America—the motion picture—may seem an unlikely enough revelation even today, a full century after the plateau of the New South and the Great Migration, jazz, blues, barbecue, and all. To the dutiful civil servant Evan Chesterman, and certainly to D. W. Griffith, whom we call the father of narrative cinema, the idea would have been unthinkable.[40] But a guy like Mark Twain—regional migrant, slave of new technology, racial cross-dresser, memorialist of a better, or at least an imaginatively alternative, Old South—would have nodded in recognition and assent, absorbing the grief and savoring the humor of the tale.

NOTES

1. Charles Musser, *The Emergence of Cinema: The American Screen to 1907* (Berkeley: University of California Press, 1990), 1. Musser's book is the most complete introduction to the earliest developments in cinema up to the nickelodeon.

2. See, for example, Pearl Bowser, Jane Gaines, and Charles Musser, eds., *Oscar Micheaux and His Circle: African-American Filmmaking and Race Cinema of the Silent Era* (Bloomington: Indiana University Press, 2001); Pearl Bowser and Louis Spence, *Writing Himself into History: Oscar Micheaux, His Silent Films, and His Audiences* (New Brunswick: Rutgers University Press, 2000); J. Ronald Green, *Straight Lick: The Cinema of Oscar Micheaux* (Bloomington: Indiana University Press, 2000); J. Ronald Green, *With a Crooked Stick: The Films of Oscar Micheaux* (Bloomington: Indiana University Press, 2004); Patrick McGilligan, *The Great and Only Oscar Micheaux: The Life of America's First Black Filmmaker* (New York: HarperCollins, 2007).

3. Jane Gaines, *Fire and Desire: Mixed-Race Movies in the Silent Era* (Chicago: University of Chicago Press, 2001), exemplifies the trend of reading *Within Our Gates* as a response to *The Birth of a Nation*. Jacqueline Najuma Stewart, *Migrating to the Movies: Cinema and Black Urban Modernity* (Berkeley: University of California Press, 2005), provides a wonderful treatment of the work of independent black filmmaking culture and reception, explicitly locating this work in the historical context of the Great Migration.

4. On the history of southern segregation, see, for example, C. Vann Woodward, *The Strange Career of Jim Crow* (New York: Oxford University Press, 1955); Grace Elizabeth Hale, *Making Whiteness: The Culture of Segregation in the South, 1890–1940* (New York: Pantheon, 1998).

5. C. Vann Woodward, *Origins of the New South, 1877–1913* (Baton Rouge: Louisiana State University Press, 1951), offers a still-influential account of the period, with particular emphasis on political and economic developments. Edward L. Ayers, *The Promise of the New South: Life After Reconstruction* (New York: Oxford University Press, 1992), attempts a more elaborate portrait of New South diversity, balancing vernacular cultures with macroeconomic and political trends. Hale, *Making Whiteness*, emphasizes the key role of consumer culture in this period. On the Great Migration, see, for example, Stewart, *Migrating to the Movies*; Carole Marks, *Farewell—We're Good and Gone: The Great Black Migration* (New York: Alfred A. Knopf, 1991). On Populism, see, for example, Woodward, *Origins of the New South*; Ayers, *The Promise of the New South*; Lawrence Goodwyn, *Democratic Promise: The Populist Movement in America* (New York: Oxford University Press, 1976). On lynching, see,

for example, W. Fitzhugh Brundage, *Lynching in the New South: Georgia and Virginia, 1880–1930* (Urbana: University of Illinois Press, 1993); Hale, *Making Whiteness*. On jazz, see, for example, Gunther Schiller, *Early Jazz: Its Roots and Musical Development* (New York: Oxford University Press, 1968); Marshall Stearns, *The Story of Jazz* (New York: Oxford University Press, 1956); Albert Murray, *Stomping the Blues* (New York: Da Capo, 1976).

6. H. L. Mencken, "The Sahara of the Bozart," *Prejudices, Second Series* (New York: Alfred A. Knopf, 1920), 142.

7. See Charlie Keil and Shelley Stamp, eds., *American Cinema's Transitional Era* (Berkeley: University of California Press, 2004), for a recent collection of essays addressing this period.

8. On the "cinema of attractions," see Tom Gunning, "The Cinema of Attractions: Early Film, Its Spectator and the Avant-Garde," *Wide Angle* 8, nos. 3 and 4 (1986): 63–70. On these other issues, see Keil and Stamp's introduction and selected articles by contributors in *American Cinema's Transitional Era*.

9. Henry T. Sampson, *Blacks in Black and White: A Source Book on Black Films*, 2nd ed. (Metuchen, N.J.: Scarecrow Press, 1995), 172. See also Jacqueline Stewart, "William Foster: The Dean of the Negro Photoplay," *Oscar Micheaux Society Newsletter* 9 (Spring 2001): 1–2.

10. Charlene Regester, "From the Buzzard's Roost: Black Moviegoing in Durham and Other North Carolina Cities during the Early Period of American Cinema," *Film History: An International Journal* 17, no. 1 (2005): 113–24, discusses black southern moviegoing and theater operation with particular emphasis on the roles of segregation.

11. See Stewart, *Migrating to the Movies*, for a detailed portrait of black Chicago's film industry in the context of a more general black public sphere.

12. For comparisons of the two films, see, for example, Gaines, *Fire and Desire* (see note 3); Michele Wallace, "Oscar Micheaux's *Within Our Gates*: The Possibilities for Alternative Visions," and Jane Gaines, "*Within Our Gates*: From Race Melodrama to Opportunity Narrative," both in Bowser, Gaines, and Musser, *Oscar Micheaux and His Circle*.

13. Tom Gunning, *D. W. Griffith and the Origins of American Narrative Film: The Early Years at Biograph* (Urbana: University of Illinois Press, 1991), provides an excellent study of Griffith's pre-*Birth* career, with primary emphasis on the development of what Gunning calls the emergent "narrator system" in Griffith's one-reel films in 1908–09 (25–28), and on the contemporary transformations within the film industry as a whole. Little work, however, has been done on the subject of Griffith's racial representations before *The Birth of a Nation*; a valuable exception is Scott Simmon, *The Films of D. W. Griffith* (New York: Cambridge University Press, 1993), especially in Simmon's treatment of Griffith's one-reel Civil War films, 104–36.

14. See Hale, *Making Whiteness*, 199–239, for a more comprehensive treatment of spectacle lynching during the segregation era.

15. I borrow these terms from Donald Bogle, *Toms, Coons, Mulattoes, Mammies,*

and Bucks: An Interpretive History of Blacks in American Films (New York: Continuum, 1973).

16. Quoted in Gerald Mast, ed., *The Movies in Our Midst: Documents in the Cultural History of Film in America* (Chicago: University of Chicago Press, 1982), 132.

17. Pearl Bowser, "Pioneers of Black Documentary Film," in *Struggles for Representation: African American Documentary Film and Video*, ed. Phyllis R. Klotman and Janet K. Cutler (Bloomington: Indiana University Press, 1999), 1–33, locates the earliest black documentary filmmaking efforts in a fluid continuum with long-practiced still photography by African Americans, and cites *A Day at Tuskegee* (1909) as the earliest black documentary film.

18. See David A. Gerstner, "'Other and Different Scenes': Oscar Micheaux's Bodies and the Cinematic Cut," *Wide Angle* 21, no. 4 (1999): 6–19. Gerstner argues: "Through the mirroring of the sequences (Mrs. Warwick/Sylvia, Mrs. Warwick/Geraldine) the fate of the black man is cast. Which way Mrs. Warwick, the philanthropist, decides to help the race is directly tied to how she ultimately understands—*an understanding inscribed through Micheaux's camera that writes the feminine body*—the African American man" (17). To Gerstner's reading I would add an observation about Sylvia during this sequence. For Sylvia herself becomes somewhat peripheral amid these transactions even though she is the primary fundraiser for a school with which Dr. Vivian is not even affiliated. Indeed, as a black woman from the South she rests at the center of all these regional, personal, and financial connections, and yet Micheaux relegates her to something like the role of cheerleader—one who celebrates Mrs. Warwick's decision to fund the Piney Woods School, but who remains on the sidelines as the real power is wielded and transferred from the white woman to black men (financially to Reverend Jacobs at Piney Woods, and authoritatively to Dr. Vivian). It is Sylvia's invisible labor that makes these transactions possible. Later, a similar process is at work during Dr. Vivian's patriotic speech and marriage proposal. Rather than focusing too closely on the particularity or depth of Sylvia's traumatic past, he thinks instead about her potential to be a good American, rendering her body secondary to the more visible racial and national figures he invokes. Sylvia thus shifts back and forth between labor and submission; she resides at the center of the film's movement even as her activities—education, fundraising, conversion, and finally marriage—have implications for those around her more than for herself.

19. Gridlestone forms an explicit link to the slave past, alluding to his father, "who owned a thousand slaves," as the figure who taught him to keep blacks in their place by any means necessary. Gridlestone's brother, too, represents a sordid legacy from slavery in his attempted rape of Sylvia, invoking a very old tradition of white men having sexual relations with slave women and producing illegitimate mulatto children. Such a tradition, of course, did not end with slavery. Thus, Sylvia's identity crisis, partially the result of her mixed ancestry, is grounded in the mythology of the sexually violent Old South.

Why, then, the intertitle's reference to the "legitimate marriage" between Sylvia's white father and a black woman? Perhaps this was Micheaux's way of rewriting history, of suggesting the cultural legitimacy of Sylvia's current cultural role. Perhaps he meant to suggest, in compliance with the genre conventions of melodrama, the honorable nature of Sylvia's character. Or perhaps the reference appeared for more mundane reasons: as a mistranslation; or as a nod to local censors who would not countenance any reference to illegitimacy. Not enough is known about the surviving print of *Within Our Gates* to verify these latter possibilities. The film was repatriated in 1988 from La Filmoteca Espanola, the National Film Archive of Spain, where it had been translated under the title *La Negra*. Its length, about one-quarter shorter than originally advertised, suggests considerable editing as a result of censorship.

20. See Miriam Hansen, *Babel and Babylon: Spectatorship in American Silent Film* (Cambridge: Harvard University Press, 1991), for a more theoretical treatment of "spectatorship" reliant on formulations of the public sphere as a normative category for film reception. My use of the term here is intended to emphasize the role of visuality not simply as it is constructed in films, but as it is practiced by individual viewers and audiences. The distinction is at some point arbitrary, though it becomes an important one in my reading of Micheaux's conception of the collaborative participation of his audience.

21. It is interesting to note that each of Dr. Vivian's references to African American military service here had been represented in film. Thomas Cripps, in *Slow Fade to Black: The Negro in American Film, 1900–1942* (New York: Oxford University Press, 1993), discusses the 1898 Edison newsreel film *Colored Troops Disembarking*, in which "black men with weapons in hand marched down a gangplank on their way to Cuba" (12). Lincoln's 1916 two-reeler, *The Trooper of Troop K*, discussed earlier, dramatized black participation in the 1916 Battle of Carrizal in Mexico. And among the considerable quantity of film of black soldiers during and after World War I, Micheaux himself may have had a hand in shooting footage of the 8th Regiment, 370th Infantry in Chicago to accompany his planned premiere of *The Homesteader* in February of 1919. The existence of these films suggests a sort of feedback loop in the narrative context of *Within Our Gates*, since one might plausibly ask to what degree Dr. Vivian's historical and racial consciousness (and, of course, that of his screenwriter, Micheaux himself) had been shaped by motion picture representations of African Americans. In presenting this historical narrative to Sylvia, Dr. Vivian raises the possibility that even as his vision of black cultural memory will survive for viewers of *Within Our Gates*, it is that memory that has already been shaped by prior images of blackness on film. Film is grounded in memory, and memory in film.

22. Blacks would not have required a long memory for this sort of awareness: there were scores of race riots in 1919 throughout the United States, most notable this time for the degree to which blacks fought back against white violence. See, for example, William M. Tuttle Jr., *Race Riot: Chicago and the Red Summer of 1919* (1970; Urbana: University of Illinois Press, 1996).

23. Frederick Douglass, *Narrative of the Life of Frederick Douglass, An American Slave*, ed. Houston A. Baker (New York: Viking, 1982), makes a special effort to

posit education as one of the indispensable vehicles in his journey from slavery to freedom. Relating the story of his own secret and quite dangerous quest for literacy as a kind of synecdoche for the achievement of emancipation in his 1845 autobiography, he advocates education more generally for the betterment of blacks. "I now understood," Douglass remarks after describing the conversation in which his master ordered his mistress to stop teaching the slave how to read, "what had been to me a most perplexing difficulty—to wit, the white man's power to enslave the black man. It was a grand achievement, and I prized it highly. From that moment, I understood the pathway from slavery to freedom" (78).

24. Quoted in Mast, *The Movies in Our Midst*, 132.

25. Ibid., 132–35.

26. "The Silent Film," *Richmond News Leader*, February 9, 1965.

27. For more thorough historical analyses of Virginia's film censorship history, including attention to Micheaux's experiences before the board, see Melissa Dawn Ooten, "Screen Strife: Race, Gender, and Movie Censorship in the New South, 1922–1965" (Ph.D. diss., College of William and Mary, 2005); J. Douglas Smith, "Patrolling the Boundaries of Race: Motion Picture Censorship and Jim Crow in Virginia, 1922–1932," *Historical Journal of Film, Radio, and Television*, 21, no. 3 (2001), 273–91. For more on southern film censorship in general, see Robert Jackson, "Fade In, Crossroads: The Southern Cinema, 1890–1940" (Ph.D. diss., University of Virginia, 2008).

28. J. Douglas Smith, *Managing White Supremacy: Race, Politics, and Citizenship in Jim Crow Virginia* (Chapel Hill: University of North Carolina Press, 2002), presents a broad social history of Virginia's racial atmosphere between World War I and 1954. Focusing more on politics than culture, Smith includes brief attention to film censorship and Micheaux, placing the board's activities squarely in a broad pattern of politically motivated, state-sponsored control of race relations and representations.

29. Commonwealth of Virginia, Office of the State Board of Censors, *Annual Report*, July 9, 1925, 2.

30. E. R. Chesterman, review of *Love Mart*, February 11, 1928. Records of the Division of Motion Picture Censorship, 1926–1968. Accession 26515, Box 53, State Records Collection, Library of Virginia, Richmond (hereafter SRC).

31. Commonwealth of Virginia, Division of Motion Picture Censorship, *Annual Report*, September 24, 1928, 4.

32. Commonwealth of Virginia, Office of the State Board of Censors, *Annual Report*, July 9, 1925, 2.

33. E. R. Chesterman to mayor of Norfolk, February 28, 1924. Records of the Division of Motion Picture Censorship, 1926–1968. Accession 26515, Box 53, SRC.

34. See "Appendix B: An Oscar Micheaux Filmography," in Bowser, Gaines, and Musser, *Oscar Micheaux and His Circle*, 250–56, for more context on the apprehensive responses of censors to these films, and on Micheaux's continuing efforts to have the films approved for exhibition.

35. Oscar Micheaux to Virginia State Board of Motion Picture Censors, Octo-

ber 14, 1924. Records of the Division of Motion Picture Censorship, 1926–1968. Accession 26515, Box 53, SRC.

36. Oscar Micheaux to Virginia Motion Picture Censors, March 13, 1925. Records of the Division of Motion Picture Censorship, 1926–1968. Accession 26515, Box 53, SRC. The subsequent quotations are taken from this source.

37. W. E. B. Du Bois, *The Souls of Black Folk* (1903; New York: Penguin Putnam, 1995), 41.

38. Micheaux Film Corporation letterhead, March 13, 1925. Records of the Division of Motion Picture Censorship, 1926–1968. Accession 26515, Box 53, SRC.

39. Commonwealth of Virginia, Office of the State Board of Censors, *Annual Report*, July 9, 1925, 3.

40. My use of the phrase "nigger in the woodpile" alludes to that of Jacqueline Najuma Stewart, who, in "Introduction: A Nigger in the Woodpile, or Black (In)Visibility in Film History," in *Migrating to the Movies*, 1–19, discusses its meaning in the contexts of the early Biograph film *A Nigger in the Woodpile* (1904) and of the history and criticism of early cinema more generally. Citing the range of meanings for the crude slang expression from the mid-nineteenth century, Stewart writes: "Thus, at a metaphoric level, this phrase serves as an apt description for the way in which early films frequently conceal and reveal Black figures, creating discomfort and disorder intended to amuse, fascinate, and/or alarm white viewers. In addition, I invoke this expression because I want to suggest that racial difference has functioned as something like the proverbial 'nigger in the woodpile' of early film history and theories of film viewer relations, including those developed by revisionist film scholarship" (5).

Hear Me Talking to You

The Blues and the Romance of Rebellion

GRACE ELIZABETH HALE

So glad I'm brownskin, so glad I'm brownskin, chocolate to the bone.
So glad I'm brownskin, chocolate to the bone.
And I've got what it takes to make a monkey man leave his home.
—BARBECUE BOB, "Chocolate to the Bone" (1928)

Why do white men want to sing the blues?
—PAUL NELSON, "Country Blues Comes to Town" (1964)

For the black southerners who made and listened to the music and took it with them as they migrated north, the blues conjured the possibility of change. The earliest blues musicians and fans had lived through the late nineteenth-century era of racial terrorism and the hardening of segregation into a new culture of oppression. Black freedom, southern whites insisted, would not mean much: the chance to work endlessly for little reward, the opportunity to "play" the "good nigger" of the white southern imagination and the minstrel stage, and the occasion to leave. On plantations, in railroad and timber camps, and in barber shops and cafes across eastern Texas, in the Delta, through the Black Belt of Alabama and Georgia, in the Carolina Piedmont, and in the region's growing cities, African Americans in the early twentieth century responded to a new music that suggested alternatives. If Jim Crow treated blacks as a mass, as a collectively inferior people, the blues resisted, asserting black individualism in a stylized and increasingly commodified form. With their sounds and words, blues musicians created a rebel persona, a romanticized black figure who said no to hard work and yes to personal pleasure. The blues rebel announced that transformation was possible, that individual black lives could not be contained and controlled by whites.

It is more than ironic, then, that later white fans understood the music as the somehow pure, "outside of history" voice of rural black southern "folk." Most of the early and influential record collectors and scholars of the blues were white fans who discovered the music in the decade after World War II. Their love affair with black racial difference, part of the same postwar moment as Norman Mailer's "white Negro" and the mostly white Beats' attraction to black jazz musicians, helped establish a second blues romance. Beginning with the work of white record collectors such as Harry Smith and James McKune and white scholars such as Alan Lomax, David Evans, and Samuel Charters, this fantasy of blues rebellion emerged most powerfully in the 1960s and early 1970s as the folk music revival ignited a new interest in the blues and young stars from Bob Dylan to the Rolling Stones recorded blues songs. These white fans took the blues persona as the truth. Rather than an artistic and commercial creation, the blues rebel became a "real" black identity, proof that African Americans—especially southern rural people "uncontaminated" by modernity—lived and felt more deeply than modern whites repressed and alienated by modern life. This romance imagined stasis instead of transformation. White blues fans acted, in music critic David Hajdu's words, "as if the point of the blues were not to cry out against suffering, subjugation and marginalization, but to preserve those things." Black people had to stay the same, authentic and pure, so that whites could experience transcendence, an easing of their own feelings of alienation.[1]

Blues Romance No. 1

An older American myth imagines economic independence as the source of individual identity. Working for oneself—a farm on the frontier, a small shop downtown, the practice of a skill such as brick laying—makes a person matter. African American musicians countered this white, male model of individualism with an alternative when they created the music that would later acquire the label the blues. In their myth, self-expression, a form of cultural rather than economic self-determination, was the act that made a person an individual. Their art created a persona that shouted: "I am still here. I exist. I exist because I struggle with the world." Early blues recordings make it clear that musicians consciously crafted this new model of individualism, but they made their alternative vision for working-class black people, not for whites.[2]

Somewhere in the Black Belt South, sometime around the late 1890s, some now-unknown black musician or group of black musicians consciously created a new form out of the mix of musical resources then available in the region. These earliest blues (now often called classic, country, or Delta blues) drew on the field hollers, work songs, and one-line songs called jump-ups that preceded them, but the new music was greater than the sum of its sources and recognizably different. In the early twentieth century, migrating southern blacks spread the blues to New Orleans, Memphis, Chicago, New York, and elsewhere, and a variety of black musicians—including vaudeville, minstrel, and medicine show performers, professional songwriters, and members of jazz bands—adopted and adapted the form. With the advent of commercial recording in the 1920s, the blues emerged as the most profitable form of working-class black popular music.[3]

In the earliest surviving recordings, which date from the 1920s, the new music employed intricate rhythms, minor and pentatonic modes, call-and-response patterns (the guitar or harmonica often answered the voice), and blue notes (flatted thirds and sevenths). Many songs used a I, IV, V chord structure for the music and a three-line, AAB or AAA, twelve-bar form for both the lyrics and music. And singers often inflected their songs with moans, screams, growls, and cries. Tapping their feet, patting their guitars or piano keys, blowing their harmonicas, and repeating lyrics and yet always changing them, they got their audiences through the "freedom" of the lynching epidemic and segregation like the work songs had gotten black people through slavery.

The first blues musicians made a living entertaining local audiences in small juke joints and cafés and at rural house parties across the Black Belt and in bars in southern river cities such as New Orleans and Memphis. For rural black southerners who did not want to or could not sharecrop or work as day laborers or domestics, playing music was one of the few ways besides preaching to earn money. The music, in this sense, was always a commercial product. Most musicians tried to please, and what working-class black audiences wanted to do was dance. Blues lyrics filled up the melody the voice sang against the guitar or the piano and decorated the beat. Musicians often linked together certain standard lines, their versions of other musicians' lyrics, and their own original lyrics and set them to their own adaptations of common tunes. In this way, they could continue playing a song as long as their audience enjoyed dancing to its beat. Lyrical unity was less important than the feel and energy a song generated. With the advent of recording, however, musicians began to think more in terms of discrete song lyrics and standard song lengths.

Blues musicians often offered their own definitions of the blues. Much early evidence comes from song lyrics. "If the blues was money, I'd be a millionaire." "If the blues was whiskey, I'd stay drunk all the time, 'cause I can't be satisfied." "You know the blues ain't nothin but a low-down shakin achin chill / Well if you ain't had em honey, I hope you never will," Son House moaned in his 1942 song "Jinx Blues." "Well, the blues, the blues is a worried heart, is a worried heart, heart disease." In an interview taped in 1946, Big Bill Broonzy insisted, "the blues is something that's from the heart—I know that, and whensoever you hear fellows singing the blues—I always believed it was a really heart thing, from his heart, you know, and it was expressing his feelings about *how* he felt to the people." Memphis Slim, in the same interview, joined in, "yeah, blues is kind of a revenge. You know you wanta say something, you wanta signifyin like—that's the blues. We all have a hard time in life, and things we couldn't say or do, so we sing it." Son House remembered the time when he first began playing the blues: "I got the idea that the blues come from a person having a dissatisfied mind and he wants to do something about it." For these musicians, playing the blues meant putting on the persona of a black individual who spoke her mind and her emotions in a world that denied not only black individuality but often also black humanity. The expression of the blues persona's particular feelings, in the stylized conventions of the form, asserted the fact that working-class blacks had feelings. The expression of the persona's particular pain and survival in spite of it announced a collective resistance and a collective survival.[4]

A great deal of blues scholarship has followed the amazingly prolific white field recorders and scholars John and Alan Lomax in simply assuming the blues is a "folk" music, an old oral tradition that rural black people seamlessly and collectively evolved from earlier musical forms. But at the moment of origin, the blues form, as the scholar Luc Sante has written, "was actually a sudden and radical turn in African-American music." Blues historian Samuel Charters has argued "that there was no sociological reason for the blues verse to take the form it did. Someone sang the first blues." The creators of the art form remain unknown, not because "the people" somehow spontaneously cried out their pain in an AAB form like a "collective sigh." The names of these musicians have been lost in the isolation, poverty, and oppression blacks faced in the turn-of-the-century segregating South and in the romanticism of early blues scholars who could simply not conceive of African American musicians as modern artists. In 1933, when the Lomaxes took their first Library of Congress–sponsored recording trip, this story of origins would have been very recent history.[5]

The earliest surviving accounts of hearing the blues, however, all place the music in the U.S. South in the first decade of the twentieth century. "Father of the blues" W. C. Handy, who made his career self-consciously promoting his own 1903 "discovery" of the blues, wrote famously of his first encounter with "the weirdest music I had ever heard": a black man "fretting his guitar with a knife to produce an eerie, sliding wail and singing about 'goin' where the Southern cross' the Dog'" while waiting for a train in Tut-wiler, Mississippi. Ma "Mother of the Blues" Rainey first heard the form the year before, in a small town in Missouri, where she was working in a tent show. "A girl from the town" performed a "strange and poignant" song about the man who had left her. Rainey learned the song from the girl and soon added it to her act. After fans repeatedly asked her what kind of music it was, she remembered later, she finally had an inspiration and answered, "It's the Blues." Jelly Roll Morton, too, heard the music around this time, in New Orleans. Mamie Desdoumes, a piano player and occasional prostitute, he remembered, performed a wailing song that had to be a blues:

I stood on the corner, my feet was dripping wet.
I asked every man I met

. . . .

Can't you give me a dollar, give me a lousy dime,
Just to feed that hungry man of mine.

Song collectors, combing the countryside since the 1870s, did not find any blues songs until after 1900. But pioneering sociologist Howard Odum, at work collecting songs in Lafayette, Mississippi, and Newton County, Geor-gia, between 1905 and 1908, recorded on wax cylinders and transcribed the lyrics to many songs that blues musicians would later record in the 1920s. Scholars interviewing elderly Delta blacks in the 1960s could not find anyone who remembered hearing the blues before 1910. The blues was not a "folk" form, around for decades and developing in isolation. It was a new musical form created by African Americans around the turn of the century.[6]

Most blues musicians and the original, pre–World War II fans that made the music into a big business were born in the South, and many grew up there. Migration, and records, however, soon circulated the music beyond local juke circuits, logging and railroad camps, house parties, and southern urban enclaves. In the 1920s, the blues became a profitable business, based in the urban North, in Chicago and New York City most importantly.[7]

The blues singers best known today—Charley Patton and Robert Johnson and Son House—Delta or country blues musicians—spent a great deal of their careers singing the blues across the local Delta scene. Robert Johnson, born in the Mississippi Delta in 1911, recorded in 1936 and 1937. His biggest hit, "Terraplane Blues," exemplified one major category of the blues: songs about sex—fights with lovers, and the sex act itself, the pleasure sex brings in spite of other troubles. Here, the rebel persona emerges in the songs' insistence that the singer is an individual because he expresses himself as a lover:

> And I feel so lonesome you hear me when I moan
> When I feel so lonesome you hear me when I moan
> Who been driving my Terraplane for you since I been gone
>
> . . . .
>
> I'm 'on' get deep down in this connection keep tanglin' with your
>   wires
> I'm 'on' get deep down in this connection hoo-well keep tanglin' with
>   these wires
> And when I mash down on your little starter then your spark plug
>   will give me fire.

But these musicians—even Patton, who was the most popular of the three in the 1930s (he died in 1934)—did not achieve much fame in the early twentieth century outside the Delta scene. They did not make the blues a nationally popular musical form.[8]

The women did that. Women blues singers such as Bessie Smith and Ma Rainey, the most popular blues musicians of their day and the artists who made the blues a commercially viable recorded music, performed "I exist because I struggle with the world" songs, too. Born in Chattanooga, Tennessee, in the 1890s, Bessie Smith became the first blues superstar. Her 1923 recording "'T Ain't Nobody's Bizness If I Do" was a huge hit:

> There ain't nothing I can do, or nothing I can say
> That folks don't criticize me
> But I'm goin' to, do just as I want to anyway
> And don't care if they all despise me
>
> . . . .
>
> If I go to church on Sunday
> Sing the shimmy down on Monday
> Ain't nobody's bizness if I do, I do.

The personal rebellion she expresses here—

If I should take a notion
To jump into the ocean
'T ain't nobody's bizness if I do, do, do, do

—takes on added meaning in the 1920s as northern urban spaces such as Atlantic City became increasingly segregated. But personal freedom here is not all about leisure time. She can give away all her money and choose to accept domestic violence, too, if she chooses:

I swear I won't call no copper
If I'm beat up by my poppa
'T ain't nobody's bizness if I do, if I do.

The blues persona Smith creates will not just live outside middle-class morality and respectability. She will live outside the law, too. Blues lyrics, in fact, do not make much of a distinction between the two. In "Beale Street Papa," also recorded in 1923, Smith's singing expresses both longing and pain over the loss of her man and yet emphasizes that her sexual expression, her existence, is her own:

Mmmm hmmmm, I'm blue
so how come you do me like you do?
I'm cryin', Beale Street papa, don't mess around with me
There's plenty pettin' that I can get in Tennessee
I still get my sweet cookies constantly.[9]

These early female blues stars sang what scholars have called classic blues, a fusion of the blues form that emerged in the South, the birthplace of many of these performers and their fans, with the more commercialized musical forms of minstrelsy and vaudeville. Smith and Rainey, both of whom danced as well as sang, used tone, gesture, and movement to act out a rebellious blues persona even when singing more minstrel or Tin Pan Alley material. Producing guttural cries and blue notes, pushing their voices to project intensity and volume, and swinging their breasts and hips, they conveyed the effect that they inhabited emotionally and physically the pain and desire and longing that their lyrics described. Sometimes, they literally acted out their songs. "Baby, I come out on that stage, dressed down! I had on a hat and a coat and was carrying a suitcase," Rainey described singing "Traveling Blues" to Thomas Fulbright, a white actor who performed in a drama company playing the same town as Rainey's show. "I put the suitcase down, real easy like, then stand there like I was thinkin'—just let'em see what I was about. Then I sing. You could jes' se them Jiggs wantin' to go some place else."[10]

Women blues singers—Smith and Rainey, as well as Victoria Spivey and Ethel Waters—completely dominated the first five years of blues recording. Blind Lemon Jefferson, a native of Texas who recorded in Chicago, became one of the first popular male blues musicians and helped open up the business for blues guitarists, most of whom were from the rural South. His 1926 recording "That Black Snake Moan," another sex song, was a huge hit. "Hangman's Blues," a popular 1928 recording, illustrates another side of the blues. Violence, too, could be an act of self-expression—murder, knifings, domestic abuse—the violence African Americans inflicted, not the violence they endured, which had the opposite effect and erased individual black identity. Jefferson sings of both kinds of violence here:

> Hangman's rope sho' is tough and strong
> Hangman's rope sho' is tough and strong
> They gonna hang me because I did something wrong
>
> . . . .
>
> Crowd 'round the courthouse and the time is going fast
> Crowd 'round the courthouse and the time is going fast
> Soon a good-for-nothin' killer is gonna breath his last.

The blues may have been highly codified and commercialized, but the blues persona did not promise transcendence. Poverty would never end. Life would never be anything but hard. Instead, self-expression in the form of sexuality, violence, and, indeed, singing about anything—these acts proved a person's existence, making a man or a woman a human and not just a sign of oppression. In these acts, working-class black people lived.[11]

In the blues, the stylized presentation of individualism almost always occurs through the use of first person in the lyrics. An entire category of blues songs took this convention one step further when musicians named their creations after themselves. In Big Bill Broonzy's 1928 recording "Big Bill Blues," he feels a hurt so bad it must belong to him alone:

> Mean my hair's a-risin,' my flesh begin to crawl.
> Ah, my hair's a-rising, my flesh begin to crawl.
> I had a dream last night, saw another mule in my doggone stall.
> Lord, there's some people say that these Big Bill blues ain't bad.

Ah, some people say that these Big Bill blues ain't bad.
Mean it must not have been them Big Bill blues they had.

In blues lyrics, the personal voice reigns.[12]

In the pre–World War II period when the blues enjoyed broad popular and commercial success, black female blues singers accompanied by jazz bands and later black male guitarists dominated the genre. Smooth, urban stars such as Lonnie Johnson and "throwback" blues artists such as Jim Jackson and Papa Charlie Jackson who also recorded minstrel songs were also tremendously popular. These were the musicians—not the now-canonical Patton and Johnson and House—who sold records. The blues comprised the most important music within the broad commercial category of "race records," which identified the race of the performer and not a clear musical style. By the late 1920s and early 1930s, however, the blues referred both to songs with a variety of structures that somehow conveyed a blues tone or sensibility and to a specific song structure. Across all these types of blues, however, musicians sang a blues persona into being—"I exist because I struggle. I exist because I have sex. I exist because I hurt other people. I exist."

Throughout the early twentieth century, the blues circulated images of black identity in direct contrast to both the communal, pious, otherworldly image of the spirituals and the comic, sentimental, or absurd images of minstrelsy. The blues conjured a black individual who was sexual and violent and anything but good, a black person free to be bad, with a dark (no pun intended) sense of humor, a tragic sense of life. The minstrel, on the other hand, played the fool for the white folks, even when blacked-up black men played the fool on the white folks. As Ralph Ellison argued so eloquently in 1958, the minstrel character, whether a blacked-up white man or a blacked-up black man, was always white. Black audiences loved minstrelsy, too. And often black performers on the local Delta juke circuit played blues songs one night and minstrelsy the next. The point is not that whites controlled one image—the minstrel—and blacks controlled the other, but that the mediums presented two different images of black identity, the black man or woman who tries to go along and the black man or woman who says no, who wants to play her own life her own way.[13]

The emphasis on individual performance in the blues in turn made sex the perfect subject and metaphor for the music and the model of individual identity it generated. Sex, like the blues itself, was a way of asserting the self in the world, of stealing some pleasure out of the grind of work and poverty.

Sex, too, was about performance. In the blues, Ellison wrote his good friend Albert Murray, "sex means far more than poontang, but the good life, courage, cunning, the wholeness of being colored, the beauty of it . . . as well as the anguish, and the deep capacity of [a character] to stand for, to symbolize it all." Historically, musical styles that stand outside of middle-class norms have often been connected with sexuality. In the blues, singing about sex made clear the rebellion at stake in the music challenged not just whites but middle-class blacks, with their emphasis on respectability, as well.[14]

The blues model of individualism—cultural rather than economic self-determination, "I exist because I express myself" rather than, "I exist because I work for myself"—was created by black women as much as black men. Like her younger friend Bessie Smith, Ma Rainey became wildly famous between 1923 and 1928. In her 1928 recording "Hear Me Talking to You" she sang,

Ramblin' man makes no change in me.
I'm gonna ramble back to my used-to-be.
Ah, you hear me talkin' to you, I don't bite my tongue.
You wants to be my man, you've got to fetch it with you when you
    come.

Smith and Rainey and other female blues singers wore fancy clothes, clothes like rich people—indeed they became rich people. They sang, "I exist and I have my own sexual desires," not just to the oppressive white world but to black men, too. Presenting themselves as sexual subjects rather than sexual objects, they announced that they made their own choices, and, in this arena of life at least, they were self-determining. In the *Chicago Defender* ad for Ma Rainey's 1928 recording "Prove It On Me Blues," Rainey is dressed like a man, surrounded by small and feminine women. The song describes her desire for sex with other women:

Went out last night with a crowd of my friends.
They must have been women, 'cause I don't like no men.
It's true I wear a collar and a tie.
Makes a wind blow all the while
'Cause they say I do it, ain't nobody caught me.
They sure got to prove it on me.

Here Rainey cuts men entirely out of the loop. Not only does she claim her sexuality but she does not need men at all. She is not always this strong. In "Victim of the Blues" (1928) she is heartbroken. In "Traveling Blues" (1928)

her man leaves her, and she threatens to kill him. In "Sweet Rough Man" she loves (both sexually and emotionally) a man who bashes her bloody. But it is always Ma Rainey, with her beautiful clothes and her powerful voice, singing that she is still here.[15]

Sounds, too, played an essential role in creating the blues "I exist" message. Rainey's studio recordings are rich in what Roland Barthes calls "the grain of the voice," the qualities that convey that a physical body has produced a sound. Rainey does not just have a deep Georgia accent; she also lisps and garbles her diction. She drops and blurs the final consonants of words. She slurs notes, moving from one to another without any clear break between the two, and uses glissandos, shifting her pitch as much as an octave within a word. She pushes her huge contralto voice until it cracks, and she moans. Rainey can wail a single note or an entire stanza. She cries "oh" or "oo" in songs such as "Levee Camp Moan" and "Ma and Pa Poorhouse Blues." And she groans on a single repeated word in "Little Low Mama Blues" and "Slow Driving Moan." Within the genre conventions of the form, Rainey's cries, growls, moans, and sighs sonically enact the blues message of individualism through self-expression. They remind listeners that voices convey meanings through sound as well as words. Other musicians produce similar effects by using their guitars, harmonica, or other instruments to imitate the human voice and by bending or bluing notes to produce microtones between the standard steps of the Western scale.[16]

Blueswomen achieved such popularity because they performed their success, the fact that they could change their identities, that they could conjure with their sound and their words the whole journey from rags and cotton, hunger and want to worldly success and freedom from the constraints of conventionality. Whether they had actually made the journey themselves did not matter, although many of them had. Their popularity did not depend upon their "authenticity," their "real" biographies, or what scholars have called the folk expression of "the Negro" and "the voice" of Africa. It reflected their embodiment of the whole exhausting journey, the turning of painful, lived history into a story of individual transformation, the way they wore all the contradictions, the sexism and the sexual freedom and their own desire here standing in for all the power relations in the world. In the moment, for the length of a song, the blues could chase the blues away. There was, of course, a whole category of blues songs about that, too, for example, Bessie Smith's "Jail House Blues."

In a segregated world in which most white people thought they knew who black people collectively were—inferior—the blues' insistence on the possibilities of individual transformation became a form of psychological resistance. In the places where organized black politics were possible—in the tobacco towns of the Piedmont and the left-labor circles of New York City in the 1930s and 1940s—musicians adapted blues songs to communicate more explicit messages of political protest, too. Sexual power relations give way in these songs to economic power relations.[17]

John and Alan Lomax collected the song "Hard to Be a Nigger" in Central State Prison Farm near Sugarland, Texas, probably in 1933, from a black inmate who said his name was Clear Rock:

Well, it makes no difference
How you make out your time.
White man sho' to bring a
Nigger out behin.'
Ain't it hard? Ain't it hard?
Ain't it hard to be a nigger? Nigger? Nigger?
Ain't it hard? Ain't it hard?
For you cain't get yo' money when it's due.

Lemme tell you, white man,
Lemme tell you, honey,
Nigger makes de cotton,
White folks gets de money.

Despite the Lomaxes' role in preserving this song, white field collectors in the South did not transcribe or record very many explicitly political blues songs. It is impossible to know now whether musicians chose not to share them, whites chose not to collect them, or musicians just did not write these kinds of lyrics often.[18]

Unionized black tobacco-industry workers made places such as Durham, North Carolina, and Richmond, Virginia, into centers of labor radicalism in the 1930s and early 1940s. Blues musicians flourished in these cities, playing songs for these workers in cafés and barbershops and even on street corners near factories as shifts changed. Complaints against cheating boss men or "captains" and unfair criminal convictions—many blues musicians played their own versions of prison or chain gang blues—multiplied, and generalized, overt indictments of white supremacy and white violence appeared. White communist and blues fan Lawrence Gellert collected many of these explicitly political songs. "Sistren an' Brethren" protested lynching and demanded resistance:

We's buryin' a brudder
Dey kill fo' de crime
We's buryin' a brudder
Dey kill fo' de crime
Tryin' to keep
What was his all de time.

When we's tucked him on under
What you gon' to do?
When we's tucked him on under
What you gon' to do?
Wait till it come
Dey's a-rousin' fo' you.

Yo' head tain' no apple
Fo' danglin' from a tree
Yo' head tain' no apple
Fo' danglin' from a tree
You' body no carcass
For barbacuin' on a spree.

Stand on you' feet
Club gripped 'tween you' hands
Stand on you' feet
Club gripped 'tween you' hands
Spill der blood too
Show 'em yo's is a man's.

Blues singers often sang for union organizing drives and to bolster morale on the picket lines.[19]

Through the 1940s, black working-class fans sustained the blues as a musical form. For them, the blues generated a rebel persona, a stylized preservation of individualism as grounded in sex, heartbreak, violence, and music in acts of self-expression. This persona made real, at least for the length of a song, the feeling that material change was possible. African Americans created this first blues romance, staking their fantasy on transformation rather than transcendence.

The "darky act," the minstrel show and all later performances of blackness that have emerged in its wake, has always been a kind of rebellion. But just exactly who rebels and what they struggle against has continually changed. Working-class white men invented minstrelsy in the 1830s and 1840s as a rebellion against new middle-class conventions of masculinity and the increasing loss of economic independence in the shift to wage labor. In the post–Civil War minstrel revival that began in the 1870s, many white Americans rebelled against the outcome of the Civil War. Minstrelsy for them expressed the loss of the Old South, romanticized as a plantation pastoral: the happy slaves, the clear and stable roles for men and women, rich and poor. Minstrelsy never worked as a one-way theft, a medium in which whites stole and adapted black cultural forms. Exchange always occurred—musical performance was and is promiscuous—and in the post–Civil War period whites both adapted earlier minstrel songs and acts borrowed decades before from black music and style and also went back to the source, back through both contemporary and past black songs for new minstrel material. In songs such as "My Old Kentucky Home" and "Carry Me Back to Old Virginia," for example, whites used African Americans' expressions of longing for family left behind on what the historian Ira Berlin has named the second middle passage, the sale of slaves from the East Coast to the new southwest frontier, for their own purposes, as a way to express their own nostalgia for their mythical Old South. The minstrel singer's borrowing of emotions generated in a different time and place to express her feelings about her own place in the world—an emotional ventriloquism—was central to minstrelsy's appeal. By the 1890s, black men themselves adopted the darky act, blacking up and dressing in drag, making money playing with white fantasies of black identity in ways that would get them killed off the stage. With its obvious artifice—the blackened faces, exaggerated mouths, and stylized expressions were never natural—minstrelsy always rebelled against reality imagined as fate. The blues rebelled against fate, too, and part of that fate for African Americans was minstrelsy.[20]

Both the blues and minstrelsy accentuate the knowingness of the performance—theatricality, illusion. On stage, for example, Ma Rainey took on many, sometimes conflicting personas. She became a blacked-up white man or a black man performing in drag, an auntie or a whore of the minstrel stage, a poor black girl from Georgia or a respectable middle-class matron. Ma Rainey became a lesbian or a dominatrix or a masochist or a nymphomaniac, a powerful woman or a slave to love. Ma Rainey became a rich white woman. (She literally *wore* money, a necklace made out of gold coins.) All of these images were performances. Some had roots in reality and some did not—no matter. Early blues fans, like black and even early white fans of minstrelsy, knew they were consuming artifice and illusion. They did not care about the real Ma Rainey. Being able to be many Ma Raineys—using her body to express different individual selves—that was power. The act of performing multiple personas made clear the precariousness of any one identity or "authentic" self.[21]

The difference between minstrelsy and the blues does not lie in the reality of the blues image of blackness. The difference lies in the fact that minstrelsy plays with white fantasies of racial and gender identity, while the blues, before the blues revival, plays with black fantasies of racial and gender identity. Minstrelsy dissolves the individual into the category of blackness, while the blues announces with little but bravado to back it up that the individual exists in the act of rebellious self-expression, exists because she breaks the rules.

The blues proposed a new model for individual identity. Rebellion did not demand an explicitly political act, and self-determination did require an economic act. Political agency and economic independence, after all, were growing increasingly unattainable for African Americans in the turn-of-the-century South, when those anonymous musicians created the blues. The public performance of psychological rebellion, the assertion of "I" against the weight of social conventions, institutions, politics, and, indeed, all relationships of power—was what was possible. The blues has deeply southern roots here. Southern segregation—named Jim Crow after a minstrel character—was all about performance: blacks' public performance of their inferiority through visible rituals of deference and visible use of inferior spaces. If whites could not ensure that every African American *was* actually inferior to every white, they could make African Americans perform inferiority everywhere. Segregation's performances erased African American individuality.

In response, the blues announced the possibility of an individual black identity. Self-expression made a man or a woman an individual, gave them some shred of agency within the limits of their world. Nothing in this model of individual identity, however, suggested that self-expression revealed some core, pure self. Nothing in the blues vision suggested authenticity. Self-expression did not mean confession. Asserting the "I" against the world did not mean exposing the inner life, some essential private self. It meant art, art in the older meaning of the term: art as skillfully making something, art as making love or fighting, art as making music. And it was significant that women, far from standing in as only the resources, both material and cultural, out of which men made their own transformations, could make this art too.

By the time of the 1950s and 1960s folk revival, the blues model of identity—"I exist because I express myself"—was traveling in two very different directions. Close to home, among black audiences with recent working-class and southern roots and among some working-class whites, too, the music conveyed the seductive power of transformation, the possibility of changing your material circumstance, your class status, your life, if just for the length of the song. For this magic to work, blues musicians needed enough talent to trap a dancing audience inside the rhythm and the melody and the words of a tune. Outside these audiences, among middle-class white kids especially, but some middle-class black kids, too, "I exist because I express myself" conjured a different kind of magic—authenticity, essence, something to hold the spinning world still, the opposite of transformation. For this magic to work, "the folk" had to be authentic or transcendent, expressing some essential truth. And they had to remain the same. Only then could these new fans experience the possibility of transformation and change. Middle-class, mostly white fans' version of "I exist because I express myself" moved in a very different direction from the route taken by black blues musicians and black working-class fans, and yet for many, ended up, bizarrely, back in the U.S. South.

NOTES

1. David Hajdu, "Blues Capitalist," *New York Times Review of Books*, May 10, 2009, 12. On the role of white scholars, fans, and record collectors in shaping the blues, see Ted Gioia, *Delta Blues* (New York: Norton, 2008); and Marybeth Hamilton, *In Search of the Blues* (New York: Basic Books, 2008).

2. On the history of the blues, I have relied heavily on W. C. Handy, *Father of the Blues* (1941; New York: Da Capo, 1969); Handy, ed., *Blues: An Anthology* (1926; rev. ed., New York: Da Capo, 1990); Ralph Ellison, *Going to the Territory* (New York: Vintage, 1986); Albert Murray, *Stomping the Blues* (1976; New York: Vintage Books, 1982); Lawrence Levine, *Black Culture and Black Consciousness: Afro-American Folk Thought From Slavery to Freedom* (New York: Oxford University Press, 1977); Amiri Baraka (Leroi Jones), *Blues People: The Negro Experience in White America and the Music That Developed From It* (New York: William Morrow, 1963); Samuel Charters, *The Country Blues* (New York: Rhinehart, 1959); Charters, *The Roots of the Blues: An African Search* (New York: M. Boyars, 1981); Jeff Todd Titon, *Early*

Downhome Blues: A Musical and Cultural Analysis (1977; Chapel Hill: University of North Carolina Press, 1994); Charles Kiel, *Urban Blues* (Chicago: University of Chicago Press, 1966); Alan Lomax, *The Land Where the Blues Began* (New York: Delta, 1993); Paul Oliver, *Blues Fell Down This Morning: Meaning in the Blues* (New York: Cambridge University Press, 1960); and Oliver, *The Story of the Blues* (Boston: Northeastern University Press, 1998); William Ferris, *Blues from the Delta* (New York: Da Capo, 1978); Robert Palmer, *Deep Blues: A Musical and Cultural History of the Mississippi Delta* (New York: Penguin, 1981); William Barlow, *Looking Up at Down: The Emergence of Blues Culture* (Philadelphia: Temple University Press, 1989); Angela Y. Davis, *Blues Legacies and Black Feminism: Gertrude "Ma" Rainey, Bessie Smith, and Billie Holiday* (New York: Pantheon, 1998); Daphne Duval Harrison, *Black Pearls: Blues Queens of the 1920s* (New Brunswick: Rutgers University Press, 1988); Hazel Carby, "'It Just Be's Dat Way Sometimes': The Sexual Politics of Women's Blues," *Radical America* 20 (June–July 1986); and Gene Santoro, *Highway 61 Revisited: The Tangled Roots of American Jazz, Blues, Folk, Rock, and Country Music* (New York: Oxford University Press, 2004). Levine, *Black Culture*, 269–70, argues that the blues are a form of self-expression that communicates the meaningfulness of working-class and poor southern black life. Still, Levine sees the blues as a communal form of expression, while I emphasize individualism. The blues is in part a form of black working-class protest against middle-class African Americans' domination of ideas about the black community. Davis, *Blues Legacies*, 42, 91, 135, argues that the image of the self that blues musicians make in their music anticipates the new conceptions of the self of the 1960s. My argument is that blues songs help create these new ideas of the self.

3. Palmer, *Deep Blues*, 41.

4. "Heritage U.S.A.," *Sing Out!* 2 (May 1952): 18. Son House, "Jinx Blues," recorded by Alan Lomax near Cormorant, Mississippi, in 1942 and available on *King of the Delta Blues* (Catfish, 2006). Big Bill Broonzy, Memphis Slim, and Sonny Boy Williamson, *Blues in the Mississippi Night* (Rykodisc, 1990). Alan Lomax recorded these three musicians talking in his apartment in New York City in 1946. Son House, "I Can Make My Own Songs," *Sing Out!* 15 (July 1965): 38–45, quotation on 45.

5. Luc Sante, "The Genius of Blues," *New York Review of Books*, August 11, 1994, quotes, 46, 52. Charters, *Country Blues*. Many scholars would insist that the names of the inventors of the blues have been lost in the way almost all names associated with oral traditions have been lost. The blues, however, moved from an oral tradition to a recorded tradition in about twenty years, a length of time short enough for oral testimony about the musicians who created the form to have survived long enough to be recorded.

6. Handy, *Father of the Blues*, 74; Sandra Lieb, *Mother of the Blues: A Study of Ma Rainey* (Amherst: University of Massachusetts Press, 1981); John W. Work, *American Negro Songs and Spirituals* (1940; Mineola, N.Y.: Dover Publications, 1998), 32; Alan Lomax, *Mr. Jelly Roll: The Fortunes of Jelly Roll Morton, New Orleans Creole and "Inventor of Jazz"* (New York: Duell, Sloan, and Pearce, 1950); Howard Odum, "Folk-

Song and Folk-Poetry as Found in the Secular Songs of the Southern Negroes," *Journal of American Folk-Lore* (July-September 1911): 255–94, and (October-December 1911): 351–96; Howard W. Odum and Guy B. Johnson, *The Negro and His Songs: A Study of the Typical Negro Songs in the South* (Chapel Hill: University of North Carolina Press, 1925); and Odum and Johnson, *Negro Workaday Songs* (Chapel Hill: University of North Carolina Press, 1926). Odum's wax cylinders have not survived. On interviewing Delta blacks in the 1960s, see Stephen Calt, *King of the Delta Blues: The Life and Music of Charlie Patton* (Newton, N.J.: Rock Chapel Press, 1994), 329. On song collectors in the late nineteenth and early twentieth centuries, see David Whisnant, *All That Is Native and Fine: The Politics of Culture in an American Region* (Chapel Hill: University of North Carolina Press, 1983). Many early song collectors, however, were looking for English and Scottish survivals and "white" folk culture and may have missed the blues. On the collectors who focused on black folk songs, see David Evans, *Big Road Blues: Tradition and Creativity in the Folk Blues* (Berkeley: University of California Press, 1982).

7. Sante, "The Genius of the Blues"; and Charters, *Country Blues*.

8. Elijah Wald, *Escaping the Delta: Robert Johnson and the Invention of the Blues* (New York: Amistad, 2004); and Peter Guralnick, *Searching for Robert Johnson* (New York: Dutton, 1989). The lyrics of Johnson's "Terraplane Blues" are available as a recording on Robert Johnson, *King of the Delta Blues Singers* (1961; reissue, Sony, 1997). Johnson died in 1938. I have studied the following published collections of blues lyrics, in addition to listening to all blues songs recorded in the 1920s and 1930s that are available (some are listed in these notes): Lawrence Gellert, *Negro Songs of Protest* (New York: American Music League, 1936); Gellert, *Me and My Captain: Negro Songs of Protest* (New York: Hours Press, n.d. [1939]); Odum and Johnson, *The Negro and His Songs: A Study of the Typical Negro Songs in the South* and *Negro Workaday Songs*; John A. and Alan Lomax, *Negro Folk Songs as Sung by Leadbelly* (New York: Macmillan, 1936); Dorothy Scarborough, *On the Trail of Negro Folk-Songs* (Cambridge: Harvard University Press, 1925); Newman Ivey White, *American Negro Folk-Songs* (Cambridge: Harvard University Press, 1928); John W. Work, *American Negro Songs: A Comprehensive Collection of 230 Folk Songs and Spirituals, Religious and Secular* (New York: Crown Publishers, 1940); and Michael Taft, *Talkin' to Myself" Blues Lyrics, 1929–1942* (New York: Routledge, 2005).

9. Bessie Smith, *Bessie Smith: The Complete Recordings*, vol. 1–5 (Columbia, 1991–1996); Davis, *Blues Legacies*. Other sources on women and the blues include Douglas, *Terrible Honesty*; Lieb, *Ma Rainey*; Duvall Harrison, *Black Pearls: Blues Queens of the 1920s* (New Brunswick: Rutgers University Press, 1988); and Dexter Stewart Baxter, *Ma Rainey and the Classic Blues Singers* (New York: Stein and Day, 1970); Carby, "'It Just Be's Dat Way Sometime'; Chris Albertson, *Bessie* (New York: Stein and Day, 1972); and Samuel B. Charters and Leonard Kunstadt, *Jazz: A History of the New York Scene* (1962; New York: Da Capo, 1981). "'T Ain't Nobody's Bizness If I Do" and "Beale Street Papa" are published in Davis, *Blues Legacies*, 342–43, 264. On blues recordings, see Robert Dixon and John Godrich, *Recording the Blues:*

1902–1942 (New York: Stein and Day, 1970). On the segregation of Atlantic City, see Bryant Simon, *Boardwalk of Dreams: Atlantic City and the Fate of Urban America* (New York: Oxford University Press, 2004).

10. Lieb, *Mother of the Blues*; Davis, *Blues Legacies*; and Thomas Fulbright, "Ma Rainey and I," *Jazz Journal* 9 (March 1956): 1–2, 26.

11. On Blind Lemon Jefferson, see Pete Welding, *Bluesland: Portraits of Twelve Major American Blues Masters* (New York: Dutton, 1991). "Hangman's Blues" is included in *Blind Lemon Jefferson: Complete Recorded Works in Chronological Order* (Document Records, 1991), vol. 3 (1928) of the four-volume set.

12. Wald, *Escaping the Delta*; Douglas, *Terrible Honesty*. On Papa Charlie Jackson, see Dixon and Godrich, *Recording the Blues*, 33–34. On Big Bill Broonzy, see William Broonzy, *Big Bill Blues: William Broonzy's Story as Told to Yannick Bruynoghe* (London, 1955); Studs Terkel, *Big Bill Broonzy, His Story*, interview with Broonzy, (n.p., n.d.), at Music Library, University of Virginia, Charlottesville; and Big Bill Broonzy, *The Blues Tradition* (1927–1932) (Milestone Records, 1985). Preston Lauterbach, a former University of Virginia graduate student, has done important and pioneering research on black audiences' love of minstrelsy and blues musicians who also performed minstrel songs for black audiences. His work, so far unpublished, has deeply influenced my thinking here.

13. Ralph Ellison, "Change the Joke and Slip the Yoke," in *Shadow and Act*, 45–59.

14. Ralph Ellison and Albert Murray, *Trading Twelves: The Selected Letters of Ralph Ellison and Albert Murray* (New York: Modern Library, 2000), 29; Davis, *Blues Legacies*.

15. "Hear Me Talking to You," 221–22; "Prove It On Me Blues," 238; "Victim to the Blues," 252; "Travelin' Blues," 252, "Sweet Rough Man," 247–48; all in Davis, *Blues Legacies*. Ad for Ma Rainey's "Prove It On Me Blues," *Chicago Defender*, 1928; and Ma Rainey, *The Complete Ma Rainey Collection, 1923–1928* (King Jazz, 1994).

16. Roland Barthes, "The Grain of the Voice" in *Image, Music, Text* (Hill and Wang, 1977); Rainey, *The Complete Ma Rainey Collection*; Lieb, *Mother of the Blues*; and Davis, *Blues Legacies*.

17. "Heritage U.S.A."; Bruce Bastin, *Red River Blues: The Blues Tradition in the Southeast* (Urbana: University of Illinois Press, 1986); Denning, *The Cultural Front*, 348–61; Titon, *Early Downhome Blues*; and Steve Garabedian, "Reds, Whites, and Blues: Lawrence Gellert, *Negro Songs of Protest*, and the Leftwing Folksong Revival of the 1930s and 1940s," *American Quarterly* 57, no. 1 (2005): 179–206.

18. "Hard to Be a Nigger" is published in "John A. Lomax and Alan Lomax, *American Ballads and Folk Songs* (New York: Macmillan, 1934), 233–34. The Lomaxes, it is worth mentioning, did not pay people for the songs they recorded and often published. On finding Clear Rock later and discovering that his name was Mose Platt, see *The John and Ruby Lomax 1939 Southern States Recording Trip Archive*, Library of Congress, Section 11, Taylor Texas, May 10, 1939, at http://memory.loc.gov/ammem/lohtml/lohome.html.

19. "Sistren an' Brethren" is published in Gellert, *Negro Songs of Protest*. Some

Hear Me Talking to You **257**

of Gellert's field recordings of protest songs are available on *Negro Songs of Protest: Collected by Lawrence Gellert* (Rounder, 1973); *Cap'n You're So Mean: Negro Songs of Protest*, vol. 2 (Rounder, 1982); and *Nobody Knows My Name: Blues from South Carolina and Georgia* (Heritage, 1984).

20. Eric Lott, *Love and Theft: Blackface Minstrelsy and the American Working Class* (New York: Oxford University Press, 1993); Grace Elizabeth Hale, *Making Whiteness: The Culture of Segregation in the South, 1890–1940* (New York: Vintage, 1999); David Rodiger, *The Wages of Whiteness: Race and the Making of the American Working Class* (New York: Verso, 1991); Ira Berlin, *Generations of Captivity: A History of African American Slaves* (Cambridge: Belknap Press, 2003); and Michael Rogin, *Blackface/White Noise: Jewish Immigrants in the Hollywood Melting Pot* (Berkeley: University of California Press, 1996).

21. Judith Butler *Gender Trouble: Feminism and the Subversion of Identity* (New York: Routledge, 1990); and Peggy Phelan, *Unmarked: The Politics of Performance* (New York: Routledge, 1993); and Phelan and Jill Lane, eds., *The Ends of Performance* (New York: New York University Press, 1998).

At the Feet of Dessalines

Performing Haiti's Revolution during the New Negro Renaissance

CLARE CORBOULD

Black Americans during the interwar years expended a remarkable amount of energy describing the history, culture, and current conditions of people in the nearby republic of Haiti. Their efforts went beyond nonfiction, with a diverse bunch of cultural producers turning their hands to the task, including librettists, composers, visual artists, filmmakers, photographers, and writers of short stories, poetry, novels, and plays. Such products were part of a cultural-political movement, known as the New Negro Renaissance, characterized by an intense scrutiny of all issues relating to black identity. Culture produced during the era challenged mainstream and dominant accounts of history, which claimed for the United States a unique position as the most progressive of nation-states, the founder of modern democracy, the place where the ideals formulated in ancient Greece finally came to fruition. Black writers and artists used a wide variety of cultural forms to campaign for adequate recognition of black Americans' past and present contributions to the American nation, but also to challenge the rhetoric that asserted America was exceptional. In bringing Haiti to life on stage and in film, black Americans drew attention to the occupation by U.S. Marines of the neighboring republic and introduced into the public sphere a sustained and serious attack on the reputation and credibility of the United States. Denouncing their homeland as an imperial overlord, not so different from the European imperial states Americans so often defined themselves against, black Americans instead pledged their allegiance to Haitians, and by extension, with other colonized people around the world.

Playwrights were fascinated by Haiti, and especially its 1791–1803 revolution, which delivered the Western Hemisphere its first independent black nation. That event was almost always sidelined in accounts of world history, Western history, and histories of the development of civilization.[1] In black American history, by contrast, it was a signal and founding event. The leading characters of that complicated rebellion and its tumultuous after-math mesmerized black Americans one hundred years after the revolution's close. Play after play focused on three men: brave, tragic Toussaint Louver-ture, betrayed by the French; self-proclaimed emperor Jean-Jacques Des-salines, deposed by a coup that brought Henri Christophe to power in the north, who in turn completed the triumvirate in twentieth-century black Americans' memory. Stage writers of the interwar years all but ignored the period of Haitian history from about 1820 to the 1920s and 1930s. Casting physically robust and often well-known male actors in the leading roles, black playwrights and directors staged a type of masculinity by and large unavailable to black American men, especially those who lived in lynching's shadow in the segregated South. Staging Haiti therefore became a way to protest against both the occupation of the small nation and also American race relations.[2]

Inspiration for bringing Haiti to life came from many places. American slaves and free people of color had celebrated the black republic's existence ever since its foundation in the revolutionary overthrow of a white slave-owning class.[3] Some blacks emigrated to the Caribbean republic, includ-ing over 2,000 people in the middle of the nineteenth century.[4] Reverence continued in the next century, for example in the naming of schools such as the Toussaint L'Ouverture Grammar School in St. Louis that writer Maya Angelou attended in the 1930s. Black activists and intellectuals vigorously promoted plays and pageants as one of the best means of improving the self-image of black Americans, especially children. When troupes staged a pro-duction—studied their lines together, made sets, sewed costumes, coaxed audiences—they forged and strengthened community ties. Most interwar pageants and many plays, especially those of just one act, dramatized the lives of famed black men and women, past and present, as well as lauding the achievements of a race whose members had mostly been enslaved just some sixty years before. In time, it was hoped, such performances would improve race relations. Putting Haiti on stage came out of this fondness for performance as a means to improve psychological health.

Haiti was in the mind's eye for a less edifying reason. From 1915 until 1934, American Marines occupied the nation, purportedly for the benefit of Haitians. Haitians themselves were not so sure. Elites on the island were affronted by accusations of poor self-government, while poor Haitians were subject to the restoration of the dreaded *corvée*, by which they were pressed into hard labor, servicing roads and other public works. Haitians and black Americans alike protested against the abrogation of Haitian sovereignty,

Figure 11.1. "'Civilizing' Haiti," Chicago Defender, February 23, 1929. Versions of this cartoon appeared at least three times between 1922 and 1929. In one, the hairy white hand of U.S. military occupation crushes a miniature woman, whose arm is held aloft in a pose reminiscent of the Statue of Liberty. Courtesy of the Chicago Defender.

especially after the Paris Peace Conference of 1919, at which the idea of national self-determination was much bandied about. Black activists and intellectuals in the United States wrote stinging critiques of the occupation in newspapers and magazines. With Haitians, they formed transnational organizations designed to bring the occupation to an end. Haiti's role as a symbol of black nationhood was of unparalleled importance, especially into the 1930s when the reputation of other black nations was tarnished—by the revelation that slavery existed in Liberia and by fascist Italy's invasion of Ethiopia.

Inspiration for staging Haiti came also from within the United States. It is hard to overstate the presence of Haiti in interwar American culture, especially when compared with the inconsequential consideration given to most places overseas. Throughout the period of the U.S. occupation of the republic, as historian Mary Renda has demonstrated, Haiti appeared on stage, in books, film, newspapers, and even on "scenic wallpaper."[5] The phenomenal expansion of mass consumer culture occurred alongside the rise of American imperial power, producing a particular fascination among Americans with the exoticism of conquered territories.[6] In most of these mainstream accounts, Haiti was a backward place where travelers could experience the primitive culture of Africa, only closer to home. These were lurid treatments of Haitian culture, sold as "reportage." Tales and images of voodoo ceremonies, cannibalism, child sacrifice, and zombies, not to mention drumming and half-naked bodies, became bestselling books and much-seen films.[7] The best-known of these cultural productions was the second full-length play in the brilliant career of Eugene O'Neill, *The Emperor Jones*. Extremely popular, the play was mounted first in 1920 in downtown New York, with Charles Gilpin playing the lead in a run of over 200 performances. It had another three New York seasons by 1926, including one starring Paul Robeson in 1924, and several in Europe. A film and opera followed in 1933. In the 1930s, Haiti continued to fascinate white theater-goers; no fewer than three federally funded Depression-era productions were set in Haiti, including Orson Welles's directorial debut in 1936, known locally as "the voodoo *Macbeth*."

Transforming people's ideas about Haiti—and black people in general— became paramount after it became clear that efforts to end the occupation in more directly political ways had failed. James Weldon Johnson, executive secretary of the NAACP, lobbied presidential hopeful Warren Harding on the back of four widely read articles published in 1920 in the *Nation* under the series title "Self-Determining Haiti."[8] Harding courted the votes of black Americans and anti-imperialists by criticizing Wilson's administration but dropped the matter soon into his term, irrespective of damning findings by a Senate inquiry in 1921–22.[9] Other than in black public life, where it appeared constantly in newspapers and journal articles, editorials, cartoons, and letters, as well as in the arts, American interest in Haiti fell away for the remainder of the decade. It was only after a massacre of Haitians in the town of Aux Cayes in late 1929—coinciding with a move in foreign relations away from Theodore Roosevelt's "big stick" and toward the "good neighborliness" of the late Hoover administration and then Franklin Roosevelt— that Americans' attention was refocused on Haiti.[10] Throughout these years, however, black artists and writers in all genres, influenced by the press and urban organizations, concentrated hard on Haitian history and culture.

Black American cultural producers seized the opportunity to reshape representations of blackness in the American public sphere. They drew on cutting-edge theories that refuted the idea that racial difference was biologically determined, positing instead that human difference could and should be explained through history and circumstance. Such ideas emanated from Columbia University's recently established anthropology department, which was under the stewardship of German immigrant Franz Boas. In doing so, they denounced claims that Haitian culture was inferior to white American culture. Instead, they heralded the creativity of a people under duress, both during the Revolution and under U.S. imperial rule. Moreover, they used their descriptions of Haitian life to reflect on black American responses to enslavement and adverse race relations in the decades since the Civil War. Finding a similarity in the cultural responses to oppressive conditions, they forged an alliance with Haitians that transcended a simple biological connection.

Black Americans' dramatizations of Haiti in the past and present could not avoid engaging in some way with O'Neill's *The Emperor Jones*. Rarely has a play generated so much commentary reflecting political issues of the day. The script centered on Brutus Jones, a Pullman train porter who has escaped jail in the United States and within two years become emperor of an unnamed Caribbean island. Jones's brutal exploitation of the natives ensures their wish to overthrow him. With rebellion mounting, Jones attempts to flee, but his progress is impeded by ghosts of his misdeeds. He is haunted at first by his recent sins and then, going back into his past, by a chain gang, a slave auction, and lastly a witch-doctor in an African setting. Jones loses his clothing, his nerve, and his sanity. Ultimately, a native kills him with a silver bullet. A tom-tom beat accompanied actors every step of the way, increasing in tempo and intensity as the play progressed.

Audience members assumed the play took place in Haiti; the setting was, in O'Neill's scathing observation in the play's preface, "an island in the West Indies as yet not self-determined by white marines. The form of government is, for the time being, an Empire."[11] If O'Neill's stage directions did not give it away, the very character of a self-proclaimed black emperor would put viewers in mind of Jean-Jacques Dessalines, the inaugural leader of the Republic of Haiti, who declared himself emperor in 1804. Some in the audience would have recognized too the bravado of the heroic character's claim that he could be shot dead by only a *silver* bullet. Another of the revolutionary heroes, Henri Christophe, who ruled the northern part of Haiti from 1807 to 1820, said the same thing and eventually, infirm and with his enemies fast approaching, took his own life in this fashion.[12]

O'Neill's protest against American imperialism in Haiti was not necessarily antiracist—Brutus Jones was hardly a model of transnational black solidarity—and yet many black theatergoers found the play profoundly moving. Visual images of black people, whether on material objects ranging from piggybanks to pancake mix or in films that took their cue from immensely popular theatrical minstrel routines, were rarely complimentary. Black viewers, who were long used to seeing themselves portrayed as buffoons, could take some pleasure in Brutus Jones's impressive military regalia and bearing. Moreover, Jones, even if his traits included stereotypical criminality and dandyism, was a genuinely tragic character who occupied the stage the whole time in a full-length play. It was no accident that when Orson Welles came to choose material for his first production, funded by the Federal Theatre Project, it was for a version of Shakespeare's *Macbeth* that harked back, in staging, setting, costumes, and themes, to O'Neill's *The Emperor Jones*. Jones may have been immoral, but, like Macbeth, at least his decisions were his own, and his fate of his own making. Jones may not have been likeable but, like Macbeth, he was powerful, reminding his Cockney sidekick, Smithers, to "Talk polite, white man! Talk polite, you heah me! I'm boss heah now, is you fergettin'?"[13]

Black audiences appreciated that while Jones on paper was a brutally exploitative imperial master, in production the play was much more about the psychological torments experienced by black Americans with a long history of violence and subjugation. Writer Jean Toomer lauded O'Neill in 1921 for achieving his purpose of "a section of Negro psychology presented in significant dramatic form." For Toomer, each individual had his or her own particular unconscious, but all were subject to group conditions, so "in fact Brutus Jones lives through sections of an unconscious which is peculiar to the Negro. Slave ships, whipping posts, and so on. . . . In a word, his fear becomes a Negro's fear, recognizably different from a similar emotion, modified by other racial experience."[14] *The Emperor Jones*, for all its faults, took the psychology of a black man seriously, thereby challenging the discipline of psychology itself, which assumed a white subject in its studies of the individual in society. Promoting the 1933 film, Robeson said that O'Neill "dug down into my racial life and has found the essence of my race. Every word he wrote for *The Emperor Jones* is true to the Negro racial experience."[15] Black American intellectuals were not only relieved to see a dramatic character on stage, but also thought the psychological elements of the play had real merit.

For some critics, the genius of O'Neill's play in production lay in its portrayal of the similarities between black Americans' experiences of slavery and its aftermath (what Black Power advocates later termed "internal colonialism"),[16] and those of people under colonial rule, whether Haitians under the command of the U.S. Marines or Africans subject to the rule of various European powers. Hubert Harrison, Virgin Islands immigrant to the United States, concurred with O'Neill in calling the play a "psychological study," but like Toomer and Robeson stressed that it was a study of a *black* man. In Harrison's view, "the external setting of the drama is really of no importance whatsoever. . . . It could just as readily be set in Africa or South Carolina."[17] Haiti linked Africans to their descendants in the United States, but their links were more than biological. Insisting on the similarity of experiences in Africa and throughout the diaspora, Harrison implied that racism in the United States was structurally similar to that of colonialism elsewhere, with similar effects on those under the thumb.[18] The experience of subjugation, justified on the basis of supposed black inferiority, was similar everywhere.

What was "true . . . racial experience" for Robeson was not to all black Americans' tastes. Some merely had reservations, as did an East Coast writer who called it an unflattering but "necessary intermediary step."[19] Others condemned the play, including a reviewer for a black nationalist newspaper, the *Negro World*, who found it utterly unsuitable to the task of representing black history, which should focus on the far more positive aspects of the past: "The Negro, with the new thought of racial respect, cannot be proud of the Negro actor, who holds his race up out of the shadows in such a limelight as that which shines in 'Emperor Jones.'. . . The man who sells the spirit of his manhood and the soul of his womanhood for the electric lights of an American Broadway and the tainted medals of the white man, is not an ideal Negro for Negro history."[20]

While that reviewer lamented the lack of uplifting themes, others found Brutus Jones's psychological torments unconvincing and were irritated by his predictable descent into an atavistic past, helped along by the constant drumming. That sound drove the "rhythmic hotness" that for white visitors to nighttime Harlem was the soundtrack to a rejuvenating trip into "precivilization."[21] A poet in the *World*, tired of overdetermined depictions of black people's responses to drumming, called for the "Death of the Emperor Jones" in the title for his 1930 poem:

I'm tired;
Weary from drums
Pounding in my ears,
Banging in my head,
Drumming in my heart,
Drums—white drums

Bursting fear
Into my brain,
Sweating agony
Over my body,
Drums, drums driving,
Driving to madness.[22]

Both the stage productions and the film version of *The Emperor Jones* were dependent on a primitivism that many in the audience found more amusing than tragic. Langston Hughes recalled being impressed with members of a 1930s audience in Harlem who had failed to admire Jules Bledsoe's rendering of the tragedy. They laughed without restraint and reportedly yelled out, "'Why don't you come on out of that jungle—back to Harlem where you belong?'"[23]

Such derision notwithstanding, O'Neill's play did a great deal to popularize an issue dear to many black Americans' hearts: the dubious basis of the United States' occupation of Haiti and the brutality of the Marines stationed there. By staging the revolution again and again, dramatists put into the public sphere a different image of Haiti than that used to justify the occupation. One of the earliest of these interwar plays was *Genifrede*, written and first performed in 1922, and published in a 1935 collection for black schoolchildren. Its author was a Washington, D.C., schoolteacher, Helen I. Webb. *Genifrede* set the scene, so to speak, for plays by black Americans that were set in Haiti and explored themes relevant to the experiences of black people in both countries (and further afield).[24] Tension built in the play with a booming cannon firing at very specific intervals, as the title character, daughter of revolutionary leader Toussaint Louverture, attempted to avert the execution of her lover, General Pierre Moyse, himself Louverture's nephew.[25] The taut atmosphere in Webb's play was very much like that in numerous one-act plays that focused on lynching and were written by black American women during the interwar period.[26] Webb's focus on the helplessness of Genifrede in the face of Moyse's death paralleled a central preoccupation in that other set of female-authored plays, which were often laid out in domestic settings with women anticipating in horror the imminent death of their sons, brothers, and/or lovers. Despite the differences between *Genifrede* and these plays—notably that Moyse is murdered by fellow black men rather than white lynchers—each counterposed the relative helplessness of black women in the face of such violence with a certain nobility among the men facing death. Webb thus linked black Americans and Haitians on the basis of a shared experience of violence. By referring to Louverture as a "courageous chief," Webb's exploration of masculinity further connected black Americans and Haitians to African men. Webb evoked tribal Africa in order to show that Haitian men, and black American men, were the descendants of proud Africans.

The search for a strong leader was an abiding theme in black American culture and politics.[27] During the 1920s and 1930s, Marcus Garvey was likened to Louverture in the pages of his organization's newspaper, and, just as Louverture had been during the antebellum period, also to George Washington.[28] A lineage of strong male nation builders, imagined to have originated with a redoubtable African masculinity, was a foremost preoccupation of Garvey's black nationalist organization, and it pervaded black American culture more widely, as the plays examined here demonstrate. One of the most straightforward ways to protest the U.S. occupation of Haiti was to dramatize a diasporic family of black men, all capable of self- and collective government. Contrary to claims by the government of the occupying forces, Haitians were not constitutionally incapable of leading and managing their own country, just as black Americans could live without the paternalism so many white Americans assumed they needed. Women's roles in these plays were almost always as adjuncts—usually wives or girlfriends—to active men. In Langston Hughes's play, first produced in 1935 and titled at different times *Drums of Haiti* and *Emperor of Haiti*,[29] the focus was again on revolutionary leaders. Whatever their faults, they were paragons of strength and courage:

DESSALINES. Then remain on guard! But not inside.
CONGO. I got you, chief.
DESSALINES. (*laughing*) Chief!
CONGO. Like in Africa, Jean Jacques—Chief.
DESSALINES. Can you remember Africa, Congo?
CONGO. Sure. I was a big boy when that English ship got hold of me.
    That's why I can do our dances so well. I learnt 'em in Africa.[30]

In Hughes's play, taking charge during the revolution restored putatively natural qualities associated with men in Africa.

Black playwrights not only depicted Haiti's leaders as strong and admirable, but also turned their talents to bringing to life those Haitian people whose names were not known. In contrast to O'Neill's play, which failed to give depth to any Haitian characters, Hughes's *Emperor of Haiti* charted Dessalines's rise to emperor but also his fall from grace, as he became in-

creasingly unpopular with most Haitians and was eventually murdered by
his rivals. In this play, those who opposed Dessalines remained committed
to the principles of the revolution, freedom and fairness for all. Hughes
portrayed these characters as identified with Africa, while Dessalines was
seduced by the Anglo-Western world:

PIERRE. I'd rather have a bugle, that's what I want.
CELESTE. For what?
PIERRE. A bugle blows pretty. All the white children have 'em.
CELESTE. The white children's free.
MARS. Anyhow, a drum can sound twenty times as far as any bugle
     ever blowed. Bugles don't belong to black folks.
PIERRE. That's how come I want one.
LULU. You can have one, honey, when we's free. . . .
CELESTE. Drums is what our gods like, though. Drums is for Legba
     and Dambala, Nanna and M'bo.
CONGO. African gods been known' drums a long time. Them tinny
     bugles just cain't reach they ears. . . .
MARS. The drum's a black man's heart a-beatin.' Tonight that
     beatin's goin' to set the Frenchmen's hair on end.[31]

The anemia of the "tinny" bugle was contrasted with the vitality of the
throbbing drums—the "black man's heart a-beatin.'" As the moment of rebellion approached, "the drums beat louder, ever spreading."[32] At the end
of the second act, they beat again, this time to signal the overthrow of Dessalines's self-indulgent court. Hughes conveyed conflict between light-
skinned mulattoes and black Haitians aurally, with sound used to mock
the upper class's imperfect mimicry of white customs. During a banquet of
state, the Bugle Boy (Pierre grown up) announces the arrival of the emperor
and his light-skinned aristocratic cronies, but the sound of his instrument
is lost in the din of the drums. "The drum," the stage directions read, was
"never silent during the rest of the scene. Its monotonous beat continues,
as if calling for one knows not what."[33] Drumming may have signaled black
atavism to some, but in Hughes's hands, it became a symbol of a masculinity that was a little closer to Africa and a lot less cowed than that of black
men in the United States, where Jim Crow racism and violence worked hard
to enforce submission. Hughes, like Webb, used Haiti to effect something
of a return to an imagined place—"Africa"—where men's masculinity went
unquestioned and their lives and bodies unharmed. The plays were more

than a protest against the occupation; they also protested the emasculation racism wrought in the United States.

Such a "reclaiming" of an imagined African masculinity was a problematic enterprise; while brute strength may have become a treasured hallmark of American masculinity by the early twentieth century, in black men it was widely considered to be dangerous.[34] According to Secretary of State Robert Lansing, black Americans, Haitians, and Liberians all possessed an "inherent tendency to revert to savagery."[35] Black militancy was therefore always a double-edged sword, at once enabling vehement protest against conditions in Haiti and in the United States (and especially forming the basis of a claim to proper and rightful citizenship, because these men were appropriately strong and independent) but at the same time confirming stereotypes about a lack of civilization among black people.

Black playwrights, like their white fellow citizens, were often fascinated with aspects of Haiti's culture they thought exotic, and were not immune to the tendency to emphasize its sensational aspects. When two university teachers, Clarence Cameron White and John Frederick Matheus, traveled to Haiti, they were enthralled by what they respectively called "The Magic Isle" and "this luxurious island paradise."[36] White was also a well-regarded composer and violinist. Matheus was a writer and expert in Romance languages. In *Tambour*, a play written just after their 1928 trip to Haiti, the female lead character, Zabette, objects to her boyfriend Mougalou's preference for drumming over spending time with her. Notwithstanding her protests, Mougalou continues to drum, half-naked, because "when I make the drums talk they speak back to me. They whisper the long lost secrets of the Congo. They tell the story of black warriors crashing thru the African jungles." Zabette, in spite of herself, "suddenly begins to tremble and quiver, her whole frame undulating with the contagion of the vibrating drums." Mougalou "thumps with a certain wild abandon, yet in perfect rhythm that is never once missed. At times he appears to fall into a trance state."[37] *Tambour* put into words and music the equation between drums, Haiti, Africa, and unshakeable savagery that had been implicit—even if equally well understood—in *The Emperor Jones*.

Drums were linked to rhythm, widely considered to be a distinctive African cultural "survival" or inheritance in the New World. Rhythm, in turn, was linked to an easy sexuality, uninhibited by generations of civilization and all the healthier for it. On first reading, Zabette and Mougalou were staple characters, drawn from Westerners' fantasies about how black

Figutre 11.2. Clarence
Cameron White,
Tambour. *Black
American playwrights,
like white Westerners,
focused their accounts
of Haiti on drumming,
dancing, and voodoo.
Their interpretation of
these practices, however,
could not have been more
different from that of most
white tourists. Clarence
Cameron White Papers,
Moorland-Spingarn
Research Center, Howard
University.*

people spent their time. Her very proximity to a drumbeat seemed to signal her descent down the ladder of civilization. And yet neither Mougalou nor Zabette was made out to be grotesque or comedic, which was usually the case in characterizations of black people on stage. While the script was not explicit about the fact that drumming and dancing were skills learnt through years of training and practice, nor did it fetishize these abilities as coming naturally to black people. Instead, drumming and dancing were signs of a culture that at the play's conclusion triumphed over the failures in Haitian politics, since the reign of the "four great founders," Louverture, Dessalines, Christophe, and Pétion, and the chaos fuelled by mercenaries known as "cacos." With Mougalou kidnapped, Zabette is about to be ravaged by his rival, but is saved by a powerful voodoo curse. The play ended with the distinctive sound of Mougalou's drumming coming from the distant hills, bringing with it the hope that he remained alive. Written in 1929 but set in 1911, just before U.S. Marines invaded, White's and Matheus's play implied that the Haitian people of the countryside would triumph yet over all oppression.

Scripts such as *Tambour* reflected a new appreciation in anthropology for that which was different, without conventional denunciations of racial inferiority. When White and Matheus collaborated on *Ouanga* (1932), an opera set during the revolutionary era, a complicated score pit the tom-tom against other instruments to symbolize the clash between African culture, specifically voodoo, and the modernizing will of Dessalines; it was the drum versus the "passionate sweep of strings and woodwinds, which sound the theme of conflict between the old customs and the new."[38] Stage directions specified the drumbeat should have a similar effect on the audience as in *The Emperor Jones*: "The insistent, measured beat of the native drums from the distant mountains ominously strikes the ear as the flamboyant tropical scene with the full force flashes upon the eye. The orchestration expresses peace and the fresh beauty of nature in contrast to the veiled threat of the booming tom-toms."[39] But alongside this familiar portrayal of primitive culture—drums in the distant hills appeared in just about every account of Haiti—there were merengues in the score. White had an ethnographer's desire to represent Haitian culture in all its variety and without judging cultural forms, whether "old" or "new," in relation to one another.[40] And although voodoo was represented in the play by drums and dancing, it was not barbaric. Rather, Matheus's script and White's score dramatized voodoo as a serious belief system, integral to Haitian life. In *Ouanga*, Dessalines met his demise because he outlawed indigenous religious practice and tried to replace it with Catholicism.

When black American playwrights, librettists, and composers treated the subject of voodoo, they intended to do more than simply titillate their audience and reassure those watching of their place higher up the evolutionary ladder. In these portrayals it did not necessarily follow that just because Haitians engaged in religious and musical practices that some assumed harked back to Africa that they were therefore a backward people. On the contrary, black American dramatists' use of voodoo was a celebration of autonomous black culture, and one borne very much of the experience of enslavement in the New World. For playwright Leslie Pinckney Hill, it was one of the "black man's necessary masks . . . a clever mystico-political organization operating powerfully upon the minds of illiterate masses."[41] Voodoo, far from being a so-called authentic survival of African culture, was a terrific example of the syncretism and adaptability that characterized black culture and formed the basis of black political struggle.[42]

Accordingly, given the environment in which culture was divided hierarchically into "high" and "low," the forms black American writers and musicians chose for representing Haiti fell squarely into the "high" category.[43]

They created operas, librettos, and in the case of Hill, 120 pages of single-spaced blank verse, a mode he declared "the only vehicle worthy of the dignity and elevation of my theme."[44] Implicitly they rejected the sensational "reportage" of Haitian customs in newspapers, bestselling travel accounts by many white Americans, and the increasingly pervasive figure of the zombie, who would come in the early 1930s to dominate a new genre of horror film.

Using these forms, artists challenged characterizations of black folk that shored up the U.S. occupation by implying they were childlike, primitive, and in need of help. As Mary Renda has shown in her account of the mutual impact of U.S. and Haitian society and ideas upon one another, the language of paternalism infused American attitudes toward their neighbors.[45] Instead, black Americans called into question the claim that the United States was an exceptional republican democracy by implicitly critiquing the version of Haitian history offered by the conquerors. Cultural renditions of their opposition echoed the stinging words of a white NAACP executive who asked, "Which is worse, to eat a human being without cooking him, as is alleged to be the custom in Haiti, or to cook a human being without eating him, as we know to be a custom in Mississippi?"[46] Leslie Pinckney Hill answered succinctly, "Haiti has come to be a sort of challenge to the democratic sentiments and preten[s]ions of our time."[47] Langston Hughes replied to the NAACP executive's question with a short satirical skit, *The Em-Fuehrer Jones* (1938). Hitler replaced Emperor Brutus Jones but similarly stumbled about the stage as if frightened in a forest, haunted by the specter of sportsmen Joe Louis and Jesse Owens.[48] In a four-page script, Hughes replaced Brutus Jones with a more historically accurate white colonizing figure, drawing a parallel between the racial ideologies that prompted American occupation of Haiti, its treatment of its own black citizens, and fascist Germany's imperial designs.

Well-to-do Haitians and black Americans collaborated in cultural critiques of the U.S. occupation of Haiti. Where elite Haitians had previously disdained "peasant" culture, they now revered it in their efforts to demonstrate a cultural national sovereignty in the face of an attack on their political sovereignty.[49] The revolution featured prominently in such collaborations, as when Dantès Bellegarde, the Haitian diplomatic envoy to Washington and the Pan-American Union, came at Arthur Schomburg's invitation to the opening of an exhibition of Haitian history and culture at the Harlem branch of the New York Public Library. "Nothing can better serve the cause of my country, so misunderstood, so particularly disparaged in the United States," wrote Bellegarde to Schomburg, "than the demonstration you intend to make." Echoing the sentiments of many central to the Harlem Renaissance, Bellegarde claimed that the exhibition would show "how a people, freed from the most brutalizing slavery, has been able to overcome all the hostility which surrounded it and attain, by its own effort, the highest culture, thus avenging the black race of the accusation of inferiority which they have dared to place against it."[50] James Weldon Johnson had said almost exactly the same thing about what art could do for improving race relations, even to erase racism, within the United States. Black inferiority could be disproved, he argued time and again, by showing that black artists could match or even surpass the creativity, ingenuity, and aesthetic sense of their white compatriots.[51]

Haitians and black Americans also joined forces to establish organizations designed to lobby the U.S. government into retreating from Haiti. These included the Union Patriotique, begun in November 1920, and the Haiti–Santo Domingo Independence Society.[52] At the basis of these societies was a new militancy that characterized postwar black politics, including, for example, better known organizations such as the Universal Negro Improvement Association. This militancy was linked closely to a particular style of masculinity that was shared, too, by cultural producers of the era, including those who wrote about Haiti. In both *Tambour* and *Ouanga*, the characters associate rebellion with manliness and link both to drums and, therefore, to Africa. By writing and performing such themes in the United States, artists completed the line of descent from African manhood to African American, via Haitian leaders and participants in Haiti's revolution. This relationship was given form in Clarence White's scrapbook of his trip to Haiti. A photo of collaborator John Matheus sitting on the steps at the base of a massive statue of Dessalines reads "J. F. M. at the Feet of Dessalines."[53]

Playwrights and composers who aimed to convey that Haitian culture was admirable, not depraved, faced a significant challenge: most people were not interested in political art. The most commercially successful stage and film productions of the era featuring or created by black Americans were those that updated the minstrel tradition into modern musicals. Such shows offered up, for runs of months at a time, half-naked bodies and thumping drum rhythms for consumption by audiences whose responses were very different depending on who they were. White Americans' assumptions about their black neighbors survived without challenge.[54] In this context, staging

Figure 11.3. Clarence Cameron White's collaborator John Matheus sitting on the steps at the base of Jean-Jacques Dessalines's statue in Haiti. Linking black American men to the heroes of the Haitian Revolution, and in turn to African chiefs, playwrights protested against official and popular ideas that black men were incapable of governing themselves. Photographs and Prints Division, Schomburg Center for Research in Black Culture, The New York Public Library, Astor, Lenox and Tilden Foundations.

productions that challenged racial prejudice was very tricky. In Clarence White's unpublished autobiography, he recalled that after winning the 1932 David Bispham Memorial Medal for an American opera composition, he contacted many people to try to interest them in producing *Ouanga*. It was discouraging, he wrote, to be informed over and over that "since the subject matter was not humorous, it might not be acc[ep]table as a vehicle for a Negro cast." A white patron organized a reading in New York for notables including Leopold Godowski, but as White discovered later, they were already keen to mount George Gershwin's score of *Porgy and Bess*. White concluded: "In fact I now think that American Producers were not interested in the idea of an all Negro Opera at this time."[55] *Ouanga* had its first full production in 1949, by an all-black company at South Bend, Indiana. William Grant Still's opera, *Troubled Island*, waited until the same year for its first outing.[56] Things were little different for black Americans in Europe. White and Matheus hoped for a London production of *Ouanga* starring Paul Robeson as Dessalines, and a film version. They may also have hoped for a Paris production with Jules Bledsoe to sing the role of Dessalines, but it all came to nought.[57] Trinidadian C. L. R. James's stage show, *Toussaint L'Ouverture*, with Robeson in the title role, played London for just two nights.[58]

Recognizing the limitations of stage performance as a means of improving ideas about black people, whether Haitian or North American, many black Americans instead attempted to mobilize the still relatively new cinema technology. Forays into film, which along with music was the most widely accessed and popular form of American mass culture, were always difficult. Film of the classical era favored caricatures of black Americans, either as stock southern plantation characters or as monsters of one sort or another.[59] Well into the interwar years, racial stereotypes pervaded popular film. *King Kong*, with its obvious racial overtones, was the hit of 1933. Horror-filled "zombie flicks," set in Haiti, began in the 1930s.[60] Mainstream film portrayed others in the African diaspora no more sensitively than it did American blacks. The many films of this ilk included Columbia Pictures' *Black Moon* in 1932, with over 250 extras running riot as a voodoo high priest prepares to sacrifice the pretty heroine.[61] *Voodoo*, filmed entirely in the West Indies, screened on Broadway promising access to sacred rites usually off-limits to white folk.[62]

Opportunities for black Americans to make or participate in independent film were few and far between. Black independent filmmakers, including Oscar Micheaux, tended to produce storylines set in the modern era that stressed the Americanness of black Americans. There were, nonetheless, efforts to bring the Haitian Revolution to life onscreen. In 1920, *Crisis* ran an advertisement calling on readers to buy stock in a new company that intended to make a "Super-Photoplay," called "Toussaint L'Ouverture," with Clarence Muse of the Lafayette Players in the title role.[63] Eight years later, a band of New Englanders, fed up with the way "in which Toussaint has been consistently omitted from histories," announced they would raise one million dollars to portray his life in a film that even the great Louverture "'would be proud [of] if he could view it.'"[64] I have not found evidence either film was ever made. Paul Robeson himself, his statements about O'Neill's realism notwithstanding, had a miserable time in the mid-1930s making films that did not allow him to portray blackness (or at least black men) in the way that he either wanted or intended.[65] Criticized widely for *Sanders of the River*, in which he played an African chief in grass skirt who was the very model of Western fantasies, Robeson said he starred in the film with the intention of using its profits to make a film in which he would play Haitian leader Henri Christophe. If that were successful, one on Menelik II, emperor of Ethiopia, would follow.[66] (Neither film came to pass.)

The closest Robeson came to portraying either hero was in a British-made film, *Song of Freedom* (1936), directed by J. Elder Wills. Here, Robeson was able finally to depict African and black cultures—and most importantly, a worldwide black fraternity—more to his satisfaction. Unusually, *Song of Freedom* featured scenes of the slave trade, including the Middle Passage, and interracial working and living on the docks in England. Robeson played John Zinga, a British dockworker whose transformation into a singing star gives him the opportunity to discover his heritage as the descendant of Queen Zinga of Casanga, an island off the west coast of Africa.[67] Once again the site for representing black culture was an island, though this time one that was closer to the African mainland than was the in-between space of Haiti.

Onstage in London in the early scenes of *Song of Freedom*, Zinga stars in the opera-in-a-film, "The Black Emperor," a superb reworking of the themes of *The Emperor Jones*. In full regalia unmistakably like that of Brutus Jones, Robeson was able finally to play a man of full stature, one interested in his ancestry and cultural heritage, whose desires are quite distinct from the exploitative ambitions of Brutus Jones. Later in the film, the character's strength is perversely demonstrated through his capacity to commit suicide, something Brutus Jones had not managed, instead wasting his bullets shooting fearfully at ghosts. And although Zinga's attitude is akin to Marcus Garvey's neocolonialism, wanting "to bring help to his people" in Africa in the form of medicine and ships ("progress" in his words), he is ultimately embraced by the natives as one of them, avoiding Brutus Jones's fate of assassination.

Although Robeson was happier with this film, it was still tinged by the primitivism that had disappointed him about his earlier works.[68] The self-serving witch doctor, in particular, was a shallow rendering of African religion that set up mysticism against Western "rationalism." The witch doctor was an exoticized creation, a character springing from the primitivist imagination that pervaded the New Negro Renaissance of the interwar years and which accounted for the "Negro vogue" on the other side of the Atlantic.

Robeson's failures in the expensive medium of film reflected the experience of those in performance genres generally. Every effort by black Americans to connect to Africa and Africans, whether directly or through stepping stones such as Haiti or "Casanga," was constrained by stereotypes as to black people's primitive nature. Those who managed to overcome it found their plays and operas went unproduced. With film, black audiences enjoyed what they could, and either ignored or booed the rest.

It was perhaps the limitations of performance genres that sent those looking to protest against the occupation or to represent blackness in more sympathetic ways to other cultural modes, too. Langston Hughes's career is illustrative here. As well as *Drums of Haiti*, begun in 1928 and reworked over twenty years, he wrote about Haiti in essays, short stories, and memoir, as well as in private correspondence. He also translated Haitian writer Jacques Roumain into English. Hughes began work on *Drums of Haiti* in 1928, before his journey to Haiti. His commentary on Haiti records his conversion from regarding it as an island on which Africa could be consumed to something rather more complicated. To be sure, in his 1956 memoir he wrote that "the upper-class Haitians who have lived abroad know all the [dance] steps of Broadway and of Paris. But the black Haitians of the soil seem to remember Africa in their souls and far-off ancestral tribes where each man and each woman danced alone."[69] As well as celebrating this apparently unself-conscious bodily memory of Africa, Hughes recognized simultaneously how economic conditions in rural Haiti affected the country's inhabitants. He was not hampered by the blinkered romanticism that blinded so many of his contemporaries to the poverty endured by rural Haitians.[70] Hughes titled an account of his 1931 trip, "In Search of Sun." The heading promised a rendition of the tropical paradise other Americans had found. Instead, it became ironic as Hughes analyzed the inequities of Haitian society, seeing for the first time how, as he put it in later years, "class lines may cut across color lines within a race."[71]

Hughes, always a great stylist and rarely didactic, reviewed U.S. imperialism through sustained attention to Haitian footwear. In "Drums of Haiti," market vendors who were formerly slaves agreed that their material conditions had improved, with the Pepper Vendor contending "Right! Some of you-all's even got shoes."[72] But that play had few performances, so Hughes used shoes as a symbol both of wealth and of misguided imperial ambitions in many genres of his writing. During his trip in 1931, he published an article entitled "People Without Shoes," a pointed critique of the unequal distribution of wealth in the republic.[73] Hughes might have been riffing on an early editorial by James Weldon Johnson, whose articles in the *Nation* in 1920 brought Haiti to the attention of President Warren Harding. Johnson explicitly criticized the U.S. government's policy of occupation, predicting that each Haitian "will no doubt seriously question whether he has gained anything, even if he has learned to wear shoes, derby hats and stiff collars."[74]

A children's book Hughes cowrote in 1932 had an appropriately ingenuous tone, but nevertheless included observations such as "pennies are scarce in Haiti."[75] The poverty of the children's family was contrasted against the "shiney pointed shoes" of those in the upper classes.[76] *Popo and Fifina* combined the two elements of Hughes's vision of Haiti: a delight in a culture that appeared to black Americans to have retained African elements in a more pure form than had their own culture, and an emphasis on poverty caused at least partly by U.S. colonization. As well as attributing the poverty of rural Haitians to the occupation, the story, as Mary Renda has pointed out, also challenged the occupation by reversing the idea that Haiti was a child in need of a father. Instead the book emphasized "strong paternal figures in the Haitian family and in Haitian history."[77] King Christophe gets a mention, when his story is told to the children by the character, Uncle Jacques, presumably named for the revolutionary freedom fighter Jean-Jacques Dessalines. In this children's tale, as in his essays, Hughes was forthright about conditions in present-day Haiti. Whereas on stage, he and his contemporaries brought to life, time and again, the heroes of the revolution and ignored most else of Haitian history, other genres enabled them to protest the occupation much more directly.

Black Americans' reappraisal of Haiti's history and culture found expression on the 1930s stage—and reached substantial audiences—thanks to federal funding for the arts created as part of Franklin Roosevelt's New Deal, designed to stimulate the depressed economy. The Works Progress Administration's Federal Theatre Project (FTP) kept alive the fascination with the Haitian Revolution. In 1936, Orson Welles made his debut directing Harlem's Negro Theatre Unit in a version of *Macbeth*, set in Haiti, with costumes and themes designed to remind audiences of *The Emperor Jones*. The play was known locally as "the voodoo *Macbeth*." On opening night, the eighty-five-piece marching band of the Monarch Negro Elks drew a crowd

Figure 11.4. Poster for Haiti. *At the conclusion of the play, black audience members cheered as Henri Christophe dispatched the last remaining Frenchmen and proclaimed the Republic of Haiti. Prints and Photographs Division, Library of Congress.*

of 10,000 people onto the streets to follow behind a banner announcing "Macbeth by William Shakespeare." Traffic remained at a standstill for an hour while the crowd enjoyed a street-side performance outside the theater.[78] Two years later, the Harlem unit of the FTP staged *Haiti*, which was resuscitated from a miserable script about miscegenation into a celebration of the anticolonial revolution. Some 74,000 tickets were sold during the show's 103-performance run at the Lafayette Theatre in Harlem.[79] Those who attended enjoyed the performance, especially when white characters were knocked out by black fists.[80] *Haiti* was also mounted in Boston and Hartford, while on the West Coast, posters enticed audiences to experience "The Black Magic of Haiti in the story of the only man Napoleon feared" in a WPA production of Henri Christophe's life in *Black Empire* (1936).[81] Both *Black Empire* and *Haiti* confirmed old stereotypes about black people's propensity to mysticism and savagery.[82] At the same time, they repeatedly conjured up strong black male leaders, played on stage by physically powerful men such as Paul Robeson and Rex Ingram, whose lists of achievement, on and offstage, were impressive. These performances thereby challenged the assertion that Haitians and other black people were childlike and in need of the care and protection of American power. These were men fit to rule.

The fascination, obsession even, with the Haitian Revolution, and with Haiti itself, as compared to other islands in the Caribbean, was due to the need to tell the stories, again and again, of strong black men who resisted white colonial authorities, who bore arms and who governed themselves in a black nation. For this reason, the characters' faults were not fatal to their fans, just as Brutus Jones had been warmly received in the early 1920s. Even well into the 1940s, the American Negro Theatre (ANT) finished its hit season with a play titled *Henri Christophe*.[83] Though the play was panned for being overly "talkative," one writer in the *New York Times* conceded nevertheless that "the story of the King of Haiti is always legitimate, and with its present-day applications no one has a better right to tell it than a Negro theatre."[84] As the play closed with a Broadway producer choosing not to exercise his option to take it downtown from the 135th Street Library theater where it was playing, another *Times* reporter noted of the ANT that "the hardy experimentalists acknowledge that the Dan Hammerman play did not quite ring the bell, [however] the group felt that the significance of the theme justified its presentation."[85]

While American marines and government officials were busy proving Haiti was childlike and in need of help, black Americans by contrast were adamant that Haitians themselves were the fathers of genuinely democratic republicanism. Playwright Leslie Pinckney Hill went so far as to claim that the story of the Haitian Revolution was salutary for white as well as black American audiences because Toussaint was responsible for ending Napoleon's desire for empire and enabling, therefore, the sale of the Louisiana territory to Jefferson and the birth of the modern United States.[86] As the brothers and sisters of Haitians, along with other "dispersed children of Africa," black Americans were the legitimate heirs to this tradition.[87] They therefore had the authority to challenge American democratic pretensions, and pointedly criticize the inequity of the U.S. state, both within and beyond its borders. For many, cultural representations of Haiti became a means to insist that they too be included as genuine citizens of the American polity.

While insisting America broaden its definition of national belonging to include its black citizens, black Americans simultaneously cast their lot with Haitians and other colonized people. Just as had the Haitians, black Americans too had developed a distinctive culture under conditions of oppression.

While the two cultures were not identical, the means of identifying as members of a racial group were similar. Drawing a parallel between their own experiences of racism and those of colonized Haitians—including resistance through the formation of culture—black playwrights exposed as farcical American claims to be an isolationist power and an exceptional nation. The United States was a colonial power like any other; in the past it had engaged in the slave trade, and an internal colonialism in the forms of slavery and segregation, while in the present it had extended its reach beyond national borders to places such as Haiti. In bringing to life the drama of the Haitian Revolution, black Americans sought to remind viewers of the ideals of the American Revolution and to insist on the need to extend those ideals to *all* American citizens. At the same time, they redefined their own citizenship away from the prevailing ideal of "100 percent Americanism" to something much more broad. While they were Americans, they were also connected to Haitians, with whom they shared a history of enslavement and resistance to oppression, and by extension, to others in the black diaspora and to people everywhere living under colonization.

NOTES

1. Michel-Rolph Trouillot, *Silencing the Past: Power and the Production of History* (Boston: Beacon Press, 1995).

2. Helen Webb Harris, "Genifrede" (1922), in *Negro History in Thirteen Plays*, ed. Willis Richardson (Washington, D.C.: Associated Publishers, 1935), 219–37; Clarence Cameron White and John F. Matheus, "Tambour," (1928 or 1929), Clarence Cameron White Papers, reel 10, Schomburg Center for Research in Black Culture, New York Public Library (hereafter Schomburg Center); Leslie Pinckney Hill, *Toussaint L'Ouverture: A Dramatic History* (Boston: Christopher Publishing House, 1928); Langston Hughes, "Emperor of Haiti," (orig. "Drums of Haiti," begun 1928), in *Black Drama in America: An Anthology*, 2nd ed., ed. Darwin T. Turner (Washington, D.C.: Howard University Press, 1994), 19–71; John Matheus, "Ti Yette," in *Plays and Pageants from the Life of the Negro*, ed. Willis Richardson (1930; Great Neck, N.Y.: Core Collection Books, 1979), 77–105; Clarence Cameron White and John Frederick Matheus, *Ouanga* (1932), no publication details, p. 25, Clarence Cameron White Papers, reel 4, Schomburg Center; May Miller, "Christophe's Daughters," (1935) reprinted in *Black Female Playwrights: An Anthology of Plays Before 1950*, ed. Kathy A. Perkins (Bloomington: Indiana University Press, 1989), 166–75. Plays written by white Americans but directed or performed in by black Americans included Eugene O'Neill, *The Emperor Jones*; William DuBois, "Haiti"; Orson Welles's 1936 production of Shakespeare's *Macbeth* at the Lafayette Theatre in Harlem; *Henri Christophe*,

by Dan Hammerman, at the American Negro Theatre, June 1945. Programs and Playbills, Rare Books and Manuscript Division, Schomburg Center.

3. Herbert Aptheker, *American Negro Slave Revolts* (1943; New York: International Publishers, 1974), 15, 43–4, 96–101, 249; Eric Sundquist, *To Wake the Nations: Race in the Making of American Literature* (Cambridge: Belknap Press, 1993), 31–36; Alfred N. Hunt, *Haiti's Influence on Antebellum America: Slumbering Volcano in the Caribbean* (Baton Rouge: Louisiana State University Press, 1988); Elizabeth Rauh Bethel, "Images of Hayti: The Construction of An Afro-American Lieu De Mémoire," *Callaloo* 15, no. 3 (Summer 1992): 827–41; Michael P. Johnson, "Denmark Vesey and His Co-Conspirators," *William and Mary Quarterly* 58, no. 4 (October 2001): 915–76, esp. 964; James Sidbury, "Plausible Stories and Varnished Truths," *William and Mary Quarterly* 59, no. 1 (January 2002): 179–84.

4. Chris Dixon, *African America and Haiti: Emigration and Black Nationalism in the Nineteenth Century* (Westport, Conn.: Greenwood Press, 2000), 177–216.

5. Mary A. Renda, *Taking Haiti: Military Occupation and the Culture of U.S. Imperialism, 1915–1940* (Chapel Hill: University of North Carolina Press, 2001), 220–21.

6. Kristin Hoganson, *Consumers' Imperium: The Global Production of American Domesticity, 1865–1920* (Chapel Hill: University of North Carolina Press, 2007).

7. Blair Niles, *Black Haiti: A Biography of Africa's Eldest Daughter* (New York: Grosset & Dunlap, 1926); John W. Vandercook, *Black Majesty* (New York: Harper Brothers, 1928); William Seabrook, *The Magic Island* (New York: Harcourt, Brace and Company, 1929); Faustin Wirkus, *The White King of La Gonave* (Garden City, N.Y.: Doubleday, Doran & Company, 1931); and Wirkus, "When I Was King" (1932), NAACP Papers, microfilm, part 11, series B, reel 36, frames 392–99, British Library, London; John Houston Craige, *Black Bagdad: The Arabian Nights Adventures of a Marine Captain in Haiti* (New York: Minton, Balch, 1933); and Craige, *Cannibal Cousins* (New York: Minton, Balch, 1934); Edna Taft, *A Puritan in Voodoo-Land* (Philadelphia: Penn Publishing Company, 1938). On these see Laënnec Hurbon, "American Fantasy and Haitian Vodou," in *Sacred Arts of Haitian Vodou*, ed. Donald J. Cosentino (Los Angeles: UCLA Fowler Museum, 1995), 181–97; and Renda, *Taking Haiti*, 229–60. Films included.

8. James Weldon Johnson, "Self-Determining Haiti," I-IV, *Nation* (August 28–September 25, 1920).

9. Johnson, *Along This Way: The Autobiography of James Weldon Johnson* (1933; New York: Penguin Books, 1990), 360; Brenda Gayle Plummer, "The Afro-American Response to the Occupation of Haiti, 1915–1934," *Phylon* 43, no. 2 (Summer 1982): 134–36; Henry Lewis Suggs, "The Response of the African American Press to the United States Occupation of Haiti, 1915–1934," *Journal of Negro History* 73, no. 1/4 (Winter-Autumn 1988): 36–37.

10. Plummer, "The Afro-American Response," 140–41; Suggs, "The Response of the African American Press," 38–39.

11. Eugene O'Neill, "The Emperor Jones," in *The Emperor Jones* (1922; London: Jonathan Cape, 1969), 145.

12. This myth appeared in May Miller's play *Christophe's Daughters*, 174; and Clarence Cameron White's music lesson plans, Lesson XVI (on Jamaica) in *Lessons & Examinations*, Clarence Cameron White Papers, reel 4, Schomburg Center. On O'Neill's mixing up of the revolutionary figures, see VèVè A. Clark, "Haiti's Tragic Overture: (Mis)Representations of the Haitian Revolution in World Drama (1796–1975)," in *Representing the French Revolution: Literature, Historiography, and Art*, ed. James A. W. Heffernan (Hanover, N.H.: University Press of New England, 1992), 248.

13. O'Neill, "The Emperor Jones," 152.

14. Jean Toomer, "Negro Psychology in The Emperor Jones," (1921) in *Jean Toomer: Selected Essays and Literary Criticism*, ed. Robert B. Jones (Knoxville: University of Tennessee Press, 1996), 6.

15. Interview with William Lundell, *Screenland* (October 1933), cited by Martin Bauml Duberman, *Paul Robeson* (London: Pan Books, 1989), 622.

16. Robert Blauner, "Internal Colonialism and Ghetto Revolt," *Social Problems* 16, no. 4 (Spring 1969): 393–408. Also see Stokely Carmichael and Charles V. Hamilton, *Black Power: The Politics of Liberation in America* (New York: Random House, 1967), esp. 2–32; Eldridge Cleaver, "The Land Question and Black Liberation" in *Eldridge Cleaver: Post-Prison Writings and Speeches*, ed. Robert Scheer (New York: Random House, 1969), 57–72; and Bob Blauner, *Racial Oppression in America* (New York: Harper and Row, 1972), esp. 1–123.

17. Hubert Harrison, "The Emperor Jones," *Negro World*, June 4, 1921. Reprinted in Jeffrey B. Perry, ed., *A Hubert Harrison Reader* (Middletown, Conn.: Wesleyan University Press, 2001), 378–83, quotation on 381.

18. Cf. Renda, *Taking Haiti*, 207; Hazel V. Carby, *Race Men* (Cambridge: Harvard University Press, 1998), 78.

19. J. Cogdell, "Truth in Art in America," *Messenger* 5, no. 3 (March 1923): 634–36, 635; Renda, *Taking Haiti*, 209–12.

20. Mrs. William A. Corbin, "Emperor Jones on the Pacific Coast," in *Negro World*, March 3, 1923, 10.

21. Ronald Radano, "Hot Fantasies: American Modernism and the Idea of Black Rhythm," in *Music and the Racial Imagination*, ed. Ronald Radano and Philip V. Bohlman (Chicago: University of Chicago Press, 2000), 459–80.

22. Haines J. Washington, "Death of the Emperor Jones," *New York World*, May 9, 1930, 11.

23. Langston Hughes, *The Big Sea* (1940; New York: Hill & Wang, 1963), 258. A *Negro World* reviewer reported that at the Harlem premiere of the 1933 film version, those in the audience did not like the film at all; see Tony Martin, *Literary Garveyism: Garvey, Black Arts and the Harlem Renaissance* (Dover, Mass.: Majority Press, 1983), 118.

24. "Howard Players Appear in Their Own Plays," *Chicago Defender*, June 3, 1922, 5.

25. Harris, "Genifrede," 221, 223.

26. See, for instance, plays in the following collections: Kathy A. Perkins, ed., *Black Female Playwrights: An Anthology of Plays Before 1950* (Bloomington: Indiana University Press, 1989); Jennifer Burton, ed., *Zora Neale Hurston, Eulalie Spence, Marita Bonner, and Others: The Prize Plays and Other One-Acts Published in Periodicals* (New York: G. K. Hall, 1996); and Kathy A. Perkins and Judith L. Stephens, eds., *Strange Fruit: Plays on Lynching by American Women* (Bloomington: Indiana University Press, 1998).

27. Wilson Jeremiah Moses, *Black Messiahs and Uncle Toms: Social and Literary Manipulations of a Religious Myth*, rev. ed. (University Park: Pennsylvania State University Press, 1993).

28. See "Hon. Wm. Sherrill Names Greatest Men of the Negro Race," *Negro World*, March 10, 1923, 2; Vere E. Johns, "Evidence From Jamaica Shows Marcus Garvey Racially Dead," *New York Age*, September 10, 1932, 7; "Garvey Planning African Empire: Black Queen Aids Garvey Plan Empire," *Evening Graphic*, November 25, 1927, L. S. Alexander Gumby Collection of Negroiana, vol. 32, Rare Book and Manuscript Library, Columbia University, New York.

29. Arnold Rampersad, *1902–1941: I, Too, Sing America*, vol. 1 of *The Life of Langston Hughes* (New York: Oxford University Press, 1986), 165–66; Tammy L. Kernodle, "Arias, Communists, and Conspiracies: The History of Still's 'Troubled Island,'" *Musical Quarterly* 83, no. 4 (Winter 1999): 487–508, 488; 1963 revised version in the Rare Books and Manuscripts Division, Schomburg Center.

30. Langston Hughes, "Emperor of Haiti," in *Black Drama in America: An Anthology*, 2nd ed., ed. Darwin T. Turner (Washington, D.C.: Howard University Press, 1994), 31.

31. Hughes, "Emperor of Haiti," 34–35.

32. Ibid., 40.

33. Ibid., 56–57.

34. Gail Bederman, *Manliness and Civilization: A Cultural History of Gender and Race in the United States, 1880–1917* (Chicago: University of Chicago Press, 1995).

35. Robert Lansing to J. H. Oliver, January 30, 1918, in Plummer, "The Afro-American Response," 130.

36. Clarence Cameron White, "A Musical Pilgrimage to Haiti, The Island of Beauty, Mystery and Rhythm," *Etude* (July 1929): 505, NAACP Papers, part 11, series B, reel 9, frames 816–17; John F. Matheus, "Precis methodique d'histoire d'Haiti; Black Democracy," review of Dr. François Dalencour's *Précis méthodique d'histoire d'Haiti* (1935) and H. P. Davis's *Black Democracy*, *Journal of Negro History* 21, no. 4 (October 1936): 433–38.

37. Clarence Cameron White and John F. Matheus, "Tambour," Clarence Cameron White Papers, reel 10, Schomburg Center. "Tambour" was produced in 1929 by the

Allied Arts Players, Boston, dir. Maud Cuney-Hare; see Bernard L. Peterson Jr., *Early Black Playwrights and Dramatic Writers: A Biographical Directory and Catalog of Plays, Films, and Broadcasting Scripts* (Westport, Conn.: Greenwood Press, 1990), 132.

38. Matheus and White, *Ouanga*, 4.

39. Ibid., 3. *Ouanga* was performed in concert form in 1932 and as a full opera for the first time in 1949. See Peterson, *Early Black American Playwrights*, 263.

40. Michael Largey, *Vodou Nation: Haitian Art Music and Cultural Nationalism* (Chicago: University of Chicago Press, 2006), 164.

41. Hill, *Toussaint L'Ouverture*, 8.

42. See Sidney Mintz and Michel-Rolph Trouillot, "The Social History of Haitian Vodou," in Cosentino, *Sacred Arts of Haitian Vodou*, 123–47. Cf. Robert Farris Thompson, "From the Isle Beneath the Sea: Haiti's Africanizing Vodou Art," in Cosentino, *Sacred Arts of Haitian Vodou*, 91–119. On the relationship between culture and politics generally see Lawrence W. Levine, *Black Culture and Black Consciousness: Afro-American Folk Thought from Slavery to Freedom* (Oxford: Oxford University Press, 1977).

43. Lawrence W. Levine, *Highbrow/Lowbrow: The Emergence of Cultural Hierarchy in America* (Cambridge: Harvard University Press, 1988).

44. Hill, *Toussaint L'Ouverture*, 7.

45. Renda, *Taking Haiti*.

46. James Weldon Johnson, no title, no date, NAACP Papers, part 11, series B, reel 8, frames 452–56; see also Johnson, *Along This Way*, 360.

47. Hill, *Toussaint L'Ouverture*, 7. Hill also wrote a pageant in 1931 called *Jethro* in which the concept of representative government was developed by an Ethiopian; for details see Peterson, *Early Black American Playwrights*, 104.

48. Langston Hughes, "The Em-Fuehrer Jones" (1938), in *Lost Plays of the Harlem Renaissance, 1920–1940*, ed. James V. Hatch and Leo Hamalian (Detroit: Wayne State University Press, 1996), 358–61.

49. Largey, *Vodou Nation*, 12; Schmidt, *The United States Occupation of Haiti*, 150–51.

50. Dantès Bellegarde to Arthur A. Schomburg (March 11, 1932), Schomburg Papers, reel 1, Schomburg Center. A copy of the speech is on reel 5. A press release containing a description of some of the exhibited items is at NAACP Papers, part 11, series B, reel 10, frame 23. In 1934 President Stenio Vincent visited the library, Arthur A Schomburg to Stenio Vincent, May 3, 1934, Schomburg Papers, reel 8. By 1938, the library held 700 titles on Haiti, see letter from Schomburg to Rene J. Rosemond, May 19, 1938, Schomburg Papers, reel 8.

51. James Weldon Johnson, "Some New Books of Poetry and Their Makers," Editorial, *New York Age*, September 7, 1918), reprinted in *The Selected Writings of James Weldon Johnson*, vol. 1, *The New York Age Editorials (1914–1923)*, ed. Sondra Kathryn Wilson (New York: Oxford University Press, 1995), 271–77, 272; James Weldon Johnson, Introduction to *The Book of American Negro Poetry*, ed. Johnson

(1922; New York: Harcourt, Brace, 1959), 9; Johnson to Clarence Cameron White (January 12, 1935), cited in Jon Michael Spencer, *The New Negroes and Their Music: The Success of the Harlem Renaissance* (Knoxville: University of Tennessee Press, 1997), 103.

52. Anon, "No. 17. Fighting for Negro Freedom in Foreign Lands," NAACP Papers, part 11, series A, reel 30, frames 532–38; a series of letters from James Weldon Johnson to Moorfield Storey between September 1920 and May 1921, NAACP Papers, part 1, reel 17, frames 312, 313, 329, 330, 337, 352; Leon D. Pamphile, *Haitians and African Americans: A Heritage of Tragedy and Hope* (Gainesville: University Press of Florida, 2001), 117–18; Plummer, "The Afro-American Response," 133; Renda, *Taking Haiti*, 191. Other organizations included the American-Haitian Benevolent Club and the Save Haiti Committee; see, respectively, Plummer, "The Afro-American Response," 135; and "Save Haiti," NAACP Papers, part 11, series B, reel 9, frame 746.

53. Clarence Cameron White Collection, Photographs and Prints, box 2, Schomburg Center.

54. See Errol G. Hill and James V. Hatch, *A History of African American Theatre* (Cambridge: Cambridge University Press, 2003), 244–49.

55. Clarence Cameron White, unpublished autobiography, typescript, p. 39, Clarence Cameron White Papers, box 209–8, folder 2, Moorland-Spingarn Collection, Howard University, Washington, D.C.

56. Kernodle, "Arias, Communists, and Conspiracies," 487.

57. Matheus to White, November 15, 1931, Clarence Cameron White Papers, reel 1; letters between White and Ona B. Talbot, November 4, 1932, reel 1, and February 5, 1934, reel 2; letter from Talbot to Paul Robeson, November 4, 1932, reel 1, all in Clarence Cameron White Papers, Schomburg Center. On the Paris production, see Mary Church Terrell, "Local Composer Wins Medal for Best American Opera," *Washington Evening Star*, May 28, 1933, 6.

58. Sheila Tully Boyle and Andrew Bunie, *Paul Robeson: The Years of Promise and Achievement* (Amherst: University of Massachusetts Press, 2001), 327, 339.

59. Jacqueline Najuma Stewart, *Migrating to the Movies* (Berkeley: University of California Press); Cedric J. Robinson, *Forgeries of Memory and Meaning: Blacks and Regimes of Race in American Theater and Film before World War II* (Chapel Hill: University of North Carolina Press, 2007).

60. E.g., *White Zombie* (1932), see Renda, 226–27; *Ouanga* (1935), set on "Paradise Island" in the West Indies, filmed initially on Haiti but moved to Jamaica, see Bryan Senn, *Drums of Terror: Voodoo in the Cinema* (Baltimore: Midnight Marquee Press, 1998), 38–40.

61. "Coast Codgings," *Chicago Defender*, May 12, 1934, 9.

62. "Film 'Voodoo' Now Running on Broadway," *Chicago Defender*, April 8, 1933, 5.

63. "Toussaint L'Ouverture," *Crisis* 20, no. 6 (October 1920): 297.

64. "Life of Toussaint to Be Told in $1,000,000 Film," *Chicago Defender*, April 28, 1928, 2.

65. In particular the film *Sanders of the River* (dir. Zoltan Korda, 1935); see "Robeson Film Called Propaganda Justifying British Imperialism," *Afro-American* (week of July 6, 1935), Gumby Collection, vol. 112; Duberman, *Paul Robeson*, 179–80. Some have been skeptical of Robeson's claim that he was duped into thinking the film more progressive than it turned out to be, see Boyle and Bunie, *Paul Robeson*, 323–27; Stewart, "Paul Robeson and the Problem of Modernism," 97–99. In any case, as Robeson told an interviewer in 1935, if a black actor wanted to work, he had to take roles "with which he is not ideologically in agreement." Cited in Carby, *Race Men*, 79.

66. "Robeson to Play King Christophe in British Production, He Reveals," *New York Amsterdam News*, October 5, 1935, 1; "Paul Robeson In Moscow," *Chicago Defender*, August 22, 1936, 24.

67. *Song of Freedom* (dir. J. Elder Wills, 1936).

68. On Robeson's feelings: Duberman, *Paul Robeson*, 204.

69. Langston Hughes, *I Wonder As I Wander: An Autobiographical Journey* (New York: Hill and Wang, 1956), 22.

70. Stephen Howe, *Afrocentrism: Mythical Pasts and Imagined Homes* (London: Verso, 1998), 83.

71. Hughes, *I Wonder As I Wander*, 28.

72. Hughes, "Emperor of Haiti," 66.

73. Langston Hughes, "People Without Shoes," *New Masses* 12 (October 1931): 12.

74. James Weldon Johnson, "Views and Reviews: Civilizing the 'Backward Races,'" *New York Age*, March 22, 1919.

75. Arna Bontemps and Langston Hughes, *Popo and Fifina*, illus. E. Simms Campbell (1932; New York: Oxford University Press, 1993), 22.

76. Charles H. Nichols, ed., *Arna Bontemps–Langston Hughes Letters: 1925–1967* (New York: Paragon House, 1980), 22.

77. Renda, *Taking Haiti*, 281.

78. "Crowds Jam Streets as 'Macbeth' Opens," *New York Times*, April 15, 1936, 25.

79. "Lafayette Incident Rebuke to Cultural Pride of Community," Press Releases of Department of Information, Record Group 69, National Archives, quoted in Rena Fraden, *Blueprints for a Black Federal Theatre, 1935–1939* (Cambridge: Cambridge University Press, 1994), 156.

80. Renda, *Taking Haiti*, 286–87.

81. John O'Connor and Lorraine Brown, eds., *"Free, Adult, Uncensored": The Living History of the Federal Theatre Project* (London: Eyre Methuen, 1980), 120.

82. E. Quita Craig, *Black Drama of the Federal Theatre Era: Beyond the Formal Horizons* (Amherst: University of Massachusetts Press, 1980), 154–61.

83. *Henri Christophe*, by Dan Hammerman, at the American Negro Theatre, June 1945, Programs and Playbills, Rare Books and Manuscript Division, Schomburg Center.

84. "Two Plays Off Broadway," *New York Times*, June 17, 1945, X1.

85. "Four Attractions to Take on Holidays," *New York Times*, June 29, 1945, 13.

86. Hill, *Toussaint L'Ouverture*, 7.

87. The title of Dantès Bellegarde's address on Haiti at the Fourth Pan-African Congress held in New York in 1927 was "Dispersed Children of Africa." See "Meeting of Noted Negroes Held Here For the First Time," *New York Amsterdam News*, August 22, 1927.

fourth coda

Spectacle, Celebrity, and the Black Body

An early twentieth-century black celebrity such as Herbert Julian, the flamboyant pilot, parachutist, and bon vivant, was inconceivable only a few decades earlier. Leaving aside the technological innovations that made his exploits possible, Julian's fame was inseparable from the glitz and glamour of the modern milieu of Harlem and the other meccas that drew black migrants in the early twentieth century. Shane White, Stephen Garton, Stephen Robertson, and Graham White acknowledge that there were black celebrities before Julian, but they had typically been race leaders or blacks noted for exceptional accomplishments. Julian's signal accomplishment seems to have been the panache of his clothes, lifestyle, and antics. By making a spectacle of himself and his life, Julian caught the attention of the black press and of the residents of his adopted Harlem. His exploits, even when they fell short of his boasts, suggested that the marvels of the modern age were not the exclusive playthings of whites. In the process, Julian came to embody, for many black Harlemites and some white New Yorkers as well, the spirit and mood of the modern era—on the make, on the move—as fully as any of his contemporaries.

Boxer Joe Louis's sensational victory over German Max Schmeling in 1938 provides a fitting conclusion. However much racism shaped Louis's career, Louis nevertheless set out to control his career to the greatest possible extent. His pursuit of self-determination was of a piece with the insistent individualism that Julian displayed and that formed the core of the blues. Louis's career also demonstrated that the verities of Jim Crow were susceptible to revision. At least some whites came to recognize that a black man could possess laudable courage, dignity, pride, and ambition. Thus, as Lewis Erenberg reveals, the blacks, Jews, leftists of all persuasions, and "patriotic" whites eager to see a symbol of resurgent Germany humbled, who cheered Louis on in 1938, were without precedent. A generation earlier boxing had enabled Jack Johnson to achieve notoriety, but Louis achieved considerably more when he defeated Schmeling. Louis crossed over, so to speak, from the world of sports to become both an African American folk hero and an American icon.

Important and far-reaching changes occurred in the politics of professional sports in the decades that separated Jack Johnson and Joe Louis. Johnson had conspicuously defied the ideology of white supremacy at its apogee. Louis, in contrast, launched his career at the same time that international politics and economic disarray prompted a revision of ideas about race and American identity. Faced with the daunting task of forging bonds in a nation previously divided by cultural issues (e.g., Prohibition and religion), race (e.g., the Ku Klux Klan), and ethnicity (e.g., immigration "reform" during the 1920s), public leaders, above all President Franklin D. Roosevelt, adopted a political rhetoric that emphasized the common economic and social needs of all Americans. Roosevelt cultivated an expansive "civic nationalism" and stressed that all Americans, regardless of ethnicity and race, belonged to a single national community. With Roosevelt emphasizing the bonds of nationhood, with Americans reeling from the effects of the Depression, and with totalitarian nationalism on the rise throughout Europe, the United States could no longer tolerate the cultural fragmentation that had characterized the 1920s. This larger political context insured that Louis's bout against Schmeling took on exceptional significance for all Americans.

The Black Eagle of Harlem

SHANE WHITE, STEPHEN GARTON, STEPHEN ROBERTSON,

AND GRAHAM WHITE

It was all so much more innocent back then. In the spring of 1923 Americans were still enraptured with the sheer romance of flight, the authorities had not yet taken control of the airspace over cities, and, seemingly, pilots were pretty much free to do as they pleased. Thus it was that late in the afternoon, on Sunday, April 30, three planes took off from Curtis Field on Long Island, maneuvered into formation, and headed for Manhattan. Clarence Chamberlin, a pioneer aviator and later transatlantic flier, piloted the lead plane and, bundled in the passenger seat with his newly purchased parachute, was Hubert Julian, a recent émigré, originally from Trinidad. Moments after the planes reached Harlem, flying low at less than 3,500 feet, the pilots exploded several noise bombs, prompting many surprised whites living in Washington Heights to take to the streets in order to discover what was going on. To most Harlem residents, however, the bombs were superfluous; for weeks, hand-painted signs emblazoned with the simple, if opaque, message "Watch the clouds," had been plastered all over the Black Metropolis. The black adventurer had rented a vacant lot on the corner of Seventh Avenue and 140th Street and had had nailed to the fence around his target placards entreating locals to "WATCH THE CLOUDS THIS SUNDAY—JULIAN IS ARRIVING FROM THE SKY HERE." The postscript—"Admission: $1.00"— was in smaller print. On the previous Sunday, Julian had made his first attempt to parachute into Harlem, but everything had gone wrong. The wind had been far too strong and, just seconds after the jump had been called off, the plane containing Julian had developed engine trouble. As a result, Julian's plane had been forced to skim along only feet above the Harlem River and swoop under the narrow span of Hell Gate Bridge before sputtering its uncertain way back to Curtis Field. Now, however, a week later, everything seemed ready.

If nothing else, Harlem loved a spectacle. Julian would later recall in his autobiography (as told to John Bulloch) that, as he and his companions flew low over the city streets, "we could see the people pouring out of every building," and that thousands of black faces "seemed to be staring up as we cruised around." The lead plane separated from its escort and almost slowed to a stall, and then, over 141st street and Riverside Drive, Julian clambered out onto the wing, lay down, and rolled off into seeming oblivion as his plane peeled away. Moments later, Julian ripped a hole in the fifteen-pound bag of flour that he was carrying, causing "a dramatic long white trail for the 500 feet or so I fell freely." That was hardly the end of the drama. Julian was garbed in skin-tight livid scarlet tights and tunic, a "devil costume" he had rented from a theatrical shop, and after his parachute opened, he unfurled a large banner that fluttered behind him announcing that "HOENIG OPTICAL IS OPEN TODAY." In the event, Julian missed his target, only just avoided serious injury on the Eighth Avenue El, and landed on the roof of the post office on 140th Street. Meanwhile, on the streets below, there was bedlam. According to the *Daily Star*, as Julian jumped from the plane, motorists commenced "a hideous din of squalling horns." Furthermore, the crush of tens of thousands of blacks looking skyward and chasing a black Mephisto rapidly descending in a parachute nearly caused several automobile accidents and did result in the smashing of several plate glass windows and the tearing from its stanchions of the iron railing around the post office. Meanwhile, Julian calmly packed up his chute, put on and adjusted a sash urging the use of a St. Louis hair straightener, descended the post office's fire escape, and jumped the last ten feet into the arms of the waiting crowd. Several blacks then hoisted the intrepid black daredevil onto their shoulders and carried him off in triumph to Liberty Hall on 138th Street. No one could ever have accused Hubert Julian of failing to make an entrance.

Liberty Hall was, of course, the headquarters of Marcus Garvey's Universal Negro Improvement Association (UNIA). It took some time for the crowd to shuffle in and settle down, but as soon as there was quiet, Julian began reading out a series of paid advertisements, each of which was greeted with roars of approval from the gathered throng. He asked those present to patronize the eye doctor whose card he was displaying on his chest and then pointed out that a department store on 138th Street, now run by blacks, was in imminent danger of being taken over by whites. Julian was in full cry, imploring his audience to support the current owners of the store, when a policeman pushed his way through the crowd and served him with a summons for disorderly conduct. A few days later, Julian appeared in court, impeccably attired as ever, in dark suit, spats, and bowler hat, with a pink flower in his buttonhole. In the event, the judge was forced to dismiss the case, but he did ban Julian from flying over New York for six months, by which time, he hoped, a city ordinance would regulate or, more likely, prevent such stunts.[1]

Six months to the day later Hubert Julian was at it again. This time his jump was partly sponsored by the Martin Saxophone Company and Wurlitzer. As he descended into Harlem, Julian played "Runnin' Wild" on a gold-plated Martin saxophone. Once more he was off target, missing a vacant lot and crashing through the skylight on the 123rd Street police station. Surprised officers drew their guns, but the on-duty lieutenant calmed everyone down by yelling out: "Oh, it's all right boys, it's just that crazy nigger trying to kill himself again." According to one account, Julian was confronted by an angry crowd whose members demanded a refund because they had seen nothing of his landing. He partly subdued, or at least confused, his detractors by informing all within earshot that the reason he was off-target was that he had been testing a new invention called the "*saxaphonaparachut tagravepreresista*." Then, with his pride ever so slightly dented, the black parachutist borrowed a nickel from someone, slipped away, and caught the subway home.[2]

These two jumps into Harlem made Hubert Julian known throughout America. He, himself, believed that the extensive newspaper coverage, often including pictures, made his name a "household word." Perhaps. Julian's fancy was particularly tickled by the *Herald Tribune*'s H. Allen Smith's christening of him as "The Black Eagle of Harlem," a sobriquet he adopted and that stuck until his death in 1983. Few could doubt that it was an improvement on the "Ace of Spades" and similar names dreamed up by headline writers in white newspapers. Even as late as the 1960s, letters addressed simply to "The Black Eagle, U.S.A." were delivered by the postal service to Julian's home.[3] Yet there was always something of the minstrel show in the way whites depicted Julian, and it was certainly the case that he played to some of the boastful stereotypes held by whites about blacks. Among most African Americans, however, he was taken rather more seriously, an attitude reinforced by his several stints flying for Haile Selassie in the 1930s. Indeed, in 1962, when Julian was languishing in a jail in the Congo, suspected of being an arms dealer, his release was organized by a Mr. Gardiner, a Ghanaian working for the United Nations. According to newspaper reports, Gardiner's first words to Julian were: "This is one of the saddest days of my life. When I was an undergraduate, I worshipped you as a hero. Most of my African contemporaries did the same."[4] The memory of those early daring descents lingered for a long time, most especially in Harlem. After interviewing all manner of people in the 1970s for *When Harlem Was in*

Vogue, David Levering Lewis wrote that "Julian's debut is still remembered by ageing Harlemites." A few pages into Toni Morrison's *Jazz* (1992), there is a half-sentence—"A colored man floats down out of the sky blowing a saxophone. . . ."—that must by then, and even more so now, have been almost totally opaque to all but a very few of her readers, still nurturing dwindling memories of the Black Metropolis in the 1920s.[5]

Hubert Julian may be now largely forgotten, but in the 1920s he was a black celebrity, one of the best-known African Americans in the United States. He was hardly the first black to thrust her- or himself into the New Nation's public sphere. Periodically, under slavery, individuals attained notoriety through their, usually violent, actions; most obviously, this was the case with Nat Turner's revolt in 1831. More interestingly, there was also a string of African Americans who gained fame because of their special talents or physical characteristics, a phenomenon that Adam Green has labeled "the tradition of eccentric virtuosity among blacks in the New World."[6] Both the poet Phillis Wheatley and Benjamin Banneker, astronomer, surveyor, and author of an almanac with an ephemeris calculated by the free-born black, were grist for the antislavery mill and became well publicized figures in the late eighteenth- and early nineteenth-century debate about the mental capacity of blacks.[7] Similarly, Henry Moss, a black man who seemed to be in the process of slowly turning white, a development of no little interest in the context of arguments about the origins of races, was exhibited to the paying public in northern cities in the 1790s and was the frequent subject of articles in the press. Charles Caldwell, a pupil of Benjamin Rush, claimed with only a little hyperbole that the name Henry Moss "was almost as familiar to readers of newspapers and other periodicals . . . as was that of John Adams, Thomas Jefferson or James Madison."[8] Thomas Wiggins (1849–1908), better known as Blind Tom, was probably autistic and, although he could barely speak, possessed a phenomenal musical memory that enabled him to replicate any piece of music played to him. In the second half of the nineteenth century, Wiggins sold out concert halls and theaters all across America, allowing his owner, who carried on controlling his former slave for decades after the end of slavery, to make hundreds of thousands of dollars out of this black prodigy.[9]

By comparison, throughout the nineteenth and early twentieth centuries, all manner of extremely articulate black leaders, such as Frederick Douglass, or even the more conservative Booker T. Washington, were marginalized by the white press. To be sure, they were interviewed and featured in occasional news stories, but coverage of their speeches and activities was limited. As Charles Ponce de Leon has noted, the way the press all but ignored in particular the eminently respectable Washington was "a curious phenomenon." At precisely this time "fawning celebrity profiles" were "becoming a staple of mass-circulation journalism and even third-rate political hacks and inexperienced ingénues fresh from the chorus line could get this kind of publicity." There was a similar terseness to the way in which the white reporters wrote about such black stars of the stage as Bert Williams and black athletes. To an extent, Jack Johnson was an exception, but the hostility of the white press to the controversial boxer was palpable. In an age of segregation, white editors assumed, probably correctly, that their readers were not interested in getting up close and personal with prominent blacks. It was on the other side of the color line, in the African American newspapers and magazines, that such figures as Douglass, Washington, and Johnson, as well as W. E. B. Du Bois and Madam Walker, achieved the status of celebrity. Given the intense concern with racial uplift on the part of many of these publications, it was also the case that usually these African American celebrities became "culture heroes," their fame enmeshed with the aspirations and hopes of ordinary black men and women.[10]

Hubert Julian was certainly linked to these earlier traditions of black celebrity. In the 1920s there was still more than a hint of Barnum associated with flight, and a black man piloting a plane, let alone launching himself into the void using one of the primitive parachutes then available, could fairly be described as an example of "eccentric virtuosity." It was also true that Julian's exploits were most extensively covered in the black press. Nevertheless, from the perspective of more than three-quarters of a century, what is most striking is everything that was different and new about Julian's fame. For a start, Julian was most closely associated with a specific urban area, Harlem, that was rapidly emerging as the Black Metropolis and the center of black life, not just in America but in the world. No one person could represent the diversity of Harlem, but the way in which Julian dared to seize the future encapsulated much of the excitement and brash assertiveness that characterized life in this northern city. Julian's embrace of modernity, his love of speed and the machine, even the way he exploited, to a quite remarkable extent, the new art of advertising, all seemed to usher in a new age for African Americans, one full of possibilities. There was, his example seemed to suggest, no particular reason why modernity had to mean that blacks were limited to jobs on the factory floor. Julian was a fascinating figure with what we would now call crossover appeal, and interest in him was hardly limited to the black population. In 1931, when the *New Yorker* first devoted one of its famous "Profiles" to a black, it was only fitting that the two-part piece was about Hubert Julian.[11]

As with so many of his fellow Harlem residents in the 1920s, Julian was a migrant. He had been born on September 20, 1897, in Trinidad, the only child of a well-to-do family that owned a cocoa plantation and a shoe factory.[12] In his autobiography he claimed to have been both entranced by the first airplane flight in the West Indies, which took place on a field just outside of Port of Spain, and devastated when the plane stalled and plummeted into the ground, killing the pilot. He later wrote, "I was horrified that the effortless, graceful flight I had watched with such fascination could end so suddenly and tragically." In fact, as David Shaftel has shown recently, Julian had already left the West Indies when, in January 1913, Frank Boland crashed a plane near Julian's home. This would not be the only time that Julian employed imaginative license in his autobiography. For all of that, there is little reason to doubt his claim that from a very early age, Julian was obsessed by planes and flight. He was educated in England and Canada, and in Montreal, just as the war ended, William Bishop, a Canadian ace who had won the Victoria Cross, taught him to fly. In November 1919, Hubert Julian became the first African American to make a solo flight.[13] He also patented a device that combined a large parachute and blades similar to those that would later be used in helicopters, that, in the event of a plane becoming disabled, was designed to allow a soft landing. His initial motive may have been altruistic, inspired, perhaps even troubled, by the crash he had heard about if not seen as a teenager, but, according to his autobiography, he sold the Canadian rights to his invention for $25,000.[14] Having proved to his family that he could make his own way, Julian decided to move to Harlem and determined that he "would arrive in America in style." As he lovingly detailed, after buying a completely new wardrobe from the best tailors, shirtmakers, and shoemakers in Montreal, Julian purchased a McFarlane limousine, hired a chauffeur, and headed off for Harlem. Not many of the myriad migrants to the Black Metropolis can have started their new life with such outrageous panache.[15]

On reaching Harlem, Julian went straight to the Elite Barber Shop on Seventh Avenue, an establishment patronized by, among others, Bill "Bojangles" Robinson, where he announced to the amusement of sundry hangers-on, passing the time by telling their lies, "I will endeavor to live by my wits, gentlemen." Julian joined in the laughter, but, as far as he was concerned, he was merely stating matters the way they were. Bankrolled beyond the wildest dreams of most black migrants, Julian deliberately set out to make himself known throughout Harlem. Initially, he moved into the five-story house of a madam—Julian later referred to this time as his "buffet flat days"—but soon established his own residence. The striking-looking young black man, resplendent in his magnificent car, cut a broad swath through Harlem life, becoming a friend of Marcus Garvey as well as a *habitué* of the swankier clubs that abounded north of 125th Street.[16] Julian also became a familiar figure to New York's flying crowd, made a few flights, and learned how to use a parachute. Julian's two jumps into Harlem in 1923 had made him a celebrity, but as far as the black aviator and parachutist was concerned they were just the beginning. He had much larger ambitions.

In early 1924 Hubert Julian started a fundraising drive to finance his long-held dream of a solo flight from New York across the Atlantic Ocean to Liberia. Advertisements in such African American newspapers as the *Amsterdam News* and *Pittsburgh Courier* solicited one dollar from every member of the race to aid this "scientific undertaking." Money trickled in, but there was, not surprisingly, some skepticism among blacks; (this was, after all, three years before Lindbergh's first solo flight across the Atlantic from New York to the rather closer Paris). Forty years later, Julian claimed, "My West Indian friends supported me as usual, but the American Negroes tried to make out I was a fraud, and that I was practising a confidence trick on them just to raise money for myself." Julian may, or may not, have been right about the divisions between American and West Indian blacks—it was certainly the case that, in his autobiography, he placed considerable emphasis on his West Indian origins in detailing his reception in Harlem—but if he was correct it was also true that American blacks were hardly the only observers who had doubts about his intentions. Not long after Julian had started advertising in the African American press he received a visit from a black man who worked for the U.S. government investigating matters relating to the mails. James E. Amos had been a valet and bodyguard for President Theodore Roosevelt, was the person responsible for making the arrest of Marcus Garvey on board the train returning to New York from Chicago, and, when he died in 1954, was the "ranking Negro FBI special agent." According to the two-part profile in the *New Yorker*, published later in 1931, Amos told Julian, "well, Major, on behalf of the United States government I beg to inform you that you either make that said airplane flight or else—." He went on to point out, in speech rendered in the way the *New Yorker* had determined that blacks spoke, that "there is a law against collectin' funds through the mail with intent to defraud. You better go ahead with yo' flight to Africa." After Amos had left, Julian turned to a man working nearby and said, "I think I'll buy that airplane."

Julian had only enough money to put a deposit down on a third-hand seaplane that aviator Clarence Chamberlin patched up as best he could. Julian then rented another vacant lot, this time on the corner of 139th Street and Seventh Avenue, and put his plane on display. A huge sign announced, "COME IN—FOR THE DOUBTING THOMASES, BEHOLD THE MIGHTY *ETHIOPIA I THAT* I AM GOING TO ATTEMPT TO FLY TO AFRICA, LAND OF OUR FATHERS. TOUCH THE PLANE AS THAT DOUBTING THOMAS WANTED TO THE HANDS OF THE LORD." Admission was one dollar. Every Sunday Julian and his workers started up the engines in front of those curious enough to pay, and in late June nearly a thousand people also paid to watch the proprietor of the *Amsterdam News*, a Miss Warren, christen the plane with a bottle of champagne. Julian was sharply attuned to the power of symbolism and acutely aware of what was going on in Harlem. Not only was he flying to Africa, but he named the plane *Ethiopia I* "in honour of the only black kingdom." Emblazoned on one side of the plane was the legend, "Dedicated to the advancement of the Negro race." Yet Julian was also aware that Harlem was not only linked to Africa but part of his adopted country, the United States of America. The flight, naturally enough, would take place on July 4th.

According to the *Negro World*, Julian's ambition had struck a chord among the residents of Harlem. It was expected that thousands of them would turn out to watch Julian take off, a level of support for the black aviator that would show "the spontaneous outpourings of a people who are anxious to demonstrate to a wicked world that what other men can do the Negro can also do." Interest in Julian's flight was hardly confined to the black press. On June 29, William Randolph Hearst's *New York American* claimed that "what Booker T. Washington was intellectually to the Negro race, so would Hubert Julian be aeronautically." The paper went on to add that "calm, smiling, Julian presents a clean specimen of young manhood, confident and capable." On the morning of July 4, the *New York World* ran a headline that blared, "NEGRO AVIATOR EXPECTS TO LAUNCH WORLD FLIGHT FROM HARLEM TO-DAY." The story began by stating that "Lieutenant Hubert Julian, M.D., of No. 106 West 139th Street, a West Indian, who has been making Harlem gasp for months by his parachute leaps" was making a "one-man airplane tour of four continents and expects to arrive at his starting point, 139th Street and the Harlem River, just thirty-one days hence." The planned route was New York, Atlantic City, South America, Liberia, Paris, London, Iceland, Greenland, Canada, and New York.

On Independence Day in 1924, somewhere between 15,000 and 30,000 people, mostly black, clambered all over wharves and docks and lined the shores of the Harlem River in search of the best vantage point. There was a festive air to proceedings. Bands played and hot-dog sellers hawked their wares. Thousands in the crowd clutched orange balloons that they were supposed to release when the seaplane left the water, although inevitably many were let loose early. Julian arrived resplendent in a blue uniform and knee-length black boots, accompanied by an aide carrying three suitcases prominently labeled "Tropical," "Arctic," and "Rainy Weather." But not everyone had come to watch the plane take off. Several men thrust themselves forward and served Julian with papers claiming that there was an attachment on the plane and that he could not leave until the balance owing, some $1,400, the *New York World* reported, had been paid. According to the *New Yorker*, Julian looked somewhat relieved and was more than willing to call the event off, but at this point the master of ceremonies, Lieutenant St. William Grant, and a prominent member of the UNIA intervened, stating, "we can get that money in ten minutes from a crowd like this." He dispatched his men in full UNIA regalia into the throng. Others, mostly West Indians, joined in, selling photographs of Julian for a dollar a piece, and the money was soon collected. Given what happened and the obvious risks of flying an antiquated plane into the emptiness of the Atlantic, there was always some doubt as to what Julian's intentions were. Seven years later, the *New Yorker* reported an alleged exchange between Julian and Chamberlin that occurred just before take-off. Chamberlin had observed that "that rowboat is heavier in the water when it's leaving the ship than it is going out. You're taking gas out of it!" Julian nodded his head and supposedly said, "It don't do to try and be *too* smart. Too much gas over your head is dangerous if you crash. I can get quite a ways on what's left."

Just before five o'clock the plane's aging engines spluttered into life, and the craft skimmed across the Harlem River and eventually lurched into the air. The crowd cheered, the band burst into music, and thousands of orange balloons soared into the hot afternoon air. Exactly what happened next is not clear. Julian later claimed that damage caused one of the plane's pontoons to fill with water, making the plane vibrate and keel over dangerously. Whatever the case, it was apparent to all that one of the plane's pontoons had fallen off within sight of Harlem. The damaged plane limped on for a short time but crashed very hard into Flushing Bay, some fifteen hundred feet from shore. Julian was fished out of the water suffering only a broken leg. According to the *New Yorker*, the denouement to the whole affair occurred soon after. Julian's first visitor in hospital was the black government agent who informed him, "Major, on behalf of the United States Government, I wish to inform you that everything is all right. You did yo' best, and if luck was against you that ain't listed among the crimes in the postal laws and regulations. I takes great pleasure in announcing we are satisfied." Amos then presented Julian with a small bouquet of tea roses and walked out of the room.[17]

Hubert Julian may have failed in his attempt to make aviation history, but he remained one of Harlem's best-known black celebrities. Periodically, for the rest of the 1920s and into the 1930s, announcements would appear in the press of plans for other heroic individual flights across the Atlantic, but nothing ever came of them. Julian busied himself making jumps and flying in Harlem and elsewhere in America, and in giving talks on black uplift to UNIA crowds. One of his most treasured press clippings was from the *New York Times*: "Whenever there is a disturbance of any magnitude in Harlem, Hubert Julian is involved in some way, either with a stunt flight or with another parachute jump." And that continued to be the case. On Sunday, November 6, 1927, the largest ever crowd in Harlem, variously estimated at between 150,000 and 200,000 persons, gathered for the funeral of Florence Mills, a truly remarkable stage performer who had died tragically young. As the funeral procession left Harlem, and later, as the casket was lowered into the ground at Woodlawn Cemetery, Julian swooped low in his plane and showered the mourners with rose petals provided by the *Amsterdam News* and Small's Paradise, a prominent Harlem club. A few years later, in August 1931, Julian dropped a bouquet of flowers at A'Lelia Walker's graveside, also at Woodlawn Cemetery.[18] It was not only for funerals that Julian's services were required. He buzzed various UNIA processions and, at Easter in 1934, flew a livid red plane low over what the *New York Times* described as a "sinuous, brilliant procession of hundreds of chanting followers" of Father Divine wending its way, slowly, through Harlem to Rockland Palace on 155th Street and Eighth Avenue. Julian addressed the crowd of some 5,000 and announced that he was about to make a world flight, "on which he would spread the message of the 'Father.'"[19] This too came to nothing.

News of Julian's attempt to fly across the Atlantic in *Ethiopia I* had spread well beyond the United States. In April 1930, an emissary from Ras Tafari, soon to be crowned Haile Selassie I, knocked on the door of Julian's Lenox Avenue apartment and offered him $1,000 per month and expenses to take part in the coronation ceremony. At a grand review, in front of an awe-struck crowd of 50,000, Julian launched himself out of a plane at 5,000 feet and parachuted to within fifty feet of Haile Selassie's throne. Even the *New Yorker* noted that "Julian was magnificent that day."[20] This was the beginning of an off-and-on relationship with Ethiopia—the lowlight of which was Julian's crashing of one of the emperor's planes—that lasted a number of years. Indeed, according to a particularly far-fetched part of his autobiography, Julian planned to shoot Mussolini, who had ordered the invasion of Ethiopia, with a cleverly concealed gun but was foiled when his inability to curb his tongue while talking to the foreign minister, Count Ciano, led to the cancellation of his meeting with the Italian dictator.[21]

In a fashion that would require the talents of a Spike Lee to do it full justice, Hubert Julian continued to make headlines for much of the rest of his life. In late 1937, Julian responded to a cablegram from a Chinese general and, according to the *Chicago Defender*, "sailed for the bomb-riddled Shanghai area, where he will fly a combat plane."[22] He was the producer of an Oscar Micheaux film, *The Notorious Elinor Lee*, which had its world premier in Harlem in January 1940.[23] Later that year he made a cameo appearance in the Finnish Flying Corps during the Russo-Finnish War. In September 1940, outraged by *Mein Kampf*, Julian cabled Herman Goering, challenging him to a duel in Messerschmitts over the English Channel. In the uneasy months after Dunkirk, the press lapped up the story about someone who wanted to stand up to the Germans. The response from Germany to Julian's telegram was, however, a deafening silence.[24] After the war, Julian set himself up in the import-export business, coming up with a scheme to buy millions of the American army's stale cigarettes that were stored in warehouses in Germany and repackage them for sale in the Far East. He then moved into business as an arms dealer and was involved in trying to sell arms in Guatemala, Haiti, Cuba, and the Congo.[25] Julian also continued to garner newspaper space. In 1964 he offered to bet Republican presidential nominee Barry Goldwater three tons of gold that he would lose the election to President Johnson. Julian was particularly taken with Lyndon Johnson. Indeed, the following year, after the Los Angeles riots, Julian announced that no American president had done "so much for the Negroes," and that the behavior of blacks in Watts had been so disgraceful that he "was giving up his home in the United States."[26] In 1966, Julian was widely reported as being one of the celebrities, along with Jim Brown, the football star, attending Cassius Clay's London fight with Henry Cooper. That, it appears, was Julian's last public hurrah. The gospel of black uplift looked increasingly dated in an age of black power, and he simply faded from view. His death in the Bronx in February 1983 went all but unnoticed.[27]

Hubert Julian was a pioneer. Previous to his arrival in Harlem about the only link blacks could possibly have with the machine and with height was as an elevator operator, an occupation in which the conditions were appalling and in which African Americans were ubiquitous.[28] For the most part, blacks could not even get jobs on the factory floor, with employers generally preferring recent European migrants. The idea that African Americans could use complicated machinery, let alone invent anything, was simply beyond the comprehension of most whites. Before Julian migrated to Harlem he had made a brief trip of a few days to Washington in order to secure the American rights to his invention. As he entered the patent office, the clerk burst out laughing and said: "What do you want to file—music?"[29]

By most accounts Julian became a very good pilot. In what appears to us to be one of the most heartfelt passages near the beginning of his autobiography, he claimed that "at the controls of a plane you feel free, complete master of your own destiny for once, clear of all the petty restrictions and annoyances of the world below. The air," he continued, "is the one place where all men really are equal, where it makes no difference what colour a man's skin may happen to be, where all that matters is your own skill." He also became much more adept at using a parachute, but, of course, it was those early wild and spectacular jumps into the Black Metropolis that made his name. He claimed in his autobiography that "my own people hailed me as a hero and pioneer, and though you may think that parachute jumps over Harlem were a strange way of working for racial advancement, I honestly believe it really did contribute something useful and valuable."[30] This was undoubtedly correct: indeed, it must be one of the few occasions in his life that Julian understated his case.

And yet Julian's love of the machine and speed was hardly the end of his embrace of modernity. From the beginning of his career, he was aware that he was staging a carefully choreographed performance, in which thousands of Harlemites were mobilized as unpaid extras, in order to create a media event. He was photographed, interviewed, and written about extensively by both the black and white press. Little wonder that John Bulloch, the collaborator on Julian's autobiography, described him as "a publicist without peer."[31] In line with the ethos of America, particularly New York, in the 1920s—the business of America is business—Julian's performances were designed to make money. Initially, the source was individuals, paying admission to get into the rented lots where he planned to land, and Harlem businesses. When he made his first jump, Julian was a walking billboard. Morticians had participated in a bidding war to secure display rights to Julian's body if the parachute did not open. The winner, who paid one hundred dollars, claimed, "It will be worth a fortune displaying the brave fool's body."[32] After the first jump, by which time he was better known, Julian cast his net rather wider, managing to secure sponsorship from Wurlitzer, Martin Saxophones, and a company that sold razorblades. Julian was prescient in recognizing the importance of advertising and very skilled—he could always talk the talk—in attracting what might be called crossover money from the other side of the color line, something that blacks would not succeed in doing really successfully until the time of Michael Jordan and Tiger Woods. As with many other modern celebrities, Julian was very familiar with the legal system and quick to have lawyers issue a writ if he felt wronged. In 1933 he sued the Hearst Press for half a million dollars, eventually settling out of court "for a considerable sum."[33] There was always an element of the huckster and the conman to Hubert Julian, and contemporary critics, including particularly commentators such as George Schuyler, with access to the newspapers were hardly slow to point out examples of this failing.[34] But it was also the case that he had fulfilled his ambition, stated so brazenly to the denizens of the Elite Barber Shop back in 1921, of living by his wits, and had done so by plunging headfirst into the twentieth century.

Julian was different from most black pioneers. Usually black individuals who challenged white domination of particular areas did so as sedately and respectably as possible. Right from the start of black legal challenges to white discrimination in New York in the 1830s and 1840s, it was the black community's most solid citizens who went to court. Similarly, in the twentieth century, Jackie Robinson and the various young black men and women who were the first to desegregate baseball or universities were constantly forced to curb their tongues and fists and be on their best behavior no matter how provoked. Julian, on the other hand, went out of his way to be as flamboyant as possible. There probably would have been a satiric edge to a lot of the press coverage of Julian anyway, but he did make it rather easier for his detractors. He tried to register his invention with the Canadian authorities under the name "parachuttagravepreresista," only to have the patent returned to him labeled "Aeroplane safety device." At the court case after his first jump into Harlem, he handed around cards to the judge and others stating that he was HUBERT JULIAN, M.D. WORLD'S CHAMPION

DAREDEVIL PARACHUTIST. He later explained that he was not a doctor and that the M.D. stood for Mechanical Designer.[35]

It is difficult to imagine more of a contrast than that between Hubert Julian and the most famous airman of them all. If Charles Lindbergh, a product of the Midwest, was almost impossibly bland and camera shy, with a politics that, as would later become apparent, slid toward sympathy with fascism, Hubert Julian came straight out of Harlem. Well before he had made clear his antipathy to fascism by tweaking Goering's nose, Julian had demonstrated a radical bent that had been shaped by the cauldron of politics in the Black Metropolis. Not for him the caution of the National Association for the Advancement of Colored People. Trying to solicit money from the association's secretary, James Weldon Johnson, for one of his flights, Julian ended up loudly reminding him of the word "Advancement" in his organization's title and suggesting that they replace it with "Defense." As Julian noted in his autobiography, "We did not part the best of friends."[36] Julian was, however, a friend of Marcus Garvey and often stumped for the UNIA. And as with many Garveyites, Julian developed a strong interest in Africa and particularly Ethiopia. Even his involvement with Father Divine was a commonplace among former members of the UNIA. What was unusual was that Julian went to Ethiopia and ended up in the service of Haile Selassie.

Politics was only the very beginning of the way in which Hubert Julian had been shaped by Harlem. There was, in addition, a distinctive style to urban black life in the 1920s and 1930s, and nowhere was this more apparent than on the streets of the Black Metropolis. Albert Murray, the writer and critic, remembered, in relation to the Harlem of this time, "The clothes you wore, the way you talked (and I don't mean just jive talk), the way you stood (we used to say stashed) when you were just hanging out, the way you drove an automobile or even just sat in it, everything you did was, you might say, geared to groove."[37] With Julian, it started with his clothes—one of the "ruling passions of my life," he claimed in his autobiography—and the care which he took over his appearance whenever he was out in public.[38] Julian was possibly the only inhabitant of Harlem whose passion for military-style uniforms—ensembles that were usually designed by himself—could relegate Marcus Garvey to the background. For his attempted flight across the Atlantic, the black aviator wore a suit of the palest blue, set off by a leather helmet, and a pair of cavalry boots of the finest make, adorned with silver spurs. Julian took similar pains with his attire whenever he gave press conferences, appeared in court, graced Harlem clubs with his presence in the

Figure 12.1. Hubert Julian in Paris with his new English plane, 1934.
New York Daily News/Getty.

early hours of the morning, or when he was simply going about his everyday life. Well ahead of the vogue for the British look, prompted both by the Duke of Windsor and the influx of West Indian migrants more attuned to what was going on in London, that energized fashionable blacks in the late 1930s, Julian modeled himself on the look of an English gentleman.[39] During the late 1920s, he even acquired a middle name—"Fauntleroy"—and began to affect a monocle. On his return from Abyssinia in 1930, the *New York Times* ran a picture of an extraordinarily dapper looking Julian "clad faultlessly in morning dress and swinging a heavy malacca stick." Five years later, on the occasion of another return from Africa, the *Times* reporter lovingly detailed Julian's attire: "a black morning coat and vest, with striped light gray trousers, black shoes and pearl gray spats, a wing collar and Ascot tie, derby hat and a beaver overcoat," topped off with an "ivory-handled black silk umbrella."[40]

As Albert Murray was well aware, though, it was always more than just clothes. There was an aggressive masculinity to the way Julian, who had a reputation as a ladies' man and was not reticent about using his celebrity, cut a swath through the women, married and single, in Harlem night clubs

*Figure 12.2. Hubert
Julian arriving in New
York on board the* Ile de
France, *1930. Underwood
& Underwood/Corbis.*

in the early hours of the morning. But for all his charm, there was an edgi-
ness to Julian's demeanor. This was a side to Julian that did not appear in
his autobiography. Soon after he arrived in Harlem, a Mrs. Edna Powell
Julian, who claimed to have been married to Julian in Canada, sued for
separation and alimony. She used Herbert Boulin, of the Boulin Detective
Agency, one of America's first black detective organizations, to investigate
Julian and serve him with the legal papers. As a result there was a considerable amount of bad blood between Julian and Boulin, a situation exacerbated when Boulin was retained to investigate one of Julian's fundraising
efforts. In May 1925, when the two met on the corner of 140th Street and
Seventh Avenue, they got into a wild brawl that lasted several minutes. The
magistrate found in favor of Boulin, who was still sporting a badly swollen
eye.[41] Toward the end of his life, this aggression became almost a travesty.
In his introduction to Julian's autobiography, John Bulloch delighted in re-
telling a story of Julian at a London restaurant. On being brought a very rare

steak, Julian "cut it open, then roared for the waiter. 'I may be black,' he said, 'but I'm not a cannibal.'"[42] Earlier, in the 1920s and into the 1930s, there had been an edge to Julian, an air of danger that went with his immaculate attire. Anyone dealing with him did well to remember that he had emerged from one of the toughest crucibles around, the streets of Harlem.

Hardly surprisingly, Julian had his detractors in Harlem and elsewhere. Right from his earliest flights in the 1920s, various commentators were quick to question the black aviator's ability at the controls of a plane. Even the *Negro World*, while supporting his attempt to fly to Africa in 1924, cautioned, "Would that Julian's skill as an airman nearly equalled his daring." A few years later, the *Inter-State Tattler*, in the middle of a fanciful piece suggesting that the huge Elks Convention meeting in Harlem should "do a Lindbergh," by which the writer meant stage a totally original aerial display, a stunt that "unless Lieut. Julian were engaged for a pilot . . . would be quite safe." By the mid-1930s many black reporters were tired of Julian's pretensions and announcements to the press of yet another flight to somewhere or other that never eventuated.

Criticism of Julian from blacks reached a crescendo over the black aviator's erratic behavior during the Italo-Ethiopian War, a cause that provoked passionate reactions among African Americans.[43] In late 1935, the *Chicago Defender* printed a full-page piece of "fiction," so thinly disguised as to be laughable, about a black airman in Ethiopia named "John Hubert" who "styled himself 'The Black Eagle.'" In the story, Hubert, who could fly and shoot the plane's weapons perfectly well but, suffering from "ground-shyness," was totally incapable of landing his craft, crashed three of the Emperor Selassie's planes and almost wrecked two others in a matter of days. In the extraordinary denouement to the piece, Hubert drove off no less than six Italian bombers intent on destroying Addis Ababa in a brilliant display of aerial combat and then landed his plane. As the white colonel ran up to the plane, Hubert asked, "Did you see that?" The black pilot brushed aside the white man's praise for his flying—he was just talking about the way he had brought his craft down to the ground. "Why, Colonel, I made a perfect three-point landing." Hubert then promptly died from his bullet wounds. An item in the *New York Age* the following year was, if anything, even less subtle. Julian, "who, unfortunately for the race, is also known as a Negro," had just announced his plans for a flight between New York and Rome. The *Age* editorialized, "We have been forced to hear Julian's idle pratings about his mythical exploits and extraordinary plans until we are sick of them." Indeed, the newspaper hoped that he would attempt the transatlantic flight "because we don't believe he can make it." The piece nastily concluded, "And if he didn't so much the better."[44]

Undoubtedly Julian's larger-than-life personality and flamboyant style, which not infrequently, particularly later on, slid off into bombast, rubbed people the wrong way, but it is also important to remember that he went where no black man had ever considered going before, and inevitably the rebuffs and taunts of a society in which racism was endemic would take their toll. Perhaps the most interesting point of comparison is with Julian's friend and sometime business partner, the great black film director Oscar Micheaux. For all their slightly old-fashioned values, both black men dared to venture into areas that most whites had unthinkingly considered to be theirs and theirs alone. Not only were film and aviation the epitome of modernity—the signal technological achievements of the early decades of the twentieth century—but they were also extraordinarily expensive activities, far too expensive, as it turned out, for African Americans to give anything but sporadic support. The result was that the careers of both men were a litany of scrimping and scraping, relying on antiquated equipment, being as creative as possible in taking every available short cut, and, inevitably, of promised films and flights that never occurred, bouncing checks, unpaid debts, and the continual threat of bankruptcy. Micheaux's biographer wrote of the director that "he knew how to stretch a dollar, and knew even better how to stretch credit," and much the same could be said of Julian. Both men were extremely gifted salesmen, and to quite a remarkable extent what they both packaged with their guileful words and images were the stories of their own lives. It was hardly surprising, then, that the third film slated for production by the Micheaux-Julian partnership was an aviation picture. "It will tell the story of my career," Julian told a *Time* reporter, "my crack-up when I tried to fly to Europe, my parachute jumping over the city, and my triumph in getting the Army to have Negro aviators." Almost inevitably the dynamic duo lost their financial backing, and the film was never made. But there can be no doubt that the legendary black director knew a cracking story, one that would make a great film, when he heard one.[45]

What, then, are we to make of Hubert Fauntleroy Julian? According to a writer in the *American Mercury* in 1940, Julian was "surely one of the more fabulous figures of our day." For Brian Urquhart, a prominent figure in the United Nations over several decades, Julian was "one of the more engaging rogues of our time."[46] But Urquhart knew him only in the postwar years, by which time he was a caricature of his former self, lurking around the world's trouble spots, always trying to put together a profitable arms deal that, if it ever came off, was only going to add to everyone's misery. Julian's later years were a story of the tropics and of failure that surely Graham Greene, who was making this territory his own in these years, could have done much with. In the decade and a half after he arrived in Harlem in 1921, Julian was a much more engaged and engaging figure. Against all the odds, his was a migrant success story: using his wits, his courage (let us not forget how dangerous flying, let alone parachuting, was in the 1920s), and his quick tongue, Julian had taken on whites at their own game and established a reputation that had spread well beyond Harlem. If Jack Johnson was the boxer, Florence Mills the actress, and Louis Armstrong the musician, then Hubert Julian was the pilot (and parachutist). And if there was always the hint of the confidence trick to Julian's schemes, this too was recognizable to most Harlemites, for the 1920s was the golden age of the con, and the Black Metropolis was awash with hustlers of various sorts.[47] Indeed, in so many ways, Julian was an exaggerated, larger-than-life version of what was going on in Harlem. But what was different, of course, was that Hubert Julian could *fly*. Scores of thousands of Harlem's residents were thrilled by Julian's parachute jumps into Harlem, or awed by the way he flew, almost ridiculously low, over some procession or other, or simply moved by his dropping of the petals over the mourners at Florence Mills's funeral. Not only, by these means, did Julian disprove the unthinking assumption, held by many Americans, that anything to do with flying would remain the preserve of whites, but he did it with a large style that ordinary men and women of Harlem could recognize as something they saw every day on 135th Street or Seventh Avenue.

In May 1927, when Charles Lindbergh flew the Spirit of St. Louis across the Atlantic in the first nonstop solo flight, he was treated to a rapturous reception.[48] And, yet, in Harlem the applause was somewhat muted. To be sure, black newspapers and magazines were mostly concerned with what was going on in the Black Metropolis, but perhaps it was also the case that Harlem already had its own pilot and that the exploits of the "Lone Eagle" seemed less impressive to those already familiar with the career of the "Black Eagle." Interestingly, at almost the same time, a new dance was emerging on the dance floors of Harlem. It was a "synthesis of European social dance traditions and the West African dance tradition of self-expression" that would revolutionize American dance.[49] The dance was, of course, called the "lindy hop." As a marketing ploy pitched at a crossover clientele the name was an act of genius, and, over the years, thousands of whites would troop up-town to the Savoy Ballroom and other venues to watch and photograph the spectacle of black dancers brilliantly performing the lindy. If Hubert Julian uttered an opinion as to the name of the dance it was not recorded, though perhaps, publicist par excellence that he was, he would have appreciated the cleverness of the dance's eventual title. Still, for someone who himself was "the black pilot," and who habitually was still energetically cutting the rug in Harlem clubs in the early hours of the morning, it is difficult not to imagine that he also would have thought that the "Black Eagle Hop" had a nice ring to it.

NOTES

1. We would like to acknowledge, gratefully, the generous support of the Austra-lian Research Council in awarding us a Discovery Grant, "Black Metropolis: Harlem 1915–1930," which enabled us to conduct the research on which this essay is based. We would also like to thank Fitz Brundage for doing the heavy lifting in organiz-ing the 2008 conference and this ensuing volume. On the romance of flight, see Joseph J. Corn, *The Winged Gospel: America's Romance With Aviation, 1900–1950* (New York: Oxford University Press, 1983). Our account of Julian's parachute jump has been pieced together from Colonel Hubert Julian, *Black Eagle*, as told to John Bulloch (London: Jarrolds, 1964), 52–55; John Peer Nugent, *The Black Eagle* (New York: Bantam, 1972), 18–22; Clarence D. Chamberlin, *Record Flights* (Philadelphia: Dorrance & Co., 1928), 239–40; *Amsterdam News*, April 18, 1923, 1; *New York Times*, April 30, 1923, 3; *New York Daily News*, April 30, 1923, 3; *Amsterdam News*, May 2, 1923, 1; *New York Age*, May 5, 1923, 1. The story from the *Daily Star* is reprinted in Allon Schoener, ed., *Harlem on My Mind* (1968; New York: New Press, 1995), 60–61 (although the date of the story is incorrect). Often the different accounts are contra-dictory. Julian remembers that there were five planes in the convoy but the contem-porary newspaper accounts state there were only three. Where possible we have fol-lowed the account written closest to the event. Julian has not fared that well in the historiography of black aviation, usually being treated as somewhere between "flam-boyant" and a "charlatan." See Von Hardesty, *Black Aviator: The Story of William J. Powell* (Washington, D.C.: Smithsonian Institution Press, 1994), which is a new edi-tion of William J. Powell, *Black Wings* (1934); Samuel L. Broadnax, *Blue Skies, Black Wings: African American Pioneers of Aviation* (Westport, Conn.: Praeger, 2007); Von Hardesty, *Black Wings: Courageous Stories of African Americans in Aviation and Space History* (New York: Collins, 2008). Julian has also been dealt with briefly by David Levering Lewis, *When Harlem Was in Vogue* (New York: Alfred A. Knopf, 1984), 111–12; and Ann Douglas, *Terrible Honesty: Mongrel Manhattan in the 1920s*

(New York: Farrar, Strauss and Giroux, 1995), 457–61. Published after we had written this article, and after the conference in October 2008, was David Shaftel, "The Black Eagle of Harlem: The Truth Behind the Tall Tales of Hubert Fauntleroy Julian," *Air and Space Magazine* (January 2009).

2. Julian, *Black Eagle*, 56–57; Nugent, *The Black Eagle*, 23–25; Chamberlin, *Record Flights*, 239–40.

3. Julian, *Black Eagle*, 56.

4. *New York Times*, August 24, 1962, 1, 5. George Schuyler devoted a whole column to pointing out how naive Gardiner was for making such a statement. See *Pittsburgh Courier*, September 8, 1962, 12.

5. Lewis, *When Harlem Was in Vogue*, 111; Toni Morrison, *Jazz* (New York: Alfred A. Knopf, 1992), 8.

6. Adam Green, *Selling the Race: Culture, Community, and Black Chicago, 1940–1955* (Chicago: University of Chicago Press, 2007), 157.

7. Winthrop D. Jordan, *White Over Black: American Attitudes Toward the Negro, 1550–1812* (Chapel Hill: University of North Carolina Press, 1968), 283–86, 449–55.

8. Shane White, *Somewhat More Independent: The End of Slavery in New York City, 1770–1810* (Athens: University of Georgia Press, 1991), 65–66.

9. Deirdre O'Connell, *The Ballad of Blind Tom* (New York: Overlook Duckworth, 2009).

10. Charles L. Ponce de Leon, *Self-Exposure: Human Interest Journalism and the Emergence of Celebrity in America, 1890–1940* (Chapel Hill: University of North Carolina Press, 2002), 69–73. The best account of blacks as "culture heroes" remains by far Lawrence W. Levine, *Black Culture and Black Consciousness: Afro-American Folk Thought from Slavery to Freedom* (New York: Oxford University Press, 1977), 367–440.

11. Morris Markey, "The Black Eagle-I," *New Yorker*, July 11, 1931, 22–25; Morris Markey, "The Black Eagle-II," *New Yorker*, July 18, 1931, 20–23. For a prescient piece on celebrity and "what, why and how persons, things break into nation's press" that mentioned Julian, see *Pittsburgh Courier*, January 20, 1934, A1.

12. Julian, *Black Eagle*, 26. According to Nugent he was only the manager of the plantation. See Nugent, *The Black Eagle*, 3. His family was well enough off to send him to a private school in Trinidad.

13. Julian, *Black Eagle*, 25–26, 28–30, 34–35. Shaftel, "The Black Eagle."

14. Julian, *Black Eagle*, 36–39, 42. According to Nugent the rights were sold for a combination of stock and $3,000 in cash. See Nugent, *The Black Eagle*, 7.

15. Julian, *Black Eagle*, 42–43.

16. Nugent, *The Black Eagle*, 10, 13.

17. Our account of Julian's abortive flight has been pieced together from a number of sources: Markey, "The Black Eagle-I," 22–25; Julian, *Black Eagle*, 59–65; Nugent, *The Black Eagle*, 27–35; Chamberlin, *Record Flights*, 240–44; *New York World*, July 4, 1924, 13; *New York Telegram*, July 4, 1924, 12; *New York Herald Tribune*,

July 5, 1924, 9; *New York World*, July 5, 1924, 13; *New York American*, July 5, 1924, 3; *Negro World*, July 5, 1924, 2; *Negro World*, July 12, 1924, 2. The *New Yorker* piece does not name Amos. For that information, see *Atlanta Daily World*, January 7, 1954, 2.

18. The *NYT* quote is in Julian, *Black Eagle*, 60. This quote was also used in a 1962 story about Julian in the *Times*, although, strangely, rather than citing itself the paper attributes the quote as, "it was said." We have been unable to find the original quote in the *Times* but did find a very similar quote—"There was a time in the early part of 1923 when every disturbance of any magnitude that occurred in Harlem was in some way involved with another parachute jump by Julian"—in the *New York Herald Tribune* which was reprinted in the *Defender*. See *New York Times*, August 24, 1962, 5; and *Chicago Defender*, July 7, 1928, 10. Bill Egan, *Florence Mills: Harlem Jazz Queen* (Lanham, Md.: Scarecrow Press, 2004), 234; *Inter-State Tattler*, August 27, 1931, 1, 12.

19. *New York Times*, April 2, 1934, 3.

20. Markey, "The Black Eagle-II," 20–23. See also Julian, *Black Eagle*, 81–91.

21. Julian, *Black Eagle*, 115–18.

22. *Chicago Defender*, September 25, 1937, 5. According to his autobiography, this was in fact the first time he was involved in an arms deal. First, he went to Paris, where an armchair he was sitting in collapsed and he broke his wrist. He never made it to China. Julian, *Black Eagle*, 120.

23. On the premier, see H. Allen Smith's account from the *New York World-Telegram*, collected in H. Allen Smith, *Low Man on a Totem Pole* (Garden City, N.Y.: Doubleday, Doran and Co., 1941), 72–81.

24. On Finland, see *Chicago Defender*, July 13, 1940, 3; Julian, *Black Eagle*, 123–28. On Goering, see "Talk of the Town" in the *New Yorker*, September 28, 1940, 14; Smith, *Low Man on a Totem Pole*, 79–81; Julian, *Black Eagle*, 133–34; Meigs M. Green, "Harlem's Fabulous Flyer," *American Mercury*, February 1941, 219–26.

25. Julian, *Black Eagle*, 141–88.

26. On the bet with Goldwater, see *Chicago Daily Defender*, September 17, 1964, 4. On Johnson and leaving America, see *Chicago Daily Defender*, August 18, 1965, 2; *New York Times*, August 18, 1965, 20.

27. *New York Times*, May 22, 1966, 221. Ann Douglas makes a point of the fact that there was "no hard evidence of his death." See Douglas, *Mongrel Manhattan*, 458. However, with the modern marvel of the Internet, it is easily possible to come up with someone stating authoritatively in Wikipedia that Julian died on February 19, 1983, in the Bronx. See http://en.wikipedia.org/wiki/Hubert_Julian.

28. On elevator operators, see Marcy S. Sacks, *Before Harlem: The Black Experience in New York City Before World War I* (Philadelphia: University of Pennsylvania Press, 2006), 113–14.

29. Julian, *Black Eagle*, 40–41.

30. For a particularly laudatory account of Julian's flying skills see an article by William Pickens in the *Atlanta Daily World*, April 25, 1932, 2. Julian, *Black Eagle*, 25, 57.

31. Julian, *Black Eagle*, 10.

32. Nugent, *The Black Eagle*, 19.

33. *New York Age*, December 30, 1933, 1. There were many other suits. In 1937, for example, Julian sued Father Divine. See Jill Watts, *God, Harlem U.S.A.: The Father Divine Story* (Berkeley: University of California Press, 1992), 155. In 1952, Julian sued *Time* magazine for $600,000 in damages over an article about Julian's arms dealings with the Guatemalan government. See *Chicago Defender*, November 22, 1952, 3.

34. See, for example, *Pittsburgh Courier*, November 8, 1930, 10; *Pittsburgh Courier*, September 8, 1962, 12. In the former piece Schuyler wrote, "I pointed out long ago that both Julian and Garvey were frauds, robbing the gullible for their own aggrandizement"; and in the latter he claimed, "Mind you, I have nothing against Julian, whom I have known for the last thirty years, as a sharp hustler."

35. Julian, *Black Eagle*, 38; Markey, "The Black Eagle-I," 23; Nugent, *The Black Eagle*, 21.

36. Julian, *Black Eagle*, 68–69.

37. Quoted in Sally Price and Richard Price, *Romare Bearden: The Caribbean Dimension* (Philadelphia: University of Pennsylvania Press, 2006), 18. See also Robert G. O'Meally, "We Used to say 'Stashed': Romare Bearden Paints the Blues," in *The Hearing Eye: Jazz & Blues Influences in African American Visual Art*, ed. Graham Lock and David Murray (New York: Oxford University Press, 2009), 173–93.

38. Julian, *Black Eagle*, 42. On the importance of clothing and style more generally in African American culture, see Shane White and Graham White, *Stylin': African American Expressive Culture from Its Beginnings to the Zoot Suit* (Ithaca: Cornell University Press, 1998).

39. Markey, "The Black Eagle-I," 25. On English look, see White and White, *Stylin'*, 251.

40. *New York Times*, November 19, 1930, 21; *New York Times*, December 14, 1935, 8.

41. *Amsterdam News*, October 10, 1923, 1; *Amsterdam News*, May 13, 1925, 1.

42. Julian, *Black Eagle*, 11.

43. For a full account of these matters, see William R. Scott, *The Sons of Sheba's Race: African-Americans and the Italo-Ethiopian War, 1935–1941* (Bloomington: Indiana University Press, 1993), 42, 81–95.

44. *Negro World*, July 5, 1924, 2; *Inter-State Tattler*, August 19, 1927, 2; *Chicago Defender*, November 23, 1935, 11; *New York Age*, June 27, 1936, 6.

45. On Micheaux, see Patrick McGilligan, *Oscar Micheaux, The Great and Only: The Life of America's First Great Black Filmmaker* (New York: Harper Collins, 2007), passim, quote is at 145; *Time*, January 29, 1940, 67–68. On the problems faced by blacks trying to raise money for any venture, see Shane White, Stephen Garton, Stephen Robertson, Graham White, *Playing the Numbers: Gambling in Harlem Between the Wars* (Cambridge: Harvard University Press, 2010), 200–222.

46. Green, "Harlem's Fabulous Flyer," 219; quoted in Nugent, *The Black Eagle*, x.

47. On the con in Harlem, see Shane White, Stephen Garton, Stephen Robertson, and Graham White, "The Envelope, Please," in *The Cultural Turn in U.S. History: Pasts, Presents, Futures*, ed. James W. Cook, Lawrence Glickman, and Michael O'Malley (Chicago: University of Chicago Press, 2008), 121–52.

48. See John W. Ward, "The Meaning of Lindbergh's Flight," *American Quarterly* 10 (1958): 3–16; Corn, *Winged Gospel*, 17–27.

49. On the lindy hop, see the excellent, Joel Dinerstein, *Swinging the Machine: Modernity, Technology, and African American Culture between the World Wars* (Amherst: University of Massachusetts Press, 2003), 250–82, quote at 258. See also, Marshall and Jean Stearns, *Jazz Dance: The Story of American Vernacular Dance* (New York: Da Capo Press, 1994), 323–34.

More than a Prizefight

Joe Louis, Max Schmeling, and the Transnational Politics of Boxing

LEWIS A. ERENBERG

On the evening of June 22, 1938, ex-champion and German national Max Schmeling clashed with sensational American titleholder Joe Louis for the heavyweight crown. This much-anticipated bout between Louis, only the second black heavyweight champion, and Schmeling, Germany's most successful boxer and the only man to beat Louis, created extraordinary excitement across the world. This was no ordinary prizefight. "The state of the . . . nation or the world can invest a sporting event with dramatic intensity such as is reached in few theatres," historian C. L. R. James noted. "When the democrat Joe Louis fought the Nazi Schmeling the bout became a focus of approaching world conflict." While Germans hoped that "Unser Max" would vindicate their nation in the eyes of the world, African Americans entrusted "Our Joe" to knock out this representative of white supremacy. Many other Americans, especially Jews angered by the rise of Nazism, rooted for the black boxer as an American hero versus totalitarianism. Befitting a match that radio announcer Clem McCarthy called "the greatest fight of 'our' generation," 70,000 spectators jammed Yankee Stadium almost to capacity. While the rich, famous, and powerful filled the ringside seats, African Americans in the grandstands rooted on their hero. Seventy million other fans listened on the radio; a German contingent arrived to support their man; and Germans at home stayed up until early morning for the transatlantic broadcast. "No championship fight since Dempsey-Tunney," noted a German reporter, "has produced such burning interest." Given the bout's political import, outside the stadium the Anti-Nazi League called for a boycott of German goods, while Communists urged fans to cheer Louis and boo Schmeling.[1]

That the fight's drama lay in a battle between a German and an (African) American allows historians to place domestic events in international perspective. With the recent rise of globalization, historians are aware that an exclusively national focus offers too narrow a lens for understanding contemporary transnational culture. Yet most attention has gone to the period after World War II when American military power expanded globally to influence other societies. Well before the war, however, American entertainment traveled the world. Moreover, as Eric Foner argues, America's relationship with the world "has also powerfully influenced the idea of freedom and its evolution at home." The struggle against Nazi Germany, for example, highlighted aspects of American racism, and "fundamentally transformed perceptions of who was entitled to enjoy the blessings of liberty in the United States." According to recent scholars, early twentieth-century American nationalism was firmly rooted in a racial hierarchy of whiteness. As an arena of white male power, boxing in the United States displayed deep hostility toward prizefighters of color. The Louis-Schmeling fight demonstrates how international conflict with Nazism's master-race philosophy challenged an American racial nationalism.[2]

While cultural historians have begun to explore the global impact of American entertainment, they have generally ignored sport in general, and boxing in particular. Americans played few sports that have had boxing's international quality. Baseball's World Series did not involve the world, and Americans participated in the Olympic Games only once every four years. The Louis-Schmeling bouts are only two examples of many international boxing contests that started in the early nineteenth century. The heavyweight match between American titleholder John C. Heenan and British champion Tom Sayers in England in 1860 drew more transatlantic attention than any other sporting event from 1830 to 1870. In the twentieth century, boxing became a lucrative mass sport in many societies and drew legions of foreign boxers to the United States. Schmeling's New York career in the 1920s and 1930s testifies to the international nature of the sport.[3]

During the 1930s, however, boxing, and sport in general, achieved a level of international politicization unheard of only a decade earlier. As liberal columnist Heywood Broun noted, the 1938 bout was "more than a prizefight." Schmeling "came into the ring as a symbol of a political philosophy" and was "expected to dramatize the new German anthropological theories and demonstrate Nordic superiority." Historians are aware that the Berlin Olympics of 1936 mixed sport and politics, but during this era the ring also was an arena where competing symbols of nationalism, race, and masculinity clashed. For Nazi Germany and New Deal America, boxers embodied a gendered dimension of national ideals, for male power seemed essential to national identity. In both countries, the Depression created problems for male and national identity that boxers helped to resolve. With millions of men unemployed, outlets for breadwinning were few and images of impotence abounded. In this atmosphere, boxers with knockout power and hence male strength served as national heroes. Louis became a superman for African Americans and then, through his international battles, a hero for white Americans, too. A product of cosmopolitan Weimar, Schmeling was remade into an Aryan superman by the Nazi regime to rescue a society weakened by inflation and depression, defeat in World War I, and foreign occupation of the Rhineland. Overcoming histories of weakness and humiliation, Americans and Germans transformed "Unser Max" and "Our Joe" into heroic masculine national symbols.[4]

While Schmeling became a German national hero, Louis symbolized an African American political and cultural awakening. With his knockout power and dignified presence, he became a folk hero and symbol of race pride. While the Louis phenomenon drew on earlier cultural revivals, such as the Harlem Renaissance and the Marcus Garvey movement, Louis's achievement moved far beyond middle-class artists and represented a national sense of unity among African Americans, rich as well as poor, southern as well as northern. As Germans attempted to reestablish national strength and regain the respect of the world, black Americans were in a process of decolonization, of rethinking the racial hierarchy that placed them at the bottom and whites at the top by virtue of race alone. Both groups sought symbols of collective revival and group pride. A successful black superhero offered a new myth of masculine fighting strength to wipe out memories of slavery, lynching, and dependence. In the 1930s and 1940s, black boxers made the sport a public expression of racial and masculine identity in a society that allowed few such opportunities. As one black columnist declared: Louis was "The Man We Want to Be." While many whites saw Negroes as minstrel figures, "Louis, simply by being the kind of young man he is, promises to eclipse the old picture of what white people think Negroes are, while insinuating a newer and true one in its place." Athletes were part of a cultural revival that, as Declan Kibard asserts of the Irish national awakening, "preceded and in many ways enabled the political revolution that followed." As black boxers dominated the ring, they contributed to a dream of a future that included strong black men on the public stage fighting back against white supremacy in athletics and everyday life.[5]

The African American sports awakening also challenged the link between race and American national identity. Unlike Germans who focused more narrowly on virulent racial nationalism in the 1930s, a broad body of Americans wrestled with a new national identity rooted in ethnic, racial, and cultural pluralism. Popular culture, CIO unions, New Deal arts programs, and a resurgent Left challenged earlier racial nationalism. Popular Front and New Deal political values also influenced sports as the Anti-Nazi League, a loose alliance of leftist and religious groups, promoted boycotts against the Olympics and Schmeling. Further, the racial nationalism that remained, especially but not exclusively in the South, deepened awareness that American racial ideas were similar to those of the Nazis. In an atmosphere of international tension, Louis became the first black hero to cross race lines to become a hero to white Americans and a widely accepted representative of American national values.[6]

The question remains how these two boxers and boxing itself managed to carry such importance in the 1930s. The answer may lie in the way that the sport mirrored the national and racial history of both societies during this era. In fact, both boxers' careers are rooted in the Depression and its effects on boxing, masculinity, and politics. By the time of their two epic matches in 1936 and 1938 they had assumed primary roles in the sport's renewal after it had suffered its "own private depression" worldwide, after reaching a high point in the United States and Germany during the 1920s.[7]

Schmeling carried German boxing to transatlantic prominence in the late 1920s, but his career plummeted during the worst Depression years of the early 1930s. Drawn to boxing as an alternative to routine factory and office jobs, Schmeling became a cosmopolitan Berliner enmeshed in a popular cult of the body. When he went to New York in 1928, he secured a Jewish manager and became a transnational symbol befitting his Weimar café circle of actors and artists. He also symbolized boxing's rise in Berlin and New York from illegal sport to mass acceptance and million-dollar gates. After World War I, thousands of Germans were introduced to the sport in British internment camps. Once outlawed as a brutal plebian activity, boxing spread quickly as part of a more open republic, where individuals were responsible for their own fate. With his own hands, Schmeling rose from the working class to wealth and celebrity. In 1930 he became the first German to win the heavyweight title, but the outcome tarnished the sport. He won his title on a foul, lying on the canvas. "My crown was without glory," he said. German fans called him the "Low Blow Champion" and described "grave damage to the testicles." A saying emerged: "I am Schmeling humiliated." Despite international success, Schmeling suffered a blow to "German honor" just as the shock of the Depression resurrected persistent fears of national disunity and male weakness associated with wartime defeat and postwar inflation. While Schmeling regained some prestige by successfully defending his title in 1931, the bout was a financial fiasco, drawing the fewest fans in championship history. In 1932 he lost the title, and then was knocked out by the Jewish Max Baer, a defeat the Nazis deplored. His career seemingly over, he fell into "a deep depression."[8]

Declining gates and Schmeling's losses signaled boxing's worldwide depression. Mediocre champions turned over rapidly, and in the Depression's depths, fans everywhere abandoned the tarnished sport. In Germany, Schmeling's fate prompted the socialist newspaper, *Vorwärts*, to ask, "Is Boxing Dying?" while Nazis blamed Jewish money lust for prizefighting's decline. Meanwhile, heavyweight boxers' links to gangsters led American fight fans to interpret the sport as part of a flawed society and exacerbated long-standing beliefs that the sport was sordid, brutal, and un-American. Mob-controlled Primo Carnera, an Italian giant of limited ability, whose fights "have been of a very suspicious character," led many fans to conclude that boxing, like business, was rigged by ruthless individuals who had no respect for anything other than money. Max Baer, Carnera's successor, embodied the failed consumer values of the 1920s. "He made wisecracks and went to parties," noted one observer, "he was Broadway, he was California and Florida." Boxing's low point paralleled the cultural and political malaise of the early 1930s. Crooked managers bent only on profit dominated the fight game. Ruthless individualism subverted community and fair play; strong men seemed hollow.[9]

While boxing suffered economically and culturally during the early 1930s, by mid-decade the sport experienced an amazing revival in both nations. When Schmeling and Louis fought for the first time in June 1936, the former was leading a German pugilistic, cultural, and political regeneration. After his string of losses, Schmeling began a successful comeback in 1934 just as the Nazis sought to restore Germany's strength and prestige. Faced with a massive depression, the regime poured money into public works and relief, created new recreational programs, and began rearmament. Having scorned international sports and mass culture—especially their American incarnations—for their weakening effects on German national character, once in power the new regime reversed itself and attempted to use the international sports arena for nationalist ends. In a populist manner, the regime courted athletes, artists, and movie stars to legitimize itself at home and abroad. In early 1933, for example, shortly after taking power, Hitler met with Schmeling. No other German politician had paid him attention despite his world title, and to meet President Von Hindenburg one "had to be from the nobility." A propaganda master, Hitler saw the athlete's interviews abroad as a way to sell the regime. "Now you can tell the pessimists out there how peaceful everything is here and assure them that we are making progress." In 1935 Hitler asked him to dissuade the American Olympic Committee from boycotting the Berlin games.[10]

Using Schmeling to publicize the regime represented the Nazi reevaluation of exercise and sports as a means to rescue Germany from defeat and demoralization. In *Mein Kampf*, Hitler argued that fighting sports would transform German young men into proper Aryans and future soldiers. In their desire to prepare German men for battle, the Nazis abandoned their preference for the German tradition of physical exercise and glorified both exercise and sport. The regime required mandatory physical education in schools and universities and promoted mass sports festivals. As Hitler declared, education should not aim at "pumping in mere knowledge, but at training bodies" to protect the nation as soldiers. A Nazi apologist noted sport was "outward testimony of a nation capable of athletic achievement and an inward maintenance of the health of the *Volk* and a promoter of the community of the *Volk*." Sport would produce the healthy racial body and the new fascist man. As an ally of politics, athletics became essential to the state. Although personally indifferent, Hitler bankrolled the Olympics of 1936 to validate the regime's beneficence and the Aryan race's physical supremacy. Eager to avenge the defeat of its manhood in the war and rescue the nation from Weimar racial and sexual degeneracy, the Nazis promoted boxing to toughen men and prepare them for battle against foreign enemies. "There is no sport," declared Hitler, "that promotes the offensive spirit, demands lightning quick power of decision, and prepares the body to take punches" as does boxing. While the Nazis distanced themselves from professional sport because of its degrading "Jewish" commercial values, they viewed professional boxers as mass heroes. As the era's best-known idol, Schmeling was invaluable as a new role model for German youth. Only athletes tied to the state could achieve greatness, while athletic success validated the state by symbolizing a renewed national culture. Sport victories, noted Schmeling, "were being converted into political currency."[11]

In their desire to purify athletics of degenerate racial influences, Nazis advocated athletic and physical training for German men, according to

Nazi sports ideologue Bruno Malitz, "for reasons of race, of blood. The aim is . . . to strengthen, to maintain, and to cultivate the German *Volk*, the Nordic race." Sport had to be purified "of the alien and weakening presence of the Jew." As he did in all other areas of cultural life, Hitler appointed party leaders to oversee professional boxing, expel Jews, Gypsies, and Afro-Germans from the sport and ensure that boxing fulfilled the regime's political ideals. All Jews were dropped from the membership rolls of amateur and professional boxing organizations, and new members had to be of "Aryan origin." Convinced that Jewish money and management corrupted sport and German manhood, the Nazis banned Jewish capital and personnel from organizing matches or managing fighters. These rules gave Schmeling serious problems, since his American manager and many friends were Jewish. He turned to the boxing authorities, who explained that restrictions on his manager applied only in Germany. Because of his associations, Schmeling had to walk a fine line.[12]

His comeback placed Schmeling at the apex of German sport, just when the Nazis were consolidating power and turning to international athletics as an integral part of their cultural and gender revolution. In 1934 he beat fellow German Walter Neusel before 90,000 spectators, Germany's largest bout ever—as *Box-Sport* declared, "in terms of sporting and publicity value, the *high point* of German boxing history." *Box-Sport* argued that the bout might have changed "opinion abroad toward the new Germany and its leader." Indeed, the match assumed the features of a party rally and Nazi spectacle, a harbinger of the Olympics. Boxing officials spoke, and Nazi groups marched about with flags aloft. For Schmeling's next bout with an American the regime helped finance a new Hamburg arena. Madison Square Garden's Jimmy Johnston complained: "the German government wants to establish its prestige in the field of sports." Germany captured the Olympics, and "now they are trying to take the world boxing championship back to Germany." American press attention led *Der Angriff* to declare Schmeling "a true flag-bearer for his country." With Storm Troopers present, Hitler salutes and the national anthem celebrated Schmeling's victory. Hitler and Minister of Propaganda and Enlightenment Dr. Josef Goebbels cabled their congratulations and invited Schmeling to the Chancellery. The large crowd, German victory, and world attention, moreover, signaled Germany's desire to replace the United States as boxing's capital. To that end, the regime played a crucial role in currency matters and financial negotiations for Schmeling's major international matches.[13]

As part of his comeback, in June 1936 Schmeling had to fight young American Joe Louis, whom boxing experts hailed as the next world champion. Just as Schmeling's comeback symbolized a German renaissance, Joe Louis's title quest signified a revitalization of American boxing and black pride during the Depression. Few historians have understood Louis's story as a Depression tale. When he turned professional in 1934 boxing had declined, sports heroes were suspect, and corruption ran rampant. Yet a hunger emerged for male sports heroes who represented something other than money and who stood apart from the ruthless self-interest that had nearly destroyed boxing. As he fought his way to become only the second African American heavyweight champion in history, Louis represented the desire of the most forgotten of forgotten Americans to take their rightful place in the American firmament. In this he became a living embodiment of the New Deal ethos. Compared to his recent predecessors, he was not only a sensational fighter, he also attracted fans of all races because of the ideals associated with his quest.[14]

When Louis first appeared on the national scene in 1935, winning twenty-three straight fights, twenty-one by knockout, and annihilating ex-champions Primo Carnera and Max Baer, he raised white fears of "a new black menace" who would challenge the white supremacy that was deeply rooted in boxing and in American life. As historian C. L. R. James asserted, "Negroes are inferior? . . . Here is one Negro who is not inferior and beat everybody who dares to challenge him." In referring to a black menace, whites recalled Jack Johnson, the first black heavyweight to win the championship and to challenge the tenets of white civilization. When Johnson wrested the title from Tommy Burns in Australia in 1908 he precipitated a crisis that revealed the white supremacist nature of the sport. Never as fully segregated as professional team sports, boxing nevertheless was an arena where white manhood dominated unfairly. From John L. Sullivan in 1882, white heavyweight champions refused to battle black contenders. Dominated by the white working class, boxing elevated poor white men to full manhood while excluding black men because they were considered less than full men, morally weak, and physically and sexually indulgent. Moreover, the white public would not pay to see black men fight. Boxing embodied the Anglo-Saxon virtues of individual will, aggression, and conquest and contempt for the humiliation of submission. With physical superiority considered a sign of racial supremacy, most whites saw Johnson's crown as a threat to Caucasian racial and national prestige and demanded that a "White Hope" defend the race's honor. As "All Coons Look Alike to Me" played, ex-champion Jim Jeffries took up the cudgels of the white race in 1910; Johnson defeated him handily. When films of the bout provoked race riots in which whites attacked blacks in revenge for their loss, Congress banned fight films to prevent subsequent riots and future depictions of black triumph over white manliness that might undermine the myth of white superiority. In attempting to enjoy the fruits of victory, Johnson challenged other racial and sexual taboos with his white wives, fast cars, and his black-and-tan cabaret. With white women and "civilization" at stake, he was indicted under the Mann Act, forced into exile, and swindled out of his title.[15]

All black heavyweights labored under the color line that was reimposed after Johnson's defeat in 1915. To avoid stimulating black unrest in the empire, Great Britain's Home Office responded to Johnson's desire to fight in London by banning interracial bouts. In the Unites States, Tex Rickard, promoter of the "White Hope" fight, used his control of Madison Square Garden's monopoly over heavyweight boxing in the 1920s to enforce the color bar to prevent riots and to safeguard the sport against possible federal or state bans. More important, this policy ensured that black contenders would not meet white champions in contests that implied racial equality. Rickard barred Jack Dempsey from defending his title against his main challenger, Harry Wills, whom *Ring* called "a clean athlete, a splendid sportsman, a boxer of high ideals who has proved himself a credit to the game and to his race." White foreigners such as Schmeling were more acceptable contenders in 1930 than any black menace. Race trumped nation. Initially reluctant to waste his time training a black heavyweight in a white-dominated sport, black trainer Jack Blackburn told Louis, "White man hasn't forgotten that poor nigger with his white women, acting like he owned the world." Common wisdom held that black fighters did not draw, which forced them to lose to white contenders to make them look good. Blackburn agreed to train Louis only if he took no easy or fixed fights, refused to rely on decisions, and aimed for the kill. "Let your fists be the referee." Louis did. His success, however, raised fears of "a dark cloud" over the heavyweight division.[16]

Initially, white anxieties about Louis appeared everywhere. Reporter Davis J. Walsh declared in the *Birmingham News* that "something sly and sinister and perhaps not quite-human came out of the African Jungle" to destroy Carnera. Davis recognized the stakes: "Africa, the dark continent, was ready to revel at the slightest notice over this amazing person who has arisen overnight to challenge and defy the white man's innate sense of superiority." Louis had the eyes of "an animal. . . . His 'strike' is something not too far from death." Even admiring northern sportswriters described Louis as an instinctual animal lacking the higher mental faculties. The *New York Sun*'s Frank Graham noted that one of Louis's great strengths was "the savage streak in him that makes him a fearsome, even a disturbing figure in the ring." As Paul Gallico put it, Louis was a "magnificent animal . . . he lives like an animal, fights like an animal, has all the cruelty and ferocity of a wild thing." To offset his fearsome power, white columnists and cartoons depicted Louis out of the ring as a minstrel figure: he loved to sleep, devoured fried chicken, spoke in dialect, and had a "kinky head." White sportswriters found it hard to accept Louis as the equal of white boxers, although few of them had highly developed minds. Most whites could not mention Louis without reference to his race: "colored clouter," "tan tornado," "Dark Destroyer," "Brown Bomber"; and most white cartoonists depicted him as a simple, slow, colored boy.[17]

Despite such racist depictions, a large portion of the black and white press portrayed Louis as the complete fighter, a smart and accomplished boxer as well as the stereotypical natural killer. This moved Louis beyond traditional categories for American fighters. As Gerald Early asserts, white boxers assumed the republican image of the honest hard worker, while black fighters were considered slick tricksters, good at defense and speed. Jill Dupont points out that Louis could box well, and he took on the image of an honest hard-working hick from the West. As a hybrid hero he challenged representations of black boxers as bodies without minds. To be a good boxer one had to train hard, to study one's craft in a serious way. For every derogatory image of Louis in the white press, there emerged a portrait of him as a black producer hero, a figure of common decency and fair play. In addition, his fluid fighting style uplifted a brutal sport to the level of art. He was poetry in motion. Observers also noted Louis was black, white, and Cherokee, and though considered a Negro, the light-skinned boxer was seen as all-American. Raising questions about racial definitions, Louis's silent, stony face, disturbing to many whites, made it clear that he was absolutely calm in the ring as he laid claim to a key element of democratic citizenship and equality—self-sufficiency. His modest, hard-working image allowed many white men to identify with him inside the ring. Louis could express their fury toward a corrupt civilization that had no use for their manhood.[18]

To offset white fears and break the color line, Louis's all-black managerial team, two clever numbers' bankers from Detroit and Chicago, carefully crafted a public mask for him. In contrast to Johnson, they formed Louis's

Figure 13.1. The Joe Louis Brain Trust—poker-faced Louis and his African American advisers. From left to right, Julian Black, Jack Blackburn, Louis, John Roxborough, and Russell Cowans. Associated Press/Library of Congress.

image as a clean-cut, abstemious, religious, and serious young man who would not offend white sensibilities outside the ring. Aware of white fears of miscegenation, his managers advised him against being photographed with white women or attending nightclubs alone. Married at twenty-one to a respectable black girl, Louis removed any hint of interracial sexual danger. Though in truth he had a large sexual appetite and spent money profligately, unlike Johnson, he was discreet. His clean-living image fit his upbringing. Reared a strict Baptist, he did not play cards, drink, or date until he was sixteen, and he abjured alcohol and cigarettes his entire career. A quiet child, Louis suffered from a speech impediment, and as a boy he stammered. The public may have thought him slow, noted his son, but he "was quick, with a dry sense of humor." However, the disability made him uneasy with strangers, especially white newsmen, and he earned a reputation for sullenness or seriousness, depending on who did the reporting. A reporter noted, "Joe Louis Never Smiles." The ring adage, "I'll let my fists do the talking," carried more weight in his case. Inside the ring, he was not to speak ill of his opponents or gloat over fallen foes. As a former amateur champ, he had little interest in mocking opponents. But his managers were not interested in creating an obsequious black man. They urged him never to act or look like a "nigger doll, a fool," but instead "like a black man with dignity," and they schooled him in proper dress and deportment.[19]

Despite white fears and condescension, Louis transformed himself into a New Deal–era working-class hero, the first black athlete to take on Galahad status. His managers knew he had to be twice as good as any white heavyweight to contend for the title, and they had him fight at least twice a month, take on all-comers, and advance within the rules of the ring. In this, Louis adopted the hallmark of American sports—one advanced by following the democratic rules of fair play. This led to admiration by even disparaging writers for his fighting ability and moral character: "As far as I am concerned," declared Davis Walsh, "it seems possible that he's the greatest fighter that ever lived." Many whites supported Louis, noted the *Chicago Defender*, and calls for drawing the color line were muted. Ring experts, the paper found, "don't speak of Joe in the same breath with Jack Johnson" and instead emphasize his gentlemanly character "to keep him from running into the race hatred and prejudice that had engulfed the bulk of Race battlers." White sportswriter Richards Vidmer argued that character was key. "Louis was as different from Johnson as Lou Gehrig is from Al Capone." He was "an ambassador of his race," taught by his managers that "the world will judge his brothers through him, and he conducts himself with immaculate care." Given boxing's sordid state, "the rise of Louis seems to possess an aura of romance that is hard to believe," noted white columnist George Clarens. "It may sound soft and sentimental . . . to talk about idealism in professional boxing," he argued, but Louis "intends to be a credit to his race and to his new profession." White columnist Jonathon Mitchell noted that his character, punching ability, and drawing power might force Madison Square Garden to "yield to a clamor for a 'mixed' fight."[20]

While the Germans banned non-Aryans from sport in the 1930s, in the United States the Depression encouraged legions of poor black and ethnic working-class youth to enter boxing for economic gain and as an outlet for aggression. Among these was Louis, whom blacks saw as the embodiment of their experience and aspirations. He had taken to amateur boxing as an identity otherwise denied him. Considered mentally slow and physically clumsy, Louis turned fast and powerful once he donned gloves. "It was love at first sight. . . . It was like power pumping through me. Maybe it's like people getting religion." Boxing appealed "because there was something professional about it" that required skill and hard work. It "was the first time I knew what I really wanted to be. At last there would be something where I could be an individual." The Depression wounded Louis's family, which had been part of the Great Migration from southern sharecropping to Detroit's industrial work. In the late 1920s his family went on relief, and Louis supplanted his stepfather as breadwinner with earnings from amateur bouts. In the Depression, fighting for what one got seemed a realistic metaphor for daily life. Louis earned merchandise checks to feed his family, and after his first big professional win he proudly repaid the family's relief debt and assumed their support. Perhaps he took this male role from his beloved Westerns. "I guess I wanted to be the big, strong, good guy and help those poor defenseless folks who needed it."[21]

By 1935, Louis led the rescue of professional boxing. As a black columnist noted, "Fistiana's new superman, Joe Louis, stands out in bold relief in the . . . gratifying sports renaissance of 1935." His nontitle bouts with Carnera and Baer earned more than had any recent title bouts. "Louis came as a modern Moses to lead the manly art out of the depths of the depression to a new 'high.'" Not only did he bring "a new era of interracial goodwill," he also brought "boxing back on a big time basis and the million-dollar gate." As *Daily Worker* sports editor Lester Rodney noted, Negro fighters Louis, Henry Armstrong, and John Henry Lewis "have roused the fans from their apathy, compelled real admiration for their talents and courage," and "restored the meaning of the word champion and pulled a dying sport to its feet." That black fighters carried the popularity and integrity of boxing on their shoulders suggests major changes afoot in American life.[22]

For all his good qualities, however, Louis would not have had a title shot had not the Depression dramatically weakened boxing. With the box office in ruins, Louis's drawing power proved essential to the sport's survival and forced the issue of the color line. Because his punching power attracted large gates, "there doesn't seem to be any wariness or regret on the part of white folks to see a colored boy moving up." With a mediocre white heavyweight crop, a million-dollar match was possible only if white champion James Braddock fought a black man. Another factor was the movement of black managers and Jewish promoters from the margins to the center of boxing in the 1930s. "Never in the history of the fight racket," noted black columnist Roi Ottley, "has a Negro piloted a Negro into such a prominent position." Louis's managers had the independent income that allowed them to compete with white managers and avoid having Louis "lose a few" to get ahead. The *Saturday Evening Post* praised their idealism: "Broadway is the kingdom of smart money," but Louis's managers "have shown astounding lack of interest in the angles."[23]

Challenges to Madison Square Garden's monopoly also helped break the color line. This challenge came from another outsider, Jewish ticket scalper Mike Jacobs, who had helped promote Garden events during the 1920s. When the Depression hurt revenues, management fired him and raised the rent on the Hearst Charity Milk Fund, sponsor of their most lucrative boxing event. Jacobs then outbid the Garden for the charity and signed the biggest attraction. Unlike the Garden's management, Jacobs had no "prejudice about a man's color so long as he could earn a green buck for him," and he told Louis he would be the first black heavyweight "without the shackles of double-dealing and racial mix-ups." Jacobs soon had Louis fighting in Yankee Stadium with the Hearst press and powerful boxing interests behind them. The two men led boxing's revival, noted one observer, "the Jewish boy who learned how to sell tickets to people, and the Negro boy born in an Alabama cabin." With press revenues down in the Depression, the Hearst chain and even southern newspapers proved willing to feature a black heavyweight capable of restoring readership and overall profits.[24]

As the first black heavyweight to contend for the title since Johnson, Louis galvanized black pride and placed the race issue squarely at the center of sports. Even before he met Schmeling, his fights carried political content. In this he exemplified "hidden scripts" that the weak used to challenge power amid the overt script of accommodation to white authority. For blacks, the Louis script was very much in the open. Boxing was an arena in which blacks could express their challenge to the racial hierarchy on a mass scale, and when Louis fought they not only followed him on radio, they flocked to stadiums in unprecedented numbers. Despite Louis's overt humility, from his first big New York bout against Carnera in spring 1935, his fights took on political overtones. Billed as David vs. Goliath, the fight occurred as fascist Italy planned to attack Ethiopia, and black Americans had begun organizing in opposition. "Louis's comparatively small frame," noted an observer, helped. Fans "always take to the smaller man against the bigger one." The press made the bout an international event. "The first battle of the next war was fought in New York City Tuesday night," declared Will Rogers, an antifascist and promoter of a pluralistic America. "Big Italy met Little Abyssinia, and Mussolini's spring drive was halted in its tracks." Further, "General Joe Louis, head of the Ethiopian forces, met Il Duce Carnera . . . and treated him like a Christian of gladiatorial days."[25]

By knocking out white opponents on a wholesale basis, Louis became a superhero who served as a model of powerful masculinity for the black masses. His migration from Alabama to Detroit, Chicago, and Harlem mirrored the black experience and strengthened communal identification. The black press's sports pages rang with pride over black athletic feats, but no one surpassed Louis in coverage. In 1935, the *Pittsburgh Courier* assigned special reporters to follow Louis's every move to satisfy the black public's interest. Black fans named babies for him and wrote poems and songs about him. One poem portrayed Louis as a modern hero:

Louis can't be compared with men of old
He's not to be classed that way. He'll fight six men and whip all of
    them
For he's trucking in a great big way.

Irene Thompson's poem, "Fistic Idol," came with a letter: "I worship Joe Louis more than Father Divine's Followers Worship Him." Black fans also bought souvenir ashtrays labeled "An Investment in Self-Respect." From 1935 to 1936, Louis's managers spent $25,000 "to keep faith with his admiring public" by hiring secretaries to answer requests for autographed photos.[26]

As someone who faced the same obstacles imposed by the white world, Louis became a hero to black entertainers and musicians who also served as symbols of pride. As Dizzy Gillespie noted, "To be a 'hero' in the black community, all you have to do is make the white folks look up to you and recognize the fact that you've contributed something worthwhile." When Louis knocked out an opponent, Dizzy "felt like I'd scored a knockout. Just because he's black like me." Solidly in his corner, black musicians poured the black community's feelings for Louis into music. No other athlete has inspired the same number of songs as those recorded in Louis's honor. In 1935 Memphis Minnie recorded "He's in the Ring (Doin' the Same Old Thing)," and that summer, Carl Martin recorded "Joe Louis Blues" just before the Baer fight. After Louis became champion, the number of songs multiplied, climaxing in Count Basie, Paul Robeson, and Richard Wright's "King Joe," which came out in 1941.[27]

Louis's victories produced great celebrations of collective race victory as communities took to the streets in a carnival mood to overturn the boundaries of ordinary life. These spontaneous celebrations engendered analysis by intellectuals eager to plumb their meaning. Richard Wright described blacks pouring into ghetto streets after Louis beat Baer. Yelling his name, they formed long, snaking lines and "wove in and out of traffic." It seemed like "a revival. . . . It was a feeling of unity, of oneness." Watching this break in the normal world, Wright saw a racial awakening as blacks recalled "four centuries of oppression, of frustrated hopes, of black bitterness." They "imputed to the brawny image of Joe Louis, all the balked dreams of revenge, all the secretly visualized moments of retaliation, AND HE HAD WON!" As Wright saw it, "Joe was the consciously-felt symbol. Joe was the concentrated essence of black triumph over white." Blacks now felt free. "Invincible! A merciless victor over a fallen foe!" This "pent-up folk consciousness" that "beats and suffers and hopes—for freedom. . . . Here's the real dynamite that Joe Louis uncovered!"[28]

In June 1936 Louis and Schmeling met to decide the next opponent for heavyweight champion James Braddock. Schmeling was Germany's standard-bearer, but Hitler was dismayed that he "wanted to wager the German name against a Negro, against whom there was apparently no chance." *Box-Sport* worried about a loss to "not even a pure Negro, but some kind of *mixed breed* between black and white," an example of America's miscegenation nightmare and Germany's fear. Fearing a Negro victory and negative publicity before the Olympics, Goebbels warned the German press to ignore the race angle. The *Volkischer Beobachter* ignored this advice, claiming that white Americans supported Schmeling as "the representative of the white race" in hopes he would halt "the unusual rise of the Negro." The paper argued that "our patriotic ambitions" were at stake, and predicted victory since Max's strength "sprang from German character" and its "special racial feeling." The regime preferred that Schmeling fight a white opponent in Germany, without his Jewish manager, but he held fast.[29]

A 10 to 1 underdog, Schmeling shocked the boxing world with a dramatic victory and cemented his place as a German national hero. Convinced that Louis was vulnerable to a right hand, Schmeling saw his opening in the fourth round and knocked him down. By the twelfth round, Schmeling had battered the tired and outgunned Louis into submission. According to James T. Farrell in the *Nation*, "a long and lusty roar acclaimed the end of one superman and the elevation of another superman to supplant him in the sports columns." Having accomplished the impossible, Schmeling became the darling of German fans and the regime. Hitler congratulated him on a "wonderful victory . . . of our greatest German boxer," while Goebbels crowed, "Your victory is a German victory." Germans now could acknowledge the victory as racial. As Goebbels told his diary, Schmeling has "fought for Germany and won. The White over the Black, and the White was a German." The *Hamburger Anzeiger* added that Schmeling's victory made him "for Americans, the savior of white boxing supremacy." Similarly, George Spandau claimed victory in a worldwide racial struggle. Had Louis won, colored peoples everywhere would have revolted. But, having checked "the arrogance of the Negro," Schmeling had restored "the prestige of the white race" and the "superiority of white intelligence."[30]

Schmeling's return home was triumphant. He flew across the Atlantic in the Hindenburg zeppelin to Frankfurt where, like an ancient German god, he descended from the skies to a huge reception. The zeppelin, a marvel of Nazi mechanical genius, was crowned by athletic success to showcase the strength of German society. After party officials hailed his triumph, he and his family flew on Goebbel's special plane to Berlin, where legions of officials greeted them. At a three-hour reception in the Chancellery, pictures of which graced newspapers and newsreels, Hitler declared, "Every German has reason to be proud." He and party officials saw the victory's propaganda value. German sports announcer Arno Hellmis noted, "Only one who is familiar with crowd psychology knows what kind of great, vital publicity Max Schmeling provides." Now his name "is spoken here exclusively in connection with his *homeland*."[31]

Eager to build on Schmeling's success, Goebbels transformed an individual victory into a national triumph by expanding the fight film and releasing it commercially to enthusiastic audiences. "Max Schmeling's Victory—a German Victory" displayed the nationalistic fervor of that Olympic summer. It also heralded a race triumph. "Telegrams poured in from Australia, South Africa, South America and the American south," the film's narrator, Hellmis, proclaims, "where the loss of a white man to a black man could be accepted only with clenched teeth, but the win caused great jubilation." No expert had believed Schmeling could beat a Louis who had youth and his race's "natural boxing talent." But Schmeling possessed iron discipline and willpower and intelligence no black boxer could match. Just before the filmic account of the bout starts, Hellmis says, "you will see a will as hard as Krupp steel that will accomplish everything." The film depicts Louis as brave but no match for the German's superior courage, strategy, and will. Special inserts in the film stressed the humiliation that "Unser Max" had faced in America. Using American cartoons, Hellmis showed how America "laughed at him, degraded him." One depicted Schmeling as mere cannon fodder, while in another, experts pointed to the bloody German lying on the

Figure 13.2. Max Schmeling comes back and becomes a German national hero and symbol of the Nazi regime. After his victory over Steve Hamas on March 10, 1935, in Hamburg, the arena erupted into a Nazi rally. At far right Joe Jacob, Max's Jewish manager, created a stir when the Nazis saw him saluting with a cigar in hand. Associated Press/Library of Congress.

mat. But the film shows him standing up to the insults to German manliness and national pride. "Against this humiliating treatment at the hands of millions, Max stood in the ring alone. He did not lose heart, he believed in his ability and his strength." After the knockout, degradation turns to respect. "This German had done what no one thought possible!"[32]

German fans saw this success as part of the rescue of German pride and the triumph of a master race. Indeed Schmeling's victory came shortly after the reoccupation of the Rhine, which expunged the memory of sexual and national violation by black French colonial troops. Both Hitler and Schmeling overcame the odds and the shame of national humiliation. In this climate, many Germans saw Louis as an instinctual fighter who lacked Schmeling's intelligence. Hans Massaquoi, an Afro-German boy, recalled his teacher's words: "Max Schmeling has demonstrated in the most convincing way that a Negro's brute strength is no match for an Aryan boxer with superior intelligence. His victory was a great victory not only for Germany but for Aryan people throughout the world." The teacher added that blacks might win some Olympic events, but they were not athletes, just "born runners and jumpers—like horses and other animals." For a German to lose to a "half-civilized people," he said, "is no more disgrace than losing to a horse. Everybody knows a horse is physically superior but mentally inferior to a man. The same is true for Hottentots from America."[33]

Although relatively dark skinned, Schmeling was the closest thing to a super athlete the Nazis had. He assumed the role of the Siegfried Hero, one of the oldest myths in German culture, the pure German hero beset by unscrupulous enemies. He became the perfect Aryan man who embodied the strength, will power, and intelligence of the resurrected nation, a man capable of destroying the racially mixed sign of pollution in the body politic. In a culture that equated money and professionalism with Jews, Schmeling, the consummate professional, was reinterpreted as fighting not for prize money but for a noble sportsman's purpose—the comeback. Now that he had triumphed, Schmeling would do what no one else had, recapture the crown and regain the world's respect.[34]

In contrast, Louis's defeat knocked him off the white press's pedestal. Initially, many white sportswriters sounded themes reminiscent of the German analysis: Louis was a naïve "boy," lacking Schmeling's intelligence and skill. Sportswriter Grantland Rice argued that "the near superman of many fights suddenly turned into a duffer . . . his elemental, jungle cunning was no match for a much superior intelligence." A *Chicago Defender* survey of southern papers found that the defeat "has been a signal for a new outburst of enthusiasm so long smoldering in their hearts." Letters to the editor used all sorts of abuse:" "nigger," "darkie," "coon," and "Sambo." Southern Congressmen, meanwhile, stopped deliberations to cheer the German's triumph. Many white northerners agreed: Louis lacked the intelligence to change his tactics. Yet he still had support among many white northerners who acknowledged the loss but saw it as a sign of an overconfident young man who had not trained well. By withstanding a hammering for twelve rounds, he disproved the adage that a Negro could not take it and hence lacked courage. Especially impressive was his refusal to alibi. "I just got beat," he said. Many predicted that he would come back even stronger. For these writers, Louis's modesty, hard work, and seriousness would carry the day. His failure, to them, came to be every man's failure—a common fate in the Depression. And as he went on to knock out other opponents, he made new fans. Here was a Depression symbol that would not quit.[35]

Louis's loss shocked the black community. Maya Angelou described what it meant whenever he was hurt: "It was our people failing. It was another lynching, yet another Black man hanging on a tree." Singer Lena Horne expressed the feelings of millions who saw their superman destroyed. On the road with Noble Sissle's Orchestra, she was hysterical at the news. Joe "was the one invincible Negro, the one who stood up to the white man and beat him down with his fists. He in a sense carried so many of our hopes, maybe even dreams of vengeance." As African Americans absorbed the defeat, rumors circulated of doping and of an affair by Louis's wife that had unnerved him. This passed quickly. Louis declared that he had been beaten fairly. Moreover, for the first time he knew what he meant as a symbol to black people. "I let myself down, I let a whole race of people down." In an experience common to Depression heroes, his failure spurred him to identify more deeply with the fate of the group—in this case the black community. "I was the only hero they had then, and heroes aren't supposed to lose." Shamed by his defeat, he vowed to come back and win the crown. Blacks forgave quickly, for Louis had experienced the humiliation and defeat that they knew every day, but he was not vanquished by it. As Louis Armstrong wrote to the *Courier*, "Joe Louis is not through." With him when he won, "we should rally around *our* Joe and encourage him in defeat."[36]

Politics and economics also facilitated Louis's comeback. The German propaganda effort turned many Americans against Schmeling. Determined to mobilize a broad antifascist coalition against a blatantly racist state, black and white leftists, many of them Jews, shifted their view of sport as a manifestation of bourgeois capitalism to one of democracy and pluralism. Richard Wright, Frank M. Davis, and the *Daily Worker*'s Lester Rodney saw Louis as a democratic hero battling worldwide fascism and Jim Crow. The Anti-Nazi League's boycott of the Louis-Schmeling bout helped cut attendance in half, and they nearly succeeded in persuading Americans to boycott the 1936 Olympics. Now the Anti-Nazi League vowed to stop a title fight between Schmeling and Braddock in 1937. Fearful that a Schmeling fight would be unprofitable, Braddock chose Louis as the only opponent who could draw a million-dollar gate. In response, the German public invested the mythic view of Schmeling with renewed meaning. Contract for a title fight with Braddock in hand, Schmeling traveled to New York for the fight in June 1937, but Braddock fought Louis instead. Insulted by this trickery, Germans charged that a Jewish cabal conspired to deny Schmeling his title and Germany its respect. To be sure, Jews were involved, but it was the threat of an antifascist boycott led by leftist and religious Jewish groups, that convinced Braddock's manager that the gate would suffer if the champ fought Schmeling in "Jewish" New York. Braddock met Louis instead, Louis won the title and broke the color line, and Schmeling was left out. Germans saw it as a Jewish conspiracy and a lust for money that had sidelined their hero bent on a noble quest and installed a "Neger" as champion.[37]

With Louis as champion, the Louis-Schmeling rematch in June 1938 brought the competing aspirations of Americans and Germans to a head and transformed Louis from a black hero into an American idol. Each combatant stood as an idealistic symbol, Siegfried and Galahad, fighting for national honor. Rising international tension since the last bout intensified interest and fed a growing sense that American nationalism was at stake. With his party firmly in power and opposition suppressed, Hitler no longer felt compelled to placate world opinion. Secure at home, he remilitarized Germany and made aggressive territorial demands on his neighbors. In March 1938 German troops annexed Austria, while Hitler continued to foment strife in Czechoslovakia. These moves fed American fears about Germany's intentions toward the rest of the world. At the same time, the regime was free to implement more ruthlessly its attack on German Jews. The rising sense of the German threat heightened concerns about the Nuremburg Laws and Nazi anti-Catholicism. Adding to the furor, just days before the bout, eighteen Americans were indicted as Nazi spies.[38]

As international tensions mounted, the bout moved from the terrain of race to the level of nationalism. As one New York sportswriter noted, publicists did not need the race angle to boost attendance: "here's a hate motif ready made." Those who saw Schmeling as "a political symbol will be desperately hopeful for his downfall." Louis also saw international events elevate him from race to national hero. "The whole world was looking to this fight. . . . Germany was tearing up Europe, and we were hearing . . . about the concentration camps for the Jews. A lot of Americans had family in Europe and they were afraid for their people's lives. Schmeling represented everything that Americans disliked and they wanted him beat and beat good." In response to the boycott threat, promoter Mike Jacobs promised to donate some of the gate to refugees and pledged Louis would avenge European Jewry. American Jews were now firmly in Louis's camp, but other white support surprised him. "White Americans—even while some of them were lynching black people in the South—were depending on me to K.O. Germany." President Roosevelt stoked the national fervor. He invited Louis to the White House and declared, "Joe, we're depending on those muscles for America." Louis was thrilled. "Now, even more, I knew I had to get Schmel-

LOOKING BACKWARD OR DO YOU REMEMBER THIS PICTURE OF JUNE THE 22ND 1938. IT IS MAX SCHMELING THE GERMAN HEAVY-WEIGHT ABOUT TO GET THE FINISHING BLOW FROM JOE LOUIS.

Kamerad!

WHAT A PITY IT WASN'T HITLER.

Figure 13.3. "The Wrong Man," cartoon, June 22, 1938. This cartoon was reprinted on the same date in 1939 with more explicit attention to the political and international implications of the bout between Joe Louis and Max Schmeling. As a result of his victory, Louis became a national hero, the first time an African American male enjoyed such widespread popularity. Boxing and nationalism merged in new ways. Library of Congress.

ing good. I had my own personal reasons, and the whole damned country was depending on me."[39]

Having been cheered by large segments of the American public in 1936, Schmeling was shocked by the shift in American opinion. Protesters met his ship with signs calling him an "Aryan Show Horse" and a symbol of a "Master Race" and urging boxing fans to "BOYCOTT NAZI SCHMELING!" Because of Hitler, "no one wanted to see me win the title." He tried to explain he was no Nazi, but New York City had turned hostile. In 1936 reporters had asked whether he was afraid of Louis, now they inquired about Nazi race policies. Schmeling's rhetoric hurt, too. According to the *Courier*, the "Nazi" boxer declared that "the black dynasty of pugilism must come to an end." Having beaten Louis, he argued that he had "a strong psychological superiority over the Negro" and had instilled strong fear in "a man of Joe's race." Louis sneered, "I only hope Schmeling will have plenty of that psychology around to use for salve when I knock him on his pants." Columnist Westbrook Pegler, who had warned against mixed-race matches in 1935, now supported a boycott because the German was cast "in the role of Nazi hero" and the Nazi idea was the "sworn enemy" of "Americanism." The Nazis practiced virulent racism and "are sworn to destroy American ideals." The *Beckley (W.Va.) Post-Herald* held that Hitler's treatment of Jews, and his aggressive threats, forced the newspaper and presumably some white readers to "choose Joe Louis, an American Negro." Weeks of tension hit Schmeling in the dressing room. He felt nervous alone. Walking to the ring, "all hell broke loose." It "was like walking a gauntlet. . . . I was . . . hit by cigarette butts, banana peels, and paper cups."[40]

Standing at the center of a global spectacle, Louis accepted his role as a national hero. In a ghost-written article, he declared that he fought not only for revenge, but, "I fight for America against the challenge of a foreign invader, Max Schmeling. This isn't just one man against another or Joe Louis boxing Max Schmeling; it is the good ole U.S.A. versus Germany." As the two combatants awaited the bell, the crowd stood for the "Star Spangled Banner," in contrast to 1910, when "All Coons Look Alike to Me" greeted Jack Johnson. Heightening the sense of nationalism, American flags were everywhere, but no swastikas were in sight. The fight was as much about nationalism as it was about race. Germans solidly backed Schmeling, their real champion against the so-called champ, but the results proved devastating to their hopes and to Schmeling's career. "From the bell, the Negro went out swinging wildly. Schmeling evaded the first hard left hook, but it took only a few seconds and the German was down." After he rose, Louis drove him to the ropes, and hit him with two hard body shots. "I was paralyzed from that point on," Schmeling said later. The action in the ring electrified the crowd. The crowd was on its feet yelling, "Kill the Nazi," as Louis battered his helpless foe for two minutes and four seconds, the shortest heavyweight title match in history. "Contrary to all Nazi racial laws," noted Richard Wright, the black boxer punched the white one "so rapidly that the eye could not follow the blows. His blows must have jarred the marrow not only in the white puppet's but in Hitler's own bones." Blacks took to the streets chanting, "Ain't you glad?" Badly hurt, Schmeling went to the hospital, while Louis, his title confirmed, established "himself as the hardest hitter and greatest heavyweight that ever pulled on a glove."[41]

In response to Schmeling's destruction by a member of an "inferior" race, Germans railed against a conspiracy. Schmeling was an Aryan sports paragon, according to *Der Angriff*, "a perfect example of athletic ambition and inner strength of character," who was beaten unfairly by "the wild drumfire of the Negro, whipped up by the white American." Ex-champ Gene Tunney was "a spy in service for Joe Louis," who urged his wild attack. Moreover, Germans charged, American boxing officials had conspired to delay the rematch while Schmeling aged. "Americans did not want a German champion," and they had used their Negro to steal the title from Germany. As one newspaper declared, "The German had prepared conscientiously for the fight against the Jewish intrigue of the American businessmen," but the cabal allowed "unser Max" to be fouled by kidney blows. Incensed, Nazi officials refused to show films of the devastating defeat in Germany. As Schmeling lay in the hospital, reports that he claimed a foul fueled the flames, but he refused to lodge an official protest. As a result, "after this defeat," Schmeling claimed, "I no longer existed for Hitler and Goebbels . . . my name simply disappeared from the newspapers." More accurately, Goebbels relegated his name to the sports page.[42]

Conversely, Louis's victory became one of the greatest symbolic triumphs in boxing history. African Americans, for example, saw Schmeling and his boasts of mental superiority as the embodiment of the white hope. His defeat proved sweet revenge against racism. Black reporter Frank M. Davis saw the symbolism: "Would the German, exponent of Aryan supremacy win," he wondered? Afterward, "shouts of joy rang to the stars," as blacks took to the streets. "It was as if each had been in that ring himself," as if all of them "had dealt destruction with his fists upon the Nordic face of Schmeling and the whole Nazi system he symbolized." Louis's victory beat the color line in boxing but also made "the struggle against it in politics, in economics, and on the cultural field, and in other spheres of the sporting world easier." Wright saw the mass celebration as "the largest and most spontaneous political demonstration ever seen in Harlem." Overjoyed that Louis "wiped out the stain of defeat," blacks "threw off restraint and fear," and defied police and property laws with "an impulse which only the oppressed can feel. The earth was theirs as much as anybody else's." By defeating the German Louis had also proved himself an American hero. "Joe Louis, son of America, son of Alabama, Black American and fighting champion," declared *Pittsburgh Courier* columnist William G. Nunn, "WE SALUTE YOU!"[43]

Louis's victory confirmed him as the "giant killer," who did what blacks wanted to do—smash white faces as symbols of the power that controlled their lives. Within the rules, Lawrence Levine argues, Louis proved his masculinity and the community's potential power. Among blacks, public awareness of their power was coalescing on a mass scale even before World War II. In all the communal celebrations there were signs announcing "a victory for democracy." It was hard even for whites to miss. In Baltimore, Russell Baker witnessed blacks writing a new script after Louis's triumph. Black residents, "seized by an instinct to defy destiny," streamed out of their homes into white neighborhoods. "Joe Louis has given them the courage to assert their right to use a public thoroughfare. . . . It was the first civil rights demonstration I ever saw, and it was completely spontaneous, ignited by the finality with which Joe Louis had destroyed the theory of white supremacy." As blacks rejoiced in his victories, they participated in dethroning notions of white physical superiority, white authority, and their own subservient condition. They were black Americans entitled to their full rights. Globally, Louis's victory delighted "colored" peoples, who saw him as a race hero against colonial oppression. South Africa's *Bantu World* celebrated Louis's destruction of the Aryan symbol, while Marcus Garvey noted that Louis had accepted the "responsibility our race has placed upon his shoulders," to triumph "in the great wilderness of prejudice." As an athlete, he was "our international leader."[44]

The white southern press also depicted the battle between a white German and a black American as a symbolic confrontation between Nazi Germany and the United States. The 1936 Olympics and Nazi aggression had much to do with the change. After Louis's victory, the southern press attacked the Nazi leadership. The *Birmingham Age-Herald* hoped that "this defeat of Schmeling will stir a little fear into the heart of German officialdom. If so, the world will be a bit happier for what a brown-skinned Alabama boy did." Despite this overall view, however, white southern reporters still portrayed Louis as a "colored boy," thus putting him firmly in his place. Even so, southern papers were often more moderate than many of their readers. Jimmy Carter recalled an incident in Plains, Georgia, that revealed his father's discomfort with black victory. Mr. Earl invited his tenants to listen to the fight on the radio by propping it in an open window so the family could listen inside, while the blacks remained outside. "My father was deeply disappointed in the outcome," Carter noted, and turned off the radio immediately after the match. Similarly, blacks in Stamps, Arkansas, knew that it was not safe to walk outside on nights when Louis won. On the other hand, Louis's posture and decorum, his public mask of staying within the rules of "his place" outside the ring, earned him some respect even in the South. Many northerners were also ambivalent, but they recognized something had changed. General Hugh Johnson, former NRA chief, noted Louis's victory disproved "this nonsense about Aryan physical supremacy," but he continued to believe that blacks were stronger than whites because they were closer to the jungle. Still, Johnson declared, "It is nothing for us to weep about and seek white hopes. . . . These black boys are Americans."[45]

The victory not only heightened American nationalism, it challenged an American national identity rooted in race. In an international conflict between fascism and democracy, white Americans were forced to choose between what historian Gary Gerstle calls racial and civic nationalism.

Rooting against the African American representative aligned one with the Nazis. As white columnist Dan Parker put it, those Americans who rooted for Schmeling based on the color of his skin were "fine advertisements for the republican form of government." Given the issues surrounding the bout, Louis's victory opened up the question of white supremacy itself. *Ring* called Louis courageous in avenging his only defeat and claimed his victory meant the complete deflation of "claims to natural supremacy of any particular race or group." Even the *Louisville Courier Journal* said, "the ludicrous Nazi myth of racial superiority suffers a knockout at the fists of Joe Louis." Jack Dempsey, who had referred to Louis as an instinctual fighter, now admitted that he equaled the "the best heavyweights of modern times," and was "clever." The sports editor of the *Detroit Times*, Bud Shaver, was more positive. Louis, he said, "has white, Indian and Negro blood in him, and to me that is all good American blood." Recognizing race mixture as a national ideal, and aware that Louis was forced to wear a mask because of American racism, Shaver argued that Louis was "far more than a superbly competent fighter. He is a challenge to tolerance in an intolerant world."[46]

The ambivalent acceptance of Louis as an American hero was only a first step for whites on the long road to redefining American national identity. But the portrayal of Schmeling as a Nazi Aryan hope put a severe dent in the white hope idea in American boxing. Promoters still sought white opponents to boost the gate, but the urgency for racial revenge to defend national honor had lost its steam. *Ring* noted that few people now assumed that "fistic victory immediately establishes one race over another." In a revealing cartoon, *Boxing News* showed "The White Hope Trail," filled with white boxers bent on fighting Louis, who stands as a giant among pygmies. Referee Arthur Donovan heard "no cry of outraged racial pride. . . . Perhaps we're a trifle more civilized than when . . . we thought pictures of a Negro slapping a white man down were dangerous to the republic, and prohibited them." Louis's triumph and the legitimacy his career brought to the once-troubled sport also contributed to the end of the federal ban on prizefight films in 1939, reversing the law enacted in the "white hope" reaction to Jack Johnson. While some southern congressmen still worried about race riots, the majority of Americans no longer saw racial honor at stake in mixed-race bouts. Equally important, blacks and whites paid to watch Louis fight a black contender in 1939. By the late 1940s it was common to see Louis in the ring against other black fighters.[47]

White depictions of Louis also changed. William Wiggins Jr. found that before the second Schmeling bout, white cartoonists drew Louis as they had Johnson: a lazy sambo, with savage, apelike features, dark skin, and kinky hair, who spoke in dialect and loved chicken. After Louis won the title in 1937 and then proved himself an American hero against Schmeling, however, the white press treated him more humanely. This shift occurred in two stages. At first, cartoonists portrayed him more realistically but projected the sambo image onto his trainer or others. Eventually, however, white cartoonists simply abandoned sambo entirely. Prior to 1938, the *Brooklyn Daily Eagle*'s Ed Hughes depicted Louis as in minstrel caricature. After Louis whipped Schmeling, Hughes drew the champion as a handsome young man with a well-proportioned body. In the eyes of many white sports cartoonists, the Brown Bomber had demonstrated his patriotism and manhood by defeating the foreign foe. Sports stories, while still condescending, stopped using dialect and ceased constantly referring in a demeaning manner to his race. After 1938 and during World War II, Louis became a credit to his race—the human race.[48]

Although talk of a rematch surfaced, war intervened. Schmeling lost credibility in the United States when the press reported that he blamed a foul for his loss. During the conflict, he became the face of the enemy. Reporters depicted Schmeling, who was a German paratrooper, as a confirmed Nazi, a commandant of Auschwitz, and the only man Louis ever hated. His fate in Germany was worse. Now that he was of limited value to the regime, his cosmopolitanism worked against him. His loss to a Negro, his refusal to hold his fights in Germany, his relationships with his Jewish manager and friends, and his intervention on behalf of various Jews with Nazi officials led to official disapproval. Alone of all German athletes he was drafted into the paratroopers at the age of thirty-six and hurt himself badly jumping into Crete. Goebbels still used pictures of him in uniform to promote the war effort in newsreels at home and abroad. However, when Schmeling refused to follow Goebbels's plan and claim that the British had abused German prisoners of war on Crete and then professed his love for America in interviews with foreign journalists, Goebbels sought to try him for treason. Initially sympathetic to a regime that promised an end to street violence and a new era of German unity, Schmeling believed he could outlast the Nazis and work them to his benefit. However, he paid the price for his independence and for getting too close to the regime. Man of the 1920s, Nazi symbol, he had tried to walk a tightrope to pursue individual sporting goals and failed.[49]

By contrast, Louis's enlistment as an army private ensured his status as an American hero who sacrificed wealth and career to defend his country. He appeared in films (*This Is the Army* and *The Negro Soldier*) and on the radio, sold treasury bonds, and fought exhibition matches to bolster troop morale. For a nation facing possible defeat after Pearl Harbor, Louis's triumph over Schmeling after his initial defeat promised national victory. Indeed, the fight lived on as a metaphor for the international conflagration and American ideals. When he enlisted, the *Chicago Tribune* declared, "Joe has a date for a return engagement with Max Schmeling." Every form of propaganda replayed the fight. Louis, like the country, had faced defeat in the first bout, but came back to decisively triumph over his Aryan superman foe. Now he was sacrificing his own comfort and title for his country, thus linking race and nation in new ways. His great moment of sacrifice came when he risked his title for the Navy Service League just after Pearl Harbor and donated his purse to the families of sailors killed or wounded at Pearl Harbor. He then did the same for the Army Service League. Although some blacks criticized him for aiding a segregated navy, he and his promoter Mike Jacobs, a Negro and a Jew, received praise for their dedication to their country. The elevation of Louis to American hero emerged in the tributes, following the bout, at the annual Boxing Writers' Association Banquet. According to former New York City mayor James Walker, Louis's personal and fistic conduct "entitled [him] to the highest title known to the American people. You are an American gentleman. . . . You have made us all proud to be Americans. . . . You laid a rose on Abraham Lincoln's grave!" The National Boxing Association president added, "Joe Louis is symbolic of America. It is not the color of his skin that counts, but the red blood that courses through his veins." All during the war, Louis's words and actions elevated him to the status of patriotic hero. He was, as a poem in *Collier's* declared, "The Man Who Named the War," by declaring, "We Are on God's Side." The poem was read in a national broadcast aired on NBC.[50]

As the most prominent black American, Louis became the symbolic center of a war defined as a defense of ethnic and racial pluralism. As a black American, however, Louis was forced to serve in a segregated unit. As he and his black boxing troupe entertained white and black American GIs in nonsegregated settings, at his insistence, Louis stood at the apex of what the war meant. Was he "Citizen Barrow," serving his nation and entitled to his full American rights? Or was he just another black man who would have to accept secondary status? To win black support for the war, the treasury bonds campaign made Louis a symbol of black success. Without touching

Pvt. Joe Louis says_

"We're going to do our part
... and we'll win because
we're on God's side"

Figure 13.4. "Private Joe Louis says, . . . 'We're on God's side,'" framing the role of the United States in World War II. At the same time, Schmeling served the nation in similar ways. National Archives.

segregation, the campaign highlighted Louis as the first American to defeat a Nazi, and black civilians responded by buying huge numbers of bonds; black pilots named their planes the "Brown Bomber." While the government recognized black patriotism without promising much, to blacks the campaign signaled that they, like Louis, were Americans and would be repaid for enduring segregation during the war by victory over oppression at home afterward. In fact, Louis told the *Pittsburgh Courier* that he hoped "our boys will get their opportunity in the Navy equal with the other boys. . . . Those Jap bullets don't have any prejudice in 'em. This war should put an end to all this foolish discrimination."[51]

In the 1930s and early 1940s boxing stood at the center of international events. The war profoundly affected American culture and society, but the Louis-Schmeling bout suggests that the beginnings of a new civic nationalism of ethnic and racial pluralism started during the Depression in response to a growing fascist threat, coupled with social and cultural changes brought on by the Depression. Germans and Americans turned to heroic male ideals to overcome histories of defeat, humiliation, and economic chaos. These supermen helped spur national revivals, but they embodied competing national ideals: the clash between Aryan purity and a developing American ideology of ethnic and racial pluralism. International conflict placed national ideals into sharp relief. Germans could embrace Max Schmeling as a symbol of national manhood more easily than all Americans could embrace Joe Louis. Early on, black Americans saw "our Joe" as a hero who defeated white supremacy at home and abroad and fought for their status as full American citizens. By claiming that Germany's superior racial culture produced Schmeling's victory, the Nazis turned the Louis-Schmeling bout in 1938 into global theater. A black American champion of democracy against a fascist foe opened the door to the questioning of racial nationalism in the United States. Adopted by the Left and American Jews as an antifascist hero, Louis became a symbol of democracy, a hybrid hero and pluralist icon as the nation went to war. That international tensions played such an important role in transforming American culture should alert historians to the importance of transnationalism in American history. In fact, as the Cold War intensified, Schmeling went from pariah to hero among Germans and Americans. The need for allies against the USSR led to his resurrection as a Coca-Cola bottler, symbol of capitalism, and friend of the United States. When he returned to the United States in 1954 to reconcile with Louis and put the Nazi racist past to rest, old foes became new friends in a new international setting. Yet international influences did not only Coca-Colonize Germany, they had profound effects on the United States. The Olympics continued as a testing ground for competing nationalisms against the USSR, and the role of black athletes as symbols of democracy would force a continual rethinking of the segregation of sport in a democratic society locked in world combat against totalitarianism. In the person of Muhammad Ali, moreover, the Vietnam War abroad and the civil rights struggles at home once more propelled boxing into the international political arena.[52]

NOTES

1. C. L. R. James, *Beyond a Boundary* (New York: Pantheon, 1987), 192. McCarthy quoted in Chris Mead, *Champion Joe Louis: Hero in White America* (New York: Scribner, 1985), 148, leafleting, 146. "Joe Louis Bleibt Weltmeister," *Stuttgarter Neues Tageblatt*, June 23, 1938, 1. For the tremendous excitement the bout generated, see Nat Fleischer, "Fleischer Picks Louis to Top Schmeling," *Ring*, June 22, 1938, Joe Louis Scrapbooks (hereafter JLS), vol. 51. Alan Gould, "Ring Experts Dizzy Trying to Pick Bout," *New Orleans Picayune*, June 21, 1938, 17, noted that representatives of fif-

teen countries, including Japan, Australia, South Africa, Argentina, Brazil, Canada, Mexico, Cuba, and seven European nations applied for press passes.

2. Kristin Hoganson, "Cosmopolitan Domesticity: Importing the American Dream, 1865–1920," *American Historical Review* 107 (February 2002): 55–56, surveys the field; as does David Thelen, "The Nation and Beyond: Transnational Perspectives on United States History," *Journal of American History* 86 (December 1999): 965–75. For studies of globalization, see Heide Fehrenbach and Uta Poiger, eds., *Transactions, Transgressions, Transformations: American Culture in Western Europe and Japan* (New York: Berghahn Books, 2000); Richard Kuisel, *Seducing the French: The Dilemma of Americanization* (Berkeley: University of California Press, 1993); Richard Pells, *Not Like Us: How Europeans Have Loved, Hated, and Transformed American Culture Since World War II* (New York: Basic Books, 1997); Rob Kroes, *If You've Seen One, You've Seen the Mall: Europeans and Mass Culture* (Urbana: University of Illinois Press, 1996); Jessica Gienow-Hecht, "Shame on US? Academics, Cultural Transfer, and the Cold War: A Critical Review," *Diplomatic History* 24 (Summer 2000): 465–94. Eric Foner, "American Freedom in a Global Age," Presidential Address, *American Historical Review* 106 (February 2001): 4, 10–11. Ragnhild Fiebig-von Hase and Ursula Lehmkuhl, eds., *Enemy Images in American History* (Providence: Berghahn, 1997). Reinhold Wagnleitner and Elaine Tyler May, eds., *"Here, There and Everywhere": The Foreign Politics of American Popular Culture* (Hanover, N.H.: University Press of New England, 2000). Wagnleitner focuses on post–World War II influence of U.S. entertainment on Austria in *Coca-Colonization and the Cold War: The Cultural Mission of the United States in Austria after the Second World War* (Chapel Hill: University of North Carolina Press, 1994). For jazz, see S. Frederick Starr, *Red & Hot: The Fate of Jazz in the Soviet Union, 1917–1980* (New York: Oxford University Press, 1983); Michael H. Kater, *Different Drummers: Jazz in the Culture of Nazi Germany* (New York: Oxford University Press, 1992); E. Taylor Atkins, *Blue Nippon: Authenticating Jazz in Japan* (Durham: Duke University Press, 2001); Phyllis Rose, *Jazz Cleopatra: Josephine Baker in Her Time* (New York: Doubleday, 1991). Especially insightful is Berndt Ostendorf, "Subversive Reeducation? Jazz as a Liberating Force in Germany and Europe," in *Revue Francaise d'Etudes Americaines*, ed. Bernard Vincent, Hors Series: "'Play It Again Sim' . . . Hommages a Sim Copans" (December 2001): 54–72. See also Paul Gilroy, *The Black Atlantic: Modernity and Double Consciousness* (Cambridge: Harvard University Press, 1993). On the role of racial and civic nationalism, see Gary Gerstle, *American Crucible: Race and Nation in the Twentieth Century* (Princeton: Princeton University Press, 2001). For whiteness, see David R. Roediger, *The Wages of Whiteness: Race and the Making of the American Working Class* (London: Verso, 1991); and Roediger, *Towards the Abolition of Whiteness: Essays on Race, Politics, and Working Class History* (New York: Verso, 1994); Alexander Saxton, *The Rise and Fall of the White Republic: Class Politics and Mass Culture in Nineteenth-Century America* (New York: Verso, 1990); Matthew Frye Jacobson, *Whiteness of a Different Color: European Americans and the Alchemy of Race* (Cambridge: Harvard University Press, 1998).

For whiteness, masculinity, and nationalism in boxing, see Gail Bederman, *Manliness and Civilization: A Cultural History of Gender and Race in the United States, 1880-1917* (Chicago: University of Chicago Press, 1995); and Gregory S. Rodriguez, "'Palaces of Pain'—Arenas of Mexican-American Dreams: Boxing and the Foundation of Ethnic Mexican Identities in Twentieth-Century Los Angeles," (Ph.D. diss., University of California, San Diego, 1999).

3. On the failure to take sports seriously, see Elliott J. Gorn and Michael Oriard, "Taking Sports Seriously," in *Taking Sport Seriously, Social Issues in Canadian Sport*, ed. Peter Donnelly (Toronto: Thompson Educational Publishing, 1997), 22–25. For Heenan-Sayers, see Elliott J. Gorn, *The Manly Art: Bare-Knuckle Prize Fighting in America* (Ithaca: Cornell University Press, 1986), 148–60. Gregory S. Rodriguez, "'Palaces of Pain'" points out that Los Angeles served as an international center for Mexican and Filipino boxers from the 1920s. On the Olympics, see Richard Mandell, *The Nazi Olympics* (Urbana: University of Illinois Press, 1987).

4. Heywood Broun, "It Seems to Me," *New York World-Telegram*, June 24, 1938, JLS, vol. 56. Barbara Keys, "Dictatorship of Sport: Nationalism, Internationalism, and Mass Culture in the 1930s," (Ph.D. diss., Harvard University, 2001), sees rising nationalism pushing the internationalization of sport in the 1930s while marginalizing competing ideals of physical culture in the United States, Germany, and the USSR. For superheroes in the Depression, see Lawrence Levine, "American Culture and the Great Depression," in *Unpredictable Past* (New York: Oxford University Press, 1993), 227–28; Bradford W. Wright, *Comic Book Nation: The Transformation of Youth Culture in America* (Baltimore: Johns Hopkins University Press, 2001), 1–29. George Mosse, *Nationalism and Sexuality: Respectability and Abnormal Sexuality in Modern Europe* (New York: H. Fertig, 1985), 153–80, stresses the Nazi obsession with masculinity. On Schmeling's enduring athletic and cultural importance in Germany, see Hans Joachim Teichler, "Max Schmeling—Der Sportler des Jahrhunderts im Dritten Reich," *Sportzeit* (2001): 7–33; Siegfried Gehrmann, "Symbol of National Resurrection: Max Schmeling, German Sports Idol," *International Journal of the History of Sport* 13 (1996): 101–13; and Robert Weisbord and Norbert Hedderich, "Max Schmeling, Righteous Ring Warrior?" *History Today*, December 31, 1992, 36–41.

5. Declan Kibard, *Inventing Ireland* (Cambridge: Harvard University Press, 1996). Theophilus Lewis, "The Man We Want To Be," *Amsterdam News*, October 5, 1935, JLS, vol. 8. Lawrence Levine, *Black Culture and Black Consciousness* (New York: Oxford University Press, 1977), 420–40, analyzes Louis's heroic role in the black community. Rodriguez, "'Palaces of Pain,'" 18–24, is the source for my view that boxing offered black boxers a public forum for the performance of masculinity and group pride. See also Thomas R. Hietala, *The Fight of the Century: Jack Johnson, Joe Louis, and the Struggle for Racial Equality* (Armonk, N.Y.: M. E. Sharpe, 2002), 168–90.

6. For views of New Deal–era popular culture as conservative, see Warren Susman, "The Culture of the Thirties," and "Culture and Commitment," in his *Culture as*

History (New York: Pantheon, 1984), 150–210; Andrew Bergman, *We're in the Money* (New York: New York University Press, 1972); Richard Pells, *Radical Visions, American Dreams* (New York: Harper & Row, 1973); and Lawrence Levine, "American Culture and the Great Depression," and "Hollywood's Washington: Film Images of National Politics during the Great Depression," in his *Unpredictable Past*, 231–55. For popular entertainment in a more insurgent vein, see Lizabeth Cohen, *Making a New Deal* (Cambridge: Cambridge University Press, 1990); David Stowe, *Swing Changes* (Cambridge: Harvard University Press, 1994); Michael Denning, *The Cultural Front* (New York: Verso, 1996); Lary May, *The Big Tomorrow, Hollywood and the Politics of the American Way* (Chicago: University of Chicago Press, 2000); Robert Sklar, *City Boys* (Princeton: Princeton University Press 1992); Lawrence Levine, "The Folklore of Industrial Society: Popular Culture and Its Audiences," in *Unpredictable Past*, 291–319. For modern dance, see Julia Foulkes, *Modern Bodies: Dance and American Modernism from Martha Graham to Alvin Ailey* (Chapel Hill: University of North Carolina Press, 2002). My views are in *Swingin' the Dream: Big Band Jazz and the Re-birth of American Culture* (Chicago: University of Chicago Press, 1998). On the pre–World War II roots of an African American awakening, see John Higham, *Civil Rights and Social Wrongs* (University Park, Pa.: Pennsylvania State University Press, 1997); Patricia Sullivan, *Days of Hope: Race and Democracy in the New Deal Era* (Chapel Hill: University of North Carolina Press, 1996); Gena Caponi-Tabery, "Jump for Joy: The Jump Trope in African America, 1937–1941," *Prospects* 24 (1999): 521–74.

7. See "Almost a New Champion," *Boston Herald*, June 27, 1935, JLS, vol. 1, for "private depression." George Mosse, *Nazi Culture, Intellectual, Cultural and Social Life in the Third Reich* (New York: Grosset & Dunlap, 1966), posits a Nazi cultural revolution to transform German society and earn it respect in the eyes of the world.

8. See Max Schmeling, *An Autobiography*, trans. George B. Van Lippe (Chicago: Bonus Books, 1998), 3–7, 12–14, 17–37 on Berlin, 43–44 on New York, 80–90 for career low points. For boxing as part of avant-garde Weimar, see David Bathrick, "Max Schmeling on the Canvas: Boxing as an Icon of Weimar Culture," in *New German Critique* 51 (Fall 1990): 113–36. For boxing as a mass phenomenon, see Erik Jensen, "Crowd Control: Boxing Spectatorship and Social Order in Weimar Germany," in *Histories of Leisure*, ed. Rudy Koshar (New York: Berg, 2002), 79–101. For more on the history of German boxing, see Knud Kohr and Martin Krauss, *Kampftage. Die Geschichte des deutschen Berufsboxens* (Göttingen: Die Werkstadt, 2000); Sepp Scherbauer, *Die Grössen Boxsport Stars* (München, 1994); and Birk Meinhardt, *Boxen in Deutschland* (Hamburg: Rotbuch Verlag, 1996). For the sport's influence on the German language, see John Willett, *Art and Politics in the Weimar Period: The New Sobriety, 1917–1933* (New York: Pantheon, 1978), 102. See Schmeling, *An Autobiography*, 59–70 for his title win, 81–83 for the German reaction. For the foul, see "Schmeling . . . Weltmeister," *Vorwärts*, June 13, 1930. For "Schmeling humiliated," see Jonathon, "Zum Weltmeister geschlagen," *Vorwärts*, June 13, 1930. For his defense's record low attendance, "Schmeling Weltmeister," *Vorwärts*, July 4, 1931. For

the shocks to male strength and the shame over defeat in World War I unleashed in renewed force by the Depression, see Wolfgang Schivelbusch, *The Culture of Defeat: On National Trauma, Mourning, and Recovery,* trans. Jefferson Chase (New York: Metropolitan Books, 2003), 196–238. Peter Lowenberg, "The Psychohistorical Origins of the Nazi Youth Cohort," *American Historical Review* 76 (December 1971), reprinted as "The Appeal to Youth," in *The Nazi Revolution,* ed. by John L. Snell (Lexington, Mass.: Heath, 1973), 93–116, argues that the Depression awakened traumas in German youth of abandonment by fathers during the war and subjection to starvation. Richard Grundberger, *The 12-Year Reich, A Social History of Nazi Germany, 1933–1945* (New York: Holt, Rienhart, and Winston, 1971), 10, notes that the Depression reinforced underlying notions that German life was chaotic.

9. Demo, "Geht der Boxsport ein?" *Vorwärts,* June 16, 1931. For corruption in American boxing, see Mead, *Champion,* 45–46, H. G. Salsinger, "Joe Louis Favored," *Detroit News,* June 25, 1935, JLS, vol. 1; John Lardner, "Lardner on Sports," *Morning (Portland) Oregonian,* JLS, vol. 1; Jeffrey T. Sammons, *Beyond the Ring: The Role of Boxing in American Society* (Urbana: University of Illinois Press, 1990), 73–95. On Baer, see Jonathon Mitchell, "Joe Louis Never Smiles," *New Republic,* October 9, 1935, 239–40.

10. For Hitler's policies to restore strength to German culture and the economy, see John A. Garraty, "The New Deal, National Socialism, and the Great Depression," *American Historical Review* 78 (1973): 907–44; David Schoenbaum, *Hitler's Social Revolution* (New York: Doubleday, 1966); and Grunberger, *The 12-Year Reich,* 28–31. Schmeling's recollection of meeting with Hitler and Hitler's words are in Schmeling, *An Autobiography,* 81–95.

11. For Hitler's quotes, see Adolf Hitler, *Mein Kampf* trans. Ralph Mannheim (Boston, 1971), on boxing, 409–10. See Schmeling, *An Autobiography,* 102, for youth role models, 139 for sports as political validation. See Bruno Malitz, *Die Leibesübungen in der nationalsozialistichen Idee* (1934), 12, for health of the volk. For physical education, see Hajo Bernett, *Unterricht an der nationalsozialistiche Schule: Der Schulsport an den höhern Schulen Preussens 1933–1940* (Sankt Augustin, 1985); and Grundberger, *The 12-Year Reich,* 287–88. John Hoberman, *Sport and Political Ideology* (Austin: University of Texas Press, 1984), 94–95, 162–68, discusses the new fascist man. Leni Riefenstahl, *Leni Riefenstahl, A Memoir* (New York: St. Martin's, 1992), 179, 188, notes Hitler's lack of enthusiasm about the Olympics until Germans won medals the first day. Keys, "Dictatorship of Sport," 138–47, discusses the shift in Nazi thinking to include international sport as well as the older German Turner tradition of physical exercise.

12. The Nazis saw the strengthened male body as a counter to deviant "Jewish" sexuality, "colored peoples," Gypsies, and homosexuals, according to Mosse, *Nationalism and Sexuality,* 170–76. For race training, see Malitz, *Die Leibesübungen in der nationalsozialistichen Idee,* 12, 37, 45; and quotes in Ralf Müller, "Max Schmeling: Seine Rolle in nationalsozialistischen Deutschland" (thesis, Deutsche Sporthochschule, Köln, 1996), 41–43, 51–53. *Box-Sport* (hereafter *B-S*), April 4, 1933, 2,

printed the rules. The Nazis also banned Afro-Germans and Gypsies from boxing to reinforce racial hierarchy and eliminate degenerate racial influences on the male body. Sander Gilman, *The Jew's Body* (New York: Routledge, 1991), 38–59 and 169–93, discusses the perception of Jewish physical traits as distinctive and degenerative. For athletes affected by the rules, see Clarence Lusane, *Hitler's Black Victims: The Historical Experiences of Afro-Germans, European Blacks, Africans, and African Americans in the Nazi Era* (New York: Routledge, 2003), 217. Arnd Krüger, "Der Einfluss des faschistischen Sportmodels Italiens auf den nationalistichen Sport," in *Sport and Politik, 1918–1939/40: Proceedings, ICOSH Seminar*, ed. Megan Olsen (Otta, 1998), 226–32, notes that the Nazis abandoned democratically elected sports clubs for the Italian fascist model of hierarchically structured, party-run sports federations. For more on the organization of German sports under the Nazis, see Hajo Bernett, *Sportpolitik im Dritten Reich* (Stuttgart, 1971), 18–37.

13. "Schmeling Schlägt Neusel," *B-S*, August 20, 1934, 5, 8. For party activity, see Müller, "Max Schmeling," 68–69. Johnston quoted on Hamas bout in *B-S*, January 14, 1935, 3. *Der Angriff*, March 9, 1935, 14. For more on Nazis and sports festivals, see Moyra Byrne, "Nazi Festival: The 1936 Berlin Olympics," in *Time Out of Time: Essays on the Festival*, ed. Alessandro Falassi (Albuquerque: University of New Mexico Press, 1987), 107–21. For the idea of Germany replacing the United States as the center of boxing, see "Schmeling Weighs Offer for Louis Fight," *New York Times*, July 9, 1935, JLS, vol. 2. Keys, "The Dictatorship of Sport," 137 n. 22; and Meinhardt, *Boxen*, 93–4, discuss the Nazi currency and tax role in international matches.

14. Sammons, *Beyond the Ring*, 96–129, notes Louis's role in the economic renaissance of boxing.

15. Al Buck, "Buck Sees ex-Champ Win on His Ring Craft," *New York Post*, June 25, 1935, JLS, vol. 1, notes the concern over the black menace, although ironically. C. L. R. James, "Joe Louis and Jack Johnson," in *C. L. R. James on the "Negro Question,"* ed. Scott McLemee (Jackson: University Press of Mississippi, 1996), 60–61. Thanks to Jeffrey Kerr-Ritchie for the source. My thoughts on the color line in boxing have been influenced by Rodriguez, "'Palaces of Pain,'" especially 3–6, 23–28; and Sammons, *Beyond the Ring*, 31–47, 76–78, 96–129. For an overview of race in American sport, see Jeffrey T. Sammons, "'Race' and Sport: A Critical Historical Examination, *Journal of Sport History* 21 (Fall 1994): 203–78. Hietala, *The Fight of the Century*, 3–128, is insightful on racism and Johnson's challenge to American society. For other excellent discussions of Johnson and his challenge to white supremacy, see Bederman, *Manliness and Civilization*, 1–5, 8–10, 41–2; Al-Tony Gilmore, *Bad Nigger! The National Impact of Jack Johnson* (Port Washington, N.Y.: Kennikat Press, 1975); and Randy Roberts, *Papa Jack: Jack Johnson and the Era of White Hopes* (New York: Free Press, 1983). The film ban is discussed in Sammons, *Beyond the Ring*, 40–46. For popular attitudes toward black athletes, see David K. Wiggins, "'Great Speed But Little Stamina': The Historical Debate over Black Athletic Superiority," *Journal of Sport History* 16 (Summer 1989): 158–85. For the refusal of white champions John L. Sullivan and James J. Corbett to fight black challenger Peter Jackson for

the title in the 1890s, see David K. Wiggins, "Peter Jackson and the Elusive Heavy-weight Championship: A Black Athlete's Struggle Against the Late Nineteenth Century Color-Line," *Journal of Sport History* 12 (Summer 1985): 290–93. For Sullivan, see Michael T. Isenberg, *John L. Sullivan and His America* (Urbana: University of Illinois Press, 1988).

16. On Wills, see Randy Roberts, *Jack Dempsey, the Manassa Mauler* (Baton Rouge: Louisiana State University Press, 1979), 141–45. For state antiboxing laws in New York, see Roberts, *Jack Dempsey*, 19; Francis Albertine, "Harry Wills, Giant Negro Gladiator, Credit to the Game," *Ring* (August 1922); quoted in Roberts, *Jack Dempsey*, 142. For more on restrictions against black contenders, see Nat Fleischer, "The Black Menace," *Ring* 14 (May 1935): 55. On the preference of foreigners over black contenders, see Sammons, *Beyond the Ring*, 73–78. For Blackburn, see Joe Louis with Edna and Art Rust Jr., *Joe Louis: My Life* (New York: Harcourt, Brace, Jovanovich, 1978), 35–37; Mead, *Champion*, 1–5. "Dark cloud," in Richards Vidmer, "Richards Vidmer's Classic Comment on Joe Louis," reprinted in *Pittsburgh Courier* (hereafter *PC*), July 6, 1935, sec. 2, p. 5. On the British Home Office, see Patrick F. McDevitt, "May the Best Man Win: Sport, Masculinity and Nationalism in Great Britain and the Empire, 1884–1933" (Ph.D. diss., Rutgers University, 1999); and James, "On Jack Johnson and Joe Louis," in *C. L. R. James on the "Negro Question,"* 60–63.

17. Davis J. Walsh, "Louis Possesses Punch and Science of Masters," *Birmingham News*, June 26, 1935, 10. Frank Graham column, *New York Sun*, June 25, 1935, JLS, vol. 1. Paul Gallico, cited in Chris Mead, *Champion*, 68. "Kinky head," in Joe Williams, [*Cleveland Press*?], June 27, 1936, JLS, vol. 1. William H. Wiggins Jr., "Boxing's Sambo Twins: Racial Stereotypes in Jack Johnson and Joe Louis Newspaper Cartoons," *Journal of Sport History* 15 (Winter 1988): 242–54 for cartoons.

18. Gerald Early, "The Black Intellectual and the Sport of Prizefighting," in *The Culture of Bruising, Essays on Prizefighting, Literature, and Modern American Culture* (Hopewell, N.J.: Ecco Press, 1994), 5–12. On being a puncher and a boxer, a killer and a craftsman, see M. Jill Dupont, "The Self in the Ring, The Self in Society: Boxing and American Culture from Jack Johnson to Joe Louis," (Ph.D. diss., University of Chicago, 2000), 327–54. On hybrid movie heroes, see May, *Big Tomorrow*, 55–99. On self-possession, see Susan Douglas, *Listening In*, 208.

19. On the rules, see Louis and Rusts, *Joe Louis*, 30, 39, 42–43, Joe Louis Barrow Jr. and Barbara Munder, *Joe Louis: Fifty Years an American Hero* (New York: McGraw Hill, 1988), 42–43; 6–8, on the speech impediment. Louis kept his many affairs, with white as well as black women, very discreet, but they ultimately ruined his marriage.

20. Davis J. Walsh, "Louis Possesses Punch and Science of Masters," *Birmingham News*, June 26, 1935, 10. For white support of Louis, see Russell J. Cowan, "Solid South Decides Joe Louis Must Be Somebody," *Chicago Defender*, April 13, 1935, 11. Quote is from "Daily Press Wants Louis as Champion," *Chicago Defender*, July 6, 1935, 13. "Richards Vidmer's Classic Comment on Joe Louis," reprinted in *PC*, July 6,

1935, sec. 2, p. 5. George Clarens, "The Pulse," *Boston Transcript*, June 26, 1935, JLS, vol. 1. Mitchell, "Joe Louis Never Smiles," 239.

21. See Joe Louis with Rusts, *Joe Louis*, 3–16, for his origins, 15–17 on Depression, 20–22 on amateur boxing, 42–44 for his chance to earn money. See also Barrow and Munder, *Joe Louis*, 21–26. On amateur boxing, see Gerald Gems, *Windy City Wars: Labor, Leisure and Sport in the Making of Chicago* (Latham, Md.: Scarecrow Press, 1997), 182–85, 193–97; and Tim Neary, "Crossing Parochial Boundaries: African-Americans and Interracial Catholic Social Action in Chicago, 1914–1954" (Ph.D. diss., Loyola University Chicago, 2004).

22. Chester L. Washington, "Chez Says 1935 a Joe Louis Year," *PC*, January 4, 1936, sec. 2, p. 5; Lester Rodney, "What Has Revived the Boxing Game?" *Daily Worker*, June 7, 1938, 8; Jack Copeland, "Looking 'Em over with Jack Copeland," *Wichita Beacon*, June 23, 1937, JLS, vol. 38.

23. Clarens, "The Pulse," JLS, vol. 1, for Louis's drawing power and the lack of opposition to him. Steve Hanagan, "Black Gold," *Saturday Evening Post*, June 20, 1936, JLS, vol. 23, for idealism and "lose a few." Roi Ottley, "Good Business Knows no Race," *Amsterdam News*, June 20, 1936, JLS, vol. 21.

24. For Madison Square Garden in the Depression, see Louis and Rusts, 47–48. On Jacobs, see Louis and Rusts, *Joe Louis*, 49–52, 134; Barrow and Munder, *Joe Louis*, 45–47, Jacobs quoted, 47. Also see Hanagan, "Black Gold." Mead, *Champion*, 35–46, discusses the battle between Jacobs and the Garden. On white southern papers' mild coverage of Louis, see Jeffrey T. Sammons, "Boxing as a Reflection of Society: The Southern Reaction to Joe Louis," *Journal of Popular Culture* 16 (Spring 1983): 22–33.

25. Caponi-Tabery, "Jump for Joy," *Prospects* 24 (1999): 521–74. For "hidden scripts," see James Scott, *The Weapons of the Weak: Everyday Forms of Peasant Resistance* (New Haven: Yale University Press, 1985). Will Rogers, "Rogers Figures Joe Louis Could Lick Il Duce, Too," *Cleveland Plain Dealer*, June 27, 1935, JLS, vol. 1. Louis Sobol, "A New School of Etiquette," *New York Evening Journal*, June 27, 1935, JLS, vol. 1; H. G. Salsinger, "Fury Grips Joe, He Ends Fight Quickly," *Detroit News*, June 26, 1935, JLS, vol. 1.

26. "Writes Song for 'Bomber,'" *PC*, June 20, 1936, sec. 2, p. 4. J. S. Hayes, "What I Think about Joe Louis and His Future Fights," *PC*, April 26, 1936, sec. 2, p. 4. Ad for Joe Louis Statue, *PC*, June 6, 1936, sec. 2, p. 5. "Louis Spends $25,000 to Keep Faith with Kid-Fans," *PC*, June 6, 1936, sec. 2, p. 5.

27. Dizzy Gillespie with Al Fraser, *To Be, or Not . . . to Bop* (Garden City, N.Y.: Doubleday, 1979), 288–89. Paul Oliver, *The Meaning of the Blues* (Toronto, 1963), 324–25. "Joe Louis 'Glorified' In Song Hit," *PC*, July 10, 1937, 13. Count Basie and Albert Murray, *Good Morning Blues* (New York: Random House, 1985), 250–51. For a song collection, see "Joe Louis: An American Hero," Rounder Records CD (82161-1106-2, 2001), liner notes by William H. Wiggins Jr.

28. Richard Wright, "Joe Louis Uncovers Dynamite," *New Masses* 17 (October 8, 1935), reprinted in *Richard Wright Reader*, ed. Ellen Wright and Michel Fabre (New

York: Da Capo, 1997), 32–34. See also Richard Wright, *Lawd Today* (Boston: Northeastern University Press, 1986), 52, 146–47.

29. Hitler's remarks quoted in Schmeling, *An Autobiography*, 111. For German concerns, see "Schmeling Departure for U. S. Practically Ignored in Germany," *New York Times*, April 16, 1936, JLS, vol 16. For the press restrictions, see *NS Presse an Weisungen der Vorkriegzeit Edition und Dokumentation*, Bd. 4/II: 1936 (München, 1936), 645–46. For "mixed breed," see "Rasse-Studien am lebenden Ojekt," *B-S*, August 19, 1935, 9. Arno Hellmis, "Heute Nacht: Schmeling-Louis," *Volkischer Beobachter*, June 18, 1936, 10. For German concerns about race mixing, see Kenneth L. Kusmer, "Toward a Comparative History of Racism and Xenophobia in the United States and Germany, 1865–1933," in *Bridging the Atlantic: The Question of American Exceptionalism in Perspective*, ed. Elisabeth Glaser and Hermann Wellenreuther (Cambridge: Cambridge University Press, 2001), 161–62. For "German character," see Ludwig Hayman, "Schmeling oder Louis?" *Volkischer Beobachter*, June 18, 1936, JLS, vol. 22.

30. James T. Farrell, "The Fall of Joe Louis," *Nation*, June 27, 1936, 836. For a description of the fight, see Max Schmeling as told to Paul Gallico, "This Way I Beat Joe Louis," *Saturday Evening Post*, September 5, 1936, 3, 10–11, 32, 34–35. For Goebbels's remarks, see Hgb Elke Froehlich, *Die Tagebücher von Joseph Goebbels*, Teil I, Bd 3/ N. 2 (München: K. G. Sauer, 2001), June 20, 1936, 112. Hicks, "Rund um den grössten Knock-out," *Hamburger Anzeiger*, June 27/28, 1936, 48. George Spandau, "Schmeling's a Cultural Victory," *Der Weltkampf*, as reprinted in English in *Crisis* 43 (October 1936): 301, 309.

31. Hellmis quoted in *Volkischer Beobeachter*, June 21, 1936, 1–2. For the receptions, see "Max ist wieder in Berlin," *Volkischer Beobachter*, June 27, 1936, 1–2; and "Luftschiff 'Hindenburg' bringt den Sieger Schmeling Heim," ibid. For Hitler's quotes, see Schmeling, *Autobiography*, 129–30.

32. All quotes are from "Max Schmeling Sieg—Ein Deutscher Sieg," 1936, Bundesfilmarchiv, Berlin. For similar treatment of the American press's "insults" to Schmeling and German honor, see "Die Pressestimmen Amerikas," *B-S* 16 (July 1936): 2.

33. *Berlin-Zeitung am Mittag*, June 27, 1936, as cited in Müller, "Max Schmeling," 100. Hans Massaquoi, *Destined to Witness: Growing Up Black in Nazi Germany* (New York: Perennial, 2001), 111–21.

34. E. H. Gombrich, "Myth and Reality in German War-Time Broadcasts," in *Film and Radio Propaganda in World War II*, ed. K. R. M. Short (Knoxville: University of Tennessee Press, 1983), 19–20; and Schivelbusch, *The Culture of Defeat*, 205–10, analyze the Siegfried hero. For an early view of Max as "one of the most cold-blooded breadwinners," see "Schmeling Boxt Schön," *B-S* 10 (March 10, 1930): 5–6.

35. Grantland Rice, "The Sportlight," *New York Sun*, June 22, 1936, JLS, vol. 23. C. Cecil Craigne, "Louis' Defeat Gives South Chance to Tell How It Felt," *Chicago Defender*, July 4, 1936, JLS, vol. 23. The reports of southern congressmen responding

to Schmeling's victory is in "Schmeling's Sieg ein deutscher Sieg," *Leipzinger Nueste Nachrichten*, June 21, 1936, JLS, vol. 23. For those who predicted Louis would win a rematch, see Paul Mickelson, "'Experts Dying Hard' on Max's Victory," *Rocky Mountain News*, June 21, 1936, JLS, vol. 22.

36. Maya Angelou, *I Know Why the Caged Bird Sings* (New York: Bantam Books, 1993), 111–15. Lena Horne and Richard Shickel, *Lena* (Garden City, 1965), 75. Louis and Rusts, *Joe Louis*, 90–93. Warren Susman, "Culture and Commitment," in *Culture as History*, 184–210, analyzes shame and commitment as a theme of the 1930s. Louis Armstrong, "Says Joe Louis Took It Like a Man, So Should We," *PC*, July 4, 1936, sec. 2, p. 7.

37. Arthur S. Evans, "The Jim Braddock-Max Schmeling Affair: An Assessment of a Jewish Boycott of a Professional Prizefight," *Journal of Sport and Social Issues* 6 (Summer 1982): 1–12. The "Jewish press" was a consistent target of the Nazis. See "Echoen von Schmeling's Sieg," *Deutsche Weckruf und Beobachter*, June 25, 1936, n. p. For more on boycotts, see Mandell, *Nazi Olympics*, 68–82. For Lester Rodney, sports editor of the *Daily Worker*, and his views of Louis, see Irwin Silber, *Press Box Red* (Philadelphia: Temple University Press, 2003), esp. 171–95. On the role of the Popular Front, see Denning, *Cultural Front*; Mark Naison, *Communists in Harlem during the Depression* (Urbana: University of Illinois Press, 1983), 204–18; Erenberg, *Swingin' the Dream*, 120–49. It is of note that the *Daily Worker* began its campaign against segregated baseball in 1936, the same year they adopted Louis as a challenger to the color line in boxing and a democratic hero.

38. Material for this paragraph comes from Gerald Astor, *". . . And a Credit to His Race": The Hard Life and Times of Joseph Louis Barrow, a.k.a. Joe Louis* (New York: Saturday Review Press, 1974), 166–67.

39. Joe Williams quoted in Mead, *Champion*, 133. Louis and Rusts, *Joe Louis*, 92, 136–39.

40. Schmeling, *Autobiography*, 140, 151–53. "Schmeling Slurs Louis, Negro Race," *Daily Worker*, June 11, 1938, 8. Edmund Boyack, "Psychological Superiority Will Beat Joe," *PC*, May 21, 1938, 1, 4. Hype Igoe, "Max Claims Fear Will Conquer Joe," *New York Journal American*, May 10, 1938, JLS, vol. 49; Louis's response is quoted in Edgar T. Rouzeau, "He Was Plain Lucky When He Fought Me for the First Time," *PC*, May 28, 1938, 1. Pegler cited in Anthony O. Edmonds, *Joe Louis* (Grand Rapids: Eerdmans, 1973), 78.

41. Louis quoted in Mead, *Champion*, 45. W. R., "Max Schmeling im Krankenhaus," *Hamburger Anzeiger*, June 23, 1938, 1. For the fight, Mead, *Champion*, 148–52. Richard Wright, "High Time in Harlem," *New Masses* (July 5, 1938): 42. Abe Newman, "Breaks All Precedents with 1 Round KO and Greatest Record Ever," *Daily Worker*, June 24, 1938, 8.

42. "Achtung! Ring Frei!" *Der Angriff*, June 22, 1938, 3; "Max Schmeling im Krankenhaus," *Hamburger Anzeiger*, June 23, 1938, 1. Schmeling, *Autobiography*, 154–56.

43. Frank Marshall Davis, "'Sepia America' Goes Wild," *PC*, July 2, 1938, 12; Wright, "High Tide in Harlem," 18–19. William G. Nunn, "Louis Had Knocked Schmeling Out before Referee Stopped Bout," *PC*, June 25, 1938, 1–2.

44. Lawrence Levine, *Black Culture and Black Consciousness*, 420–40. Russell Baker, *Growing Up* (New York: Cogdon and Weed, 1982), 206. The postfight celebrations became such a ritual that editorials appeared: "Future of 'Our Champions' Menaced by 'Celebrations,'" *PC*, July 16, 1938, 4, 24. Marcus Garvey, "Joe Louis," *Black Man* 3 (July 1938): 1.

45. *Birmingham Age-Herald*, June 24, 1938, 14; as in Sammons, "Boxing as a Reflection of Society," 29–30. The Carter anecdote and Maya Angelou's recollections of Stamps, Arkansas, are in Gilmore, "The Myth, the Legend and Folklore of Joe Louis," 265–66. Hugh Johnson, "Finds Hitler's Vaunted Aryanism Took Knockout along with Schmeling," *Chicago Daily News*, June 24, 1938, JLS, vol. 56.

46. Dan Parker, "Der Feuhrer of Speculator," *Daily Mirror*, June 18, 1938, JLS, vol. 50. Ted Carroll, "A Great Champion Arrives," *Ring*, June 1938, JLS, vol. 54. Editorial, "Joe Stands Supreme," *Ring*, June 1938, JLS, vol. 54. *Louisville Courier Journal*, June 24, 1938, JLS, vol. 54. Bud Shaver, "Joe Louis A Challenge to Tolerance in an Intolerant World," *Detroit Times*; reprinted in *PC*, July 2, 1938, 15. Also see "Schmeling's Kampf," *PC*, June 24, 1938, JLS, vol. 56. See Gerstle, *American Crucible*, 128–86, for the more inclusive American national identity.

47. Daniel M. Daniel, "The Ring's Globe Trotter," *Ring*, September 1937, JLS, vol. 40. George Winn, "In the Editor's Corner: Heavyweights on Parade," *Boxing News*, June 1938, JLS, vol. 56. Arthur Donovan, "The Referee Fights Three Men," *Saturday Evening Post*, September 10, 1938, JLS, vol. 57. On the film ban, see Sammons, *Beyond the Ring*, 118–20.

48. William H. Wiggins Jr. "Boxing's Sambo Twins," 242–54. Ed Hughes, "Another Case of 'Bad Hands,'" *Brooklyn Daily Eagle*, August 17, 1935, JLS, vol. 4. For the shift in sportswriters descriptions, see Mead, *Champion*, 181–87. For Jimmy Cannon's remark, see Alexander Young Jr., "Joe Louis, Symbol, 1933–1949" (Ph.D. diss., University of Maryland, 1968), 158.

49. For Schmeling after his defeat, see Schmeling, *Autobiography*, 161–70; and Volker Kluge, *Max Schmeling: Eine Biographie in 15 Runden* (Berlin: Auftau-Verlag, 2004), 324–50.

50. *Chicago Tribune*, January 11, 1942; as cited in Mead, *Champion*, 221. James Edmund Boyack, "Louis Hailed at Writers' Banquet," *PC*, January 31, 1942, 17. James Edmund Boyack, "It Took Joe Louis to Give the War a Name with a 'Punch,'" *PC*, May 16, 1942, 17. On his wartime role, see Lauren Rebecca Sklaroff, "Constructing G.I. Joe Louis: Cultural Solutions to the 'Negro Problem' during World War II," *Journal of American History* 89 (December 2002): 958–83; Dominic J. Capeci Jr. and Martha Wilkerson, "Multifarious Hero: Joe Louis, American Society and Race Relations during World Crisis, 1935–1945," *Journal of Sport History* 10 (Winter 1983): 5–25.

51. For the Treasury Bonds campaigns, see Lawrence R. Samuel, *Pledging Alle-*

giance: American Identity and the Bond Drive of World War II (Washington, D.C.: Smithsonian Institution Press, 1996). For Louis and radio campaigns, see Barbara Dianne Savage, *Broadcasting Freedom* (Chapel Hill: University of North Carolina Press, 1999), 88–89, 161–62. "Joe Louis Hopes Biased Naval Policies Will End," *PC*, January 17, 1942, 4.

52. For an excellent article on Coca-Cola in Germany, see Jeff R. Schutts, "Born Again in the Gospel of Refreshment? Coca-Colonization and the Re-making of Post-war German Identity," in *Consuming Germany in the Cold War*, ed. David Crew (Oxford: Oxford University Press, 2003), 121–50.

Contributors

Davarian L. Baldwin is Paul E. Raether Distinguished Professor of American Studies at Trinity College. He previously taught at Boston College. He is the author of *Chicago's New Negroes: Modernity, the Great Migration, and Black Urban Life* (2007) and is currently at work on two new projects, *Land of Darkness: Race and the Making of Modern America* and *UniverCities: How Knowledge Institutions Are Transforming the Urban Landscape.*

W. Fitzhugh Brundage is William B. Umstead Professor of History at the University of North Carolina, Chapel Hill. He is the author of *Lynching in the New South* (1993), *A Socialist Utopia in the New South* (1996), and *The Southern Past* (2005), for which he won the 2006 Charles Sydnor Prize and the 2006 Lillian Smith Award. He has also edited three collections of essays: *Under Sentence of Death: Essays on Lynching in the South* (1997), *Where These Memories Grow: History, Memory, and Regional Identity in the American South* (2000), and *Booker T. Washington and Black Progress: "Up From Slavery" 100 Years Later* (2003).

Clare Corbould is Larkins Research Fellow and Senior Lecturer at Monash University. Previously she was lecturer in history at Macquarie University and at the University of Sydney. She is the author of numerous articles and essays as well as *Becoming African Americans, 1919–1939* (2009), which was shortlisted for the 2009 New South Wales Premier's General History Prize and was named a *Choice* magazine Outstanding Academic Title in 2009. She is currently working on two projects, a study of sociologist Ophelia Settle Egypt and a biography of James Weldon Johnson.

Susan Curtis is professor of history and the director of interdisciplinary studies at Purdue University. She is the author of *A Consuming Faith: The Social Gospel and Modern American Culture* (1991), *Dancing to a Black Man's Tune: A Life of Scott Joplin* (1994), and *The First Black Actors on the Great White Way* (1998).

Stephanie Dunson, formerly professor of English and African American culture at the University of Rhode Island, is the director of writing programs at Williams College. As an academic writing specialist, Dunson has served as writing center director at Mount Holyoke College, as faculty associate of the Bard College Institute for Writing and Thinking, and as a private writing consultant for scholars at Yale University, Columbia University, and Hampshire College. She has also taught in the Graduate

Liberal Studies Program at Wesleyan University and at the University of Massachusetts.

Lewis A. Erenberg is professor of history at Loyola University, Chicago. He is the author of *The Greatest Fight of Our Generation: Louis vs. Schmeling* (2005), *Swingin' the Dream: Big Band Jazz and the Rebirth of American Culture* (1998), *The War in American Culture* (1996), and *Steppin' Out: New York City Nightlife and the Transformation of American Culture, 1890–1930* (1984). He has been a fellow at the National Humanities Center, Fulbright Distinguished Chair in American Culture at the University of Salzburg, and Fulbright Senior Lecturer at the University of Munich.

Stephen Garton is Challis Professor of History and dean of the Faculty of Arts at the University of Sydney. He is the author of four books and over sixty articles and book chapters. He has written extensively in the fields of medicine, crime, social policy, war, and repatriation, primarily in the Australian context. More recently he has begun to research the history of imprisonment and psychological classifications of criminals in North America, publishing an article on parole in Georgia in the *Journal of Social History* in 2003. His most recent book is *Histories of Sexuality: Antiquity to Sexual Revolution* (2004).

John M. Giggie is assistant professor of history at the University of Alabama. He previously taught at the University of Texas, San Antonio, where he won the Presidential Award for Distinguished Achievement in Teaching. He is the author of *After Redemption: Jim Crow and the Transformation of African American Religion in the Delta, 1875–1915* (2008) as well as numerous essays and articles. He also edited *Faith in the Market: Religion and the Rise of Urban Commercial Culture* (2002).

Grace Elizabeth Hale is associate professor of history at the University of Virginia. She is the author of *Making Whiteness: The Culture of Segregation in the South, 1890–1940* (1998), for which she won the Willie Lee Rose Award from the Southern Association of Women Historians and the Phi Beta Kappa Book Award from the University of Virginia. In addition to writing numerous articles and essays, she is the author of *Rebel, Rebel: Outsiders in America, 1945–2000* (forthcoming).

Robert Jackson is assistant professor of English at the University of Tulsa. The recipient of Ph.D.s in English and history from New York University and the University of Virginia, respectively, he is the author of *Seeking the Region in American Literature and Culture: Modernity, Dissidence, Innovation* (2005), as well as numerous articles. He is currently completing *Fade In, Crossroads: The Southern Cinema, 1890–1940* for publication.

David Krasner is associate professor of theater at Emerson College. He previously taught at Yale University. His books include *A Beautiful Pageant: African American*

Theatre, Drama, and Performance in the Harlem Renaissance, 1910–1920 (2002); *A Blackwell Companion to Twentieth-Century American Drama* (ed.) (2004); *African American Performance and Theater History: A Critical Reader* (coed.) (2001), winner of the 2002 Errol Hill Award from the American Society for Theatre Research for the best book; *Method Acting Reconsidered: Theory, Practice, Future* (2000); and *Resistance, Parody, and Double Consciousness in African American Theatre, 1895–1910* (1997), winner of the 1998 Errol Hill Award.

Thomas Riis is Joseph Negler Professor of Musicology and director of the American Music Research Center at the University of Colorado, Boulder. His book *Just Before Jazz* (1995), devoted to African American Broadway shows, received an ASCAP–Deems Taylor Award in 1995. He edited a complete edition of the first major African American Broadway musical, 1902's *In Dahomey* (1996), and is the author of *Frank Loesser* (2008). He has been a Fulbright Senior Scholar at the University of Luenburg, Germany, and was president of the Society for American Music (2009–10).

Stephen Robertson is senior lecturer in the Department of History at the University of Sydney. Robertson has published widely on childhood and sexual violence in early twentieth-century New York City. His articles have appeared in the *Journal of the History of Sexuality, Journal of American Studies,* and *Law and History Review.* He is also the author of *Crimes against Children: Sexual Violence and Legal Culture in New York City, 1880–1960* (2005).

John Stauffer is chair of the Program in the History of American Civilization and professor of English and African and African American studies at Harvard University. He is the author of *Giants: The Parallel Lives of Frederick Douglass and Abraham Lincoln* (2008), which was a History Book Club featured selection and the winner of the Iowa Writers Award and a Boston Book Club prize; and *The State of Jones* (2009), which was a *New York Times* bestseller and was nominated for the Pulitzer Prize. His other books include *The Writings of James McCune Smith: Black Intellectual and Abolitionist* (2006); *The Problem of Evil: Slavery, Freedom, and the Ambiguities of American Reform* (with Steven Mintz, 2006); *Meteor of War: The John Brown Story* (with Zoe Trodd); and *The Black Hearts of Men: Radical Abolitionists and the Transformation of Race* (2002), which won the Frederick Douglass Book Prize and the Avery Craven Book Prize and was the Lincoln Prize runner-up.

Graham White is professor of history at the University of Sydney. He is the author of books on the political history of the New Deal as well as a number of collaborative works on the history of African American culture, including *Stylin': African-American Expressive Culture from Its Beginnings to the Zoot Suit* (with Shane White, 1998) and *The Sounds of Slavery: Discovering African American History through Songs, Sermons and Speech* (2005).

Shane White is professor of American history at the University of Sydney. He is the author or coauthor of *The Sounds of Slavery* (2005), *Stories of Freedom in Black New York* (2002), *Stylin': African-American Expressive Culture from Its Beginnings to the Zoot Suit* (with Graham White, 1998), and *Somewhat More Independent: The End of Slavery in New York City, 1770–1810* (1991). He is currently an Australian Research Council Professorial Fellow, 2006–10.

Index

Green, Adam, 127, 294
Greene, Graham, 309
Greenfield, Elizabeth, 77, 78
Griffith, D. W., 166, 213, 216, 220, 221, 228, 232
Griffiths, Julia, 72
Guest of Honor, A, 133, 140
Gunning, Tom, 217

Hagenbeck and Wallace Circus, 156
Haiti: and African American culture, 259–81; opposition to occupation of, 260–62, 272–73; inspiration for *Emperor Jones*, 263–66; influence on Langston Hughes, 267–69, 272, 277–78; as depicted in *Tambour*, 269–71; as depicted in *Ouanga*, 271; as depicted in film, 275–77; as depicted in theater, 278–80
Haiti, 279
Haiti–Santo Domingo Independence Society, 273
Hajdu, David, 240
Hamburger Anzeiger, 331
Hamilton Club (Chicago), 164
Hammermann, Dan, 280
Handy, W. C., 9, 17, 19, 20, 24, 243
"Hangman's Blues," 246
Harding, Warren G., 262, 278
"Hard to Be a Nigger," 250
Harlem, 26, 28, 35, 138, 272
"Harlem Rag, The," 139
Harney, Ben, 147
Harrison, Hubert, 265
Hartford, Conn., 82
Haverly's Genuine Colored Minstrels, 56
Hawaii, 80
"Hear Me Talking to You," 248
Hearst, William Randolph, 298, 303
Hearst Charity Milk Fund, 328
Hebdige, Dick, 114
Heenan, John C., 316

Helena, Ark., 199
Helena, Mont., 80
Hellmis, Arno, 331
"Hello, Ma Baby!," 134, 138
Henderson, Fletcher, 24, 28
"Heroic Slave, The," 76
"He's in the Ring (Doin' the Same Old Thing)," 329
"He's Up Against the Real Thing Now," 61
Hicks, Charles, 151, 153
Higham, John, 125
Hill, Leslie Pinkney, 271, 272, 280
Hirsch, Irving, 141
Hitler, Adolph, 272, 320, 321, 330, 331, 336, 338
Hoffman, Carl, 133
Hogan, Ernest "Reuben Crowders," 10, 104, 137, 139, 140, 153
Hoke, Rev. James H., 204
Hollywood, 100, 218
Holstein, Casper, 177
Homesteader, The, 179, 219, 220
Horne, Lena, 334
House, Eddie James "Son," Jr., 242, 244, 247
House Behind the Cedars, The, 231
Howard University, 18, 56
"How 'Ya Gonna Keep 'Em Down on the Farm (After They've Seen Paree?)," 167
Hughes, Ed, 341
Hughes, Langston, 35, 266, 267, 268, 272, 277, 278
Huntington, W.V., 152
Hutton, Laurence, 148

Illinois, 16
Improved Order of Red Men, 164
Incidents in the Life of a Slave Girl, 79
In Dahomey, 99, 110, 112, 141
Indianapolis, 16, 27
Indianapolis Freeman, 116, 150

Ingram, Rex, 279
Institute of Musical Arts, 124
Inter-State Tatler, 307
Intolerance, 228
Irwin, May, 140
"It Don't Belong to Me," 55
"It's Tight Like That," 32

Jackson, Dan "The Embalmer," 177
Jackson, Jim, 247
Jackson, John L., 118
Jackson, Papa Charlie, 247
Jacksonville, Fla., 18, 156
Jacobs, Harriet, 67, 79, 80
Jacobs, Max, 342
Jacobs, Mike, 328
"Jail House Blues," 249
James, C. L. R., 275, 315, 322
James, Henry, 83
Jamestown International Exposition
   (1907), 6
Jazz, 294
Jefferson, Lemon Henry "Blind Lemon,"
   32, 246
Jefferson, Thomas, 228, 280, 294
Jeffries, Jim, 165, 166, 323
"Jinx Blues," 242
"Joe Louis Blues," 329
John Hertel Company (Chicago), 204
Johnson, George W., 22, 155, 218, 219
Johnson, Gen. Hugh, 339
Johnson, J. Rosamond, 136, 139, 153
Johnson, Jack, 20, 28, 34, 35, 171, 179,
   289, 290, 295, 309, 322, 325, 326,
   337, 340, 341; cultural significance
   of, 165–66
Johnson, James Weldon, 18, 19, 110,
   126, 138, 162, 168, 273, 278, 304
Johnson, John "Mushmouth," 177
Johnson, Lonnie, 247
Johnson, Lyndon B., 301
Johnson, Noble, 218
Johnson, Robert, 243, 247

Johnston, Jimmy, 321
Jolson, Al, 28
Jones, Henry "Teenan," 177
Jones, Peter P., 173, 218
Joplin, Scott, 2, 7, 17, 19, 128, 129, 130,
   136, 140, 141; early career of, 128–29;
   in Sedalia, Mo., 129–32; cultural
   ambitions of, 133–36
Jordan, Joe, 140
Jordan Marsh, 102
Julian, Herbert, 1; celebrity of, 291–310;
   parachute exploits of, 293; arrival
   in Harlem, 296; planned solo trans-
   Atlantic flight of, 297–300; and
   Ethiopia, 300–301; flamboyance
   of, 307; criticized, 307–8

Kansas, 16
Kansas City, 26, 27, 152
Kaplan, Amy, 100
Kasson, John F., 127
Kean, Edmund, 148
Keaton, Buster, 57
Keith, B. F., 102
Kentucky, 72
Kibard, Declan, 317
"King Joe," 329
King Kong, 275
"Kismet Rag," 133
Kramer, A. Walter, 136
Kristeva, Julia, 117
Ku Klux Klan, 35, 167, 221, 290

Lafayette Players, 275
Lafayette Theatre (Harlem), 279
Lane, William Henry, 8
Lansing, Robert, 269
Last Darky, The, 104
"Laughing Song, The," 22, 155
Law of Nature, The, 174
Lawrence, Kans., 10
Lead Belly (Huddie William Led-
   better), 26

Quality Amusement Corporation, 27

Queen City Band, 130

Radio Corporation of America (RCA),
31

Ragtime: origin of, 129–32, 154–55;
performers in Europe, 157–58. *See
also* Joplin, Scott

Ragtime Ballet, 133

Ragtime Review, 133

Railroad Porter, The, 173, 217

Rainey, Ma (Gertrude Pridgett), 214,
244, 246, 248, 249, 250, 251

RCA Victor, 30

Realization of a Negro's Ambition, The,
174

"Real Thing, The," 83

Remick, Jerome H., 22

Renda, Mary, 261, 272, 278

Reno, 165

Respectability: African Americans and,
9–10; of cakewalk, 115–16; of ragtime,
124–25, 132, 133–35; and Great
Migration, 159–61, 171, 173

Rice, Edward Le Roy, 154

Rice, Grantland, 333

Rice, T. D., 46, 47, 48, 53, 106

Richard, George Lewis "Tex," 323

Richmond, 250

Richmond News-Leader, 229

Riggers, J. S., 156

Ring, 323, 340

Ringling Brothers' Circus, 156

*Rising Tide of Color Against White
World Supremacy, The*, 168

RKO Pictures, 31

Roanoke, Va., 16

Robeson, Paul, 32, 34, 35, 262, 275,
276, 279, 329

Robinson, Bill "Bojangles," 34, 296

Rodin, Auguste, 5, 29

Rodney, Lester, 327, 334

Rogers, Alex, 57

Rogers, J. A., 172

Rogers, Will, 328

Rolling Stones, 240

Roosevelt, Franklin D., 35, 262, 278,
290, 335

Roosevelt, Theodore, 140, 164, 174, 226,
262, 297

Rosa Pearle's Paper, 134, 135

Rossini, 148

Roumain, Jacques, 277

Roye, Edward James, 83

Rufus Rastus, 139, 140

"Runnin' Wild," 293

Rush, Benjamin, 294

Rust College, 198

Rutgers University, 34

Rye, Howard, 157

Saint-Gaudens, Augustus, 5

St. Louis, 16, 27, 133, 138, 140, 152, 260

St. Louis Argus, 218

St. Louis Louisiana Purchase Exposition (1904), 135

St. Petersburg, 157

Salome, 8–10

Salsbury, Nate, 102

Sanders of the River, 276

San Francisco, 16, 17

Sante, Luc, 242

Saturday Evening Post, 328

Savoy Ballroom (Harlem), 310

Sayers, Tom, 316

Scarry, Elaine, 68

Schmeling, Max, 35, 316; boxing career
of, 318–21; Louis-Schmeling bout
(1936), 330–33; Louis-Schmeling
rematch (1938), 334–35; effects of
loss, 337–38, 341. *See also* Louis,
Joe

Schomburg, Arthur, 272

Schuyler, George, 303

Scott, James, 129

Sears, Roebuck and Company, 102, 175

Lamar Cecil, *Wilhelm II: Prince and Emperor, 1859–1900* (1989).

Carolyn Merchant, *Ecological Revolutions: Nature, Gender, and Science in New England* (1989).

Gladys Engel Lang and Kurt Lang, *Etched in Memory: The Building and Survival of Artistic Reputation* (1990).

Howard Jones, *Union in Peril: The Crisis over British Intervention in the Civil War* (1992).

Robert L. Dorman, *Revolt of the Provinces: The Regionalist Movement in America* (1993).

Peter N. Stearns, *Meaning Over Memory: Recasting the Teaching of Culture and History* (1993).

Thomas Wolfe, *The Good Child's River*, edited with an introduction by Suzanne Stutman (1994).

Warren A. Nord, *Religion and American Education: Rethinking a National Dilemma* (1995).

David E. Whisnant, *Rascally Signs in Sacred Places: The Politics of Culture in Nicaragua* (1995).

Lamar Cecil, *Wilhelm II: Emperor and Exile, 1900–1941* (1996).

Jonathan Hartlyn, *The Struggle for Democratic Politics in the Dominican Republic* (1998).

Louis A. Pérez Jr., *On Becoming Cuban: Identity, Nationality, and Culture* (1999).

Yaakov Ariel, *Evangelizing the Chosen People: Missions to the Jews in America, 1880–2000* (2000).

Philip F. Gura, *C. F. Martin and His Guitars, 1796–1873* (2003).

Louis A. Pérez Jr., *To Die in Cuba: Suicide and Society* (2005).

Peter Filene, *The Joy of Teaching: A Practical Guide for New College Instructors* (2005).

John Charles Boger and Gary Orfield, eds., *School Resegregation: Must the South Turn Back?* (2005).

Jock Lauterer, *Community Journalism: Relentlessly Local* (2006).

Michael H. Hunt, *The American Ascendancy: How the United States Gained and Wielded Global Dominance* (2007).

Michael Lienesch, *In the Beginning: Fundamentalism, the Scopes Trial, and the Making of the Antievolution Movement* (2007).

Eric L. Muller, *American Inquisition: The Hunt for Japanese American Disloyalty in World War II* (2007).

John McGowan, *American Liberalism: An Interpretation for Our Time* (2007).

Nortin M. Hadler, M.D., *Worried Sick: A Prescription for Health in an Overtreated America* (2008).

W. Fitzhugh Brundage, ed., *Beyond Blackface: African Americans and the Creation of American Popular Culture, 1890–1930* (2011).